WITHDRAWN

Sara Coleridge,
A Victorian Daughter

Sara Coleridge by Samuel Laurence, 1850. From the frontispiece of Edith Coleridge, *Memoir and Letters of Sara Coleridge*, 1873

Sara Coleridge,
A Victorian Daughter
Her Life and Essays

❖❖❖❖❖❖❖❖❖❖❖❖❖❖❖❖❖❖❖❖❖❖❖

Bradford Keyes Mudge

Yale University Press

New Haven and London

Set in Berkeley type by The Composing Room of Michigan, Inc.
Printed in the United States of America by Vail-Ballou Press,
Binghamton, New York.

Library of Congress Cataloging-in-Publication Data

Mudge, Bradford Keyes.
Sara Coleridge, a victorian daughter: Her life and essays /
Bradford Keyes Mudge.
p.   cm.
Bibliography: p.
Includes index.
ISBN 0-300-04443-7 (alk. paper)
1. Coleridge, Sara Coleridge, 1802–1852.   2. Women and
literature—Great Britain—History—19th century.   3. Fathers and
daughters—Great Britain—History—19th century.   4. Coleridge,
Samuel Taylor, 1772–1834 —Editors.   5. Authors, English—19th
century—Biography.   6. Editors—Great Britain—Biography.
I. Coleridge, Sara Coleridge, 1802–1852. II. Title.
PR4489.C2Z78   1989
821'.7—dc19   88-37427
                                                                              CIP

The paper in this book meets the guidelines for permanence and
durability of the Committee on Production Guidelines for Book
Longevity of the Council on Library Resources.

10   9   8   7   6   5   4   3   2   1

Yet Hope still lives and oft, to objects fair
In prospect pointing bids me still pursue
My humble tasks:—I list—but backward cast
Fain would mine eye discern the Future in the Past.

Sara Coleridge, "To my Father"

CONTENTS

ILLUSTRATIONS

PREFACE

When, in the closing lines of her poem "To my Father," Sara Coleridge claims that "Hope still lives and oft . . . / . . . bids me still pursue / My humble tasks," she assumes a characteristically self-effacing attitude about her literary labors, labors which, in the years between her father's death in 1834 and her own in 1852, required prodigious effort on her part but brought relatively little public acclaim. Her "humble tasks," her numerous scholarly editions and her long, densely written introductions and appendixes, are, however, humble only in two related senses: first, in that they assume female authorship to be a transgression of the well-established codes of propriety that celebrated and enforced women's intellectual, emotional, and economic selflessness; second, in that they position themselves by choice in the margins of precedent literary, philosophical, and theological texts. If the first assumption presupposes a female "virtue" endangered by authorship, a virtue offered as compensation for across-the-board inequality, then the second valorizes one type of authorship over another, championing the "original" text over whatever subsequent critical or editorial interpretations collaborate in its reception history. Both assumptions, of course, are complicated and conflicted ideological positions that vary depending upon the class, culture, and sex of those involved. Whereas, however, the first remains largely specific to eighteenth- and nineteenth-century Anglo-European societies, and is for that reason easily identified and analyzed, the second is still very much with us, structuring our critical methods and influencing our critical pronouncements. Thus it is that scholars have tended to accept Sara Coleridge at her word and assume without question her humble position in the literary scheme of things.

This book will argue that our understanding of nineteenth-century women's writing, of its relationships to those constraining codes of female propriety, has been severely compromised by our own hierarchical notions of "literary" and "nonliterary" value. In other words, Sara Coleridge's humble tasks should be considered anything but humble; they were, at the time, complicated strategies by which an extremely intelligent woman uninterested in writing fiction and partial to theology and philosophy both exercised her mind and attempted to influence her contemporaries. Worried by the social unrest of the Chartist years, Coleridge's daughter intended her father's works to provide a stabilizing influence upon a decidedly unstable early Victorian public. That this attempt was complicated by a troubling relationship to her father, by addiction to opium, and by acute depression and recurrent hysteria makes her story of particular interest to social historians and romanticists alike. Moreover, Sara Coleridge's importance as a purveyor of literary values, as one whose "business of life" it was to educate her contemporaries in Coleridgean truth, offers an explicit challenge to conventional ideas about literary production and reception as it raises a series of pressing questions about needed changes in literary historiography.

In keeping with its unconventional subject, this book assumes a slightly unconventional shape. It is at once a biography, a critical study, and a selected edition of essays. It reads the life of Sara Coleridge by focusing on the patterns of ideas and concerns that recur throughout a representative selection of her essays. Supplementing the study of those patterns with an understanding of both the personal tensions and the institutional constraints that worked to marginalize her as a nineteenth-century woman of letters, it argues that she wrote and rewrote her father's literary life as a way of controlling her patrimony and redefining her own unusual intellectual career. First and foremost an act of historical revision and recovery, this book also includes an appendix in which appear seven of Sara Coleridge's most interesting and least available essays. Of these, three essays—"On the Disadvantages Resulting from the Possession of Beauty," "Nervousness," and "On Mr. Wordsworth's Poem Entitled 'Lines Left on a Yew-tree Seat'"—are being published for the first time. Three others— "[On the British Constitution]," "Reasons for Not Placing 'Laodamia' in the First Rank of Wordsworthian Poetry," and "[The Autobiography of Sara Coleridge]"—were published in 1873 by Sara's daughter, Edith Coleridge, but were expurgated, to varying degrees, of their more strident passages. Because of the availability of the original manuscripts, those passages have all been restored. One essay—"Reply to Strictures of Three Gentlemen upon Carlyle"—exists only as it was published by Edith; it is included here because of its central importance in understanding the strategy behind Sara Coleridge's public veneration of her father.

All of Sara Coleridge's manuscript essays, all of her diaries, and a significant number of her letters are housed at the Harry Ransom Humanities Research Center of the University of Texas at Austin, where they form part of the extensive Coleridge Family Papers. To Cathy Henderson, Ken Craven, Tom Zigal, Dave Oliphant, and Pat Fox of the HRHRC, I am indebted for indispensable advice and constant good will. I would also like to thank the Victoria College Library, University of Toronto, and the British Library in London. Thanks go as well to Robert Woof of the Dove Cottage Library in Grasmere, to Jonathan Wordsworth for a spirited breakfast discussion about female illness in the nineteenth century, and to Molly Lefebure for an attentive and valuable reading of the manuscript. I am especially grateful to Mrs. A. H. B. Coleridge and the Coleridge estate for permission to quote from the previously unpublished material.

A version of chapter 1 appeared originally in *Tulsa Studies in Women's Literature* and a significant portion of chapter 5 in *The Wordsworth Circle*; I would like to thank the editors of both journals for permission to reprint. I would also like to thank Doug Kellner, Louis Mackey, and Rodger Gathmann of the Philosophy Department of the University of Texas at Austin. Thanks go as well to the English departments at the University of Texas and the University of Colorado at Denver. Elihu Pearlman, John Ostheimer, Sharon McCoy, and Cy Frost at Denver offered assistance and support. To the English Department at Texas, I owe special thanks. Evan Carton, Andy Cooper, Kurt Heinzelman, and Walt Reed assisted from beginning to end in a variety of capacities. To Kurt and to Clare Colquitt, both of whom labored from draft to draft with much patience and good sense, and to Andy, whose encouragement was and continues to be a mainstay, my gratitude fast approaches that which could prove embarrassing to us all. To Jane Marcus and Jerome McGann my debt is similarly ungainly: one could not ask for better teachers, and from beginning to end, this book is inscribed with great admiration for their scholarship, their integrity, their politics.

Finally, I am grateful to my parents for their unconditional support and thoughtful guidance through a process which must have seemed at times unnecessarily arduous.

ABBREVIATIONS

Aids(1825)	S. T. Coleridge. *Aids to Reflection in the Formation of a Manly Character*. London: Taylor and Hessey, 1825.
Aids(1843)	S. T. Coleridge. *Aids to Reflection in the Formation of a Manly Character*. London: William Pickering, 1843.
BL	British Library
BL(1817)	S. T. Coleridge. *Biographia Literaria*. 2 vols. London: Rest Fenner, 1817.
BL(1847)	S. T. Coleridge. *Biographia Literaria*. 2 vols. Edited by Sara Coleridge. London: William Pickering, 1847.
BL(1907)	S. T. Coleridge. *Biographia Literaria*. 2 vols. Edited by John Shawcross. Oxford: Oxford University Press, 1907.
BL(CC)	S. T. Coleridge. *Biographia Literaria*. 2 vols. Edited by James Engell and W. Jackson Bate. London & Princeton: Princeton University Press, 1983. *The Collected Works of Samuel Taylor Coleridge,* vol. 7.
C&S(CC)	S. T. Coleridge. *On the Constitution of the Church and State.* Edited by John Colmer. London & Princeton: Princeton University Press, 1976. *The Collected Works of Samuel Taylor Coleridge,* vol. 9.
CC	*The Collected Works of Samuel Taylor Coleridge*. Edited by Kathleen Coburn. London & Princeton: Princeton University Press, 1969–
CL	*Collected Letters of Samuel Taylor Coleridge*. 6 vols. Edited by Earl Leslie Griggs. Oxford & New York: Clarendon Press, 1956–71.

CN	*The Notebooks of Samuel Taylor Coleridge*. Edited by Kathleen Coburn. New York, Princeton, & London: Princeton University Press, 1957– .
DC	Derwent Coleridge
DCL	Dove Cottage Library
Diary	Henry Crabb Robinson. *Diary, Reminiscences, and Correspondences of Henry Crabb Robinson*. Edited by Thomas Sadler. New York: AMS, 1967.
D Wordsworth	Ernest de Selincourt. *Dorothy Wordsworth*. Oxford: Clarendon Press, 1933.
EC	Edith Coleridge
EOT(1850)	S. T. Coleridge. *Essays on His Own Times*. 3 vols. Edited by Sara Coleridge. London: William Pickering, 1850.
EOT(CC)	S. T. Coleridge. *Essays on His Own Times*. 3 vols. Edited by David V. Erdman. London & Princeton: Princeton University Press, 1978. *The Collected Works of Samuel Taylor Coleridge,* vol. 3.
ET	Emily Trevenen
Fr(CC)	S. T. Coleridge. *The Friend*. 2 vols. Edited by Barbara E. Rooke. London & Princeton: Princeton University Press, 1969. *The Collected Works of Samuel Taylor Coleridge,* vol. 4.
Griggs	Earl Leslie Griggs. *Coleridge Fille: A Biography of Sara Coleridge*. London, New York, & Toronto: Oxford University Press, 1940.
HC	Hartley Coleridge
HC Letters	*Letters of Hartley Coleridge*. Edited by Grace Griggs and E. L. Griggs. London, New York, & Toronto: Oxford University Press, 1941.
HNC	Henry Nelson Coleridge

HRHRC	Harry Ransom Humanities Research Center, The University of Texas at Austin.
JTC	John Taylor Coleridge
Lord Coleridge	Lord Coleridge. *The Story of a Devonshire House*. London, 1905.
Lucas	*The Letters of Charles Lamb*. 3 vols. Edited by E. V. Lucas. New Haven: Yale University Press, 1935.
Marginalia	S. T. Coleridge. *Marginalia*. 5 vols. Edited by George Whalley. London & Princeton: Princeton University Press, 1980. *The Collected Works of Samuel Taylor Coleridge*, vol. 12.
Minnow	*Minnow Among Tritons: Mrs. S. T. Coleridge's Letters to Thomas Poole*. Edited by Stephen Potter. Bloomsbury: Nonesuch Press, 1934.
ML(1873)	*Memoir and Letters of Sara Coleridge*. 2 vols. Edited by Edith Coleridge. London: Harry S. King, 1873.
ML(1874)	*Memoir and Letters of Sara Coleridge*. Edited by Edith Coleridge. New York: Harper & Brothers, 1874.
MN	S. T. Coleridge. *Notes, Theological, Political, and Miscellaneous*. Edited by Derwent Coleridge. London: Edward Moxon, 1853.
MW Letters	*The Letters of Mary Wordsworth, 1800–1855*. Edited by Mary Burton. Oxford: Clarendon Press, 1958.
N&L	S. T. Coleridge. *Notes and Lectures upon Shakespeare*. 2 vols. Edited by Sara Coleridge. London: William Pickering, 1849.
NL	*New Letters of Robert Southey*. 2 vols. Edited by Kenneth Curran. New York: Columbia University Press, 1965.
PW(1834)	S. T. Coleridge. *The Poetical Works of Samuel Taylor Coleridge*. 3 vols. Edited by H. N. Coleridge. London: William Pickering, 1834.

PW(1852)   S. T. Coleridge. *The Poems of Samuel Taylor Coleridge.* Edited by Derwent and Sara Coleridge. London: Edward Moxon, 1852.

PW(1912)   S. T. Coleridge. *Coleridge Poetical Works.* Edited by Ernest Hartley Coleridge. 1912; reprint ed., London: Oxford University Press, 1973.

Ramos   *The Letters of Robert Southey to John May, 1797 to 1838.* Edited by Charles Ramos. Austin: Jenkins, 1976.

Recollections   Edith Coleridge. *Some Recollections of Henry Nelson Coleridge and his Family.* Torquay: Fleet Printing Works, 1910.

Reed   Henry Reed. "The Daughter of Coleridge." *The Literary World* (January 1853). Reprinted in *Sara Coleridge and Henry Reed.* Ithaca, 1937.

Remains   *The Literary Remains of Samuel Taylor Coleridge.* 4 vols. Edited by H. N. Coleridge. London: William Pickering, 1836–39.

RS Life   *The Life and Correspondence of Robert Southey.* 6 vols. Edited by Charles Cuthbert Southey. New York: Harper, 1851.

SC   Sara Coleridge

SFC   Sara Fricker Coleridge

SH Letters   *Letters of Sara Hutchinson.* Edited by Kathleen Coburn. Toronto: University of Toronto Press, 1954.

SM   S. T. Coleridge. *The Statesman's Manual.* Edited by R. J. White. London & Princeton: Princeton University Press, 1972. In S. T. Coleridge, *Lay Sermons, The Collected Works of Samuel Taylor Coleridge,* vol. 6.

STC   Samuel Taylor Coleridge

Towle   Eleanor Towle. *A Poet's Children: Hartley and Sara Coleridge.* London: Methuen, 1912.

TT   *Specimens of the Table Talk of the Late Samuel Taylor Coleridge.* 2 vols. Edited by Henry Nelson Coleridge. London: John Murray, 1835.

VCL   Victoria College Library, University of Toronto

W Letters   *The Letters of William and Dorothy Wordsworth.* 7 vols. Revised, arranged, and edited by Alan G. Hill. Oxford: Clarendon Press, 1967–

W Prose   *The Prose Works of William Wordsworth.* 3 vols. Edited by W. J. B. Owen and J. Worthington Smyser. London: Oxford University Press, 1974.

WW   William Wordsworth

Sara Coleridge,
A Victorian Daughter

Introduction
Sara Coleridge and the Politics of Literary Revision

Re-vision—the act of looking back, of seeing with fresh eyes, of entering an old text from a new critical direction—is for women more than a chapter in cultural history: it is an act of survival. Until we can understand the assumptions in which we are drenched we cannot know ourselves.

Adrienne Rich, *"When We Dead Awaken"*

Such are the chief historical events of my little life, up to nine years of age. But can I in any degree retrace what being I was then—what relation my then being held to my maturer self? Can I draw any useful reflection from my childish experience, or found any useful maxim upon it? What was I?

Sara Coleridge, *Untitled Memoir*

Writing on Sara Coleridge in September 1940, Virginia Woolf recognized the tragedy of a life lived only to a fragment of its potential.[1] Like her father's "Christabel," Sara Coleridge became for Woolf an "unfinished masterpiece" whose genius was much in evidence but whose circumstances conspired against completion, stifling talent and denying possibility. The intimidating shadow of a brilliant father, the early death of a beloved husband, and the unending demands of parenthood all served to thwart the intellectual energies of a woman who by the age of twenty-two had mastered six languages, published two books, and had proven herself in many ways the most Coleridgean of Coleridge's offspring.[2] Yet according to Woolf whatever accomplishments were achieved—several children's books, a few essays, even the impressive editorial projects—pale in comparison to what might have been.[3] Continually interrupted by the demands of female duty, Sara was a "heaven-haunter" unable to translate her visions into the words of men: she was "diffuse," "indefatigable,"

1

"incomplete" (114–16). Although more educated and more articulate than the imaginary "Judith" from *A Room of One's Own,* Sara became for Woolf another of Shakespeare's sisters, a silent heroine whose muffled story haunts our understanding of the past as it challenges the myths of our present.

Woolf's backward glance at Sara Coleridge was not without its jolt of recognition, for the daughters of educated men understood one another, and the modernist daughter of the Victorian scholar and the Victorian daughter of the Romantic poet were closer than it first appeared. Sara died in 1852, some thirty years before Woolf's birth, but good friends of hers would visit Little Holland House and enjoy the company of Woolf's grandmother and her various great-aunts. Had Sara lived, she might well have joined them and perhaps taken to Aunt Julia Cameron, the eccentric and indefatigable photographer, or better yet to Aunt Anny, Thackeray's daughter and valued editor. In any case, because history was always for Woolf a kind of dusty mirror, the image of Sara Coleridge, the blurred features of S. T. Coleridge's real life Christabel, could not help but capture Woolf's own reflective gaze. Their profiles, after all, were surprisingly similar. Both were "clever" daughters of well-known men of letters;[4] both had had to struggle for an education while brothers enjoyed the universities; both had been encouraged to believe in traditional female selflessness and in marriage as their only suitable employment. Not surprisingly, both suffered anxiety, insomnia, and "madness."[5]

There were, of course, important differences, differences Woolf could use to measure her progress and distance herself from the similarities. Sara, for instance, did not have Bloomsbury. When she moved from her birthplace at Greta Hall, Keswick, to London following her marriage in 1829, she left behind "Uncle Southey" and "dear Mr. Wordsworth" and the freedom to spend her mornings as she chose. She said goodbye to the Lakes and her various "projects" and to a certain Romantic sensibility. In turn, she acquired an affectionate husband, economic security, and ten years of uninterrupted pregnancy. She became a proper Victorian lady, keeping her husband's house in order and writing poems for her children rather than herself. Like a significant number of other women in the early nineteenth century, she suffered from hysterical fits and addiction to opium. Yet, regardless of ill health, she always read voraciously—primarily literature but also history, philosophy, economics, and theology.

When her father died in 1834, Sara was overcome less by grief than guilt, for Coleridge had hardly been a responsible parent, and his daughter, like many neglected children, internalized his neglect. Years later Sara would freely admit that she had known both Wordsworth and Southey "more intimately" than she had her own father (Reed 63), and it was no secret that Coleridge had lived with his youngest child only a brief period—a period measurable in months. Nevertheless, her sorrow was acute and her sense of duty well defined: she leapt to his defense. With her husband (and first cousin), Henry Nelson Coleridge, she began an editorial project which would last almost twenty years and which would successfully counter De Quincey's charges of plagiarism and the widespread rumors of Coleridge's irresolute self-indulgence. Together they sold "Esteesee" in the image of the Victorian sage, not as the poet but as the theologian and political philosopher, the author of *Aids to Reflection, Lay Sermons,* and *On the Constitution of the Church and State.* Time and again, they published works designed to emphasize Coleridge's moral vision; even more so than J. C. Hare, F. D. Maurice, or John Stuart Mill, they were responsible for transforming a dissolute poet into a respected philosopher, and a fragmentary and miscellaneous corpus into, as Leslie Stephen later phrased it, the "centre of intellectual light in England."[6]

When her husband died in 1843, Sara took over the Coleridge literary estate and increased her editorial labors, publishing *Aids to Reflection* (1843), *Biographia Literaria* (1847), *Notes and Lectures Upon Shakespeare* (1849), *Essays on His Own Times* (1950), and *The Poems of Samuel Taylor Coleridge* (1852). Each new edition was accompanied by a lengthy introduction or appendix in which Coleridge's theories were explained, defended, or qualified. In addition, Sara began writing reviews, essays, and poetry. She became friends with Joanna Baillie, Elizabeth Barrett Browning, Anna Jameson, F. D. Maurice, William Gladstone, Henry Taylor, and Aubrey de Vere. She continued her studies in philosophy, history, and theology. By 1850, she was an established figure among the London literati, as comfortable discussing politics with Carlyle or Macaulay as she was sharing literary gossip with Henry Crabb Robinson. After her own death in 1852, Sara left thousands of pages of unpublished manuscripts—essays, letters, journals, poems, and long theological dialogues in the style of Landor's *Imaginary Conversations.* Most were fragments.

Woolf could understand fragments. Thus, Sara's twenty-six-page autobiography, written as she lay suffering from breast cancer in September 1851, became a telling document. Looking closely at the series of dots which end the memoir in midsentence, Woolf found an apt symbol for a woman who, like her father, was fated to "complete incompletely" (118), but who, unlike her father, would receive little recognition for her labors. Toiling in the service of Coleridge's reputation, Sara pieced together his fragments at the price of her own. But Woolf saw too that although fettered by duty, Sara nevertheless discovered a kind of freedom in her editing. It was there she "found her father, in those blurred pages, as she had not found him in the flesh; and she found that he was herself" (115). Editorial work became "not self-sacrifice, but self-realization," a pathway to completion, a process by which father and daughter, separated throughout their lives, found themselves and each other in a labyrinth of words.

Yet Woolf might have wondered to what degree that self-realization was accomplished at the expense of self-expression. After finishing her monumental edition of her father's *Biographia Literaria* in 1847, Sara confided to her diary a passage that Woolf would have known:

> No work is so inadequately rewarded either by money or credit as that of editing miscellaneous, fragmentary, immethodical literary remains like those of STC. Such labours cannot be rewarded for they cannot be seen— some of them cannot even be perceived in their effects by the intelligent reader. How many, many mornings, evenings, afternoons have I spent in hunting for some piece of information in order to rectify a statement—to decide whether to retain or withdraw a sentence, or how to turn it—the effect being negative, the silent avoidance of error. The ascertainment of dates, too, and fifty other troubles of that kind, causes much work with very little to shew for it. It is something to myself to feel that I am putting in order a literary house that otherwise would be open to censure here or there. But when there is not mere carelessness but a positive coldness in regard to what I have done, I do sometimes feel as if I had been wasting myself a good deal—at least so far as worldly advantage is concerned. [Diary (28 Oct 1848)][7]

Having worked for over a decade to repair her father's reputation, Sara grew dissatisfied with her "reward" and began late in life to question the value of her efforts. The endless concern with the minute particulars of someone else's corpus granted satisfaction, but of a distinctly subservient sort. Her phrasing— "putting in order a literary house"—tropes nicely on the domestic parallel; both sets of chores demand a prescribed selflessness that tends to "waste" original talent. "What," she laments, "*might* I have been?"

Clearly, the self-realization achieved in and through editorial labor was not the uncompromised union Woolf suggests, but a far more complex phe- nomenon—psychologically, socially, and historically—and one that stands at the center of a web of familial events rarely cause for speculation. This book explores that complex phenomenon in detail and argues that these familial events are of crucial importance both to a better understanding of Romantic literary history and to a subsequent and much-needed rejection of the Romantic paradigms that continue to structure our critical practice.

II

Woolf's essay was occasioned by the publication of Earl Leslie Griggs's 1940 biography of Sara Coleridge, *Coleridge Fille,* and although polite and compli- mentary, her review was no doubt intended to offer at least a partial corrective to his solid but unimaginative account. Adding to Henry Reed's "The Daughter of Coleridge" (1852), Edith Coleridge's *Memoir and Letters of Sara Coleridge* (1873), and Mrs. E. A. Towle's *A Poet's Children* (1912), Griggs's biography painted a formal portrait over their rough and often inaccurate sketches. A scrupulous researcher, he made extensive use of the unpublished material, preferring whenever possible to let the remains speak for themselves. But however sympathetic, Griggs was unable to realize anything more than a general and very distant understanding of his subject. Sara Coleridge would always be a "distinctly minor figure" (vii), and his biography as a result seems to envision itself as one long, definitive footnote to a universally accepted and unchanging "History" of great men and great events. Griggs gives no indication that Sara Coleridge's life offers anything more than a "minor" glimpse back to a famous father, and certainly no suggestion that her life might continue to speak to the present, interrogating the very "History" which has condemned her to obscurity.

Reconstructing the people and patterns of history from another set of assumptions, Woolf knew that to focus solely on the "major" was to rely upon a limited set of criteria and let innumerable questions go begging. She had mocked the tunnel vision of male historians in *A Room of One's Own* (1929) and had recognized that such self-assured selectivity was dangerous, inappropriate, and silently obfuscating.[8] She knew too that the real story often begins rather than ends with its supposedly minor details:

> And, like so many of her father's works, Sara Coleridge remains unfinished. Mr. Griggs has written her life, exhaustively, sympathetically; but still . . . dots intervene. That extremely interesting fragment, her autobiography, ends with three rows of dots after twenty-six pages. She intended, she says, to end every section with a moral, or a reflection. And then "on reviewing my earlier childhood I find the predominant reflection. . . ." There she stops. But she said many things in those twenty-six pages, and Mr. Griggs has added others that tempt us to fill in the dots, though not with the facts that she might have given us. [111, Woolf's ellipses]

In Sara Coleridge's life, Woolf saw a mystery which Griggs's biography helped more to intensify than alleviate. His assurance as to both the status and details of his subject could not keep the questions at bay. On one level, then, the series of dots symbolized a failure to complete, an inability to make or do what might have been; as such, they signified a radical lack and nothing more. Sara's own writings could not, Woolf realized, rival her father's: "Like her father she had a Surinam toad in her head, breeding other toads. But his were jewelled; hers were plain" (116). Considered formally, Sara's productions were, to use Griggs's phrase, "distinctly minor." On another level, however, as Woolf also realized, the dots punctuated a faded tale illegible to her eyes, a muted story very much a part of the heard melodies of great men and great events. In the latter case, the dots defeated critical self-assurance, represented something just beyond her grasp, and so constituted a focal point into which all perspectives collapsed. Those mysterious dots thus wisely subsumed Woolf's own possible interpretations: with so much left unrecorded, with a life reduced to dots on a page, it became pointless to argue whether Sara Coleridge was the unfortunate victim of an oppressive society or a grateful martyr to the spirit of her father—always the ". . . dots intervene."

If Virginia Woolf erred in her assessment of Sara Coleridge, she did so by too quickly accepting a mystery for which she thought there was no explanation. Written only six months before her suicide, Woolf's essay is unusually resigned to its own limitations; it is reluctant to question Griggs's use of the unpublished material and pessimistic about the possibilities for historical reconsiderations of "minor" women writers. However "sympathetic" Woolf finds Griggs's portrait, his brand of historiography aids and abets the very cultural forces that worked to marginalize Sara Coleridge as a nineteenth-century woman of letters. And, however qualified by its palpable sadness, Woolf's own acceptance of Sara as a fragmentary "Christabel" performs an analogous function, condemning Sara (albeit benevolently) with hierarchical standards of "taste" capable of flexibility but incapable of rejecting "style" and "taste" altogether.

Put another way, both Griggs and Woolf employ a system of valuation (more generally historical for the former, more specifically literary for the latter) that presupposes the necessity of public performance, of "great works" produced by artistic or intellectual "genius." That system cannot accommodate the fragmentary and miscellaneous remains of Sara Coleridge without immediately pronouncing them a failure. The result for Woolf was a double bind: she recognized a victim of cultural prejudice, of institutionalized prohibitions against women, only to have her aesthetic standards, which were necessarily canonical even when revisionist, tell her there were ample reasons for the "minor" status handed down by "History." In short, a desire for historical revision warred against the unchallengeable supremacy of "Art" and its accompanying (and unavoidable) dependence upon formalist hierarchy.

Consider, for example, another of Woolf's late essays, one particularly appropriate to this study of Sara Coleridge, "The Art of Biography."[9] There, by way of a discussion of Lytton Strachey, she explores the question, "Is biography an art?" The answer is no. The reason is that "the novelist is free; the biographer tied" (188). The latter's work "is made with the help of friends, of facts"; the former's "is created without any restrictions save those that the artist, for reasons that seem good to him, chooses to obey." Although the categories do in practice overlap, a distinction remains: biography is a "craft" rather than an "art" (191). While biography is necessarily limited by its extratextual referentiality, art is "a free world where facts are verified by one person only—the artist himself" (193).

As the masculine pronouns suggest, there is already a serpent lurking in Woolf's Eden, and, at the essay's close, when Woolf puts biography on a "lower level" just beneath the "intense world of the imagination," that serpent squirms more fully into view: "We are incapable of living wholly in the intense world of the imagination. The imagination is a faculty that soon tires and needs rest and refreshment. But for a tired imagination the proper food is not inferior poetry or minor fiction—indeed they blunt and debauch it—but the sober fact, that 'authentic information' from which, as Lytton Strachey has shown us, good biography is made" (196). The imperial "we" is a giveaway. To whom could it refer if not to a select few whose wide reading and good judgment guarantee their positions as purveyors of taste and tradition? Acclimated to sublime heights, they return intermittently to the world of "sober fact" to take a breather from their heady exertions and to recheck historical grounding.[10] The latter is an admittedly important process; "inferior poetry" and "minor fiction" were unquestionably for Woolf historical events worthy of scrutiny. But they were also corrupt (and corrupting) imaginative products: like the serpent in the garden, they promised knowledge but threatened purity. They were, as Woolf remarked elsewhere, "as great a menace to health of mind as influenza to the body."[11]

The "intense world of the imagination," it would seem, was not entirely free. However feminist its orientation, however much its dependence on and allegiance to the world of "sober fact," it remained structured by gradations of taste, standards of judgment which, at a moment's notice, could separate the "genuine" from the "inferior," the "major" from the "minor." It presupposed, in other words, the romantic belief in the otherworldliness of art, in the unquestioned and unquestionable superiority of certain imaginative artifacts over their more explicitly historical and specifically cultural counterparts. This belief, the ideological legacy to which both Virginia Woolf and Sara Coleridge were heir, has been described and exposed most succinctly by Jerome McGann in his influential study *The Romantic Ideology: A Critical Investigation* (1983). There he writes:

> Romantic poetry pursued the illusions of its own ideas and Ideals in order to avoid facing the truths of immediate history and its own Purgatorial blind. . . .
>
> When reading Romantic poems, then, we are to remember that their ideas—for example, ideas about the creativity of Imagination, about the centrality of the Self, about the organic and processive structure of natural

and social life, and so forth—are all historically specific in a crucial and paradoxical sense. . . . In the Romantic Age these and similar ideas are presented as transhistorical—eternal truths which wake to perish never. The very belief that transcendental categories can provide a permanent ground for culture becomes, in the Romantic Age, an ideological formation—another illusion raised up to hold back an awareness of the contradictions inherent in contemporary social structures and the relations they support. [134]

The legacy of romanticism, according to McGann, adopts "fundamental illusions" as categorical givens, "ideological formations" as transcendental verities, and "historical strategies" as ahistorical truths: "Literary criticism," he warns, "too often likes to transform the critical illusions of poetry into the worshipped truths of culture" (135). Sara Coleridge, I will argue, like Virginia Woolf, worked hard at "transform[ing] the critical illusions of poetry into the worshipped truths of culture." Paradoxically, however, such efforts ran counter to the very processes of reading and writing in which both women were engaged. The complexity of these contradictions speaks directly to contemporary criticism and questions the sanctity of our collective illusions.

Regardless, then, of Virginia Woolf's political commitments, of her hatred for patriarchy and her disgust at the hegemony of the literary canon (not to mention of "History" in general), she could not renounce her belief in the liberating world of art or her distrust of "minor" literary works like those of Sara Coleridge. Woolf could not abandon the security of "Literature" as a category objectively verifiable and ideologically unfettered. To do so would be to relinquish "art" for "propaganda" and "disinterestedness" for "unreal loyalties" (*Three Guineas* 85–144). It would also be to turn her back on the one Victorian institution that had provided the means by which she could escape from the incestuous house of her father and from the stultifying role of Victorian woman.[12] To question the degree to which Woolf's aesthetics worked to suppress her more radical politics is not to slight the power of what Jane Marcus has emphasized as the three dominant strands of Woolf's thought—"the mystical, the 'Marxist,' and the mythical";[13] but it is to see how the tension between Woolf's need for aesthetic standards and her desire for historical revision necessarily raises questions first about the use of major/minor distinctions in literary studies and then about possible alternative systems of critical valuation. In other words, Woolf's struggles to evaluate the writings of Sara Coleridge suggest that as long as the literary and the nonliterary remain presupposed and unmediated critical categories, then corresponding distinctions between major and minor will follow logically. Through hard work and harder polemics the literary can indeed be redefined to include "minor" writers—the politically, the sexually, the ethnically disenfranchised. But the revisionist critic usually argues that the heretofore marginalized work has been marginalized only because of a previous failure to perceive exactly how the work embodies the scene of its struggles: the "minor" writer is shown to be as complex, subtle, engaging, or powerful as the "major" writer but on significantly different terms, the relevance of which becomes apparent only after contextual redefinition. Such a move challenges the values of the literary without questioning the framework itself. If, however, the historicity of the idea of the literary is admitted as a conceptual given, then normative examination yields to a functional analysis of significantly broader scope. Or, to put it more succinctly, once historicized, the idea of the literary loses its transcultural status; it steps down from the sublime heights of romantic idealism and is reintegrated into the cultural marketplace.[14]

Sara Coleridge lived her life in the cultural marketplace, and however marginalized by her sex, she played an integral part in the literary economy of early-nineteenth-century Britain. To assume with Woolf that Sara's fragmentary and miscellaneous writings signify only the tragedy of weak will and wasted talent is to deny the meaning of a life caught between private need and public expectation; between the middle-class aspirations of an established Devonshire family and the aristocratic pretensions so much a part of the English literary world. Moreover, it is to ignore the complex processes of production and reception that constitute the making of literary value—both then and now.

III

Had Virginia Woolf examined the beginning of the 1851 fragment as closely as she had its ending, she might have ventured a more conclusive opinion about the stature of "minor" literary women, for Sara Coleridge's autobiography begins neither with a polite greeting to a familiar audience, nor with a formal introduction to the whole of the reading public. Rather, the memoir opens with an informal note to Sara's daughter, Edith:

My dearest Edith,

I have long wished to give you a little sketch of my life. I once intended to have given it with much particularity, but now *time presses*—my horizon has contracted of late. I must content myself with a brief compendium.

I shall divide my history into Childhood, Earlier and Later; Youth, Earlier and Later; Wedded Life, ditto; Widowhood, ditto; and I shall endeavor to state the chief Moral or Reflection suggested by each—some maxim which it specially illustrated, or truth which it exemplified, or warning which it suggested.[15]

Although in 1851 she was well known in London literary circles as an accomplished author and editor, although she could claim acquaintanceship with the most influential thinkers of her day, and although she had spent her first twenty-five years among three of the most famous literary families in Great Britain, Sara's autobiography was not written as a public document. Addressed specifically to Edith, the epistolary memoir was intended to be both a familial record and a cautionary tale, at once a private genealogy preserving the maternal line and a moral exhortation passing along the wisdom of age. Paradoxically, then, a life replete with the experiences of which popular memoirs were made found its expression in a private discourse that assumed its own exclusion from the very "History" in which it had participated.

Not all writing, of course, has to aspire to publication, and Sara, then suffering from the horrors of cancer, had numerous reasons for not wanting to undertake an exhausting project. Nevertheless, just a few weeks after beginning her autobiography, she abandoned it in order to devote herself exclusively to a new edition of her father's poems. Such a decision was perfectly in keeping with Sara's attitudes about female authorship and with her devotion to the reputation of her father; for like the autobiography itself, her decision to labor on his behalf rather than her own only emphasizes that writing by women in the early nineteenth century was often reluctant to call attention to itself, that publications by women were often seen as embarrassments necessitated by financial difficulty, and that women's "histories"—the essays, the poems, the journals, the diaries, the records of their lives—were often written in the margins of the very texts they themselves had helped to produce.[16] As Sara explained in her diary several years before actually beginning her fragmentary memoir, "Sometimes I have had thoughts of an autobiography. I believe the life of any individual, related sincerely & accurately in its more characteristic features—an abstract giving the quintessence of the individual's experience—would be interesting and valuable. But then the difficulty would be to avoid exposing others in explaining oneself" (Diary [3 Nov 1848]). For Sara, "explaining [her]self," making herself "interesting and valuable" to her audience, was concomitant with "exposing others," a betrayal that highlights the sacrosanct boundary between public and private even as it suggests the extent to which Sara's own "experience," the "quintessence" of her intellectual and emotional life, was "explain[able]" only to the detriment of family and friends. Thus, to tell her own story would be by definition to challenge stories already told and to violate respected codes of female propriety. There were, however, alternatives, and this book will trace the various strategies Sara Coleridge used—consciously and unconsciously—to "tell her own story" without violating societal expectation. As her essays demonstrate time and again, a nominal subservience to patriarchal authority can be used effectively to empower the woman writer.

Had Virginia Woolf, for instance, paused to consider the significance of Sara's opening remarks to her daughter, she might have recognized the degree to which women's writing in the early nineteenth century was marked indelibly by paradox. Like the all-pervasive and massively influential ideal of "femininity," which paradoxically celebrated an angelic womanhood so as to control its demonic netherside, female authors writing in the years following the French Revolution—authors lauded as assertive, enlightened, and ideologically untrammeled—often experienced the same tensions and contradictions that conflicted their less articulate sisters. Mary Poovey has eloquently demonstrated, for example, that even the most famous women writers of the period—Mary Wollstonecraft, Mary Shelley, and Jane Austen—battled the spectre of the "proper lady."[17] Analyzing the ideologies of style and narrative in their "major" works, Poovey qualifies their "artistic" achievement by explicating the psychological, historical, and political tensions inherent in early-nineteenth-century female authorship. Her analysis—one indispensable for understanding the context within which Sara Coleridge lived and worked—explores key contradictions at the heart of popular notions of female propriety:

> The period during which Mary Wollstonecraft, Mary Shelley, and Jane Austen wrote constitutes . . . a critical phase in the history of bourgeois ideology and thus provides a particularly revealing perspective upon the way in which lived and imaginative experiences are informed by ideological contradictions. This was the period in which the French Revolution represented a dramatic symbol of social and economic changes that seemed to threaten England as well. As such, it provoked both explicit challenges to the political inequality inherent in English patriarchal society and adamant defenses of the whole system. . . . As a consequence of these forces, the social order based on patronage gradually gave way, between the 1790s and the 1830s, to the practices and pressures of individualism. As competition and confrontation replaced the old paternalistic alliances of responsibilities and dependences, women in particular found their position becoming increasingly anomalous; for in some very practical ways women had always been protected by the values and allegiances of paternalism, and now, as exemplars of paternalistic virtues, they were being asked to preserve the remnants of the old society within the private sphere of the home. In doing this, however, early nineteenth-century women epitomized within their own "virtues" one of the fundamental contradictions of bourgeois ideology. For both their idealized helplessness and the domestic life they kept separate from the marketplace were increasingly at odds with the competitive spirit that was rapidly transforming every other sector of English society. [xv—xvi][18]

Pushing the scope of her analysis past the boundaries favored by such influential studies as Sandra Gilbert and Susan Gubar's *Madwoman in the Attic* (1979) and Nina Auerbach's *Woman and the Demon* (1982), Poovey situates the literary firmly within its conflicted cultural and economic context. She extends the psycholiterary concerns of Gilbert and Gubar past the sociomythic focus of Auerbach into the unabashedly political (and economic) context of a changing cultural system. After carefully charting the psychopolitical tensions embedded within Wollstonecraft's *Vindication of the Rights of Men,* for example, Poovey concludes that "despite her valorization of self-assertion, what Wollstonecraft really want[ed was] to achieve a new position of dependence within a paternal order of her own choosing" (67). Such a reading acknowledges both the security of "paternalistic virtues" and the "pressures of [a rising capitalist] individualism" so as to restore to the literary text (and, one might add, to the critical text as well) the complexity of its contradictions.

Unlike Mary Wollstonecraft, however, Sara Coleridge spoke out stridently for the paternalistic virtues as manifested in the writings of her father; she was, moreover, singularly responsible for packaging and dispensing Coleridge as the patriarchal remedy needed to cure the social ills of the 1830s and 1840s. Yet, in the same way that Wollstonecraft's "radical" doctrines contain evidence of their author's allegiance to an older "paternal order," so Sara's comparatively reactionary writings contain strategies of accommodation and subversion through which she exercised a growing need for "unladylike" self-assertion. Born in the same year that her father renounced the French cause and advocated war against Napoleon, a recantation less opportunistic than representative of a widespread apostasy, Sara came of age during a period of pronounced political conservatism, a period marked by a powerful opposition to the ideas and events of the 1790s. No longer was the intellectual climate conducive to vindicating the rights of women. Thus, like Mary Shelley, who evidenced a sense of propriety stronger than that felt by her mother, Sara harbored deep misgivings about the status of female authorship. Nevertheless, by the time she composed her autobiography in 1851, she had become extremely adept at manipulating editorial privilege for her own benefit and redefining the very patrimony to which she swore allegiance.

The multiple redefinitions enacted in and through Sara Coleridge's editorial labors complicate Gilbert and Gubar's idea of the "anxiety of female authorship" both by expanding the area of inquiry to include noncanonical texts and by challenging the traditional, Romantic notions of literary creation that continue to structure our critical enterprise. In other words, I agree with Margaret Homans that "the Romantic tradition makes it difficult for any writer to separate sexual identity from writing" and that "where . . . literary tradition normatively identifies the figure of the poet as masculine, and voice as a masculine property, women writers cannot see their minds as androgynous, or as sexless, but must take part in a self-definition by contraries" (3). Unlike *Madwoman in the Attic,* which also strongly endorses the above tenets, Homans's pioneering study, *Women Writers and Poetic Identity* (1980), insists on the importance of "comparing not so much the achievement as what precedes achievement, the process that leads to a sense of poetic vocation or identity" (9). This emphasis on process allows Homans to uncover the complex double bind at the heart of Dorothy Wordsworth's poetic efforts and to greatly expand the boundaries of the literary critical enterprise. While indebted to the work of both Gilbert and Gubar and Margaret Homans, I will argue that Coleridge's daughter provides yet another, and to my mind more revealing, example of the complexities of female literary production in the early nineteenth century. Whereas Dorothy Wordsworth was, according to Homans, successfully constrained by the "phallologocentric" ideologies of Romanticism, Sara Coleridge found in her editorial work an unusually effective solution to the pervasive prohibitions against women intellectuals, a solution that well illustrates what Elizabeth Janeway has termed "the powers of the weak."[19]

However adept at strategies of editorial self-aggrandizement, Sara Coleridge has of course never been considered a "major" figure by literary historians—for two reasons. First, her sense of female propriety forbade the forceful assertion of the Romantic "genius" so quintessentially represented in her father, and neither a propitious political climate (as in the case of Wollstonecraft) nor financial need (as in the case of Shelley and Austen) forced Sara to violate cultural prohibitions. As a result, all of her various works—poems, letters, introductions, appendices, reviews, and informal essays—position themselves by choice in the margins of other more authoritative, precedent texts. Second, her championing of paternalistic virtues has proved predictably off-putting to revisionist historians who are drawn to more outspoken "minor" writers. Strongly influenced by the very patriarchal standards they wish to revise, many feminists have chosen to ignore the strategies by which the majority of nineteenth-century women deflected and appropriated male power.[20] Such revisionism uncritically assumes the primacy of "literary" creation and the power of the imagination, ignoring the complex processes of production and reception that govern what kind of "literary" text is valued at what critical moment and for what ideological reasons. Even so astute a critic as Mary Poovey, for example, elects to perform her analyses only on canonized texts, although—as she would perhaps argue—those texts, by virtue of their privilege, are more strategically valuable as sites of sociopolitical revision. Nevertheless, the obvious question remains: why revise a Sara Coleridge when so much remains to be done for a Harriet Martineau, a Maria Edgeworth, or a Fanny Wright—not to mention Wollstonecraft, Shelley, or Austen?

The not so obvious answer is that Sara Coleridge occupies a unique position among women intellectuals of the nineteenth century. Not only was she instrumental, as this study will demonstrate, in the production and marketing of a celebrated Romantic poet and philosopher; she was also an unacknowledged collaborator, a daughter who used her father's fragmentary remains as a *raison d'écrire*, as an opportunity for the expression of her own considerable intellectual talent. She wrote and rewrote his literary life as a way of controlling her patrimony and redefining her marginal career as a woman of letters: she was at once the dutiful daughter and the domineering matriarch, the proper lady and the woman writer. Like Jane Austen and Mary Shelley, Sara Coleridge subscribed to the feminine ideal; but like Mary Wollstonecraft and Harriet Martineau, she had little desire to write domestic fictions. At heart, she was a religious philosopher, capable of studying the most abstruse metaphysics without boredom or fatigue. But in fact, she was a woman caught between her allegiance to inherited patriarchal ideals and her desire for an engaged and productive intellectual life. More so than the "major" literary women who overcame their anxiety of authorship to produce "great works" in designated genres, or the "minor" ideologues who learned to articulate their dissatisfactions in tracts now generally ignored by literary historians, Sara Coleridge pursued a career that allowed her to enact the very paradoxes in which she was enmeshed: editorial duty was both subservience and mastery: and she could, with relative freedom, alternate between "angel in the house" and "virago of the press"—to use a phrase that she herself applied to Martineau.

More important than editorial paradox, however, are the ways in which Sara Coleridge's life and work dramatize the importance of literature and literary criticism to the shifting class structures of England's infant industrial economy. The Coleridges, like the Southeys and Wordsworths, were distinctly middle class, and yet the later conservatism of all three poets, a conservatism that Sara vociferously defended, involved at least in part the appropriation of aristocratic ethics by a bourgeois literati desirous of a greater cultural influence. As Arno Mayer has convincingly demonstrated, the "old regime" was by no means dead—either in 1800 or in 1850—nor were the class divisions of the mercantile period suddenly erased by the changing economy.[21] Rather, the English aristocracy successfully assimilated itself to the new industrialism—encouraged by a self-interested middle class:

> Whereas the nobility was skilled at adaptation, the bourgeoisie excelled at emulation. Throughout the nineteenth and early twentieth centuries, the grand bourgeois kept denying themselves by imitating and appropriating the ways of the nobility in the hope of climbing into it. The grandees of business and finance bought landed estates, built country houses, sent

their sons to elite higher schools, and assumed aristocratic poses and life-styles. They also strained to break into aristocratic and court circles and to marry into the titled nobility. Last but not least, they solicited decorations and, above all, patents of nobility. These aristocratizing barons of industry and commerce were not simply supercilious parvenus or arrivistes who bowed and scraped for fatuous honors from the parasitic leisure class of a decaying old order. On the contrary, their obsequiousness was highly practical and consequential. [13–14]

Crucial to this process, as Mayer emphasizes, was the ownership of "high culture":

As part of their effort to scale the social pyramid and to demonstrate their political loyalty, the bourgeois embraced the historicist high culture and patronized the hegemonic institutions that were dominated by the old elites. The result was that they strengthened classical and academic idioms, conventions, and symbols in the arts and letters instead of encouraging modernist impulses. The bourgeois allowed themselves to be ensnared in a cultural and educational system that bolstered and reproduced the *ancien regime*. In the process they sapped their own potential to inspire the conception of a new aesthetic and intellection. [14]

Although Mayer does not discuss the importance of literature to the realignment of class ideologies during the first half of the nineteenth century, the connection should be obvious: Sara Coleridge inherited bourgeois values and championed them throughout her career. She was convinced, she informed her cousin Frank Coleridge, both "that there should be a class who make literature the business of their lives" and that she herself was of such a class (Letter [1 Feb 1844]). It was her "duty," her "moral responsibility," to educate her contemporaries and spread Coleridgean truth. The numerous volumes of her father's writings that appeared between his death in 1834 and her own in 1852 offer testimony to her labor.

The realignment of class ideologies during the first half of the nineteenth century renders Poovey's notions of female propriety somewhat problematic. Such codes must not be seen simply as universal ideals of uniform significance, codes of male origin designed to foster female submission, but rather as codes whose significance varied depending upon the social positions of those (men and women) affected. Sara Coleridge, for example, like many of her middle-class contemporaries, was caught in the paradoxical position of having to reinforce class distinctions at the very moment she promoted a universal (and bourgeois) morality derived from aristocratic norms. She distanced herself from Mary Wollstonecraft but respected Madame de Staël. Consequently, certain

kinds of literature—especially her father's—which represented relatively con-
servative ideological positions actually empowered her as a writer and thinker,
more so perhaps than many feminist historians would choose to acknowledge.
On the other hand, her "collaboration" with her father was also a collaboration
with the aristocratic desire to reformulate a nascent industrial society along the
lines of its agrarian precursor. Or, to put it another way, the modesty of
feminine literary production contrasts sharply against the boldness with which
women were put to work in the factories, and Sara Coleridge's complicities with
conservative ideology should give us pause even as we applaud the determina-
tion and ingenuity required "to tell her own story." To recognize, then, the
degree to which gender issues were defined by shifting class allegiances is to
complicate the problems of nineteenth-century female authorship by rethink-
ing which women writers actually held what kinds of literary power and within
what social and political context.

So it is that the incomplete autobiography, written specifically to daughter
Edith and abandoned in favor of one last editorial tribute to S. T. Coleridge,
represents more than simply a fragmentary mystery composed by another
"minor" woman writer. As I argue at length in chapter 6, Sara intended the
record of her life to exemplify and espouse Coleridgean principles, but she
discovered instead that the experiences she recalled threatened the order she
wished to impose: the painful memories of a negligent parent failed to reconcile
themselves to a comforting retrospective vision of Coleridge the Victorian sage.
In short, the father she had experienced was less attractive than the philosophy
she had created. And so the autobiography breaks off in midsentence: "On
reviewing my earlier childhood I find the predominant reflection. . . ." There
she stops, choosing to leave unfinished a private memoir to her daughter in
order to begin a new edition of her father's poetry and yet another introductory
essay in which she would interpret, as she had done so many times before, the
man who had come to represent the spirit of her age.

Her essay, however, although very much a tribute to paternalistic virtues,
was precipitated more by desperation than devotion. As Virginia Woolf could
not have known, Sara's autobiography was written in the midst of a crisis of faith
that had begun during the early summer of 1851 and was by that September
reaching its zenith. Characterized by depression, insomnia, and raging hys-
terical fits, her illness is recorded in her diary, where entries indicate that it was
part of a larger pattern of doubts concerning those institutions which had
molded her life. Earlier suspicions about the value of "putting in order" some-
one else's "literary house" bred in turn further suspicions which, when encour-
aged by the agonies of cancer, led her to question God's omnipotence and her
own possibilities for salvation. Thus, Woolf was right to suspect a mystery
lurking behind those concluding dots. But she was wrong to assume that they

automatically inscribed an inadequacy and that that inadequacy necessarily prohibited further scrutiny.

IV

Sara Coleridge spent the greater part of her life "putting in order a literary house" only to realize on her deathbed that she could have built her own. Her autobiography is an attempt at revision, at looking back, at seeing with fresh eyes how she might have laid new foundations instead of refortifying the old ones put down by her father. Virginia Woolf built her literary house on sites cleared by Sara Coleridge and women like her; Woolf looked back to the "lives of the obscure" in order to find her own tradition, her own line of women writers working in the shadows of great men and great events. Even though she was convinced of their "invincible mediocrity," she persisted; she read their memoirs, their diaries, their "inferior fiction," and their "minor poetry." They revised her understanding of history; she revised the way they were understood. It was, in Adrienne Rich's words, a mutually beneficial "act of survival."

The process of revision continues. To revise Virginia Woolf revising Sara Coleridge is to extend the act of survival; it is to question Woolf's unquestioned tenets as well as to champion her political and artistic integrity. It is also to question the paradigms which structure our own critical activity and to wonder about the possibilities for a cultural studies less dependent upon exclusionary standards and more receptive to the varied and often fragmentary voices of history. Sara Coleridge's fragmentary voice should remind us that literature is a social construct, an institution deployed in favor of the cultural status quo. Her voice encourages us both to reconsider the complexities of women's roles in the nineteenth-century publishing industry and to complicate traditional notions of literary production and reception. To recover Sara Coleridge's "own story," then, is not to have the last word on a "minor" subject or to define that which has previously escaped definition; it is instead to offer yet another reading, another revision of women's literary history. This book reads Sara Coleridge's life and work in an attempt to understand the intricate connections between authorship and collaboration, between empowerment and marginality, between feminism and history.

"Castles in the Air"
Education, Romance, and the Beauty of the Soul

The childhood and early womanhood of Sara Coleridge were spent under the generous guardianship of her uncle, Southey, in whose house at Keswick she, with her mother and brothers, had a happy home for many years. During that period she also enjoyed the fatherly intimacy of Wordsworth, and very often was his companion in long rambles through the beautiful region where the poet dwelt—listening to his sage discourse with the earnest ear of thoughtful youth. . . . Under such propitious guidance, or in the joyous fellowship of her brothers or of her sisterlike cousins, did she learn to hold communion with nature, and thus was her poetic soul strengthened. . . . this child of genius.

Henry Reed, "The Daughter of Coleridge"

This is the Age of Taste if not of Reason: we all visit picturesque scenery, scramble up rocks, & brace "the pelting of the pitiless storm" in hunting lakes & waterfalls; we pore over collections of pictures, striving with might & main to admire what ought to be admired and vice versa; we discuss the merits of actors, dancers, & singers with a view to display our own exquisite taste if not profound knowledge of the arts of acting, dancing, & singing; and [we] acquire weak eyes (one of the most fashionable juvenile diseases) by hurrying through an endless succession of novels, poems, & new publications of all sorts; in such an age is it not wonderful that Beauty, the great object of Taste, should be more than ever the theme of admiring eyes & tongues.

Sara Coleridge, "On Beauty"

On Christmas Day 1802, Coleridge wrote a short letter to Southey announcing the birth of his third child, a daughter: "I arrived at Keswick, with T. Wedgewood, on Friday Afternoon—that is to say, yesterday—& had the comfort to find that Sara was safely brought to bed, the morning before—i.e. Thursday ½ past six, of a healthy—GIRL! I had never thought of a Girl as a possible event— the word[s] child & man child were perfect Synonimies in my feelings— however I bore the sex with great Fortitude—& she shall be called Sara" (CL 3:902). For Coleridge, as for many of his contemporaries, the male child was an asset, the female a liability, one a blessing, the other a disappointment. In Coleridge's case, the disappointment was so insignificant in the abstract as to be almost inconceivable, barely "a possible event." But in its actuality that event became so demeaning and demoralizing that it required a good dose of paternal "Fortitude" in order to restore emotional equilibrium. A male child, after all, would carry his father's name proudly out into the world and, with good fortune, into history. A female child, on the other hand, could only, under the most ideal conditions, marry well, leaving the house of her father for that of her husband, relinquishing her name, becoming the property of another man.[1] Whereas males were educated at the grammar schools and universities and then freed to capitalize on acquired talents, females were "polished" at home and schooled in social skills and domestic management. If the opportunities for matrimony were missed, the unattached woman continued as a financial burden to her family, a perennially unemployed "old maid"—loved, pitied, often resented.

Greta Hall had, in effect, two old maids. The first, Mary Fricker Lovell, Sara's aunt, was widowed in 1796 and ungenerously provided for by her husband's family. As a result, much of the financial responsibility fell to Southey, who labored with characteristic industry to provide the needed assistance. The second, Mrs. Coleridge, of course remained married to and supposedly supported by the errant poet. Nevertheless, Coleridge's financial (and parental) irresponsibility forced her to reside at Greta Hall with her children and without her husband, largely dependent upon Southey for security and guidance. In the years between Sara's birth in 1802 and her father's last visit to the Lakes in February 1812, Mrs. Coleridge lived with her husband less than two years. After the 1812 visit neither she nor her daughter would see Coleridge again until January 1823. This separation was complicated by irregular correspondence: Coleridge was so lax during Sara's childhood and early adolescence that he often allowed years to elapse between letters.[2]

Because of her own difficulties, then, Mrs. Coleridge was especially concerned for her young daughter and saw to it from the very beginning that Sara was given a rigorous education. For although Coleridgean apologists from the Wordsworths on have painted her as a petty, selfish, small-minded woman, Mrs. Coleridge was in fact both clever and enterprising—and, unlike her husband, most capable of perseverance on behalf of her children.³ Writing to Thomas Poole in August 1810, for example, Mrs. Coleridge intimates her hopes for Sara's regular study:

> S.T.C. has been here the last four or five months, and I am sorry to add that in all that time he has not *appeared* to be employed in composition, although he has repeatedly assured me he was. . . . Yet, I must not say that his abode here has been without some advantages to us, for as soon as he came, finding his daughter was desirous of learning Latin, which she had begun, he thought it a good opportunity of teaching both her and her Mother the Italian Language while he staid: I was rejoiced at this offer but was afraid he would not persevere, and I am convinced he would very often have put off the child, when he could not find an excuse to send us *both* away when our tasks were ready.—Sara has read through a little book of Poems in that Language, many of which she can repeat, and we are now trying the PASTOR FIDO. [*Minnow* 11–12]

Even though Coleridge left for London two months later, mother and daughter persevered in their studies, and when he returned to Keswick in February 1812, on what would be his last visit to the Lakes, he was most impressed with the accomplishments of his nine-year-old daughter:

> Little Sara does honor to her Mother's anxieties, reads French tolerably & Italian fluently, and I was astonished at her acquaintance with her native Language. The word 'hostile' occurring in what she read to me, I asked her what 'hostile' meant? And she answered at once—Why! inimical: only that inimical is more often used for things and measures, and not, as hostile is, to persons & nations.—If I had dared, I should have urged Mrs. C. to let me take her to London for 4 or 5 months. . . . [S]he is such a sweet-tempered, meek, blue-eyed Fairy, & so affectionate, trust-worthy, & really serviceable! [*CL* 3:375]

As Coleridge's somewhat patronizing reference to his wife implies, Mrs. Coleridge—more than any of the other residents of Greta Hall—encouraged Sara's regular and systematic study. Even Dorothy Wordsworth gave grudging approval: "Her mother is an excellent teacher *by Books,* for Sara is an admirable scholar for her age. She is also very fond of reading for her amusement—devouring her Books—yet she is childlike and playful with children" (*W Letters* 2:526).

There were other encouragements besides those offered by Mrs. Coleridge. Brothers Hartley and Derwent had left Greta Hall for Mr. Dawes's grammar school in the fall of 1808, and their experiences must have excited Sara's curiosity and competitiveness. Unlike her "idle cousins," she was not content to let her brothers parade their superiority without a challenge; denied their formal education, she was forced to scavenge for her knowledge but did so with energy and obvious enjoyment. "She is an excellent Scholar," Mrs. Coleridge remarked to Poole, "& no trouble to teach, her brothers teach [her] in the holidays, so she picks up a little knowledge between us all—her father is very good to her when he is here, & complimented me on her progress in Italian etc. She can read a little French, and she is learning Latin, we have no Music yet" (*Minnow* 20). At first it must have been a simple kind of game, a "playing at school" in imitation of her absent brothers and in naive agreement with their notions of her inferiority as a female. But as Sara's genius asserted itself, as she became increasingly adept at her daily lessons and at pleasing her elders with her precociousness, the game would have had to change. She would have had to realize that she was competing successfully on forbidden turf, forbidden not in the sense that she was unequivocally denied access but that her presence there was unusual, and to the males of her family, somewhat amusing. Hartley, for example, was far from encouraging; he tended to be protective of his learning and at times snide and condescending. And so, as Sara grew older, the game became increasingly complex. Knowledge was not available simply for the taking; it had to be taught, and teaching a young girl had its own protocol: instruction was neither a right nor a privilege but a favor granted by those whose priorities lay elsewhere.

If Sara's intellectual propensities made for an unusual situation, that situation was complicated further by her weak health. Brothers and uncles might occasionally raise a mocking eyebrow over "little Sara's" studies, but it was the women of Greta Hall and Allan Bank who persistently questioned the wisdom of her labors. Time and again, Mrs. Coleridge's letters from this period adopt a defensive posture in regard to her daughter's activities: "She cannot be left at night—she is also quite langu[id and] her appetite and spirits have forsaken her—we must have recourse to some [?] Port wine to give her wonted elasticity—poor little love! She is but a tender creature and because she is rather forwarder in her books than most of the little Girls around us—the wise Mamas, forsooth, insist upon it, that she is killed with study—but although she is fond of improvement—she is far *fonder* of play [*Minnow* 26]. With the rigors of education perceived as a major threat to the child's delicate constitution, Mrs. Coleridge felt it necessary to defend herself and her daughter by proving that Sara was not a victim of an overbearing parent, one "killed with study," but a normal, happy little girl. To Thomas Poole she explained,

> Derwent and Sara begin to grow rather faster than [they] did at any former
> period; but the latter is so delicate that I [dare] not let her study much;
> indeed she has always had her full share of play, & certainly more pleasure

than falls to the lot of children in general; for Southey chuses to take the children on the water whenever a party is going from the house and as this generally lasts all day, and occurs pretty often they certainly have too much of this sort of thing during the summer; & Sara is almost half her time at Greta-bank with Miss Calvert where she rides on horseback often and plays more than half her time: I trouble you with these trifles, to shew you that she is not made ill by books; for I have not the slightest doubt if anything ill should happen to this dear child there would not be wanting persons to say, that she had been kept too close [at her studies]. [*Minnow* 41–42]

Frail enough that Mrs. Coleridge could imagine her early death, Sara was not ill enough to be denied schooling. Like Wordsworth, who saw Sara's learning as insurance against the possibility of spinsterhood,[4] Mrs. Coleridge firmly believed in the value of her daughter's studies and seriously questioned whether Sara's health was being adversely affected to the degree maintained by "the wise Mamas."

While the opportunities for play were many and while Sara seemed to enjoy the amusements of childhood as much as the labors of her lessons, Greta Hall was nevertheless a highly structured educational environment. "We keep a regular School," Mrs. Coleridge reported to Poole in February 1814, "from ½ past nine until 4 with the exception of an hour for walking and an half hour for dressing—Mrs Lovel keeps school in a small room for English and Latin—and the writing and figures—french—italian &c are done with me in the *dining room* with the assistance of Aunt Eliza—and Southey teaches his wife and daughters to read spanish in the study and his son Greek—should we not all be very learned!" (*Minnow* 29). The makeshift school at Greta Hall prospered, and Mrs. Coleridge's hopes for a "learned" household were soon realized. A year after Sara's mother wrote the above, Southey boasted of his pupil's success in a letter to John Estlin: "Sara has received an education here at home which would astonish you. She is a good French and Italian scholar, a tolerable Latinist, and is now learning Spanish. She has begun music also, and is said by those who are competent in the subject to display most extraordinary talents for it" (*NL* 2:119).

Thus with her mother's encouragement, Sara quickly outdistanced her fellow students and challenged Hartley's reputation as Keswick's leading child prodigy. In the process, the young scholar managed to precipitate some ill will. "The Coleridges are all scholars," Dorothy Wordsworth admitted, "but there is not one of them wholly free from affectation" (*W Letters* 3:141).[5] Yet Dorothy's real complaint was not as much with Sara as with her mother, who, in Dorothy's eyes, was unfit as a parent. Mrs. Coleridge's "lady-like" manners and worldly aspirations produced "a delightful scholar . . . eager in the pursuit of knowledge" but discouraged "the wild graces of nature" which Dorothy valued so much in her brother's children (W Letters 3:320). Sara was educated but sickly, cultured but devoid of "natural wildness": "[Young Sara] is to come in Spring, and Mrs. C is desirous to put off the evil day, for she dreads the contamination which her lady-like manners must receive from our rustic brood, worse than she would dread illness, I may almost say *death*. As to poor little Sara, she has behaved sweetly ever since her Mother left her, but there is nothing about her of the natural wildness of a child. She looks ill and has a bad appetite" (W Letters 2:373). Mrs. Coleridge's dread of the Wordsworths' rustic improprieties is likened by Dorothy to a fear of disease, which, for all its priggish concern about "contamination," paradoxically produces a child so lacking in "natural wildness" as to be the quintessence of ill health. Considering that women of learning supported themselves only when absolutely necessary, only, in other words, when destitute, the ill-health resulting from rigorous (and unnatural) study seemed to Dorothy a foolish price to pay for an ultimately useless and extravagant luxury.

For Wordsworth's strong-minded sister, the young Sara had, by 1809, already become a convenient figure through which to read the elder Sara's faults. At first, Dorothy's animosity evidenced itself in general remarks about the recurrent illnesses at Greta Hall, remarks that could always find substantiation in specific references to the youngest Coleridge. "I believe," Dorothy wrote in November 1803, "Sara Coleridge was never in a passion in her life, she is the very soul of meekness . . . but poor thing! she has been exceedingly ill as have all C's children and all the children at Keswick" (W Letters 1:419). As Sara matured, her diminutive stature became the focus of attention and a measurement against which Dorothy could judge her own healthy household:

> My brother says he should scarcely have known Sara. . . . She is thin and very small. Our baby is twice her size. [W Letters 1:475–76]

> Sara is a pretty Creature, her eyes are beautiful, and her whole figure is very elegant—but she is such a *little little* thing beside our Johnny. [W Letters 1:486]

> I could not help grieving. . . . [Sara] is puny in appearance, very diminutive, and has not a healthy appetite. I think it likely she will be a clever child, and though I must own that she is far less interesting than she was a year ago, yet she grows exceedingly like her Father. [W Letters 1:608]

What began as familial pride in the trifling issues of bodily health and stature quickly became part of the larger, well-established tensions between the two households. Sara's growing intellectual appetite served only to emphasize her continued ill health and raise eyebrows concerning her mother's competence as a parent.

Significantly, Dorothy's distrust of female scholars is echoed in scattered remarks on female education made by Coleridge himself during the spring of 1814. Although he was largely incommunicado and hence exerted no direct influence on his daughter's development, Coleridge would soon become the dominant intellectual presence in her life. His views, then, perhaps motivated in some way by Sara's example, are extremely important as guides both to his later attitudes about Sara's marriage and to his understanding of the role of women in society, an understanding which Sara would in fact support but one against which she would chafe. Unknown to her, on April 2, 1814, the *Felix Farley's Bristol Journal* published the following advertisement:

> MR. COLERIDGE has been desired by several highly respectable Ladies to carry into effect a plan of giving one or two lectures, in the morning, on the subject of FEMALE EDUCATION, of a nature altogether practical, and explaining the whole machinery of a school organized on rational principles, from the earlier age to the completion of FEMALE EDUCATION, with a list of the books recommended, &c. so as to evolve gradually into utility and domestic happiness the power and qualities of Womanhood. Should a sufficient number of Ladies and Gentlemen express their design to patronize this plan, Mr. Coleridge will hold himself ready to realize it. [CL 3:474–75]

This brief statement is all that remains of a lecture most likely never given. It suggests, however, that Coleridge, like Wordsworth and Southey, conceived of female education as a process in the service of "practical" ends—in other words, a process which begins with a defined and unalterable sense of "the powers and qualities of Womanhood" inextricable from their "utility" within the "domestic" context. If education for men encouraged the ability to take responsibility and make decisions in the world, female education was to encourage the avoidance of responsibility and the acceptance of decisions already made: the domestic sphere was by definition subordinate to its worldly counterpart and so dominated by an imposed set of patriarchal regulations.[6]

Not surprisingly, Coleridge was concerned first and foremost with the education of his sons. Hartley went to Merton College, Oxford, in 1815 and visited regularly at Highgate during his vacations. Derwent stayed on at Mr. Dawes's school until September 1818 and then became a tutor for a family in Lancashire until he secured a position at St. John's College, Cambridge, in 1820. He too visited his father at Highgate. Sara, on the other hand, remained at Greta Hall. Her only excursions were to the Wordsworths at Rydal Mount, frequent visits facilitated by a general easing of tensions between the two households.[7] The truce was a result both of Coleridge's prolonged absence, which effectively removed a major source of contention, and of the friendships which grew among the various sets of children, in particular the friendship of Sara Coleridge, Edith Southey, and Dora Wordsworth. Celebrated in William Wordsworth's 1828 poem, "The Triad," those ties would have been important to a girl growing into womanhood without the company of her brothers or the security of a stable family. Yet Sara never adopted the less studious ways of her companions.[8] In fact, regardless of irregular health and the constant temptations of her friends, she pursued her studies with increasing enthusiasm and a sense of urgency, fueled in part by her brothers' uncertain prospects; for although Coleridge was full of concern and advice for his sons, he was unable to provide substantive assistance. Hartley went to Oxford because of efforts by Southey and Wordsworth; Derwent was provided for by J. H. Frere.[9] But where Coleridge proved ineffectual, his sixteen-year-old daughter surprised family and friends with her enterprising diligence.

More than a year before Frere sent Derwent to Cambridge, Sara was already dutifully at work on a translation which she hoped would generate the necessary funds. The idea had been Southey's. He had suggested to Derwent during the fall of 1818 that a translation of Martin Dobrizhoffer's book on Paraguay, *Historia de Abiponibus* (1784), might be successful enough to bring some fame to its translator while providing money enough for the university. More interested in mathematics than the Indians of South America, Derwent was unenthused but without alternatives. When Sara eagerly volunteered her assistance, he agreed, thankful no doubt for help of any kind. According to Mrs. Coleridge, "Derwent began the first vol: and Sara . . . began the third," each completing equal portions by the time Frere's offer was made. Once Derwent learned of his good fortune, he immediately dropped the translation, and it was presumed his sister would do the same. Such was not the case. As Mrs. Coleridge reported to Poole in November 1821, "When Sara found a stop was put to it, she felt disappointed, and said, she liked the employment 'of all things,' and her uncle approving her specimen, said, if she chose, to finish it, at her *leisure,* she might, but she must not be disappointed if nothing was gained by it, and she must *not work too hard*" (*Minnow* 89–90). Southey's concern for his niece's health proved unnecessary. According to her mother, Sara did not "suffer from too intense application" but emerged from her labors "in better health than I have ever known her." In fact, if there were any unpleasant side effects, they occurred only after she finished the project: "so fond is she of literary employment that she feels quite at a loss for her last winter's amusement."

As the quotations suggest, Sara's literary "employment" first had to be redefined and divested of all intrinsic value before it became permissible. She could finish her project only "at her *leisure*," only, in other words, if she renounced it as a worldly activity of some merit ("nothing was [to be] gained by

it") and reconceived it as mere "amusement," as an activity tangentially impor-
tant to her own life and negligibly important to the lives of others. To consider
the situation in this way is not to deny that Southey's qualifications were
motivated by a genuine concern for Sara's health but to see that his concern
expressed itself in terms of preconceived notions of the value of female educa-
tion and "employment" and was thus necessarily blind to the possibility that
Sara's labors could be the cure rather than the cause of her bodily complaints.
For Southey, women's "duties" did not include the "business" of literature, and
a young girl who liked literary work "'of all things'" was destined for a rude
awakening.[10]

An Account of the Abiphones, an Equestrian People of Paraguay was published
anonymously by John Murray in January 1822, only weeks after Sara's nine-
teenth birthday. It offers testimony to her industry and talent as well as to her
affection for her brother Derwent, who received a substantial portion of her
£113 earnings. The translation was not, however, widely acclaimed, but it did
spark well-earned praise from a small audience, including some respectfully
humorous remarks from Charles Lamb. Writing to Southey, Lamb begins by
commenting on an allusion to Sara that Southey had included in his *Tale of
Paraguay*: "The compliment to the Translatress is daintily conceived. Nothing is
choicer in that kind of writing than to bring in some remote impossible parallel,
as between a great Empress and the unobtrusive quiet soul who digged her
noiseless way so perseveringly thro' that rugged Paraguay mine. How she
Dobrizhoffered it all out, it puzzles my slender Latinity to conjecture" (Lucas
3:22). Although Sara "Dobrizhoffered it all out" largely on her own, Derwent
nevertheless deserved his gratuity. Whereas Hartley, in Mrs. Coleridge's words,
"always discourage[d] his sister's erudite propensities," goading her with the
refrain "*Latin* and *celibacy* go together," Derwent "encourage[d] & instruct[ed]
her," less willing perhaps to see her only as a commodity on the marriage market
(*Minnow* 82). During the fall of 1819, for example, they read together in Tacitus,
Livy, Virgil, Cicero, Ariosto, Tasso, and Dante; and one senses that even though
Derwent spent most of his time tutoring in Lancashire, he and his sister had
become much closer as a result of their collaboration on Dobrizhoffer. With
Hartley at the height of his short-lived academic career and traveling in the more
illustrious circles of Oxford and London, Derwent and Sara must have derived
needed consolation from their new intellectual relationship.

By the time Coleridge read through his daughter's translation in January
1822, Hartley's star had already fallen. During the early summer of 1820,
Hartley learned that his fellowship at Oriel College, Oxford, would not be
approved. He had received the award in April 1819 and had become a proba-
tionary fellow of Oriel for one year, at the end of which, in a merely routine

procedure, he was to be elected an "Actual Fellow" of the college. Hartley's behavior during that year, however, proved unsatisfactory, and in late May 1920 he discovered that he would be unable to qualify at the formal procedure in October. Accusing him of multiple irregularities, the most severe of which was repeated "intemperance," the authorities of Oriel suggested he resign and avoid the disgrace of public humiliation. Choosing to defend himself against what he felt to be unjust charges, Hartley refused to resign and before long enlisted his father's support. Coleridge, who suffered his son's misfortune greatly and who would later assert that it was one of his life's greatest sorrows, came to Hartley's defense and campaigned actively against the charges.[11] But Oriel was implacable, and in late October Hartley was publicly denied his fellowship and given £300 reparation, which, with Coleridge in full accord, he stridently refused to accept.

Hartley's failure at Oxford was a severe blow to the entire Coleridge family, and its repercussions continued to be felt for years. Mrs. Coleridge, for example, when she learned of the lost £300, remained unconvinced of the value of symbolic gestures. The matter was debated in letters, and, as a result, she finally received the money in January 1823, largely through the efforts of John Taylor Coleridge, Sara's first cousin and future brother-in-law. But in January 1822, the month Sara's translation was published, Coleridge was worried less about Hartley than Derwent, who, it appeared, was following too closely in his elder brother's footsteps. Embracing the dilettantism popular among his college friends, Derwent allowed his examinations to fall below parental standards. To make matters worse, he then wrote a spirited defense of his alleged "Coxcombry," as Coleridge had termed it, which succeeded only in further offending his father. Sara, by comparison, should have been a comfort to the distracted poet feverish with worry about his wayward sons. Yet oddly his letters during this period are without reference to his daughter. That the two were occasional correspondents is highly likely but uncertain; at the very least, they would have communicated through an intermediary—Mrs. Coleridge. In any case, the surviving records make no mention of Sara's publication until August 1832, when Coleridge remarked in passing, "My dear daughter's translation of this book is, in my judgment, unsurpassed for pure mother English by anything I have read for a long time" (*TT* 2:81). The reason for this silence may have had less to do with insensitivity or preoccupation than with what was for him simply a matter of priorities. As he had explained it to Derwent several years earlier, "In your and Hartley's welfare for the next three or four years all my Heart is fixed— not that I do not tenderly love and yearn after your dear Sister: but I know not what I can hope to effect for her in the present state of my circumstances" (*CL* 4:799).

II

Coleridge's relationship with Sara was to change. Having long considered a trip to the south, expressly to reunite father and daughter, Mrs. Coleridge finally completed the necessary arrangements and left Greta Hall with Sara on November 6, 1822. The journey would last some eight months, only three weeks of which would be spent at Highgate; but when Sara returned to Keswick in June 1823, she would no longer be the innocent wunderkind made "uneasy" by an eccentric father and her own uncertain prospects.[12] She would return a young woman experienced in the ways of London society, confident in her abilities, and more sympathetic to the erratic and idiosyncratic ways of her father. She would also return committed to a decision that was to determine the course of the next twenty years, a decision that would prove both a great blessing and an irrevocable curse.

On their journey south, mother and daughter stopped first in Derby to visit the Evans family and then at Coleorton Hall to visit Sir George and Lady Beaumont. Sir George, an artist and patron of the arts, had met Coleridge during the summer of 1803 and Wordsworth a short time later. Cultured and aristocratic, the Beaumonts remained friendly with both families for many years: Sir George provided occasional financial support and Lady Beaumont regularly exchanged long, newsy letters with Mrs. Coleridge and Dorothy Wordsworth.[13] Even their well-informed correspondence, however, failed to prepare Lady Beaumont for the shock of seeing Sara. The "Highland Girl," as William Collins represented her in an 1818 painting,[14] had since yielded her youthful innocence to a mature beauty, and Lady Beaumont was quite taken: "I never saw at her age such a delicate little sylph, so thoughtful, yet active in her notions, she would represent our ideas of Psyche or Ariel, Juliet would be too material, but she looks so delicate I should tremble at her becoming a wife or mother." (*W Letters* 4:187n). The notes of praise sounded here are the first of what were to become by the end of the trip an entire symphony in honor of Sara's beauty. Lady Beaumont, Charles Lamb, the Gillmans, Coleridge himself, all were charmed by her delicate features and her serious but unassuming manner. Weak health enhanced Sara's slight build and gave her an otherworldly aura, an ethereal beauty which seemed to deny her physicality and encourage comparisons to sylphs or fairies. As Hartley remarked years later, "Sara was always so completely unique, so perfectly a Fairy, a being belonging neither to time or space, so like the etherial vehicle of a pure spirit, a visible soul (I remember once when she was sitting at the Piano-forte at Greta Hall she told me I was a *visible fool* for saying so) that I cannot image any thing like her, which is not completely the same" (*HC Letters* 156). Such "etherial" beauty was much in keeping with the standards of the day: it displaced the bodily in favor of the

spiritual and celebrated the "angel in the house" over its demonic coun-
terpart.[15]

The reports drifting back to Keswick were so lavish in their praise that
Southey found it necessary to interject his displeasure. The offending party was
Lady Beaumont, who had evidently offered to hold some kind of social event in
Sara's honor: "If Lady Beaumont has formed any indiscreet scheme of showing
off Sara, I am afraid Mrs. C. would enter into it too readily, & set down any
caution which might come from me, to a wrong motive. Most probably her
warm manner of speaking has been interpreted more literally than it was meant.
But I believe the Wordsworths are going to Coleorton, & they will prevent this
kind of mischief" (CL 5:268n). Exactly what "scheme" disturbed Southey is
unclear, but his paternal concern emphasizes that the trip to London was a rite
of passage, a coming-of-age quest for the experiences of the big city, for social
approval, and for firsthand knowledge of the absent father, the eccentric and
enigmatic Sage of Highgate. That Southey should be protective and querulous is
understandable given both his patriarchal lordship over Greta Hall and his
informed wariness of the Coleridgean monologue. Sara was old enough, South-
ey knew, to choose her own "father" and to become corrupted, if she desired, by
the fashionable life of London.

After a short visit with Derwent at Cambridge and a long stay with the
Clarksons at Playford Hall, Mrs. Coleridge and Sara finally arrived at Moreton
House, Highgate, on January 3. For the first time in ten years, father, mother,
and daughter were together in one room; and their reunion would have been
awkward as well as emotional—perhaps anticlimactic. Sara, unfortunately, left
no account of the meeting, and Mrs. Coleridge would later report to Poole only
that the stay at Highgate was of "the greatest satisfaction to all parties" (Minnow
99). Nor did Coleridge himself wax eloquent. Writing that same evening to
Charles Aders, he simply noted, "my Daughter (a sweet and delightful Girl) is
with me" (CL 5:267). Thus, for whatever reason, Sara's visit at Highgate remains
almost completely shrouded in silence. If there were causes for celebration, if
there were intimate discussions and genuine good feelings, none of the three
participants felt compelled to record the details.

The Coleridges' arrival at Highgate coincided with the arrival of two other
Coleridges equally intent on paying their respects to the poet. John Taylor
Coleridge and Henry Nelson Coleridge, Sara's first cousins, visited with their
uncle on December 28, 1822, and returned to Moreton House on January 5
specifically to meet their relatives from the north. Both had heard the rumors of
Sara's beauty and erudition and wished to appraise her for themselves. The
eldest of the two brothers, John Taylor, was an aspiring lawyer, a father of two
small sons, and a man of refined literary tastes. Already a frequent visitor at
Highgate, he deeply respected the intellectual powers of his uncle. His younger

brother, Henry Nelson, was only four years older than Sara. He had just begun reading for the law, after having distinguished himself at King's College, Cambridge. More urbane and self-assured than his brother, Henry enjoyed playing the rake, at least with his sister Fanny, to whom he sent this account of his first meeting with Sara:

> John and myself walked out to Highgate after morning church on Sunday, and got wet through. My uncle received us joyfully on the stairs, and led us into the drawing room, where were Sara and her mother. John swore he would kiss Sara, before he arrived, which I strenuously advised . . . I knew I should not have courage enough for it. But he quailed at the moment of trial, and though her lips are sufficiently tempting, yet he did not kiss her. I contented myself with a most affectionate, prolonged diminuendo and crescendo squeeze. . . . She is a lovely creature; small, but not in the least diminutive or dwarfish; her figure perfectly proportioned; her hair like Mary's [John Taylor's wife] and her eyes like a dove's; fair with a nice carmine; little features. Mrs. C. is not prepossessing; she was wonderfully kind and attentive and watchful; I even read *design* in her eye. She dressed most unbecomingly. Sara neat and elegant. . . . She does not seem at all formidable; you need not alarm yourself. She uses no hard words and seems very ordinary in her wishes and thoughts. I will engage five to one, she commits waste in the heart of the Special before a week is over; and truly let not the Special despair; he will find this little sylph of Ulleswater sufficiently susceptible, if I do not mistake. And God bless her! she has not a shilling to cross her [palm] with. [Letter (Jan 1823)]

The insouciance would not last, and if we are to assume that Henry refers to himself as the "Special," then his prophecy proved surprisingly accurate, for the "little sylph" wasted no time in casting her spell. On March 21, some two weeks after Sara and her mother had left London for Ottery, Henry made this entry in his diary:

> Sara and myself are solemnly engaged to each other. She promised never to marry any one but me. She wrote me, while in London, two notes, which I keep under lock and key, and gave me two ringlets of her hair, which I had made into two rings; one of them with my own hair intertwined with hers and set round with pearls I gave to her the last morning, when we parted, and the other, her own hair entirely, I keep myself. She took from her own neck a coral necklace, which I now wear round mine. I wrote her four letters. She has since communicated the whole affair to Fanny. . . . She advises us to keep the matter a secret till I can claim Sara without a chance of refusal.

In less than three months' time, Sara had met and secretly engaged herself to the man she was to marry six and a half years later.[16]

For the young lovers the weeks passed in a flurry of activity. Operas, exhibitions, dinner parties, and excursions of all sorts kept Sara far busier than she had ever been at Keswick. Everyone, it seemed, was desirous of meeting Coleridge's brilliant daughter. One of the oldest friends of the family, Charles Lamb, answered what must have been in his circle a common query: "Yes, I have seen Miss Coleridge, and wish I had just such a—daughter. God love her—to think that she should have had to toil thro' five octavos of that cursed (I forget I write to a Quaker) Abbeypony History, and then to abridge them to 3, and all for £113. At her years, to be doing stupid Jesuits' Latin into English, when she should be reading or writing Romances. Heaven send her Uncle do not breed her up a Quarterly Reviewer!" (Lucas 2:370).[17] Lamb was also to record Sara's departure from London a few weeks later: "The she Coleridges have taken flight, to my regret. With Sara's own-made acquisitions, her unaffectedness and no-pretensions are beautiful. You might pass an age with her without suspecting that she knew any thing but her mother's tongue. I don't mean any reflection on Mrs. Coleridge here. I had better have said her vernacular idiom. Poor C. I wish he had a home to receive his daughter in. But he is but as a stranger or a visitor in this world," (Lucas 2:374). The close of the passage strikes an appropriate note, for although the primary purpose of the trip south had been to reacquaint father and daughter, they actually—either by accident or design—spent very little time together.[18]

Whatever the reason, whether Coleridge was in fact as ill as he maintained, or whether he used his illness as an excuse to retreat from wife and daughter, whose company he might have found disquieting for any number of reasons, evidence indicates that he was a less than gracious host. In late March Coleridge sent this apology to Mrs. Aders:

My dear Madam

It is an ill wind that blows no good. Grievously did I moan under the illness, that now supplies or rather precludes my apology, and which during the whole of my dear Girl's stay in town confined me to my chamber—Even while she & her Mother were at Highgate, I never had the power of going to town with them—& during the 5 weeks' interval between their leaving Highgate & returning for *one* day to take their parting Leave for Devon, I never saw them—. [CL 5:271]

Illness often "supplie[d]" Coleridge with convenient apologies, or, more accurately, it was the ever-present excuse that explained and condoned inactivity, self-indulgence, and social infractions of all sorts.[19] The emphasis given to the *"one"* day" out of five weeks that Coleridge did manage to see his daughter encourages Mrs. Aders to sympathize with the invalid and wonder how his wife and daughter could desert him at his hour of need.

Although letters fail to reveal why Sara and her mother decided to move to John Taylor Coleridge's house after only three weeks at Highgate, they do suggest that accommodations at Moreton House were not without problems. Henry Nelson Coleridge's letter to his sister Fanny, for example, implies repeatedly that while surface relations seemed amiable, there was nevertheless a palpable undercurrent of tension. "He and his wife are kind," Henry observed, "but I suppose it is only surface work." For evidence, he noted that "Mr. and Mrs. C. do not even use the same sleeping room. Hum!" The Gillmans, Coleridge's benefactors, also seemed "kind," but their situation "*must* be irksome." Then, in a postscript on the back of the envelope, he speaks again of Sara: "You would split to hear the way I *Romanced* to Sara! It amused me so myself, that once I slightly tittered, which she took for a nervous and enthusiastic motion. My Uncle does not seem very affectionate towards her."

Regardless of his complaints to Mrs. Aders, Coleridge was not ignored during the five weeks that mother and daughter spent with John Taylor Coleridge. He was invited to dinner twice and both times refused, once in a manner so harsh he had to write back and apologize for having suggested that the invitation was not sincere (*CL* 5:267–68). One can only wonder, then, about the reasons for his displeasure. Perhaps he felt himself not to be receiving the proper attention or respect. Perhaps he was jealous of the time Sara and Henry spent in each other's company. Or perhaps he thought his daughter too quick to voice Southey's opinions when she should have been more deferential to his own.[20] Most likely, Coleridge found Sara an uncomfortable reminder of his own failures as a parent. Standing before him in all her charm and intelligence, she was very much a figure of perfection, certainly more successful in her way than either Hartley or Derwent, and yet she was the child least Coleridge's own. He could claim a certain influence over his sons: he had taught them, lived with them, worried about them, and suffered over them. In his own way he had been a father to them. But for Sara he had done nothing. His paternal claim was purely biological, for in the word's more important sense, she had been "fathered" by a community, by her mother and brothers, by the Southeys and the Wordsworths, and by all the illustrious visitors who took the time to engage her in conversation or scribble in her commonplace books.[21] Thus, for Coleridge to find his only daughter, whose birth had been for him barely "a possible event," now grown into an attractive, intelligent, industrious, and unassuming young woman, possessing the very qualities he had tried unsuccessfully to instill in his sons, would have been to confront a powerfully disturbing irony.[22]

After leaving London on March 5, Sara and Mrs. Coleridge traveled to Ottery St. Mary, Devon, where they visited with all of the various "Ottery Coleridges."

No doubt Sara was especially pleased to meet Henry's father, Colonel James Coleridge, and his sister, Fanny. The colonel, ignorant of Sara's attachment to his son, wrote glowingly of his niece: "Sara is indeed a sweet creature, and she has attached herself to me, and indeed to us all. Fanny is delighted with her." Mrs. Coleridge, on the other hand, fared less well: "We get on with Mrs. Sam and let her run on about all the literary World. And I begged her not to think ill of me because I only read the Bible, search the Encyclopaedia, etc., etc. I shall not quiz her for the love I feel for her Daughter."[23]

From Ottery they went to Exeter and to Bristol and then to Nether Stowey, where they spent the month of May with Mrs. Coleridge's old friend Thomas Poole. By the third week in June, mother and daughter were back at Rydal Mount for a short visit with the Wordsworths before returning to Greta Hall. They had been traveling nearly eight months and had completed a circuit of approximately a thousand miles. But the trip could not be considered over until Dorothy Wordsworth had passed judgment on the results: "The Maid of Paraguay and her Mother wait for me to go out. They arrived on Saturday morning and are to leave us tomorrow. The young creature has returned to her native mountains unspoiled by the admiration that has been showered upon her— indeed I think her much improved" (*W Letters* 4:200).

Sara was pleased to be back at Greta Hall. Although her affection for Henry was genuine, it was too new for her to feel anguish over their separation, and she cheerfully settled down into the old Keswick routine—reading, writing, and "rambling." Southey was still addicted to his "morning constitutional," and Sara and Edith were retained as his companions. Now more than ever, their discussions ranged over politics, religion, history, and of course, literature. Only "affairs of the heart" were taboo. But for the present Sara did not mind; she was eager to begin a new project. While she read voraciously (more romances than before), maintained a large correspondence, and earned her keep by helping to instruct the young Southey children, she still needed a project of her own, something to divert her mind from Henry's letters and from the uncertainties of his health and income.[24] Southey suggested the sixteenth-century memoirs of Chevalier Bayard and wrote to John Murray, "that *pert man*," as Sara described him, about the possibilities for publication (Letter: SC to JTC [14 Dec 1823]). Murray agreed to the plan, and Sara began translating from the French in late November.

While the *Memoirs* were only a third the length of Dobrizhoffer's travelogue and would be published in one volume (at Murray's insistence), the work was actually much more difficult. Bayard had been a genuine "knight in shining armor," and true to his fictional type, he had had one series of adventures after another—all recorded in great detail. The obscure military terms and the seemingly endless numbers of people and places kept Sara busy. "In these

Memoirs," she told John Taylor Coleridge, "the names and persons in Italy are so Frenchified and completely disguised, that I am obliged to hunt in Guicciardini and other old authors, for their true spelling" (Letter [14 Dec 1823]). Describing her daughter's "amusement" to Thomas Poole, Mrs. Coleridge noted Sara's "passion[ate]" labor: "she is never weary of turning to books of reference, Dictionaries, (of which this library furnishes several in old french) &c. Many of the Chevalier's exploits were acted in Italy so that she has immense folios of Italian Histories to look into, all of which is an amusement and a thing for which she seems to have a passion" (*Minnow* 111). The extent of Sara's interest in her subject was actually greater than her mother suspected: "I am quite enamoured of my hero," Sara admitted to her cousin, "the more so as he reminds me of my first love, Amadis de Gaul, over whose dreadful adventures I used to cry (unreproved then)" (Letter: SC to JTC [20 Jan 1824]).[25]

By January 1824, when Sara wrote the above, tears were in fact being shed but not over a fictional romance. Unlike Amadis de Gaul, who fought unrelentingly against the emperor of Rome for the hand of his (English) lover, Henry Nelson Coleridge preferred to wait until he had established himself in the law and could afford a wife—however long it took. Sara was in full agreement and not compelled by any sense of urgency, nor was she averse to the separation, believing as she did in Henry's constancy. But she was very disturbed by having to keep their relationship a secret, for secrecy of that sort necessitated minor deceptions on a daily basis. Endowed with a strong moral sense and an equally strong sense of duty, Sara found it difficult to be duplicitous with her closest friends and relatives. To make matters worse, John May, Jr., an almost-lover of whom Sara had thought herself free, proved persistent in his attentions and unmoved by her attempts to make an end to what from the beginning had been a nonexistent relationship. All of these personal anxieties were compounded by Sara's profound disappointment in Derwent's sudden decision to abandon Cambridge for a temporary teaching post at the Plymouth School. The strain manifested itself physically as a "weakness in her eyes," a low-grade infection which kept her from Bayard and so in turn encouraged further despondency. As Mrs. Coleridge reported it:

> She is, at present, dear child, a little *under a cloud,* not without hope, however, of some bright days hereafter. She has been afflicted for the last 6 months with a weakness in her eyes, which, to her, is one of the greatest afflictions that could befall her, inasmuch, as she is not permitted to use them above half the day, so that the other half is passed in dejection and sometimes in tears, which increases the weakness: there is very little appearance of defect in her eyes, so that some of her friends believe it is only nervous, and I myself believe that if not *wholly induced,* the disorder is

greatly *increased* by the state of her spirits, which have suffered great depression for a long time past, and I do not think she ever has been thoroughly happy in her mind since the shock occasioned by poor H[artley]'s failure: her more recent troubles have been on D[erwent]'s account and in respect to *that affair* of her own, of which I gave you a hint in the spring, since the youth [John May] *will* persevere, and now affects to think himself ill used: he now wishes to keep up a correspondence as *Brother & Sister,* she has not replied to the last two letters. [*Minnow* 109–10]

The cloud did not dissipate either that winter or the following spring. Even John May's admission of defeat could not bring Sara out of a depression which had numerous causes and which she herself could only partially understand. So she translated Bayard, wrote Henry, instructed her cousins, and read an astounding number of romances. But the skies continued to darken.

In June the storm broke. Henry had intended to visit the Lakes that summer and spend time with Sara at Greta Hall, but ill health forced him instead to Ottery St. Mary for several months of much-needed rest. While at home, he ignored his own advice and confronted his father with the fact of his engagement, hoping for understanding and perhaps for the financial assistance necessary to realize his pledge. It was a mistake, for the colonel, though fond of Sara, was adamantly opposed to the match, primarily for economic reasons: Henry needed more security than his penniless cousin could ever provide. Henry himself remained unconvinced, and John Taylor Coleridge was given the chore of informing Sara as gently as possible of her "disengaged" status. Sara replied,

According to current notions of *honour,* I may be disengaged, but my own *feelings* will never permit me to think myself so;—in the eye of the world I might be justified in bestowing my affections elsewhere since Henry cannot assure me of his hand as well as his heart; but after what has passed between us, after the vows that we have interchanged, *I must ever think* that for either of us to make such a transfer, while the attachment of the other party remained undiminished, would be a faithless & falsehearted thing; & I have the less scruple in making this declaration because I think that Henry's ill health may render him in more ways than one, less likely to make what the world calls a *good match* than he otherwise might do;— though I would not have him know that I should consider *him* as guilty of any breach of honour or feeling were he to make another and more prudent choice. . . . For my own part, I knew from the beginning that there was but little chance of our being ever united—I knew also that if I entered into the sort of negative engagement which Henry wished, for an indefinite term, till he should think it advisable to ask his father's consent, such a plan would probably prevent my settling in life, as it is called, altogether, & be the spoiling of my future, as the phrase is; for a man may marry almost when he chooses, but with a woman, especially one in my situation, the season is soon past & after dedicating my affections to him for so long a time how could I calculate upon stifling them all of a sudden and marrying another?—No! when I gave my heart to him I gave it for good & all, & never will I take it back till I perceive that he is weary of the gift: then I certainly will never trust any of his sex with it again. . . . Such being my feelings . . . nothing that may be said by any one with regard to this affair can have the slightest power to weaken or strengthen them. [Letter: SC to JTC (17 Aug 1824)]

In addition to revealing Sara's strong character and logical mind, the letter makes clear that her "notions of honour" were based on otherworldly standards acting in open disregard of worldly consequences. She was not naive about her prospects or ignorant of her risks or unaware of her lack of influence. Yet by appealing so obdurately to "honour" and the unassailable purity of "feeling," she effectively wields the very worldly influence she pretends to have renounced. No familial pressures, she argues, could ever "disengage" a spiritual commitment: "nothing that may be said by anyone with regard to this affair can have the slightest power." By using what was to become a favorite strategy, Sara finds worldly power by denying it. Against her, even the Ottery Coleridges were forced to concede defeat.[26]

Emotional turmoil notwithstanding, Sara progressed rapidly on the Bayard *Memoirs,* and by September, some eight months after getting started, she was already correcting proof. But Bayard was only a small part of her life, the only part that appeared always in control, always effortless, always exciting. In contrast, her health and spirits deteriorated steadily. Her eyes became weaker, her sleep more irregular, her tears more frequent. "She is extremely thin," Dorothy Wordsworth wrote: "I could not but think of a lily Flower to be snapped by the first blast, when I looked at her delicate form, her fair and pallid cheeks. She is busy with proof sheets,—a labour that she likes,—yet I should be glad if it were over, and she could be employed and amused at the same time without exercising her mind by thought and study" (*W Letters* 4:274). By the end of the year Bayard was done, Henry was traveling in the West Indies, and her engagement appeared stronger and more stable than ever before. But Sara's health—physical and psychological—continued its downward slide, a decline exacerbated in part by experiments with opium.

Although it is unclear exactly when Sara first began using the drug, most likely it was by late 1824 already contributing to her depressions. The first explicit reference to opium, however, occurs in a letter she wrote to Mary Calvert on October 19, 1825:

I have suffered more bodily pain & discomfort in the course of the last five weeks than I ever remember to have done in my life before;—one could bear up well enough during the day if it were not for the exhaustion produced by so many disturbed uneasy nights;—I am unable to sleep at all without laudanum, which I regret much, though I do not think I shall find any difficulty in leaving it off. [Letter DCL]

On November 5, she wrote to Derwent, "Mr Dequincey is again on social terms with the Wordsworths—he is well & in tolerable spirits & has left off opium, but Miss W. fears he will take to the horrid drug again—*horrid* I call it when thinking of him & some others but in me this is rather ungrateful as it has done me much good & no harm—and I might exclaim with Mrs O'Neil, 'Hail lovely blossom that can'st ease the wretched victims of disease.'" The opium would not continue to do Sara "much good & no harm," for in addition to fragile health and keenness of intellect, she would eventually share with her father an addiction to the drug. At first, her usage was no doubt irregular, but by the mid-1830s her diaries reveal a life tortured by addiction. Fortunately, she would learn—as her father had done—to control her dependency; the lesson, however, would be a hard one. Mrs. O'Neil's poetical assurances notwithstanding, the "lovely blossom" snared its own "wretched victims."[27]

Letters from the period reveal that Sara's anxiety was tripartite: her health, her work, and her engagement. But no one concern assumes the overriding importance of a first cause. Instead, glimmers emerge of a larger and more deeply rooted discontent. Writing to Derwent on November 26, 1824, having just argued that the newly restabilized relationship with Henry was found to improve her health, Sara paused to wish for the simple pleasures of an extended brother-sister relationship: "You have been very good indeed lately in the writing way: long & hard have I looked for letters from you my dear brother; your too long ones were very agreeable in most things, & the affection you express for me gives me sincere delight. I have often thought of Mr Lamb & his sister & wished our fate would be like theirs: but I will not trust myself with you till you are past the marrying age: a brother's wife I never can consent to live with." Retreating from her future marriage and its seemingly overwhelming complications, Sara desired the sanctity of a "safe" arrangement without the constraining duties of wife and mother. Several months later, in another letter to Derwent, she explained herself more clearly: "I should have been happier, with my taste, temper, and habits, had I been of your sex instead of the helpless, dependent being I am. The thing that would suit me best of anything would be the life of a country clergyman—I should delight in the studies necessary to the profession & am sure I should not dislike or obviate from the duties of it. . . . I should not marry" (Letter: [6 June 1825]). While unable to reject the patriarchal definition of "woman" responsible for the "helpless, dependent being" she had become, Sara nevertheless yearned for freedom and self-sufficiency. That her health continued to deteriorate in 1825—all her optimistic predictions to the contrary—only emphasizes that her illness was both capitulation and protest, both an admission of her "dependent being" and an expression of profound dissatisfaction with her lot.

When Sara's second book, *The Right Joyous and Pleasant History of the Facts, Tests, and Prowesses of the Chevalier Bayard, the Good Knight without Fear and without Reproach,* appeared early in 1825, she was already at work on a third. But this time her labors were not for publication. Worried about her health, Southey insisted that her new project, the "Memoirs of Jean de Troye," be undertaken solely as an "amusement" and without the pressures of deadlines, proofs, and printers.[28] Such a restriction, Southey would have argued, only enforces the simple and uncontested fact that "literature is not," as he would later tell Charlotte Brontë, "the business of a woman's life."[29] Now aware of Sara's engagement, Southey saw no reason why she should continue her literary labor: for "such employment," he explained to John Rickman, "disqualif[ies] her for those duties which she will have to perform whenever she changes from the single to the married state" (*NL* 2:280). These strictures, as repressive and unenlightened as they now seem, were to Southey commonsensical, and most likely they confirmed what Sara had begun to realize only after returning form London—that regardless of her intellectual skills, regardless of her industry and her publications, the social standards of her class required "duties" else-where. Thus, it is hardly surprising that her health continued to deteriorate in proportion to her constricting "amusements."

But Sara's mind was not easily captivated by domestic matters, and during the spring of 1825 she began for the first time to study theology with some seriousness. She read Charles Butler's *Book of the Roman Catholic Church* (1824) and Southey's response. *Vindicae Ecclesiae Anglicanae* (1826). She also read Blanco White's *Practical and Internal Evidence against Catholics* (1825) and as-sorted works by Samuel Clarke, Thomas Cranmer, and Richard Hooker. The most important tract, however, and the one that would gradually redefine her intellectual interests away from Southey's pedantic historicism and the dusty Anglicanism that came with it, was her father's *Aids to Reflection.* The book appeared in May, and Sara read and reread it all that summer and early fall. Although initially she found "much of it . . . worse than Greek," she persisted, digging through the more troublesome passages time and again until satisfied with the Coleridgean ore extracted: "I am delighted," she informed her brother Derwent, "with all I can understand" (Letter: SC to DC [20–22 Oct? 1825]). At first, however, her reactions had been mixed, but because all adverse criticism has been carefully cut from her letters, it is impossible to know the precise nature of her objections. Most likely, she adopted Southey's line and faulted the abstruse and "over-laboured" metaphysics, for elsewhere, like Southey, she had lamented her father's inability to write "popularly" (NL 2:300).[30] Yet the details of her complaints are in many ways beside the point, for Aids to Reflection was to exert a lasting effect: the book opened a new and challenging world—religious philosophy—as it offered glimpses into the mind of a man Sara still needed very much to understand.

Henry Nelson Coleridge was due to return from the West Indies in early fall, and Sara had been looking forward to spending the winter and much of the following year in town. But in October whooping cough descended like the plague on Greta Hall, and before long all of its inhabitants were ill. Sara, predictably, suffered the most and the longest; as a result, her journey had to be postponed until the next year.[31] As compensation, she began translating Cervantes but was again dissuaded from her labors by Southey, who insisted that the plays "must be translated into verse" (Letter: SC to DC [Nov 1825]). Not prepared to imprison the Spaniard in rhyme, Sara was given another, and supposedly comparable, "amusement"—the cataloguing of Southey's immense library.[32] "We are making a catalogue," Sara informed her friend Elizabeth Crumpe, "of all my Uncle's books, which consist of about 6000 volumes, every one of which is obliged to be taken down (some by aid of a stepladder, others by kneeling & stooping), brought from all parts of the house where they are dispersed, arranged alphabetically & according to size and subject, written down & replaced" (Letter DCL [3 Feb 1826]). It was, as she noted, "rather dreary work."

For the Coleridges, the new year began in furor over two seemingly unrelated events, both of which would prove important to the changing status of Sara's engagement. First, in January, Derwent announced his intention to marry "as soon as may be."[33] His fiancée was Mary Pridham, a young woman from Plymouth whom neither Coleridge nor his wife had met. Both parents reacted immediately and with great dismay. Mrs. Coleridge wrote, "I hope no child of mine will marry without a good certainty of supporting a family. I have known so many difficulties myself that I have reason to warn my children" (CL 6:546n). Reporting back to Derwent three days later, Sara described her mother as "plunged into one of those bogs of doubt & discomfort" (Letter: SC to DC [2 Feb 1826]). But Mrs. Coleridge's reaction was mild in comparison to her husband's. "My dearest Derwent!" Coleridge exclaimed,

> *Experto credes?*—That the most heartwithering Sorrow that can betide a high, honorable, morally sensitive and affectionate-natured Man, (a guilty conscience expected) is: to have placed himself incautiously in such a relation to a Young Woman as neither to have it in his power to discontinue his attentions without dishonor & remorse, or to continue them

without inward repugnance, and a future *life* of Discomfort, of vain Heart-yearnings and remediless Heart-wastings. . . . For God's sake, think and think again before you give the least portion of your own free-agency out of your own power! You give away more than Life. [*CL* 6:546–47])[34]

While the pros and cons of Derwent's engagement were still being hotly debated, Henry Nelson Coleridge published an account of his recent travels, *Six Months in the West Indies* (1826), which served almost instantly to redirect family anxieties in a new direction. The Ottery Coleridges were the first to express displeasure with the book's "laughing Epicureanism," objecting in particular to an "inappropriate" portrayal of an esteemed family matriarch (Lord Coleridge 142). They saw to it that the book was reissued in a "revised edition" without the offensive passages. Of the Keswick Coleridges, only Hartley shared their stuffy disdain. Writing to Derwent, he confided,

> *Entre nous*—I wish the dear girl had form'd another attachment. Worldly considerations apart, I do not think the author of the *Six Months' Residence* the likeliest person in the world to accord with the exquisite tenderness and susceptibility of her moral and physical constitution. Ever[y] lover, who had had the education of a gentleman, must be delicate, but our Sariola will require delicacy in a husband. . . . The *Six Months,* is very clever, and tolerably sensible, but there is a flippancy, a vulgarity about it, which I cannot esteem. It might have past in a magazine article, written in a feigned character, but surely it suits not the accredited confidante and relative of a Bishop. [*HC Letters* 93]

Mrs. Coleridge thought *Six Months in the West Indies* "lively" (*Minnow* 97), as did her husband, who, although bothered by occasional "offensive images, Sweating &c," confessed to having "received both amusement & instruction from it" (*CL* 6:560).[35] But one passage in particular did irritate Coleridge, a passage that he thought might be taken—by uninformed readers—to be a reference to Sara. Henry had written, "I love a cousin; she is such an exquisite relation, just standing between me and the stranger to my name, drawing upon so many sources of love and tieing them all up with every cord of human affection—almost my sister ere my wife" (117).

A chance complaint to Mrs. Gillman about the possibilities for misreading the passage sparked her confession of having heard vague rumors of an attachment between the cousins. Coleridge, hurt because he was not informed of Sara's involvement, immediately sent a letter of inquiry to Greta Hall. It concluded: "I have no fortune to leave, no *trust* of this kind in the transfer of which I have any interest of duty: and therefore it has ever been my fixed principle in respect of marriage that after my children have reached the years of discretion—

as a friend, I was ready to give them my best advice if it were asked while it be of any service; but as a Father, I had only my Prayers and my Blessings to give" (*CL* 6:590 and *n*). The noble selflessness only partially hides Coleridge's displeasure, and mother and daughter each urgently wrote to assuage his feelings and explain a secrecy adopted with his own best interests in mind. Their letters have not survived, and so exactly how traumatic Sara found the confrontation remains a matter of conjecture. It is safe to assume, however, that the spring of 1826 was one of the most difficult periods of an unusually difficult engagement and that by early summer Sara must have been both relieved to have her engagement common knowledge and pleased about the possibilities for a more open, honest relationship with her father and her fiancé.

Sara began her long anticipated trip to London in late July. Like her journey of three years earlier, this trip marked the beginning of a new stage in her life. Whereas in 1823 she had been a youth of twenty inexperienced in the ways of the world, now she was in every sense an adult. She had weathered the worst storms of her engagement, seen another book through the press, and survived a debilitating series of illnesses and depressions. So during those last weeks before her departure, she would have been eager to escape the routines of Greta Hall and excited by the prospects of London. Yet she was neither too eager nor too excited for literary labor. Before leaving Keswick she wrote what is to date the earliest of her surviving manuscript essays, a twenty-six page meditation on female beauty. The essay emphasizes her intellectual preoccupation with questions of female identity and status as it illuminates the personal anxieties of an intelligent and attractive woman coming of age in an openly sexist society.

III

Sara's essay, "On the Disadvantages Resulting from the Possession of Beauty," is, as its title indicates, an argument against the traditional views of female appearance that celebrate physical beauty as the highest expression of personal excellence.[36] Maintaining that the "Age of Reason" has given way to the "Age of Taste," and that "Beauty, the great object of Taste," has never before had "more numerous or more ardent votaries," Sara begins by playfully criticizing the fashionable pursuits of her contemporaries:

> We all visit picturesque scenery, scramble up rocks, & brave "the pelting of the pitiless storm" in hunting lakes & waterfalls; we pore over collections of pictures, striving with might & main to admire what ought to be admired and *vice versa*; we discuss the merits of actors, dancers, & singers with a view to display our own exquisite taste if not profound knowledge of the arts of acting, dancing, & singing; and [we] acquire weak eyes (one

of the most fashionable juvenile diseases) by hurrying through an endless succession of novels, poems, & new publications of all sorts; in such an age is it not wonderful that Beauty, the great object of Taste, should be more than ever the theme of admiring eyes & tongues.

Beneath the lighthearted prose hides a self-consciously autobiographical subtext. The quotation, from Coleridge's "Monody on the Death of Chatterton," situates the poet within precisely those romantic sensibilities his daughter wishes to reexamine. Moreover, the power Coleridge enjoys as a spokesman for the "Age of Taste" is counterbalanced by Sara's self-deprecating allusion to her own "weak eyes," one of "the most fashionable juvenile diseases." If Coleridge is a high priest, then his daughter is the devout follower—but one hardly blind to the dangers of worship.

The "ardent votaries" strive "with might & main to admire what ought to be admired," and yet they lose rather than gain from their efforts. While the popular pastimes seem harmless, they in fact encourage a celebration of beauty which extends beyond the mere appreciation of "picturesque scenery" to an obsessive concern with "personal appearance." For many young women, Sara argues, physical beauty is rendered "daily more & more the object of their . . . aims and wishes, indeed the engrossing concern of their thoughts & lives." Such obsession is encouraged by art in general and by "the rage for novel reading" in particular: "It is natural for the young female reader to long for the silken eyelashes & the Grecian features which generally constitute the chief charm of the heroine, and enable her to reign triumphantly in all hearts. And there can be no doubt that the consciousness of exciting pleasure, of chaining attention, of awakening emotions akin to love, & that immediately & without effort, is an exhilarating & almost intoxicating sensation, to some tempers the most seducing of all Earth's painted bribes, the most delicious of all her 'grief-engendering joys.'" The power that enables fictional heroines "to reign triumphantly," Sara realizes, is itself largely fictional, and at the end of her first paragraph she proposes to consider "whether Beauty be productive of the most pain or pleasure, benefit or injury to those endowed with it."

While unconvinced that beauty is a complete liability, Sara does wish to unmask the simpleminded view that "Beauty of person . . . tend[s] to make its possessor estimable & happy." To do so she explores the processes by which envy, vanity, and general disquietude all result from a societal preoccupation with "personal advantages." The victims, she concludes, are not limited solely to those beautiful women who deludedly assume superiority on the basis of their looks, but instead encompass all women who are convinced physical beauty is the only marketable female commodity: "How wretched that poor girl whose happiness is dependent on the varying though faithful report of her mirror! But are the lovely & elegant alone subject to such grievous thraldom? Have ill favoured damsels no anxieties respecting personal appearance? To be wholly exempt from them, I regret to say, is for women almost impossible:—a freedom from such petty cares is the enviable privilege of the other sex (a privilege however which they sometimes meanly abandon, becoming voluntary slaves to their glass & toilet)." "Freedom from petty cares" is for women "almost impossible" because beauty is the most convenient standard for evaluation and because it is by definition hierarchical, always asserting itself against (and over) its debased counterpart. Thus, as Sara emphasizes, "the superior beauty of one member" invariably becomes "the source of uneasiness to all parties." Until women find a way to escape society's obsession with appearance, she concludes, beauty will remain "unfavourable . . . to the formation of an estimable & amiable character."

Having established that "personal graces" are more often relied upon "as a cover for faults and deficiencies, or a charm to divert attention from them, than as an incentive to add inward to outward excellence," Sara argues in the remainder of her essay for the necessity of cultivating that "inward . . . excellence." Women must educate themselves so as to counter the "unnatural nurture" of cultural myths and establish respect for their mental and moral capabilities. As long as women remain "satisfied or absorbed with the contemplation of their outward image," they will never be able "to hold up the mirror to their minds." They will remain objects in need of admiration:

> If we address the conscious fair ones we shall generally be regaled with syllables gently ejected as if they were too large and coarse & rough hewn for the delicate mouth:—we must listen to dying falls or a sustained falsetto treble key more wearisome to any but spell-bound ears than the roughest intonations breathed forth naturally and without attempt: the desire and consciousness of admiration is seen to influence every look and gesture—their very gait betrays it—they mince as they go and put out their feet as if each step were to fall under the cognizance of observing eyes. By nothing are sense & dignity so completely banished from the countenance and demeanour as by vanity, which bids the eyes open not to see but to be seen, and the feet move not so much for the purpose of locomotion as of betraying the fair proportion of an ankle.

Without the stability of "inward excellence," beauty succumbs to vanity, renouncing "natural" unselfconsciousness for mindless affectation.

In contrast to "the conscious fair ones" who are aware of and acquiesce to their status as sexual objects, Sara postulates a class of "unconscious beauties" but immediately doubts whether such creatures could ever exist. For evidence, she cites Sir Walter Raleigh's description of a beautiful Indian encountered in the New World: "In all my life I have seldom seen a better favoured woman: she was of good stature, with black eyes, fat of body, of an excellent countenance, her hair almost as long as herself, tied up again in pretty knots, and it seemed she stood not in that awe of her husband as the rest, for she spake and discoursed, and drank among the gentlemen and captains, and was very pleasant, *knowing her own comeliness, and taking great pride therein*" (emphasis SC's). After pointing out that Sir Walter's "fair Savage" would have failed to achieve the same success had she been transported into English society, Sara then makes a crucial point: "Sir Walter's handsome brunette, however, seems to have derived some solid advantages from her charms:—where a general feeling of gallantry does not proceed, where 'allegiance and fast fealty' are not professed unto '*all* womankind,' beauty must indeed be an enviable endowment." The paragraph ends here without further comment, but the suggestion is that beauty becomes an "enviable endowment" only when it allows women the right to participate in the male world, when it encourages the self-confidence necessary for women to "discourse" with men on an equal footing. This "solid advantage," however, is impossible where "a general feeling of gallantry" professes "allegiance and fast fealty" to all women because, Sara implies, idolatry on the basis of physical appearance encourages competition among women and discourages the development of intellectual skills.

Although quick to lampoon affection and valorize the intellect, Sara refrains from pressing her argument. She does not openly propose the equality of the sexes or exhort women to compete in the marketplace. Voting rights, female education, control of property, marriage strictures, all remain nonissues, invisible sources of an unacknowledged dissatisfaction lurking beneath a bantering, witty style. Sara was unable, in other words, either to affirm or deny the ringing exhortation that concludes Mary Wollstonecraft's 1792 polemic *Vindication of the Rights of Woman*: "Let woman share the rights, and she will emulate the virtues of men; for she must grow more perfect when emancipated, or justify the authority that chains such a weak being to her duty."[37]

Having championed "character" over "appearance" and "intellect" over "ornament," Sara then orchestrates a conclusion which progresses in two well-defined stages. First, time is introduced as the great corrective; it historicizes both the possessor of beauty and the standard itself, demystifying the transitory advantages of being beautiful and the taste responsible for determining that beauty. "The pleasure derived from beauty," she writes, "is at the best a dependent uneasy precarious gratification, which holds its existence by the eyes of others." Similarly precarious are the modes of evaluation: "whatever Burke may affirm with regard to fixed principles of taste . . . Nature seldom produces a 'set of features or complexion' whose pretensions to elegance & loveliness are viewed in the same light, or nearly the same, by all beholders. . . . The fact is that in every age and country the ideas of mankind have varied on the subject."

By stressing the historical over the psychological, Sara destabilizes the idea of beauty as an unquestioned aesthetic norm and so prepares the way for the restabilizing gesture of her conclusion. Returning to the earlier emphasis on "inward excellence," Sara uses Bacon's point that the "best part of beauty is that which a picture cannot express" to argue for the far superior "beauty of the soul":[38]

> I would almost say that though external beauty does not, in my opinion, tend to produce any corresponding internal loveliness, yet the soul which is all symmetry, wherein there is "no disproportion," will, in some degree, mould the body to its likeness. Be this as it may, beauty of expression is far above that of favour, colour, or motion. But we are taught to admire a lovely flower, a glowing landscape,—why then should we be checked from admiring that object wherein, as Whither says, form and colour give most delight, "a worthy woman's face"?—because by fastening our attention too exclusively on what is external we overlook in the woman what we are in no danger of doing with regard to the flower and the landscape—the beauty of the soul.

These concluding lines displace the historical in favor of the theological and provide a spiritual corrective to what Sara refuses to see as solely a political and social problem. In other words, while clearly dissatisfied with the contemporary modes of evaluating women and aware of the degree to which men are responsible for female vanity, she nevertheless retreats from a direct confrontation with patriarchal law and offers instead a solution that alleviates the symptoms but spares the disease. Such a strategy allows her to criticize her oppressive role without abandoning the security of its shelter, without incurring patriarchal wrath—in particular, the wrath of a Coleridge, Southey, or Wordsworth.

Sara's "Essay on Beauty," then, is hardly the "girlish composition" E. L. Griggs describes (40). Rather it is a skilled attempt at accommodation by a young woman trying to preserve her integrity and pride without ostracizing herself from family and friends. Undeniably, the essay evidences a strong dissatisfaction with the pedestal on which its author had been placed. Written by a woman John Gibson Lockhart labeled "the very ideal of a novel heroine,"[39] Sara's essay nevertheless rejects all such popular mystification as deluded and pernicious, thus emphasizing how objectionable she found the empty flattery of sexual stereotyping. Her position also suggests how difficult it must have been for a woman who loved her studies "of all things" to accept the fact that such labors were no longer permissible, and that duties as wife and mother were soon to eclipse literary "amusements." But if there is dissatisfaction in Sara's essay, there is also resignation. She could not bring herself to challenge the dominant ideology, and so, like generations of women before her, she sought the relative freedom of a spiritual life as an alternative to earthly oppression. Yet her resignation was not blind martyrdom; as we have seen, what was overtly submissive was often covertly efficacious.

IV

Sara left the Wordsworths at Rydal Mount on the morning of July 27, 1826, hoping to arrive at Highgate within the week. Unfortunately, soon after setting out she fell ill and decided, following the advice of her mother, to return to Greta Hall for several weeks of rest before resuming her journey.[40] In early September, she set out once again and arrived without further trouble at Highgate on September 17. On the twenty-first Coleridge wrote glowingly of his new houseguest to his friend C. A. Tulk: "I shall have the opportunity of introducing my Daughter to you, who arrived here on Sunday last—and is all, the most ambitious Father could desire—if his ambition was within the circle of *wise* wishes—with the exception only of her "bodily strength—tho' (the Author of all good be thanked & glorified!) she is in much better health, than I had ventured to anticipate" (*CL* 6:617). Ironically, the "ambitious Father['s]" sole regret—his daughter's lack of bodily strength"—was fast becoming their strongest bond. Coleridge's first surviving letter to Sara, undated but most likely written during the weeks just before her arrival, gives an account of Swedenborg's theory of dream spirits (*CL* 6:615–16). This letter is clearly a response either to Sara's direct request for information or to her general complaints about what had become by this point a chronic affliction—recurrent nightmares. As one equally obsessed with matters of health, Sara was discovering that she had more in common with her father than she originally suspected. She also found that visiting at Highgate without her mother lessened the tension considerably. Moreover, although Coleridge was still not entirely pleased by her decision to marry, such differences were quickly—if not finally—resolved.

Regardless of eased tensions, Sara stayed with her father only until October 8. She then moved to John Taylor Coleridge's house at 65 Torrington Square, London, where she began a flurry of social activities that would continue largely unabated for the next twelve months. While these were exciting diversions after the long months at Greta Hall, Sara soon found that they distracted her from the chief object of her visit and her first priority—Henry. Writing to Derwent in early January 1827, she complained, "Entre Nous I wish all the dinner parties in the Red Sea that separate me from my dear friend. . . . I felt it was impossible to love him better than I did in absence, but I feel the chain grow tighter and tighter every day" (Letter [6 Jan 1827]). The "chain" of affection bonding Sara to Henry must have appeared durable to others as well, for early in the year, Colonel James Coleridge finally gave in to his son's wishes and approved the match. As soon as Henry established himself in the law, he was free to marry. Henry's financial independence, however, was still years away. Pleased with the colonel's decision but apprehensive about another long separation, Sara was quick to put her feelings into words:

> My childish and girlish castles in the air are now exchanged for others which have you for their object—to contribute to your daily comfort and pleasure—that is the earthly goal toward which all my hopes and wishes are turned. Shall I ever reach this goal? Sometimes I think it would be greater bliss than I ought to expect in this life: to judge from my present feelings, from the tumults of deep delight I have felt in your society, & from hearing the sound of your beloved voice, I know & feel sure, that if to this were added a sense of security & permanence, if the sad perspective of parting, of possible disasters & various dreaded contingencies were not before us, my condition could be one of real happiness. [Letter: SC to HNC (9 Feb 1827)][41]

Read quickly, the lines seem exuberant, hopeful, and committed: tender sentiments born of a four-year separation. Yet closer reading reveals a tone of willed resignation, and the closing qualifications firmly temper the preceding enthusiasm. The "castles in the air" speak both of hope and delusion, of dreams come true and dreams proved false. The fear of failure implicit in her question— "Shall I ever reach my goal?"—and in the word "sometimes" is seemingly negated by an attitude of total compliance, first to her fiancé, her "earthly" master, and then by extension to God, her heavenly master. But this servility is not completely passive. Her closing judgment, with its careful qualification of present pleasures as decidedly less than "real happiness," counterbalances the passivity of submission with the activity of suffering. Through suffering, Sara indirectly attains the unattainable happiness by keeping it ever present as a standard of measurement. Such a subtle martyrdom fulfills the required submission to both husband and God yet humbles the former in the process: the "security & performance" are in God's power, not Henry's. By emphasizing divine authority and the comparative benefits of the heavenly world, Sara aligns herself with the Omnipotent and sits in vicarious judgment on Henry and their less-than-perfect attachment. Suffering permits the subtle exercising of power without threatening the traditional model of female passivity.

Henry responded to Sara with strong affection and unperturbed optimism. By nature less conservative than his fiancée, he had at times incurred her displeasure and that of her family, but his genuine good will always regained their favor. His greatest miscalculation was doubtless the publication of *Six Months in the West Indies,* but by 1827 all was forgiven, and he was free to pursue his romance. Although few letters from the period have survived, a commonplace book of Sara's gives an unusual account of their courtship. From a poem by Henry written in its opening pages, we learn how the book came into his possession:

> The mistress of this book
>   Did lend it once to me,
> That I might therein look
>   Her own pure heart to see;—
>
> Because her modest tongue
>   Could never say the things
> Which to herself she sung
>   In her lone imaginings.

The book was not returned immediately; in fact, Henry's extensive commentary on Sara's original entries—which range from October 1819 to April 1825—indicates that it was given to him in December 1826 and not returned until October 20, 1827. Of her three commonplace books, this was her most private, and giving it to Henry was a gesture of intimacy, although it contained nothing more personal than favorite poems. Henry, however, did not limit his commentary to the poetry but proceeded to more sensitive concerns. In the margin of an Italian love sonnet, he wrote, "If my passion for you, Sara, is not pure, then human love can never be so. There is appetite in it; it is the tongue of lambent flames which speaks to *Sex;* but appetite is subordinate to reason with me, and scarcely any thing else but an effect to an intense desire to actualize my affection. I am sick for complete Union" (December 1826). Although more feverish than most of Henry's contributions (which include an eight-page formal essay on the history of love), this entry nevertheless represents the general nature of his concerns. Sara's book provided an outlet for his unvoiced frustration, a place where he was free to speak his feelings without fear of censure. Yet the passage is laden with insecure self-justifications. Rather than deny, ignore, or simply acknowledge his physical passion, Henry argues for its "purity" and insists on its subordination to "reason." His "appetite," supposedly controlled by higher faculties, works not for itself but to "actualize" the preexistent purity of his "affection": it becomes an unavoidable "effect" of an irreproachable cause. Instead of using the spiritual to sanction an informed melancholy, as Sara had, Henry uses an ideal to sanction lust.

The clearest presentation of Henry's opinions on love is to be found in the eight-page formal essay, which he began at midnight on New Year's Eve 1827.

Well organized and at times unbearably condescending, his entry is an overly polite refutation of what he sees as Sara's "old-fashioned" Platonism. "People," he begins, "especially young women, talk about Platonic Love, but they know not what they say." Platonism is only the "first stage" in the "Theory of Love," and its conception of love "is not human" but "merely an inter-appetency of Spirits" which falsely denies the body and its needs. "Dante and Petrarch," he continues, "may exemplify the second or middle stage, when the love had become human, but was for the most part uninspired by any real passion." This second stage, he argues, is characterized by "a want of depth." The last stage and the one which "perfect[s] . . . the Theory of Love" is exemplified by "the work of English Poets" who, according to Henry, properly realize the interdependency between spiritual and physical love. He summarizes: "Beauty is the virtue of the Body as Virtue is the beauty of the Mind; therefore that Love is imperfect which rejects either one or the other." Thus, Henry's eight-page polemic ends precisely where Sara's "Essay on Beauty" begins—with a popular rationale for the idolatry of female appearance.

In another entry written some eight months later, Henry explained his understanding of female anatomy from a slightly different perspective: "Have you ever supposed how mysteriously symbolical of or analogous to the patient being of a woman, is the peculiar conformation of her body? How her budding prominence of bosom is the [source?] and region of her unspeakable tenderness of Heart,—reaching out, as it seems, with a flood of the milk of human kindness;—and how on the other hand (I speak reverently on a sacred subject!) the . . ." The above passage was inked out, presumably by its author, who realized that even his "reverent" approach to his "sacred subject" was liable to cause offense. The ten lines following this passage are almost indecipherable. But the last four lines are relatively easy to read: "The truth is a man's desire is for the woman; & a woman's desire is for the desire of her husband; at least in all modest females." Was Sara in fact the "modest female" of Henry's dreams, or was Henry more reluctant than his fiancée to relinquish romantic fantasies, his own juvenile "castles in the air"? In either case, as his authoritative tone makes clear, Henry's "castles" were the stuff of patriarchal dreams, solid fantasies built on old foundations—legitimate, superior, and smug.

When Henry returned the commonplace book to Sara on the evening of October 20, he was not only optimistic about what he called their "perfect love" but also about her taking up the book again to record her intimate feelings. His last inscription reads: "I shall return this book to you this evening. When I see it again, let it have been enriched a thousandfold: Make it your friend, your confessional, your notebook. Write everything in it that has any reference to the heart; bonnets and ribbons may be discussed elsewhere; we must keep this for things of a higher more secret and more ethereal birth. Dearest partner of my affections, we *are* fortunate in our perfect love." Sara never made another entry in the book. Not inclined to discuss intimacies and especially reticent where matters of sex were concerned, she was no doubt offended by many of Henry's entries. His "perfect love," after all, was incommensurate with her own understanding of female beauty, and she must have been put off by his affected manner and superior tone. Perhaps the torn-out pages at the book's beginning—bracketed on either side by pages in her fiancé's hand—are testimony to her ire.

By late November, Sara was back at Greta Hall, relieved to have escaped the "crowded parties" of the city for the lakes and mountains of her home.[42] She settled immediately into her familiar routines, and from all accounts the next year and a half were spent in excellent health and without crises of any sort. In June 1828, Mrs. Coleridge had little to report to Thomas Poole: "Sara has been, on the whole, in good health since her return. Her marriage is, I suppose, very distant, for her cousin is young in the Law, and though it is thought that he may pass a brilliant career when his talents are known, it must take some years to establish him, and the friends of both are solicitous that they should not settle until an adequate income is insured. There is nothing but patience for them" (*Minnow* 144).

For the next twelve months, Sara and Henry were content to be patient.[43] But in the early summer of 1829, Henry felt his situation was secure enough for marriage, and he began pressuring Greta Hall for an August wedding. Initially, both Mrs. Coleridge and Sara agreed: Sara's health was strong, and although Henry's was not, he argued convincingly against further delays. In late June, however, Henry was forced to resign his position as secretary to King's College because of administrative cutbacks. A sizable portion of his income would be lost, and Mrs. Coleridge was not pleased: "This resignation has been a great grief to me, and occasioned great opposition to their immediate union, on the female part, but we gained nothing by resistance, and the thing is, it seems, to take place, relying on an increase of business, and on his being made Reporter to the New Court of Equity next year which w[oul]d fully compensate for the loss of the S-ship to the new College" (*Minnow* 147–48). As the passage indicates, Henry found an alternative source of income and quickly resolved the dilemma. The data was set for September 3.

The day of the wedding was unusually clear, and according to Mrs. Coleridge, all went smoothly (*Minnow* 151–54). The ceremony was performed by John Wordsworth, the poet's son and Sara's childhood playmate. Many of their good friends arrived for the celebration, and the party afterwards continued until four in the morning. Mrs. Coleridge, however, was the only member of the immediate family in attendance. Sara's father remained at Highgate with the Gillmans, too ill to make the journey. Nor did her brothers attend. It was left to

Southey to give the bride away. But it was Coleridge, characteristically, who had the last word. On the day of Sara's wedding, he inscribed for his daughter a presentation copy of Soethby's folio volume, *Georgica Publii Virgilii Maronis Hexaglotta* (1827):

> After my decease this splendid volume presented to me by William Soethby, Esqr (and not the only mark of Regard and Kindness that I have received from this accomplished Scholar and truly worthy Man) is to belong, and I hereby give and appropriate it to my beloved and loveworthy child, Sara Coleridge. And I hope and trust that she will never willingly part with this volume or alienate the same. For if she should marry and should have a Daughter, it is my wish that this volume should descend to *her,* or (if Sara have daughters) to her eldest Daughter, who is to regard it as a Memento provided by her maternal Grandfather, that her dear Mother's accomplishments and her unusual attainments in ancient and modern Languages, were not so much nor so justly the objects of admiration as their co-existence in the same Person with so much piety, simplicity and unaffected meekness— in short, with a mind, character and demeanour so perfectly feminine. [CL 6:692]

The book is both a wedding gift and a bequeathment; it situates one transition—marriage—with another—death. Such a gesture subordinates Sara's wedding ("if she should marry") to Coleridge's illness and so inscribes familial tension beneath paternal good will. Yet Coleridge's gift is itself a "property" to be handed down from generation to generation, a legacy that justly celebrates his daughter's "unusual attainments" but one which defuses those attainments by defining them within "a mind, character and demeanour so perfectly feminine."

Her father's inscription suggests that Sara's "accomplishments" were over and that her marriage signaled the end of an aberrant intellectual career. Such was not to be the case.

"The House of Bondage"
Marriage, Motherhood, and the Death of Coleridge

She was not caressing in manner, nor did she encourage any demonstrativeness in those around her. But this does not imply that she was in the least degree cold or indifferent. Once, when I was taken with some childish illness, I saw a look of terror on her face, and thought, with a sudden strange sense of awe, "Does mama care for me as much as that?"

Edith Coleridge, Recollections

Imagination, as we all know, is part of every human mind, or state which it is capable of passing into—an imaginative habit must proceed from that which is innate, but depends in some measure on the will of the individual. [P]oetic genius—and a powerful imagination—are rare gifts, but imaginativeness can hardly be called uncommon quality, & more or less, imagination belongs to all.

Sara Coleridge, "On Wordsworth"

Sara and Henry's marriage began only after their arrival in London in mid-October 1829. For although they spent five happy weeks honeymooning in the Lake district—a week at Patterdale, a week at Rydal Mount, and three weeks back at Keswick—that idyllic period was a fictional interlude between expectation and fulfillment, between the fantasy of marital bliss and the actuality of domestic tribulation. It was for Henry an introduction to the beauties of northern scenery, his first and only extended visit to the homeland of the Lake poets. More interested in his uncle's theology than his poetry, Henry was a man of urban sensibilities, a Victorian academic sympathetic to but distanced from the rustic Nature of Wordsworth and Southey. For Sara, on the other hand, those five weeks signaled her farewell to family and friends, to childhood haunts and intellectual projects, and to a certain romantic sensibility unavoidably a part of

52

Keswick and its environs. Genuinely sorry to be leaving Greta Hall, she nevertheless felt no regrets; she had acquired an affectionate husband, economic security, and the freedom to begin a family of her own. As she explained it to her fiancé on the eve of their wedding, "You will not, I know, grudge a few tears to my dearest mother, to dear Keswick, dear Greta Hall, and its dear and interesting inmates. These changes, these farewells, are types of the great change, the long farewell, that awaits us all hereafter. We can not but be thoughtful upon them. Yet I know and feel that *this* change is to be infinitely for the better" (*ML* [1874] 58).

Some months later, however, Sara's new situation afforded Hartley the opportunity to reflect more critically upon her last years at Greta Hall:

Most glad am I, at all events, that she is out of the house of bondage, and a house of bondage Greta-hall was to her, not by any fault, far less from any intention of its proprietors, our excellent Uncle and Aunt, but from her own excessive, I might almost say, morbid delicacy. Tho' she could not but know, that both she and our Mother were doing daily services, much above the price of reciprocal favors, and that their presence was a perpetual motive of good and kindly feelings, tho' they knew that their absence would be regretted and the house never look like itself without them, an uncomfortable sense of obligation, always lay like an incubus on their gratitude. They were afraid to move, to speak, every wrinkle of that blood-ill-temper which disorders not diminishes Aunt S.'s benevolence, even sometimes the young lady airs of our Lady Cousins, seem'd to their feverish apprehensions like a warning to depart. But *N'importe,* she is I hope, a happy wife, and will be ere long a happy mother. [*HC Letters* 108–09]

According to Hartley, Greta Hall was a "house of bondage" not only because of an obstreperous aunt or a haughty cousin's occasional "warning to depart," but more because of Sara's own "excessive" sensitivity, "her own . . . morbid delicacy," which internalized tensions and remanifested them as self-destructive physical and psychological ailments. Although he implies that Sara's "bondage" at Keswick was largely self-induced, Hartley, no doubt like Sara herself, expected marriage with Henry to provide the needed corrective to her "feverish apprehensions." "[T]here is an urgent expediency in her acquiring a home of her own," Hartley had written several months before Sara's departure; and he still expected that once settled in London, she would find her "excessive" worries quickly displaced by "domestic happiness" (*HC Letters* 98). In other words, he assumed that Sara was, like the heroines of sentimental fiction, eager for and constitutionally capable of the "happily ever after" of an ideal marriage.

Mrs. Coleridge, however, less in awe of marriage than her son, viewed Sara's change of situation with a more cautious eye. Writing to Thomas Poole in July

1829, she noted, "It seems her lot to dwell [in London]; which w[oul]d be no matter of regret to either of us, if she were a strong woman, and had not such decided habits fitting her for a quiet life in the country. A Barrister's wife sees but little of her husband, so that Sara will be transported from a *too* bustling family, to one of utter loneliness, except from occasional visitors—she thinks she shall find plenty of employ, and amusement, for her leisure and I pray that she may find it so" (*Minnow* 147). If Hartley took it for granted that Sara's "morbid delicacy" resulted directly from her ambivalent status at Greta Hall and that marriage would provide the proper blend of freedom and duty needed to cure her "excessive[ness]," then Mrs. Coleridge voiced the opposite opinion— that given Sara's health and Henry's occupation, her daughter was more likely to be entering a "house of bondage" than escaping one. Sheltering a "*too* bustling family," Greta Hall was nevertheless more desirable than "utter loneliness," a state Mrs. Coleridge rightly feared would prove injurious to a woman of Sara's temperament. But even Mrs. Coleridge was unprepared for what lay ahead.

After a few months with the John Taylor Coleridges at Russel Square, Sara and Henry moved into 21 Downshire Hill, Downshire Place, Hampstead. It was, according to daughter Edith, "a tiny cottage," well suited for their "frugal housekeeping" and not far from Coleridge's own residence, the Grove (*ML* [1874] 59). Although father and daughter were now minutes apart, little more than a short walk across the fields, their separation continued, for Coleridge was frequently too infirm for even short excursions, and Sara, while in good health, went out only rarely. As Dorothy Wordsworth reported to Henry Crabb Robinson (with some disparagement), "They cannot see much of each other. To *walk* is impossible—and to be otherwise conveyed far too expensive for a young Lawyer's wife" (*W Letters* 5:243). Dorothy's ironic jibe notwithstanding, walking did in fact become, if not impossible, then at least difficult, for early in 1830 Sara discovered she was pregnant. Self-conscious about her condition, she remained at home, read Homer, art history, and the latest *Quarterly Reviews,* and received occasional visits from Joanna Baillie and Maria Jane Jewsbury.

Almost immediately after learning of her pregnancy, Sara decided that she was unfit to raise a child without assistance and that her mother, then residing with Derwent and Mary at Helston, should move permanently to Downshire Hill. As requested, Mrs. Coleridge arrived in September, at the beginning of her daughter's confinement, and presided over the birth of Herbert Coleridge some four weeks later. On October 8, she described the event to Poole: "Yesterday forenoon, about 11 o'clock Sara was safely brought to bed of a boy who, with his mother, is going on well. He is about the middle size, a little more than 8 pounds in weight. All parties seem satisfied with his appearance, but his father thinks he [is] too much like himself to be pretty; he *wished* for a girl, but is too happy at the well-doing of his wife to care, very much, about the sex of the Child for she is *better than could have been expected*. . . . Poor father at Highgate, has been very nervous about her, he will now be relieved" (*Minnow* 163). As Mrs. Coleridge's relief at Sara's successful delivery makes clear, giving birth in 1830 had its risks, and for a woman of Sara's slight build and frail constitution, the routine dangers were increased considerably. It was obvious to Dorothy Wordsworth, for example, that Sara's pregnancy was "no cause for joy" (*W Letters* 5:243). Similarly, Lady Beaumont had thought her "so delicate I should tremble at her becoming a wife or mother" (*W Letters* 4:187n). Yet regardless of the obvious dangers, regardless of her husband's concern and her own better judgment, Sara was to be pregnant six more times during the next ten years. Twice she would complete her full term and give birth to children who lived only a few days. And despite repeated mental and physical breakdowns, she would have no respite from pregnancy until the onset of her husband's fatal illness in 1841.

In December 1830, however, Sara was still very much excited by her new maternal responsibilities and, in order to assure her own attentiveness, began a diary to record the vicissitudes of her son's first years. A "healthy child but not pretty," young Herbert experienced all the minor ups and downs of a normal baby, and the diary faithfully monitors his progress, at first only alluding to the health of his mother. Ironically, Sara admits in her initial entry to what would soon become a pattern—that immediately following the delivery she suffered from an inexplicable "weakness" and depression: "I have never got quite strong since my confinement. I know not whether nursing keeps me down. I have plenty of milk. I take a pint of ale and a little gin & water at night, occasionally a glass of port wine—sometimes a glass of table beer. During the first month I took a little spirit with egg in the morning" (21 Dec 1830). To Emily Trevenen she confessed extreme lassitude and "despair of being entirely healthful and strong" (Letter [Dec 1830])—in other words, a marked reluctance to reassume her role as the dutiful wife and mother. Nevertheless, with Mrs. Coleridge's assistance, Sara managed to control her "despair" and keep the domestic routines at 21 Downshire Hill running smoothly.

By the summer of 1831, Sara's health had deteriorated dramatically, and she decided that nursing was ruining her constitution. Although Hartley could make jokes about "little tugging Piggy-wiggies" (*HC Letters* 129), diary entries confirm how difficult Sara found the constant demands of motherhood and suggest that her illness was largely a reaction against the self-sacrifice of pregnancy and child care, a reaction whose causes were carefully concealed behind more socially accepted patterns of female infirmity.[1] To add to her worries, Henry had become convinced that the Reform Bill, then struggling for passage, was the result of a revolutionary fervor soon to erupt into open violence. In October, he informed Robert Southey that "we are all pretty well agreed here that a revolution has commenced & is moving fearfully fast" (Letter [31 Oct 1831]).[2]

Henry should perhaps have been more attentive to signs of discontent closer to home, for although Sara appeared satisfied with her new life, that satisfaction was illusory, merely the calm before the storm. By November 1831, she was pregnant again, and in July of the following year she gave birth to a daughter. Edith Coleridge was christened on August 9, an occasion marked by a rare family get-together and by the appearance of the child's illustrious grandfather. According to his wife, the old philosopher was in fine form and "talked incessantly for full five hours" (*Minnow* 165). Both Sara and her mother agreed that Coleridge's "animation" was largely due to his recent "emancipation from the opiate thraldom," a feat pronounced by Coleridge himself to be a "medical miracle" (Letter: SC to ET [12 Aug 1832]). This miracle was predictably short-lived, and Coleridge soon reverted to old habits. Even so, the lesson was evidently lost upon Sara: in six months' time she too would be trapped within the vicious cycles of "opiate thraldom."[3]

Immediately after Edith's birth, the diary begun ostensibly to follow the health of Sara's children becomes devoted almost wholly to her own, and for the first time her illness is not described solely as a physical affliction. On September 12, she recorded, "My nervous debility rather unpleasant. Symptoms increased so much that I was obliged to think seriously of [not] feeding my darling. . . . I now only nurse 5 times a day & must make further reduction as I am weak & miserably nervous & fluttered." Eight days later she noted, "Since the 12th I have been going on very sadly. Disordered bile accompanied with derangement of the nervous system is my complaint. Stomach & bowels out of order, great weakness, nervousness, shiverings & glowings &c." When Henry returned to Hampstead at the end of the month, he found his wife's "derangement of the nervous system" well advanced. She had left off nursing altogether and could neither sleep nor eat. For relief she took laudanum and began reading through the collected works of Ben Jonson. On doctor's orders, Henry arranged for an immediate departure to Brighton, where, it was hoped, the sea air and change of scenery would effect a cure.

Mrs. Coleridge described the trip as "one of the most weary journeys I ever experienced" (*Minnow* 170). Things began badly, she maintained, because Henry, in order to leave more "air" for his wife, insisted on sitting outside the carriage. While he endured nothing more serious than torrential rain, Mrs. Coleridge was left alone to deal with the frantic invalid: "I had far the worst of it, for she said, oh, I shall go into convulsions if I cannot get out! the rain pouring the whole way, yet, at any change of horses she darted out and walked rapidly up and down the road like one distracted. On our arrival we sent for Mr Laurence who ordered a warm bath, a blister on the nape of the neck, and other things . . . I shall never forget that night" (*Minnow* 170). Sara's mother was understandably upset about her daughter's illness, especially when the stay at Brighton proved to have little effect upon the often violent symptoms. She was particularly disturbed, as was Sara herself, by her inability to comprehend the nature of the affliction. Without the rudiments of psychology, it was impossible to map intricate interrelationships between mind and body, much less between social strictures and female sickness. While hysteria had been considered a recognizable disease since the beginning of the eighteenth century, its causes and cures were still hotly debated. Some medical theorists considered the illness directly linked to "utero-uterine irritation" and advised everything from leeches to ovariotomies.[4] Others claimed it was a matter of uncontrolled passion and weak will; they advised firm discipline and public reprimands.[5] In any case, consensus was rare, and as a result, Mrs. Coleridge could no more understand the reasons behind her daughter's hysteria than could Sara's doctors, for whom blisters and leeches still represented sound medical treatment.

Yet it is Mrs. Coleridge rather than her daughter who provides the information necessary to understand Sara's nervous "derangement." For although the patient left detailed accounts of her daily fluctuations, she rarely speculated during this period as to the causes of her complaint. In a weak moment, she would plead with her husband for "a three years respite from child-bearing," but she generally avoided discussing her desires or blaming anyone else for her "weakness": all was pious self-denial (Letter: SC to HNC [24 Sept 1832]). Mrs. Coleridge, however, in her typically newsy letters, often said more than she knew. Consider, for example, a passage from her letter describing the trip to Brighton: "God grant that she may be soon herself again. Before she left H[ampstead] she w[oul]d sit in a Carriage (wh[ich] we hired by the hour to drive on the Heath with the children and the nurses) and never speak one word to the poor babes the whole time." Sara had indeed temporarily lost "herself"; she had exchanged the role of the sentimental heroine patiently awaiting her fiancé for the less glamorous part of the traditional wife and mother, the selfless "angel in the house" whose desires were expected to conform to those of husband and offspring. By all contemporary accounts, fictional and otherwise, this latter role should have been her greatest achievement, the long-awaited realization of her female "nature," the "happily ever after" of every woman's dream.[6] Why then the chilling silence in the carriage? Why the unexplained distance from her "poor babes"?

For Sara, the transition from maiden to matron had been swift and unquestioned. She had left behind "Uncle Southey" and "dear Mr. Wordsworth" and all her various books and projects, acquiring in their place a husband, a home, and the many responsibilities of a "proper lady." Even Mrs. Coleridge was surprised by the sudden transformation: "You cannot imagine how odd the change in Sara's habits appear to me—so different to those of her maiden days. Reading, writing, walking, teaching, dressing, mountaineering, and—I may add, for the latter 10 years of that state—*weeping*—were her daily occupations with occasional visiting—Now, house orders, suckling, dress and undress— walking, sewing—morning visits and receiving—with very little study of Greek, Latin, and English—(no weeping!) make up . . . her busy day" (Letter: SC to ET [12 Aug 1832; SFC's note affixed]). Written only weeks before Sara's September 1832 collapse, Mrs. Coleridge's remarks express bewilderment about but support for the change in her daughter's activities. However "odd" the new habits, they do not seem to cause emotional distress—"no weeping!"— and for that Mrs. Coleridge was grateful. But clearly Sara's abandonment of reading, writing, and teaching appeared curious to her mother; it was decidedly out of character for Greta Hall's most serious student and puzzling if only because of the rapidity with which the transformation had occurred.

Mrs. Coleridge's puzzlement was understandable given the circumstances. In order to become the proper wife, Sara had willingly sacrificed her intellectual interests; she had adopted the restrictions and self-denials of marriage because they promised a higher freedom concomitant with established codes of female propriety. She had of course subscribed to such codes even in her youth, but at least at Greta Hall she had had the freedom to pursue her interests, to spend her mornings as she wished. Now busy with two small children and a demanding husband, those years of dedicated study must have seemed wasted—mean- ingless preparation for monotonous duties. Yet Sara did not and could not vocalize her discontents; she was ideologically committed to marriage and motherhood, and however strong her misgivings, they were dutifully repressed and rechanneled into more appropriate behavior.

And so Sara's nervous illness continued unabated for more than two years, from September 1832 to January 1835. Her worst period occurred during the first six months of 1833 when she gave herself up to opium and hysteria, throwing two "fits" a day, sleeping only every third night, and eating so little that her menstrual cycle stopped completely. By February, she was convinced her "bodily powers [were] all going" and that she was unable to sit up—much less walk—for more than twenty minutes a day (Diary [19 Feb 1833]). From all accounts, her "sad hysterical dejection" remained beyond the control of patient and doctors alike, an inexplicable and overpowering "weakness" that robbed her of all energy, all enthusiasm, all pleasure (Letter: SC to HNC [21 March 1833]). Frequently in letters to friends, she appears self-indulgent and highly theatrical: "O this dreadful restlessness of body—this deep dejection—nay, often blackening into despair!—I have a thousand strange bodily feelings— perpetually varying, yet ever most alarming and distressing; but even that is nothing to the despondency of mind" (SC to ET [12–16 Oct 1832]). However "alarming and distressing," Sara's illness did provide her with advantages more beneficial than mere sympathy, for by the spring of 1833, she had discovered how her affliction could be used to escape domestic duties and to ensure long periods of productive isolation: she began once again to read and write with a passion.

It is no accident that daughter Edith's *Memoir and Letters of Sara Coleridge* (1873) waits until 1833 to begin its epistolary autobiography, for during that year the primary emphasis of Sara's letters gradually shifts from the personal and the familial to the abstract and the intellectual. Having no desire to expose any part of her mother's private life, Edith edited a two-dimensional portrait of a proper Victorian bluestocking, Coleridge's gifted daughter decorously acting out his legacy. But the relentlessly intellectual, often abstruse letters of Edith's edition illustrate—in spite of their editor—how important it was for Sara to find a forum for her ideas, an outlet for her energies, a place in which she could discuss the most recent works of literature, history, or theology without violating the prohibitions against women writers. Within the safe space of her correspondence, Sara found she was free to indulge secret desires and to exercise her mind as well as her pen.

According to Mrs. Coleridge, her daughter spent the year 1833 "in a very weak and low condition, utterly helpless; always on the Sofa, & reading from morning to night" (*Minnow* 178). Although proud of Sara's intellect, Mrs. Coleridge assumed that reading provided a necessary escape from the trials of illness and that once the illness abated normal domestic duties would resume. Sara, however, was rediscovering old interests and would never again lose herself completely in motherhood. While she would play an active and eager part in the education of her children (publishing, as a result, two children's books), she devoted most of her time to the careful monitoring of current intellectual events. Unlike the years at Greta Hall, where, under Southey's tutelage, she had followed his interests back to obscure South American travelogues and to sixteenth-century French memoirs, she now preferred to read her contemporaries: she studied the literary debates, researched the theological controversies, and considered with particular interest all works by women.

Although Sara's wide reading had naturally included many books written by women, it was not until 1833 that she began to study women's writing as a distinct subgenre of contemporary literature. For the first time, her critical voice assumes the self-assured, often strident qualities which would later characterize her best pieces. Perhaps because she felt more at ease with women's works, or perhaps because her epistolary criticism allowed for a brusque informality, Sara relinquished the posturing, conventional, distinctly well bred tone of her "Essay on Beauty" and began to express herself clearly and forcefully. To Emily Trevenen, for example, she wrote of an old family friend, Joanna Baillie:

Our great poetess, or rather the sensible, amiable old lady that *was* a great poetess thirty years ago, is still in full preservation as to health. Never did the flame of genius more thoroughly expire than in her case; for though, as Lamb says, "Ancient Mariners," "Lyrical Ballads," and "Kehamas" are not written in the grand climacteric, the authors of such flights of imagination generally give out sparkles of their ancient fires in conversation; but Mrs. Joanna Baillie is, as Mr. Wordsworth observes, when quoting her non-feeling for Lycidas, "dry and Scotchy"; learning she *never* possessed, and some of her poetry, which I think was far above that of any other woman, is the worse for a few specks of bad English; then her criticisms are so surprisingly narrow and jejune, and show so slight an acquaintance with fine literature in general. Yet if the authoress of "Plays on the Passions" does not now write or talk like a poetess, she *looks* like one, and *is* a piece of poetry in herself. [*ML*(1874) 71]

When measured against Sara's high expectations, against her distinctly romantic understanding of "the flame of genius," Joanna Baillie was found wanting, as was Hannah More, whose *Coelebs in Search of a Wife* (1809) "throw[s] the garb of Dulness over the form of Religion to enforce it in a tale so dry and formal" (Letter: SC to HNC [3 Oct 1833]). One of Emily Trevenen's favorites, Elizabeth Sandford, suffered a similar fate: her writings, Sara argued, "are sensible and well expressed—but any sensible, well educated woman might have penned the same."[7]

The codes of female decorum to which Sara subscribed discouraged any behavior that drew unnecessary attention to individual women—and that of course included authorship. As Sandra Gilbert and Susan Gubar have argued, writing by women in the early nineteenth century was by definition an encroachment upon male territory and so was accompanied by its own distinctive "anxiety of authorship" (*Madwoman* 45–92). Even successful women writers were embarrassed about and made apologies for their work. Hannah More, for instance, in a passage with which Sara would have agreed, expressed a cultural commonplace:

But there is one *human* consideration which would perhaps more effectually tend to damp in an aspiring woman the ardours of literary vanity . . . than any which she will derive from motives of humility, or propriety, or religion: which is, that in the judgment passed on her performances, she will have to encounter the mortifying circumstance of having her sex always taken into account, and her highest exertions will probably be received with the qualified approbation, *that it is really extraordinary for a woman.* Men of learning, who are naturally apt to estimate works in proportion as they appear to be the result of art, study, and institution, are apt to consider even the happier performances of the other sex as the spontaneous productions of a fruitful but shallow soil.[8]

To write publicly, then, was to risk "mortification," and it is not surprising that both Hannah More and Sara Coleridge preferred to publish anonymously, to erase their sex from the title page in order to sidestep the unwanted attention that challenged both their literary productions and their "femininity." But while Sara was deeply influenced by the kind of conduct books made popular by Hannah More, Elizabeth Sandford, and later Sarah Ellis,[9] she was also a child of romanticism and believed wholeheartedly in the individual genius and the powers of the imagination—qualities that were shared, she would later argue, by women as well as men. If female authors were to violate social codes by participating in the literary marketplace, if they were to transgress the limitations of womanhood, their art had better be "gifted" enough to justify the infraction: they had better possess "the flame of genius." Thus Sara's criticism of Elizabeth Sandford—"any sensible woman might have penned the same"— evidences a crucial ambivalence. Like Hannah More, Sara articulates both a fear of public "mortification" and a secret desire for women to take the risk and prove their intellectual equality. More important perhaps, her remarks suggest that only Sara's discovery of pure "genius," of women whose talents exceeded her own, could justify the abandonment of her studies for the routines of marriage. She needed to index her own abilities against defined standards; one way or another, silence had to be rationalized.

Because the pious platitudes of the conduct books could never seem to compensate for their own presumption, the very presumption they themselves so seriously lectured against, Sara was forced to look elsewhere for her women of "genius."[10] Early in 1833, recently bedridden but intellectually engaged, she discovered the author with whom she would carry on a passionate love/hate relationship for the next twenty years—Harriet Martineau. Martineau, of course, was in many respects an unlikely candidate for the object of Sara's interest.[11] Outspoken where Sara was reticent, radical where Sara was conservative, political where Sara was spiritual, Martineau was a perfect alter ego for Coleridge's modest daughter, just the sort of lively companion that Henry would have abhorred and never permitted within their social circle. Within the world of books, however, Martineau's companionship was legitimately attained and just as legitimately enjoyed.

Born in 1802, some six months before Sara, Harriet Martineau had suffered through an unhappy childhood in a large, middle-class Norwich family. Her plain looks and awkward stature made her an object of fun for other children, a torment exacerbated by early deafness. Encouraged by her brother James, later an important religious philosopher, Martineau began writing for the *Monthly*

Repository, the largest of the Unitarian periodicals. Three years before Sara's "Essay on Beauty," Martineau had published an article "On Female Education" in which she too argued against female vanity: "When woman is allowed to claim her privileges as an intellectual being, the folly, the frivolity, and all the mean vices and faults which have hitherto been the reproach of the sex, will gradually disappear. As she finds nobler objects presented to her grasp, and that her rank in the scale of being is elevated, she will engraft the vigorous qualities of the mind of man on her own blooming virtues and insinuate into his mind those softer graces and milder beauties, which will smooth the ruggedness of his character."[12] Martineau's argument is strikingly similar to that of Sara's un-published essay. Both authors are dissatisfied with current standards of female valuation, and both offer intellectual and religious alternatives that avoid di-rectly challenging the sexual hierarchy. This agreement, however, had been the result of two very different experiences. Whereas Sara's beauty had caused her to be the unwanted center of attention, the object of praise or blame equally superficial in its understanding of her character, Martineau's lack of beauty had resulted in ridicule and neglect: both were victims of the same system but in entirely different ways.

The consensus between the two women was predictably short-lived. Mar-tineau's plain looks and lack of money made marriage unlikely and employment unavoidable.[13] As a result, she followed her intellectual interests, publishing widely and with increasing irreverence. Sara's beauty, on the other hand, led her very quickly into marriage and motherhood. By 1833, Sara was an invalid and Martineau was in the midst of her *Illustrations of Political Economy,* twenty-five volumes of overly enthusiastic dramatizations of Adam Smith's theories. Sara read them with interest and then queried Emily Trevenen:

> Do you read Miss Martineau? How well she always succeeds in her por-traits of children, their simplicity and partially developed feelings and actions; and what a pity it is that, with all her knowledge of child nature, she should try to persuade herself and others that political economy is a fit and useful study for growing minds and limited capabilities—a subject of all others requiring matured intellect and general information as its basis! This same political economy which quickens the sale of her works now, will, I think, prove heavy ballast for a vessel that is to sail down the stream of time, as all agree that it is a dead weight upon the progress of her narratives, introducing the most absurd incongruities and improbabilities in regard to the dramatic propriety of character, and setting in arms against the interest of the story the political opinions of a great class of her readers. And she might have rivaled Miss Edgeworth! What a pity that she would stretch her genius on such a Procrustes bed! [*ML*(1873) 71–72]

According to Sara, Martineau does well with traditional female subject matter—"knowledge of child nature"—but compromises her "genius on such a Procrustes bed" as political economy. Had she remained within her capabilities, Martineau "might have rivaled Miss Edgeworth." Not surprisingly, Sara felt that the imaginative realm of literature was in danger of being contaminated by overtly political intentions, just as the peculiarly female domain of children's fiction was damaged irreparably by its inclusion of traditionally male subject matter. Admittedly one of the "most powerful female writers," Martineau was faulted nonetheless for her "lack of feminine modesty and real religious feeling" (Letter: SC to Mrs. Henry Jones [nd]).

When Sara wrote the above in late 1833, she was still very much an invalid, still confined to her sofa for most of the day, and still dependent upon opium for relief from her nervous symptoms. Although intellectual interests were permanently revived, she remained completely and obsessively absorbed in the details of her own health. Moreover, she was pregnant again. On Christmas day, she made the following entry in her diary: "I suffer less than this day last year—but am sadly weaker & I fear a more confirmed invalid. But this day my Saviour was born into the world to redeem us from spiritual not from bodily evils. Oh God! I pray that I may think more of the wants of the immortal part & take less thought for the morrow as regards the health of my body." The pious plea for spiritual strength made from within a diary devoted to the careful monitoring of physical symptoms enacts the paradox at the heart of Sara's illness. It valorizes the spiritual over the bodily, the immortal over the temporal, the religious over the political. It denies the self and all claims for selfish, worldly power. Yet the redemptive gesture is based on an irradicable dualism: suffering may encourage otherworldly vision, but it is at root a bodily, temporal, and political activity. Sara's suffering displaces the world only by first residing in it. Thus her illness, her inexplicable and overpowering "weakness," is, like her diary, at once the epitome of self-denial and a celebration of subversive self-aggrandizement. It accepts the common definition of woman as weak and emotional and selfless only to push that definition to the point of its own inversion. Sara's illness restructured the domestic hierarchy so as to privilege the invalid: it exempted her from required duties, it allowed her to read and write, it made her the center of attention and the object of sympathy, all without compromising her status as the "proper lady." In short, chronic illness satisfied a whole series of desires normally denied the middle-class matron, but not without exacting recompense: it was the safest form of protest and the most dangerous.

In January 1834, Sara gave birth to twins, Florence and Berkeley. They lived only a few days, and their death plunged Sara further into depression and hysteria.[14] For the first time, diary entries indicate that Sara was aware of and upset about her heavy use of opium. Throughout the spring, she tried unsuccessfully to decrease her dosage, but each time the drug was reduced violent symptoms would return and necessitate additional "relief." Ignorant of the physiology of addiction, Sara faulted her own weakness of will and so battled against an endless cycle of reduction/illness/resumption.

Regardless of private hardships, Sara maintained public spirits; her letters throughout the spring are filled with excited commentary on recent books. To her husband, whose law practice forced him to reside four or five days each week at Lincoln's Inn, she wrote primarily of topics relating to the education of their children. Henry was a moral disciplinarian who thought even minor infractions deserved lengthy sermons on duty and obedience. Sara, equally concerned with teaching religious values, preferred firm action to equivocal words: "Don't fancy that children will listen to lectures, either in learning or morality. Punish a child for hurting his sister, and he will draw the inference that it is wrong, without a sermon on brotherly affection. Children mark what you *do* much more, and what you say less, than those who know them not imagine."[15] To her other correspondents, however, she tended to range more widely over topics of current interest:

> The Story without an End [by F. W. Carove] I have seen notices of in reviews but have not read. We are provoked that the Committee of L[iterature] and E[ducation] have not published Derwent's sermons and *have* published one of [Charles] Simeon's. . . . [John] Wilson was a bold man—How that [Evangelical] party must abominate his 'Margaret Lyndsay' in which their tone and language is so strongly reprobated. . . . Crabbe's life by his son is very interesting, and it is quite the work of the *son* of genius: sometime fresh and peculiar in the *air* of the thing, though without the power and brilliancy of the father's mind. [Letter: SC to ET (27 April 1834)]

Sara's theory about the dissipation of the power of "genius" certainly held true for both Hartley and Derwent. Hartley's irresponsible and erratic behavior continued to cause his family much sorrow; and although Derwent had done well for himself and his family, Sara was not impressed by his plodding mind or his affected manners.[16] Whether or not the theory held true in her own case, however, still remained to be seen.

II

During the spring and summer of 1834, Sara's literary and critical efforts were not limited solely to those included in her letters. For some time, she had been composing verses for her children: it was enjoyment for her, education for them. Many of the poems taught history:

William I surnamed "the Conqueror" (1066)

> It happ'd in one thousand and sixty-six
> That William the Norman claimed this land:
> The laws of England he could fix,
> But could not his rebel sons command.

Edward I surnamed "Longshanks" (1272)

> One thousand two hundred and seventy-two
> Edward the First a King was made;
> Wales he did by arms subdue,
> When he came back from the far Crusade;
> He warred in bonny Scotland, too,
> Wallace was into his hands betrayed.

Others taught geography:

> Plantain and Banana
> Grow in hot Guiana;
> There the Chocolate is found—
> Parrots in the woods abound.

Still others taught Latin vocabulary:

> A Father is *pater,* a mother is *mater,*
> A sister is *soror,* a brother is *frater;*
> A child should obey both his father and mother,
> And brothers and sisters should love one another.

> In Latin *fructus* is a fruit,
> And *bacca* is a berry,
> And *mespilum* the medlar brown,
> And *cerasus* a cherry.

Sara wrote hundreds of such poems, all of which were carefully copied onto sturdy cards and given to her children. At her husband's insistence, she selected enough for a small volume, and in September 1834 J. W. Parker published *Pretty Lessons in Verse for Small Children.* Although the book sold extremely well, going through five editions in as many years, Sara was never enthusiastic about its success and considered it little more than a family project.

Not all of Sara's poems, however, were purely didactic or exclusively for children. In "Poppies," a poem whose inclusion in *Pretty Lessons* she later regretted, Sara juxtaposes Herbert's childish innocence to her own adult "sorrows of the night," producing in the process a complex and revealing lyric in the manner of Blake, the one romantic poet Sara never read:

> The Poppies Blooming all around
> My Herbert loves to see,
> Some pearly white, some dark as night,
> Some red as cramasie;
>
> He loves their colours fresh and fine
> As fair as fair may be,
> But little does my darling know
> How good they are to me.
>
> He views their clustering petals gay
> And shakes their nut-brown seeds.
> But they to him are nothing more
> Than other brilliant weeds;
>
> O how should'st thou with beaming brow
> With eye and cheek so bright
> Know aught of that blossom's pow'r,
> Or sorrows of the night!
>
> When poor mama long restless lies
> She drinks the poppy's juice;
> That liquor soon can close her eyes
> And slumber soft produce.
>
> O' then my sweet my happy boy
> Will thank the poppy flow'r
> Which brings the sleep to dear mama
> At midnight's darksome hour.

Like Blake's *Songs of Innocence and Experience,* Sara's poem explores the tensions between a fragile, naive purity and its fated confrontation with the disillusionment and sorrow of worldly wisdom. The central image, of course, is that of the ambivalent poppy—"Some pearly white, some dark as night." The child sees only "brilliant weeds" and knows nothing of "that blossom's pow'r" or of his mother's "long restless[ness]." But the issue is not simply one of knowledge. The threat of death inscribed within both the poppies and the recurrent images of night and sleep increases the emphasis on maternal self-sacrifice and suggests a causal relationship between Herbert's health and his mother's illness, between his pampered innocence and her misery. When, at the poem's conclusion, the boy is envisioned as thanking "the poppy flow'r," he does so with an ironic understanding of the parental price paid for the "beaming brow" of his youth. Education, he discovers, is more than a matter of botanical fact.

Derwent and Mary were predictably displeased with "Poppies." Given Coleridge's well-known troubles with opium, it was a mistake, they felt, to offer the prying public further evidence of family weakness: the poem was an unfortunate breach of propriety that could not but hurt the Coleridge name. Sara apologized: "the Poppy poem in 'Pretty Lessons' should have been left out—some other doggerel substituted—but I was poorly" (Letter: SC to ET [Jan? 1835]). Evidently, the Derwent Coleridges did not object to Sara's other "doggerel," even though the image of the melancholy mother haunts the volume from beginning to end and ironically challenges the very notion of "Pretty Lessons" espoused in the title. Melancholia was one thing, apparently, and opium another. Had Derwent read Sara's poems more closely, however, he would have discovered that many of the lessons were not so pretty, a fact even more true of the poems she decided not to include for publication:

> I envy the beasts that are seeking their prey
> And the vile slimy reptile that crawls in my way,
> Yon carolling bird makes his joy to be heard
> Ah! now he's falling! —he carols no more!
> His sporting & singing and soaring are over
> Yet I envy him still as he falls on his nest
> With the sharp pointed arrow stuck deep in his breast.

As such lyrics attest, motherhood for Sara, regardless of her pronouncements to the contrary, was a deeply ambivalent experience, but one whose tensions and resentments did eventually find their qualified expression.

The process of education depicted in *Pretty Lessons* must be seen in conjunction with another phase of Sara's own education occurring simultaneously. While she was patiently writing out poems for her children, she was also extending the opportunities for intellectual exercise afforded by her correspondence. No longer content only with the spontaneous, free-style criticism of informal letters, she began writing practice essays which she could then rethink and rewrite at her leisure before sending them off to her correspondents. Sometimes the essay or dialogue would be incorporated into the letter proper; on other occasions it would be enclosed separately. One of the first of these epistolary essays, a long dialogue entitled "Nervousness," is an attempt to confront and comprehend the nature of her "nervous affliction."[17]

For some years, Sara had realized that her illness was both physical and psychological, "a disease in the mental powers—not madness—yet in some respects akin to it" (Letter: SC to HNC [13 Nov 1832]). Having suffered through numerous cures and almost as many doctors, she decided it was time to put into perspective the often conflicting theories of her medical men and to assert her "own judgment" in the matter of "hysterical illness." As she explains in her prologue,

> After some years of suffering from derangement of the nervous system[,] I have satisfied myself that there is no all competent tribunal. . . . We must listen with a clear & candid spirit to the opinions of all persons of strong natural sense and receive the fruits of their knowledge & experience; but in the end our own understanding . . . must determine in the last resort. We may err, for there is no human infallibility: but depend on it . . . we shall be our own counsellors, if we will but be true to ourselves, & if we have full *information* on the subject in question. Our advisors will differ among themselves; we *must* exert our own judgment to chuse among them; let us also exert it to review their advice. [L]et us give a fair trial to each particular suggestion on matters connected with medical science, but, for the shaping of our general course, for our view of the subject in all its bearings, we must take instructions chiefly from our own *best* selves.

In the dialogue, Sara's "best self" is personified as the "Good Genius," and into his mouth she puts "the results of [her] long deliberations on the subject of those disorders which affect the mind but do not radically & directly impair the Reason." The Good Genius is queried by the "Invalid," who, as the voice of Sara's doubts and anxieties, asks about many of the dilemmas facing nervous sufferers. The dialogue, then, affords a rare opportunity to watch two halves of the same personality confront each other over the problematics of female illness.

The prologue is a manifesto of sorts which immediately defines the intended audience—"we who are weak & miserable"—and urges their collective self-assertion—"we shall be our own counsellors." Although Sara maintains that advice should be heeded from those with "strong natural sense," she makes clear that the individual's "understanding . . . must determine in the last resort": "we *must* exert our own judgment." Admittedly, invalids are by definition hampered in their attempts to evaluate their situations; they are "continually tempted to stray from the narrow path of prudence & self control." But because nervous afflictions are so complex, because the causes are many and the treatments varied, simple answers are suspect and medical science is not entirely to be trusted. While for Sara the issue remained undeniably one of duty, it was a duty redefined by the individual sufferer and not subservient to traditional medical opinion.

The dialogue opens with a discussion of the causes of nervous illness, and the Good Genius is quick to point out that the human body is so complex, so "full of mystery," that the assigning of first causes dangerously simplifies the problem and thus generates a series of dubious conclusions. Dogmatic exactitude, the Genius argues, must yield to the careful weighing of probabilities. The Invalid concurs: "Nervous derangement manifests itself by so many different symptoms that the sufferers themselves are puzzled what to make of it, and others, looking at it from different points of view make wrong judgments on the case. Those who perceive only how it affects the mind are apt to forget that it also weakens the body; those who perceive that it is a bodily disease wonder that it should produce any alteration in a well regulated mind." The Good Genius then articulates what was for Sara a crucial distinction: "Mania is also a disease in which the mind is affected through the body; but in the sort of nervousness which we are here discussing[,] Reason, Free Will, & consequently responsibility remain, while what may be called the more sensuous part of the mind, feeling emotion, partakes of the morbid conditions of the body." Madness was a disease of the reason, nervousness a disease of the emotions. The latter left the patient's intellectual abilities unimpaired but wreaked havoc upon the feelings. Nervousness was, in other words, "a derangement of the senses," "a morbid state of sensation," in which the sufferer could be deluded by "the morbid conditions of the body" but was not without "the full use of the reasoning power."

Sara's distinction between madness and nervousness allowed her to rationalize what would have been unacceptable behavior under normal circumstances: "Just as the body is constantly simulating some organic disease[,] so the agitated spirits induce the appearance of certain tempers . . . & occasion conduct which looks as if it were principled by envy, discontent, cowardice, or the weakest & blindest self love." In fact, the nervous sufferer needs the authoritarian reprimands of an "expert" physician less than the more sympathetic treatment of one skilled in the "nurse like arts": "To infuse confidence, to suggest hopeful considerations, to soothe irritation, to amuse & relieve by temporary shifts & amusive novelties . . . which can only be suggested by one who has taken pains to know the patient's peculiarities of body & mind—and to do all this with the authority of one who has a name for curing nervousness— all this you will say is the business of a nurse rather than a physician—but I believe it is by such nurse like arts that many a physician has gained immense practice." Twenty years before the birth of Freud, Sara recognized the need for psychiatric skills in the treatment of women's illnesses. Those simpleminded practitioners who "appl[ied] one specific to all cases," who refused to explore the interconnecting "peculiarities of body & mind," were, in the words of the Good Genius, mere "Quack[s]."

Quacks, evidently, made much of the benefits of habit, preaching regular exercise or constant bedrest depending on the individual case. Sara's Invalid, however, remains unconvinced: "I am constantly told that habit is everything—

but I have not found that perseverance was rewarded by success when I endeavoured to continue the practices of health." The point, of course, was not simply to persevere or not to persevere but to recognize how complex were the ailments of nervous sufferers. As the Good Genius puts it, "Advisors are too apt to forget that the law must be limited by the state of the sufferer—as sufferers are to think the law is to be abrogated when it ought only to be modified."

One law of particular concern for Sara was that which governed the use of laudanum. No longer able to ignore her dependence on the drug or its unpleasant side effects, Sara had the Invalid raise the issue as a problem for both patient and doctor alike: "Another case of conscience with me is in regard to the use of stimulants and narcotics, particularly laudanum. Every medical man speaks ill of the drug, prohibits it, & after trying in vain to give me sleep without it, ends with prescribing it himself." In one of the longest speeches of the dialogue, the Good Genius responds,

> In these cases we must try to make out whether the suffering or the remedy be really the greater evil, being honest with ourselves in this inquiry[;] if we decide in favour of the palliative, it will be our duty to use it as cheerfully & thankfully as we can—not diminishing the relief it affords by dwelling upon the degree of mischief which it may probably be going to the constitution. . . . What we do thus cautiously & rationally can never become a bad mental habit, . . . and it is the liability to become a habit that is the chief evil of laudanum taking, rather than the bodily effects. But we must never suffer it to become a habit—but every time we have recourse to it [we] must ask ourselves if it really be as necessary as it was at first: we must never think of taking it to procure positive comfort, but only to ward off obstinate sleeplessness, and that not so much on account of the immediate suffering as the after injurious effects of irritation and fatigue.

Without a physiological understanding of addiction, Sara could rationalize the use of laudanum as an unpleasant "duty" to be endured "cheerfully" by one whose self-conscious regulation of the drug insured that it had not yet become a "bad mental habit." In other words, because laudanum was seen as morally corrupting but not physically addictive, Sara had to insist that it was a necessary evil completely under control by her rational faculties: it was a "useful temporary expedient" never employed "to procure positive comfort." To admit otherwise, to confess either enjoyment or dependence, was to confess both moral weakness and mental laxity.

After considering the benefits of other "stimulants" and discussing the popular fallacy that nervousness is solely an upper-class disorder, the Invalid and Good Genius return in conclusion to a more general assessment of "nervous derangement." Once again, the importance afforded "Reason" as the mental corrective for an inescapable bodily weakness emphasizes how Sara indulged the physical while denying it, denied the domestic while celebrating it, and celebrated the intellectual while engaging it. "Mental stimulus," the Good Genius argues, "will produce wonderful effects upon the body in cases of functional derangement. A strong excitement has even suspended for a time the pain and powerlessness produced by gout." The Invalid quickly concurs: "Mental medicine is [not] applicable only to the mind." By exercising her "Reason," the nervous invalid acts out a "cure" that was in fact an end in itself, for illness was at once protest and capitulation, a self-aggrandizing martyrdom that found a worldly efficacy by repudiating all claims to worldly power. Through illness, Sara escaped from one proscribed social role into another, but she found in her (dis)ease the very cure for which she had been searching.

III

Sara's essay on nervous derangement was begun during her father's final illness in July 1834. Coleridge, like his daughter, had long evidenced an inordinate preoccupation with matters of health. Paradoxically, that obsession made his death on July 25 an even greater shock for family and friends. As Sara explained it to Hartley,

> Gradual as our dear father's decline has been its termination has seemed sudden even to us & is a surprize to his friends in general. None but the Gillmans have ever known the extent of his weakness & suffering & they did not anticipate his removal this summer. As Henry says—his illness did not look like that of another man. The life & vigour of his mind so illuminated his house of clay that few people, especially strangers who only saw him at his best times, perceived its decaying condition. And then in the midst of bodily feebleness & frequent pain he seemed to be by no means deprived of enjoyment . . . : the chair or even the bed was no prison to him & he was conscious that his better part could scarcely be said to have grown old. [Letter VCL: SC to HC (5 Aug 1834)]

Once begun, however, Coleridge's decline was rapid:

> On the Saturday fort-night before his last illness Henry brought a good report of him. . . . On the evening of the 19th he appeared very ill & on Sunday came a note—which I opened—Henry being at Church. We sent to him there & and he went to Highgate immediately. My dear father had often seemed near death before so that it was not impossible that he might rally. Still from the tone of the note I mourned him as one about to be taken from us. Henry returned in a few hours. My father since he first felt his end

approaching had expressed a desire that he might be as little disturbed as possible. He took leave of Mrs. Gillman & did not wish even to see his beloved friend Mr. Green. . . . Henry, however, was resolved to enter his room & see him for the last time. He was just able to send his blessing to my mother & me, though he articulated with difficulty & speaking seemed to increase his pain. Henry kissed him & withdrew—never to see him living again. [Letter VCL: SC to HC (5 Aug 1834)]

Sara was not able to visit her father, and she did not attend the funeral on August 2. But she was by her mother's account "deeply affected" (Letter: SC to ET [19—25 July 1834; SFC's note affixed]). Henry concurred: "My poor Sara," he reported to Robert Southey, "is much shaken [and but] . . . slowly mending" (Letter BL: HNC to RS [25 July 1834]).

However "shaken," Sara did not allow her personal grief to precipitate yet another nervous collapse. In fact, her health and spirits suddenly improved, and from the evidence in her letters, Sara's sorrow appears to have been as much for the deceased philosopher and the death of his philosophic system as for her deceased flesh-and-blood father. She confided to Thomas Poole more than she perhaps realized:

> We mourn not only one near and dear taken from our sight but the extinction of a light such as will never beam over our earthly path again— It has made this world more spiritual and the next in some sort more visible to our apprehension—"the feeling of this loss can ne'er be old." But there was everything in the circumstances of his departure to soothe our regret and we feel happy in the hope that his writing will be widely influential for good purposes. All his views philosophical and theological may not be adopted, & the effect of his posthumous works must be impaired by their fragmentary condition, but I think there is reason to believe that what he has left behind him, published and unpublished, will introduce a higher & more improving mode of thinking and teach men to consider some subjects on principles more comprehensive and accordant to reason than has hitherto been done. Immediately popular they can never be—but their exposition of truth may mould the opinions and tinge the feelings of hundreds who have never read the words themselves. [Letter BL: SC to TP (5 Sept 1834)].

Her father's death or, more exactly, the "extinction" of his philosophic "light," suddenly provided Sara with a new raison d'être, the maintaining and defending of Coleridge's intellectual reputation. As her enthusiasm attests, such duty was not without its rewards, and several weeks before her letter to Poole, she had urged Hartley to think of Coleridge's passing as ultimately salutary for parent and children alike:

Too often the inheritance of a great name inspires little more than an unfruitful pride—pride in the celebrity rather than in that which merited it, and it is valued as giving a degree of lustre and significance to those who have none that is unborrowed. Its due effect should be to inspire high aims . . . a desire to make the worthiest use of whatever talents may be intrusted to our charge, even though they be of the humblest description. It is very generally thought that in your case genius has been inherited or if genius be not transmissible, shared by the gift of nature. But *all* the children of genius who have lived at the fountain of that light which it is hoped may eventually help to enlighten the world should seek to prove the beneficial influence of it by their own character and bearing, and that though their powers may be of the common order, they have not thrown away their uncommon advantages. [Griggs 93]

Although Sara's intent was clearly to urge her dissipated brother to mend his ways, she carefully asserts her own claim to the Coleridgean legacy, arguing that "*all* the children of genius" should "help to enlighten the world" through the example of "their own character and bearing." Also palpable in the passage is a newly discovered sense of responsibility for and excitement about her father's "genius." Coleridge's death paradoxically granted his daughter both new duties and new freedoms—the duty to protect and maintain his fragile reputation and the freedom to remake his law according to her own design.

Consider, for example, a letter from Sara to Emily Trevenen written on the day of Coleridge's funeral. It includes only passing references to Coleridge and no full account of his death. Instead, Sara presents a detailed assessment of contemporary female authors, evoking her father not to lament his demise but to use his authority for the purpose of establishing her own critical discourse:

I can not see in [Hannah More's] productions aught comparable to the imaginative vigour of Mrs. J. Baillie, the eloquence and (for a woman) the profundity of M. de Stael, the brilliancy of Mrs. Hemans (though I think *her* over-rated), the pleasant broad comedy of Miss Burney and Miss Ferrier, the melancholy tenderness of Miss Bowles, the pathos of Inchbald and Opie, the masterly sketching of Miss Edgeworth (who like Hogarth paints manners as they grow out of morals, and not merely as they are modified and tinctured by fashion), the strong and touching, but sometimes coarse pictures of Miss Martineau, who has some highly interesting sketches of childhood in humble life, and last, not least, the delicate mirth, the gently hinted satire, the feminine, decorous humour of Jane Austen, who if not the greatest is surely the most faultless of female novelists. My Uncle [Southey] and my Father had an equally high opinion of her merits—but Mr. Wordsworth used to say . . . he could not be interested in productions of that kind. . . . Indeed, you will acquit me of any affected pretense to originality of criticism when you recollect how early my mind was biased by the strong talkers I was in the habit of listening to. The spirit of what I sport on critical matters, though not always the application, is generally derived from the sources that you [are aware?] of. Yet I know well that we should not go by authority without finding out a reason for our faith; and unless we test the opinions learned from others with those of the world in general, we are apt to hold them in an incorrect, and at the same time a more strong and unqualified way than those do from whom we have derived them. [Letter: SC to ET (3 Aug 1834)]

While Sara no doubt grieved for her father, his death was nevertheless a kind of liberation: she could now claim her patrimony, her relationship to and knowledge of "the strong[est] talkers" in the early nineteenth century, without violating propriety and without fear of reproach or censure. She could, in her words, "test . . . opinions learned from others" against "the world in general." In short, she was free to evaluate that which had previously stood exempt from her evaluation.

Sara's intellectual excitement during the fall of 1834 was fueled in part by the furor over Coleridge's status as poet and philosopher. The *Poetical Works* had appeared in January, and because of the author's recent death reviewers were scrambling to place timely assessments in their favorite journals. First to appear, in the August number of the *Quarterly,* was Henry's flattering review of his uncle's poetry. Calling Coleridge "the most imaginative of the English poets since Milton," Henry has often been given credit for single-handedly establishing Coleridge's poetic reputation. That was hardly the case. Although well-received, Henry's review was followed almost immediately by De Quincey's notorious four-part serial in *Tait's Edinburgh Magazine.* De Quincey's account of Coleridge's intellectual shortcomings was a powerful if uneven indictment, and it sparked Sara's ire; but she was even more infuriated by its tactless descriptions of her mother:

> My Father's errors arose from weakness of the will alone, but Dequincey's fall has been effected by an irritable vanity as well as the proneness to self indulgence. . . . The impression which the account of my mother would leave is that she is a mean-minded unamiable woman with some respectable qualities and that my Father married her from opportunity rather than much attraction of hers. My mother's *respectability* it did not rest with him to establish: her attractions he greatly under-rates and the better points of her temper and understanding are not apparent in his partial sketch. [Letter: SC to HNC (Sept 1834)]

His "partial sketch," according to Sara, completely misrepresented her mother's personality:

[My mother] never admires anything she does not understand. Some women, like Mrs. Wilson and Mrs. Wordsworth, see the skirts of a golden cloud—they have unmeasured faith in a sun of Glory—and a sublime region stretching out far beyond their ken—and proud and happy to think that it belongs to them, are ready to give all they have to give in return. This faith—this docility is quite alien to the Fricker temperament. . . . But to say broadly or to imply unreservedly that she is harsh-tempered or narrow minded (that is, of an ungenerous spirit) or more unintellectual than many women who have pleased my Father is to misrepresent the subject. [Letter: SC to HNC (20 Sept 1834)]

De Quincey's "misrepresent[ations]" jolted Sara out of the complacent routines of her life at 21 Downshire Hill. She put aside her own reading and writing and began instead to follow the accounts of her father with keener interest. Encouraged by her husband, she systematically reread Coleridge's works, measuring what she knew of his personal weaknesses against what she was learning of his philosophical strengths.

While De Quincey's "shameless" essays irritated her more than many of the other reviews, Sara by no means limited her attention to the serial in *Tait's*. Reacting against John Wilson's generally favorable portrait of Coleridge in *Blackwood's*, she complained to Henry,

He is a fool to speak of my Father's *master*. . . . Wordsworth the master of Coleridge indeed! This is gross flattery of the living Bard. . . . He may say the one is a greater poet than the other if he will, but this, methinks, is an incorrect way of expressing the opinion: both as to reputation and enlightenment of mind I believe my Father conferred at least as much as he received in that quarter, for it was the nature of his genius to overflow on all around. Mr. Wordsworth is indeed "on his own ground as an uncomparable talker" but he did not give out all the riches of his mind with the same uncalculating profusion (without taking thought for a future work) as my Father was wont to do. Besides which their styles are not alike. One great man will gain something from another, but no man furnished my Father so largely as with justice to be called his master. [Griggs 107]

Of J. A. Heraud's piece in *Fraser's Magazine,* she wrote, "There is a great deal of coarse flattery of our friends at the Grove [the Gillmans] and a sort of defying recklessness of *our* feelings. . . . Then there are silly anecdotes told of him [Coleridge] in a silly trashy imitation of the Notes in Blackwood. . . . What can be the delicacy of the man who pens such stuff of one who has children living!" (Letter: SC to HNC [3 Jan 1834]). It was clear to Sara that something must be done, some plan of action taken, some type of organized defense begun. Two months after the death of Coleridge, she wrote to her husband, "STC's works must be reissued [but not] . . . disjointed and unaccompanied. Let them be set forth . . . with the complete scheme of arguments which convinced his own mind. Then let them be taken to pieces and examined grain by grain. . . . If they will not stand a fair test of that kind, they ought to be condemned. . . . If they are true they will prevail in the end" (Letter [30 Sept 1834]).

Sara was headstrong but not precipitant. Rather than lower herself and her husband to the level of undignified journalistic bickering, she decided to begin a long-term editorial campaign. In addition to her "motherly duties," which now included the writing of a long prose fairy tale (published in 1837 as *Phantasmion*), she assisted Henry with his edition of *Table Talk* (1835) and began transcribing her father's notes for what was later to become the four volumes of the *Literary Remains* (1836–39). Although instrumental in the planning and publication of both works, Sara received no public acknowledgement: both were officially edited by Henry, and he felt no compunction about neglecting to mention his wife's labors, either on the title page or in the preface, where he graciously thanks a number of his friends. In private, however, Henry freely admitted his debts: "All your remarks & alterations on my poor proofs are just—do what you like with them, & I am thankful. You are much superior to me in fineness of feeling & discrimination, I willingly acknowledge" (Letter [12 Sept 1834]).[18] Henry's "willing acknowledg[ments]" notwithstanding, Sara remained the invisible force behind the ongoing process of her father's canonization.

When *Table Talk* appeared in the spring of 1835, its reception was mixed, largely because Henry's ultraconservative politics had molded his uncle's conversations in ways that the more Whiggish Coleridgeans found objectionable. Hartley was one of many who reprimanded his brother-in-law for a far too simplistic portrait of Coleridge's political opinions:

His conversation when I was last in the habit of hearing him authorized me to think that he did perceive the necessity of deep and vital changes, not in servile compliance with the spirit of the age,—(an odious phrase) but to approximate the practice of the constitution to its Ideal and final cause he certainly did hold, or I grievously mistook him, that though the government did work well according to the money getting commercial principles of the economists who assailed it, it did not work well morally, did not perform its duty to God or to the divine in Man, did not supply those demands of human nature, which are at once rights and duties. He did express strong indignation against the selfishness and short sightedness of the governing classes, a selfishness modified and mollified indeed by much kindness and good-nature,—not controlled or balanced by any clear principles. He utterly condemn'd I know, to his latest hour the system which considering men as things, instruments, machines, property, does not in effect make them so. [*HC Letters* 189]

Defending her husband, Sara argued what would become *the* Victorian solution to the problem of Coleridge's political vacillations:[19]

> One of my father's Whig friends insinuates that if he had told his own story, he would have told it more Whiggishly. The spirit of party is "father to this thought"; it is not true. Henry is a man of honor, though, as some may think, an illiberal Tory. I refer such objectors to my father's little work on "Church and State." Could he, who had such an "idea of the constitution of Church and State," think more favorably of the Reform Bill, and of the projected alienation of Church property, than he appears to have done in Henry's publication? I can truly re-assert what has often been asserted before, that my father was no party man. He cared for no public man or ministry, except so far as they furthered what he considered the best interests of the country. "He had a vision of his own," and he scrupled not to condemn and expose the acting Tories if they ran counter to it. He was no lover of great and fine people—the pomps and vanities of this world were distasteful to him rather than otherwise. He had lived in a cottage himself, and he loved cottages, and he took a friendly interest in the inhabitants of them. He thought himself a true friend to the people in upholding the Church, which he considered the most popular institution in the country. [*ML*(1874) 110]

According to his daughter, Coleridge was "no party man"; he was instead a philosopher, a metapolitician whose abstruse systems at once defined the political arena and distanced him from it. Correctly perceiving that Coleridge's reputation would suffer in proportion to the strength of his political affiliations, Sara used his singularly most unpopular characteristic, his densely philosophic prose, to grant him exemption from but mastery over the political debates which threatened to engulf him.

Sara would later employ this same strategy in her appendix to the 1843 *Aids to Reflection* and in her introductions to the *Biographia Literaria* (1847) and *Essays on His Own Times* (1850). But her "solution" is also very much in evidence in an unpublished essay on Wordsworth written during the summer of 1835. Entitled "On Mr. Wordsworth's Poem 'Lines Left on a Yew-tree Seat,'" Sara's essay marks an important juncture in her life, the beginning of a life-long commitment to the defense of her father's works and the first step out from under the paralyzing depressions and nervous illnesses that plagued her throughout most of her marriage. Although Coleridge's name is never mentioned and Sara's position is in many ways her own, the firm implementation of

Coleridgean tenets makes the piece both an unacknowledged tribute to her father's memory and an important confrontation with his potentially debilitating legacy.

The essay itself is less a meditation on "Lines Left on a Yew-tree Seat" than a treatise on the role of the poet in society. As the opening distinction makes clear, Sara's interest is not in Wordsworth's "poetical philosophy," in his theories of composition and aesthetics, but in the "philosophic nature of his poetry," the ways in which his verse both embodies certain principles of philosophy and provides the vehicle for the reader's recognition of those principles. Reacting against an 1834 review of Wordsworth's *Poetical Works,* Sara insists that the reviewer has ingeniously overread the poem in question only to misconstrue the poet's intentions and his intended audience.[20] This objection leads naturally from an elucidation of the poem to a broader consideration of Wordsworth's role as poetic philosopher.

One of the fundamental strengths of the philosophical poet, according to Sara, originates in his proper understanding of the soul of man, not of some men but all men. With such an understanding he is then able to communicate his truths to the world. The submissive and unsophisticated reader, Sara argues, "may sometimes read aright from very simplicity, that is, from resigning himself completely to the will of his author, and not being seduced from submitting to . . . the suggestions of an autocratic spirit." While the highly intelligent reader may understand poetry in all its complexity, nevertheless "there is something which the understanding alone will not recognize, and which may be felt by persons of very little power and compass of thought." As the use of the term "understanding" suggests, the philosophic foundations are of Coleridge's construction, but where we would expect to have "reason" introduced as a corrective, there appears a slight modification: "Imagination, as we all know, is a part of every human mind, or a state which it is capable of passing into—an imaginative habit must proceed from that which is innate, but depends in some measure on the will of the individual. [P]oetic genius—and a powerful Imagination—are rare gifts, but imaginativeness can hardly be called an uncommon quality, & more or less of Imagination belongs to all."

Knowing her father's system as well as she did, Sara used it to facilitate her own ends. Seeking to prove the universal effectiveness of Wordsworth's philosophical poetry, she chose to emphasize the role of the imagination over that of the reason, yet she at no time strayed beyond her father's jurisdiction. Although the understanding and the reason are often treated as parts of one binary opposition, Coleridge did make clear their interrelationship with the imagination:

Of the *discursive* understanding, which forms for itself general notions and terms of classification for the purpose of comparing and arranging phae-

nomena, the Characteristic is Clearness without Depth. It contemplates
the unity of things in their *limits* only, and is consequently a knowledge of
superficies without substance. . . . The completing power which unites
clearness with depth, the plenitude of the sense with the comprehen-
sibility of the understanding, is the IMAGINATION, impregnated with
which the understanding itself becomes intuitive, and a living power. The
REASON . . . as the integral *spirit* of the regenerated man . . . re-
generateth all other powers . . . the REASON without being either the
SENSE, the UNDERSTANDING, or the IMAGINATION contains all three
within itself. [SM 69–70]

As this passage indicates, the imagination is subordinate to the reason; the latter
is a "living power," self-conscious and in part analytic, while the former is more
passive and instinctual. But as chapter 13 of the *Biographia* makes clear, the
imagination itself operates along a continuum, with both the primary and the
secondary imagination capable of profound insight. Without elaborating on her
father's distinction, Sara makes the imagination into a power innate in all men
and insists that it can be the vehicle of revelations more profound than those
achieved by the understanding. Thus, when the reviewer argues that parts of
Wordsworth's poetry are only applicable to and intended for "another philo-
sophic poet, or rather a pupil apt for becoming such," she can accuse him of an
unspiritual elitism, of recognizing neither the breadth of Wordsworth's philo-
sophic vision nor the "duty" inextricably a part of his poetic process.

As the essay progresses it becomes more stridently religious, arguing not
only for Wordsworth's spiritual awareness (she refers to his "Essay, Supplemen-
tary to the Preface"), but also for a philosophical understanding of that aware-
ness. Possessing attributes that far exceed the "finite understanding," the imag-
ination allows all men to "soar upward in love of God and move abroad in love
of God's creation." Because the imagination is part of the human soul, great
poetry should—and Wordsworth's poetry does—speak to each and everyone
of their common spiritual concerns. That this position actually extends the
views of Coleridge is demonstrated by a revealing use of an unacknowledged
quotation. Speaking of the "mystic strain" embodied in "My heart leaps up,"
Sara writes, "But even those for whom it is not intended, those who have not
'been accustomed to watch the flux and reflux of their inmost nature, to venture
at times into the twilight realms of consciousness, and to feel deep interest in
modes of inmost being, to which they know that the attributes of time and space
are inapplicable and alien, but which cannot be conveyed save in symbols of
time and space,' . . . must acknowledge the vividness of sensation and percep-
tion when the powers of the mind are new and the greater warmth of the
emotions when the mind is in early spring." The "vividness of sensation and
perception" perceived by even the most nonmetaphysically disposed readers

manifests a poetic power which unites both the imaginative and the spiritual and so communicates divine love. In other words, the transcendent experience which Coleridge, in the passage from which the excerpt originates (BL[CC] 2:147), would grant only to the most privileged of psychic explorers, his daughter insists is available to all. Coleridge too had been discussing Wordsworth's poetry, making the same claims about the content of the "Intimations Ode" that the reviewer had of the "Yew-tree Seat." His daughter's revision thus negates the context of his original argument subtly but firmly and appropriates his theories and his authority to advance her own position.

Having espoused her theory of the democratic imagination, Sara next confronts the reviewer's objections to Wordsworth's moral philosophy. Praising pragmatism, the reviewer had disagreed with the poem's "noble sentiments" and had maintained that "the operation of the harsher sentiments of our nature" has a necessary place in the "every-day intercourse of ordinary man with man." Such an admission, Sara argues, traps man within his baser nature—his flesh— and denies his potential for transforming spiritual truths into worldly actions: "We should look on every living thing in a benign spirit, condemning and despising the evil that may be in any individual but having no unkind affection toward the individual himself." Because she holds that all men share the same potential for spiritual insight, Sara finds the reviewer's elitist notions of virtue and justice highly objectionable: "I cannot believe that a different quality as well as different quantity of virtue is to be expected from different persons." Never very far from the argument is her prime example, the moral philosopher and Christian poet, Wordsworth, whose art is rightly conceived in terms of his responsibility to his fellow man. The philosopher/poet must speak from an ethical awareness; "his duty as a man of genius is included in his duty as a Christian." Thus defined, the poet is both philosopher and man of action; his poems are designed both to please and to perform moral services in the world.

The essay's concluding paragraph completes the transformation, making Wordsworth into a poetic priest and his poems into verse gospel. Once again playing an essential role, the imagination is emphasized as that divinely ordained power "by which the nature of man is refined and glorified." But the essay is considerably more than a reiteration of Coleridge's flattering assessment of Wordsworth at the close of the Biographia Literaria. For although Sara agrees with her father that the imagination is Wordsworth's strongest gift, she goes on to argue for Wordsworth as a philosopher speaking to all—men and women, rich and poor, educated and unlettered. Such an argument works to the benefit of father and daughter alike. On one hand, it includes Coleridge by implication in the same category defined for Wordsworth and rescues him from the petty squabbling of party politics; on the other, it guarantees Sara the right to appreciate and evaluate "works of genius" without fear of reproach, without fear of having violated the codes of female propriety that denied women access to critical discourse. The crucial paradox is that Sara must first dislodge her father's idea of select audience before establishing a position from which she is able to argue for him as a "philosophic poet." Or, put another way, any formal defense or explication of her poetic "fathers"—Coleridge, Southey, Wordsworth—enacted a transgression against that which she was seeking to defend or explicate, a transgression that one way or another had to be rationalized.

Coleridge's death ended the possibility of paternal reproof, of either an authorial claim to an original intention or a fatherly insistence on a properly female behavior. At the same time, his death left an immethodical and fragmentary philosophical system much in need of restoration: there were materials to edit and accusations to refute. Sara found herself free both to claim her patrimony and interpret it, or, more accurately, to claim it *by* interpreting it.

CHAPTER FOUR

"The Great Art"
From Madness to Matriarchy

*[S]he shared with Hartley . . . an absolute indifference to purely worldly stan-
dards and worldly ambitions. The approving appreciation of a friend was of far
greater value than the acclamations of a crowd. Her unusual gifts were gladly
used to expound, adapt, criticize, or interpret the minds and works of others. She
had no desire to attain celebrity by a creative exercise of her intellectual powers.
In her only long original work they were employed in children's service.*

Eleanor Towle, A Poet's Children

*It is painful to be unable to understand one's suffering, to translate it into an
intelligible language, and bring it distinctly before the mind's eye. But it is
already a sign that we are no longer wholly subdued by its power when we can
analyze it, and make this very indefiniteness an object of contemplation. This
evinces a degree of mastery over that which has of late been a tyrant. And if "to
be weak is miserable" (oh, how often have I thanked Milton for that line!), to
exercise any kind of power, or have any kind of strength, is so far an abatement
of misery.*

Sara Coleridge, Letter to Arabella Brooke

January 1836 began inauspiciously for the residents of 21 Downshire Hill,
Hampstead; for although the children remained healthy and Sara's spirits con-
tinued to improve, Henry's father, Colonel James Coleridge, died on the tenth
after a long and trying illness. It was an event that marked both the end of a
generation and the culmination of a year and a half of unexpected sorrow for the
Coleridge family: the poet's death, it seemed, had triggered a series of related
misfortunes. Charles Lamb, family friend and indefatigable humorist, had died
suddenly several months after Coleridge; and writing to Henry, Sara empha-
sized her sense of a greater loss: "I connect him with my poor father, Words-
worth, Southey, [and] Lloyd. It seems as if two links of a chain were broken, and

one is forcibly reminded of the fragility of the whole" (Letter [3 Jan 1835]).[1] A year later, the "fragility of the whole" had become all the more pronounced, and Sara confided to Derwent that her father-in-law's death caused her "to revert even more frequently than I should have otherwise done to the suffering & deathbed of our . . . beloved and revered parent" (Letter [20 Jan 1836]).

Yet Sara's melancholy musings on the death of her father occupy only a fraction of a very long and newsy letter. After mention of her "revered parent" and a brief description of the colonel's funeral, she dwells at length on what was for her perhaps the more interesting news:

> Dora . . . gives a sad account of Miss W. "Nothing," she says "seems to give her pleasure—not even the sight of her dear brother—often and often he comes down from her room, his eyes filled with tears, saying 'Well! all I can do for her now is to heat her nightcap—I have done it twenty times within the last ¼ of an hour—that seems to her a momentary pleasure, and that is some comfort.' If abscesses do not form on the brain, of which there is some danger, Mr. Carr thinks she may live for years, but this is a melancholy prospect, for if her mind is to continue in its present state one and all of us would *joyfully* see her laid by that beloved Aunt who is gone before in our own quiet Churchyard in Grasmere." Accounts of poor Aunt Southey are little if at all better than this—the consolation is that she evidently does not suffer: she never finds the time heavy, . . . and seems to be always in a waking dream.

In January 1836, Dorothy Wordsworth and Edith Southey were both considered "mentally deranged" by family and friends.[2] "Poor Aunt Southey" had suffered a nervous collapse in September 1834, and soon thereafter her affliction, at least by her husband's account, "assumed a decided form of madness in its most frightful manifestations" (Ramos 266). In early October, she was forcibly removed from Greta Hall and committed to a York mental asylum, William Tuke's renowned "Retreat."[3] Seven months later she returned to her home physically "well" but psychologically "uncured": "Her bodily health is so much improved," Southey wrote, "that in that respect indeed she may be said to be well;—but there is no other improvement. Yet tho hope is over, anxiety is not;—the character of her malady is to be pleased with nothing, & to oppose everything that is proposed; of course all our management is required" (Ramos 277). Until her death in November 1837, the perennially obstreperous Edith Southey required her husband's constant "management." She became, as he later put it, "[my] long tragedy" (Ramos 287).

Rydal Mount, meanwhile, was faring no better than Greta Hall. Dora Wordsworth, Dorothy Wordsworth, and Sara Hutchinson had all spent the spring of 1835 battling a formidable series of illnesses. Dora, suffering from "inflammation of the spine," soon put the worst behind her, but on June 23 Sara Hutchinson died after a severe bout of rheumatic fever (*SH Letters* 436–37; *MW Letters* 148). Almost immediately, Dorothy, long thought the sickest of the three, began a slow recovery. It quickly became apparent, however, that she, like Edith Southey, had undergone some kind of mental shock. In August, Wordsworth reported to Catherine Clarkson, "My poor Sister languishes in her sick room and mostly upon her sick bed, how long she may yet have to struggle we cannot foresee—her weakness is deplorable, but of acute pain we hope she has not much to endure; I say hope for her mind since Sarah's departure has been so confused as to passing events, that we have no distinct knowledge of what she may actually have to support in the way of bodily pain. She remembers and recollects all but recent things perfectly" (*W Letters* 2:755). Wordsworth's fears as to Dorothy's "confus[ion]" were soon confirmed, and in a letter to Samuel Rogers several weeks later, he admitted,

> My dear Sister, in bodily health, is decidedly better, though quite unable to stand. Her mind, however, is, I grieve to say, much shattered. The change showed itself upon the death of dear Miss Hutchinson, but probably was preparing before. Her case at present is very strange; her judgment, her memory, and all her faculties are perfect as ever, with the exception of what relates to her own illness, and passing occurrences. If I ask her opinion upon any point of Literature, she answers with all her former acuteness; if I read Milton, or any favourite Author, and pause, she goes on with the passage from memory; but she forgets instantly the circumstances of the day. [*W Letters* 2:758–59]

Dorothy's "case" does indeed appear "very strange." With "her judgement, her memory, and all her faculties" as "perfect as ever," it seems curious that she could "forget instantly" all about the "circumstances of the day"—and yet retain "her former acuteness" in other matters. For whatever reason, she denied the present and preserved the past, becoming a kind of parodic embodiment of her brother's poetic philosophy, an idiot child with a rich and bountiful cultural knowledge.

Reports of Dorothy's "shattered" mind quickly reached London, and in November Sara relayed the sad news to Emily Trevenen: "Mrs. Wordsworth's last letter which we have seen gave an affecting account of Miss Wordsworth—it is strange that there should be such a 'partition in her mind.' On some subjects it appears that she can speak as well as ever, and yet she talks and behaves in a manner which proves that there is an imbecility in her intellect, as to its general operations" (Letter [28 Nov 1835]). First Edith Southey and then Dorothy Wordsworth succumbed to what their contemporaries agreed was a type of "mental derangement." And although "imbecility" seems far too harsh a term to describe Dorothy's illness, it was clear that both women had been adversely "affected" and that by 1836 neither Greta Hall nor Rydal Mount could make any claim to domestic happiness. The house of romanticism, it seemed, had more than one madwoman in the attic. Writing to John May in August 1835, Southey noted the changed circumstances: "Miss Wordsworth, whose death has been looked upon as likely any day for the last two years, still lives on, Her mind, at times, fails now . . . so that at this time Wordsworth's is a more afflicted house than my own. They used to be two of the happiest in the country" (*RS Life* 6:271–72).

As her letters indicate, Sara was not overly disturbed by reports from the north. While she no doubt gleaned details from her correspondence and followed the latest developments with some care, her life in London was sufficiently distant from the lives of Edith Southey and Dorothy Wordsworth to ensure that their "madness" did not disrupt her domestic routines. She could not have read, for instance, Dr. Belcombe's official assessment of her aunt's mental health, and so could not have measured the similarity between their respective situations or contemplated the paternalistic discourse of "moral management" that defined women's "madness" in mid-nineteenth-century Britain.[4] Dr. Belcombe wrote:

> The mental disease under which Mrs S[outhey] labours, arises from general irritation of the nervous system; & tho she may consider herself, & perhaps feel, very unhappy from being from home, I have little doubt that were you [Robert Southey] to be here, the idea that she had induced you to come at expense & inconvenience to yourself, would be the next thing to prey upon her mind. . . . Mrs S. appears to me to have been some time labouring under the incipient stage of this malady, & what we now witness is the more acute form of it. She is nevertheless in some respects better, being more manageable, more tractable,—has eaten her food more regularly, & occasionally betakes herself to some employment. Under the most encouraging auspices, time will be required but no exertion in the medical or moral management shall be spared—[5]

Nor could Sara have read the verses that Dorothy Wordsworth began composing during the early years of her illness and continued to compose and recite throughout her so-called imbecility:[6]

> No prisoner am I on this couch,
> My mind is free to roam,
> And leisure, peace and loving friends
> Are the best treasures of an earthly home.

Such gifts are mine, then why deplore
The feeble body's slow decay,
A warning mercifully sent
To fix my hope upon a surer stay?

And may I learn those precious gifts
Rightly to prize, and by their soothing power
All fickle murmuring thoughts repress
And fit my fluttering heart for the last hour.

[*D Wordsworth* 388–89]

If Dorothy's poem enacts the female invalid's version of "Lime-Tree Bower my Prison" and recalls Sara's essays "Beauty" and "Nervousness" (in addition to hundreds of her pious diary entries), then Dr. Belcombe's diagnosis establishes the generative context, the institutional voice of the male medical profession whose duty it was to treat (and define) female maladies, to make "more manageable [and] more tractable" its "disturbed" patients.

According to Elaine Showalter, whose most recent book, *The Female Malady: Women, Madness and English Culture, 1830–1980,* persuasively rewrites medical history, "The triple cornerstones of Victorian psychiatric theory and practice were moral insanity, moral management, and moral architecture. 'Moral insanity' redefined madness, not as a loss of reason, but as deviance from socially accepted behavior. 'Moral management' substituted close supervision and paternal concern for physical restraint and harsh treatment, in an effort to re-educate the insane in habits of industry, self-control, moderation, and perseverance. 'Moral architecture' constructed asylums planned as therapeutic environments in which lunatics could be controlled without the use of force" (29). Indebted to the work of Michel Foucault, Showalter sensitively unweaves the intricate threads of nineteenth-century psychiatric discourse in order to expose the hidden power relations that worked to reinforce patriarchal myths of womanhood.

Although "moral architecture" had yet to be realized, by 1835 "moral insanity" and "moral management" were already well-established, largely because of William and Samuel Tuke's pioneering work at the York Retreat. "Moral insanity," as Dr. James Prichard defined it in 1835, involved "a morbid perversion of the natural feelings, affections, inclinations, tempers, habits, moral dispositions, and natural impulses, without any remarkable disorder or defect of the intellect, or knowing and reasoning faculties, and particularly without any insane illusion or hallucination."[7] By this definition, "[un]natural" behavior of almost any sort, particularly that which violated or threatened established social values, could be construed as a type of madness, requiring as a corrective—in Dr. Belcombe's words to Robert Southey—"moral management."

To recognize "moral insanity" as an operative subcategory of early-nineteenth-century notions of "madness" is also to recognize that Edith Southey and Dorothy Wordsworth were not certifiably "insane" by contemporary standards, that their illnesses were inscribed within larger paradigms of female "disorders," and that their prescribed treatment—"moral management"—involved a strong reassertion of patriarchal power and female subservience. It is also to recognize that their illnesses were in part a protest against the oppressive social codes that structured and constrained women's lives at Greta Hall and Rydal Mount. "The character of [Edith's] malady," Robert Southey wrote, "is to be pleased with nothing, & to oppose everything that is proposed; of course all our management is required." Similarly, as Dora noted to her Aunt Dorothy, "Nothing seems to give her pleasure—not even the sight of her dear brother." That such protest was at its origin ambivalent is undeniable. Madness, as Shoshana Felman has pointed out, is "quite the opposite of rebellion"; it is "the impasse confronting those whom cultural conditioning has deprived of the very means of protest or self-affirmation."[8]

Sara Coleridge had been negotiating this "impasse" since the onset of her illness during the first years of married life. Her "nervous derangement," she explained to Henry in 1832, was "a disease in the mental powers—not madness—yet in some respects akin to it" (Letter [13 Nov 1832]); and her dialogue on nervousness, as I have argued, was a sustained effort to differentiate between madness as a disease of the reason and hysteria as a disease of the emotions. It was also an attempt to comes to grips with an increasingly troublesome opium addiction. The death of Coleridge in 1834 jolted Sara out of an intellectual self-absorption that exploited illness in order to escape maternal duty, but that lacked a distinct goal or purpose other than the acquisition of knowledge for its own sake. Coleridge's death simultaneously pushed Sara into the literary politics of the day as it gave her a fixed point of reference, a body of literary and philosophical writings that she could adapt for her own purposes and then use as a legitimate reason for transgressing the accepted codes of female decorum and entering the public debate.

Ironically, several years before her lapse into "moral derangement," Dorothy Wordsworth took partial credit for Sara's recovery: "Her father's death rouzed her, but before that she had profited by my advice and plain speech, as I heard from both herself and others—and she now seems determined to be well, and God grant that she may, for it is a deplorable thing to see a young creature, who seems to have every wish of her heart gratified, give up to fanciful despondency" (D Wordsworth 392). Dorothy was correct that Sara was "determined to be well," but she was incorrect to assume that Sara had "every wish of her heart gratified," or to expect that once "rouzed" Sara would leave behind her "fanciful despondency." Sara's illness varied in intensity throughout her life but never completely abated. It was not a series of specific ailments or distinct periods of physical and/or psychological turmoil. Rather, it was a constant and irradicable part of her character—not only the background against which the events in her life occurred, but more accurately the constitutive context which defined and generated those events. Sara's illness was first and foremost the acting out of a cultural stereotype, the ethereal "angel in the house" whose weak constitution bespoke spiritual purity and appealing otherworldliness. It was also in part a violent protest against the selfless matriarch who was expected to live in and through her husband and progeny. But for Sara especially, illness was a symbolic reenactment of her own status as marginal intellectual; her (dis)ease both provided the opportunity for intellectual activity and confirmed the deviance that activity represented.

II

Regardless of its inauspicious beginning, 1836 progressed with Sara more intellectually active—and consequently in better spirits—than she had been in almost five years. She labored over her father's marginalia and continued to be an indispensable aid to, if not the driving force behind, Henry's ongoing edition of the *Literary Remains*. With equal care, she monitored contemporary criticism of her father's work, kept up with writings by women, and began revising her long fairy tale, "Phantasmion," for publication. Infuriated by Thomas Allsop's *Letters, Conversations and Recollections of S. T. Coleridge* (1836), she regretted that her husband had not taken legal action: "What Mr. A. has done," she complained to Emily Trevenen, is "(not to speak of its impropriety and indelicacy) illegal. Henry might have obtained an injunction to restrain the publication of the *letters* as was done in the case of some of Lord Byron's" (Letter [7 Jan 1836]).[9] During this period, she also wrote at length on Joanna Baillie's new dramas and Felicia Hemans's status as poet: the former was psychologically "too unrealistic," the latter "too stiltified and apostrophical" (Letters: SC to ET [7 Jan 1836]; and SC to Mrs. Henry Jones [1836]). As always, Sara continued to devote at least some part of her day to the education of her children, five-year-old Herbert and three-year-old Edith.

By spring, Sara's activities had somewhat slackened. She suffered a mild case of the flu over Easter and found herself in mid-April once more battling hysteria and depression. To her diary she confided, "Weeping again! Worst day that I have had since I began to recover from my hysteric malady . . . lower today than ever" (Diary [25 April 1836]).[10] A June visit from Emily Trevenen temporarily restored her spirits, and throughout the summer she managed to keep up with all her projects. By August, however, she was dreading a long-anticipated trip to Ottery. Hating travel and not overly fond of her Ottery relatives,

Sara had been postponing the trip for years—always pleading ill health. Against her better judgment and in deference to her husband's wishes, she set out with her children for Ottery in late August. It proved a costly error.

Sara arrived at Andover "ill and foreboding," at Ilminster in "a terrible state of nervous agitation," and finally at Ottery St. Mary "in great misery" (Diary [Aug 1836]). The whole of her stay at the Frank Coleridges' Manor House was marred by illness: she journeyed as far as the garden only once and took many of her meals in the privacy of her room. She continued, however, with her work on Coleridge—preparing a new edition of *Aids to Reflection,* reading the latest American assessments of her father (sent along by Pickering), and worrying about the rumored indiscretions of Joseph Cottle's forthcoming volume, *Early Recollections: Chiefly relating to the late Samuel Taylor Coleridge.* But most of all she worried about the five-day, 160-mile trip back to London.

On October 14, Sara set out with her two young children and their nurse, Anne Parrott. Henry, unfortunately, could not accompany them due to pressing business commitments in the opposite direction. At the end of the first day, Sara stopped at Ilchester, where she collapsed in tears and declared herself unfit to proceed. She sent her children back to Ottery and informed her husband of the situation:

> Your feelings will be sad when you hear that I cannot proceed with my journey. God in heaven, to whom I fervently pray, knows that I cannot. I was much worse after arriving yesterday—in hysterics frequently had no sleep last night, and in attempting to set out today found I could not do it. I mean that I was in such a state—so weak, tongue furred, stomach flatulent & sick, so that I cannot keep myself up with food, and altogether so ill that if I put a further force upon my nerves, I know not what will happen. I *cannot* bear the misery. I never suffered as I have done for 24 hours. Judge kindly of me my beloved, & write to comfort me at Ilchester. *Indeed* I would go if I could. I would suffer pain—but their terrors are too dreadful & my prostration too great. If I am now quiet I shall gradually recover but if I proceed I never shall. . . . My notion is that I may after a time return to Ottery and be in Aunt Luke's house or some lodging for the winter. This is dreadful—the separation from you but it cannot be helped. [Letter (16 Oct 1836)]

"God in heaven" acknowledged the severity of Sara's illness and the wisdom of her stopping in Ilchester, but it was Henry's kind "judg[ment]" that she most needed. Thus, the "dreadful . . . separation" was presented not as a matter of choice but of necessity: "it [could] not be helped."

Sara remained at Braine's Inn, Ilchester, for a full month, suffering through the worst period of nervous hysteria she would ever endure. Letters written daily to her husband make clear that her physical symptoms improved almost immediately—allowing her to resume her copious reading and writing with a clear head and vigorous hand. They would reappear instantly, however, whenever Henry fixed a date for her departure. Alternating between hysterical appeals and rigorous logic, Sara fought with admirable skill for the right to remain exactly where she was:

> Give me advice—but do not counsel me to proceed. Indeed I am too ill. . . . I fret about the money which all this will cost. But can I help it? O write affectionately to me. A weight will be off my heart when you have told me I have done my best. Indeed Indeed I have. [Letter (16 Oct 1836)]

> Say that I may rest here till my shattered nerves have recovered some degree of tone, and I shall be happy: but assuredly that will not be in ten days, nor perhaps in ten weeks. For the rest of my life I would keep my expenses within the closest bounds possible. In your first letter you spoke as if my feelings, "my suffering and apprehension *for the time*" were the points in question. Is that a fair statement? O no! It is the permanent prostration of nervous power, the continual recurrence of nervous miseries & weaknesses which paralyze the body & mind that are the evil. A stage lower than I now am life would be a burden, and of this I am perfectly certain that any attempt to travel for a considerable time hence would produce what I dread. [Letter (19 Oct 1836)]

> Dreadfully sick this morning. All my symptoms worse. Spirits at the lowest ebb. O this is a severe trial to us all—God help us through it. But while the fear of this dreadful journey is before me, I see not how I am to recover. [Letter (7 Nov 1836)]

> Your *expressions* my love are fond & gentle, but you virtually deny all my requests, which nothing but absolute necessity induced me to prefer. The loss of money will bear almost as heavy on me as on you, & the misery of causing so much affliction . . . is only overpowered in me by such a bodily pressure as no *human being* could resist. . . . I am not now pleading to remain here till that time [Christmas], but I must tell you that were it possible it *would* be of the greatest service. The journey being at a distance my mind would be calm though sorrowful; time would bring strength: my nerves would be further advanced from the period of vaginal shock, & thus my horror would *not* be so great as it is now. [Letter (10 Nov 1836)]

Sara explained repeatedly to Henry that her illness was both physical and emotional, and as the reference to "vaginal shock" suggests, she had from the outset implicated her reproductive organs as a contributing factor in her "nervous derangement." Suspicious discharges (which Sara labeled "albifluores" or "whites") confirmed an indisputable "irritation of the uterous, either as a cause or accompaniment of general nervous weakness" (Letter: SC to HNC [3 Nov 1836]). Strategic references to this affliction kept Henry's exasperation in check and substantiated (biologically) her emotional fluctuation: "My nerves have more phases than the moon—*varium et mutibile semper femina:* I seem to be moon struck, and infected with her changeful disposition—but her changes are all lovely, mine all distressful" (Letter: SC to HNC [3 Nov 1836]).

Sara's spiritual being was "infected" with a female body; its changing rhythms were a disease that confirmed her weakness, her inferiority, her subservience. Choosing to place her faith in the otherworldly power of her (feminine) spirit, she could at times manifest an intense physical self-loathing. Writing in anger to Henry, who refused to understand her predicament, she lashed out: "I reject all those burning expressions which suggest themselves to my mind in crowds & will endeavour to write only at the dictation of that highest mind which has nothing in common with the body. O who will deliver me from this body of death! Now indeed I do intensely long, like my poor father, to have my imprisoned Spirit released from this tabernacle of weakness & misery" (Letter [10 Nov 1836]). Sara sequestered herself in the upper rooms of Braine's Inn and acted out an allegory of self-immolation deeply rooted in Christian tradition. She took refuge in the purity of her "highest mind" and turned away in disgust from her "body of death." As the reference to her father suggests, Sara's anger justified itself by appealing to paternal precedent as well as to divine authority. Thus, Henry, in trying to exercise his influence as husband, found himself at a considerable disadvantage: traditional allegiances were being deployed for non-traditional purposes.

Not all of Sara's complaints, however, were voiced in traditional terms; nor was the female body the only object of her loathing. Occasionally her rage found an image that unleashed the various resentments normally shielded by her resigned spiritualism, exposing in the process the unacknowledged subtext of her apparent misogyny: "O this Devonshire visit has been a black vulture which for two successive summers came every now & then, as I sate in the sun, to cast grim shadow over me, & give me a sight of his beak and claws. Now he holds me down upon the ground in his horrid gripe: I am even yet struggling for breath & liberty: if I ever get alive out of his clutches I will drive the monster away and when he comes near me again he shall be received on the prongs of a pitch-fork" (Letter [6 Nov 1836]). The depiction of "this Devonshire visit" as a "black vulture" aims a well-directed synecdoche at her husband (the visit was to *his* family and at *his* insistence) while evoking rape and cannibalism as acts synonymous with female illness. The victimized invalid is at once violated and consumed by her (male) disease, pinned to the ground and hopelessly overpowered. Nevertheless, she "struggl[es] for breath & liberty," and should she escape she promises her oppressor a fate that is perhaps an image of her own disgust at wifely compliance—impalement "on the prongs of a pitch-fork."

Much of Sara's time at Ilchester was spent reading and writing. She continued to revise "Phantasmion," edit *Aids to Reflection,* and transcribe her father's marginalia. In addition, she read assorted works of theology and literature. Harriet Martineau's *10th Haycock* inspired what was by this point a characteristic response—disgust for her politics, respect for her "genius":

> The concentrated essence of Unitarian presumption, Sectarian bitterness, & Radical profligacy! It has all the ghastliness of Hogarth's most horrid pictures without their truth. The furious rhapsody against the Trinity & for the voluntary system, or against the opposers of it, is as shocking in spirit as it is horrible in literary taste. . . . Yet . . . there are interesting touches and some evidence of genius, of what order I do not say, but certainly of genius: and . . . there will be some value and curiosity in them hereafter, as signs of the 19th Century, and reflections of a remarkable individual mind. [Letter: SC to HNC (6 Nov 1836)][11]

Martineau's "Radical profligacy!" was soon counterbalanced by freshly printed copies of the first two volumes of the *Literary Remains* that Henry arranged to have sent to Ilchester in early November:

> How delightful are the "Remains"! I quite grieve to find the pages on my left hand such a thick handful. One wants to have such a book to dip into constantly, and to go on reading such discussions on such principles and in such a spirit on a thousand subjects.
>
> It does not seem as if the writer was especially conversant with this or that, as Babbage with mechanics, and Mill with political economy; but as if there was a subtle imaginative spirit to search and illustrate all subjects that interest humanity. Sir J. Mackintosh said that "STC trusted to his ingenuity to atone for his ignorance." But in such subjects as my father treats of, ingenuity is the best knowledge.
>
> Like all my father's works, the "Remains" will be more sold at last than at first. Like alum, these metaphysical productions melt slowly into the medium of the public mind; but when time has been given for the operation, they impregnate more strongly than a less dense and solid substance, which dissolves sooner, has power to do. [ML(1874) 132–33]

To depict Coleridge as the philosophic Father "impregnat[ing]" the "public mind" is to worry less about the financial success of his new editions than the political efficacy of his teachings. Sara, like Henry, wanted her father's works to provide a corrective to the social unrest personified by Martineau; Sara wanted not to sell Coleridge's "ingenuity" as an intellectual commodity, but to nurse it back to health and dispense it as a general philosophic cure to a specific political illness.

The Great Reform Bill of 1832 had turned out to be little more than a temporary compromise, and the disillusionment following the Poor Law of 1834 and the economic hardships of 1833–36 was building into what would soon become the Chartist movement. Coleridge's conservative philosophy, Sara hoped, would help to stem the tide of reform, to divert the growing social unrest with a resigned spiritualism that preached subservience and piety to the lower classes. In the same way that she denied her unruly body the chance to assert a stable independence apart from her domineering mind, Sara denied the body politic its chance to free itself from the established oligarchy. But just as she was forced to acknowledge the (male) evil of the "black vulture" and the female "genius" of Martineau, Sara would eventually have to confront the disturbing netherside of her father's political views and the positive possibilities of her own female genius. She could escape the role of invalid by nursing his reputation back to health; she could mother his mind instead of her children's and thereby earn a modicum of public recognition and the power to reconceive her intellectual patrimony; but she would eventually have to recognize that the limited freedom she enjoyed as her father's disciple and editor was purchased at the price of her own individual accomplishments.

Sara's stay at Ilchester ended on November 17, when Henry arrived and escorted his wife back to Hampstead. The entire experience had been genuinely miserable for her but not always in the ways she suggested. While she was indeed ill intermittently during the five weeks at Braine's Inn, her illness was part of larger dissatisfactions that led her to seek separation from husband and family. That Mrs. Coleridge repeatedly queried her daughter as to her use of opium and that Sara repeatedly denied the charges with vigor points to an obvious possibility. Molly Lefebure, in her well-known study of Coleridge and opium, convincingly demonstrates that the addict often seeks refuge away from the prying eyes of family and friends while complaining vociferously of abandonment and neglect.[12] But whatever the role opium played in Sara's collapse at Ilchester (and it was, after all, her father's drug, just as addiction was their shared misfortune), that collapse must be recognized as a temporary impasse between familial duty and individual desire, between the "madness" of Edith Southey and Dorothy Wordsworth and the "genius" of Harriet Martineau, between the self-denying roles of daughter, wife, and mother and the self-asserting roles of editor, author, and intellectual. Nervous illness was indeed an impasse between alternatives, a chance to negotiate the problematic terrain between "sickness" and "health," between madness and matriarchy.

III

The period of convalescence after Sara's Ilchester breakdown lasted some five months. "[O]nce more lying on the longed for little bed in Mama's little room at 21 Downshire Hill," she enjoyed a peaceful and productive spring (Diary [23 Nov 1836]). It was, in fact, one of the most intellectually stimulating periods of her life. "Phantasmion" had been finished and sent to press in late January, and although Sara was already at work on a new edition of *The Friend,* she found time to study the theological debates generated by what her contemporaries were beginning to call "the Oxford Movement."[13] Before long, she was completely immersed in the sermons of John Henry Newman and trying to decide for herself whether he was the savior or the scourge of the Anglican Church. His style, she remarked to Emily Trevenen, is "evidently the product of a highly cultivated taste, which rejected much, and abides by that which expresses the thought in the purest and most unencumbered way" (Letter [23 March 1837]). More than to style, however, Sara was attracted to his ideas, though not without important reservations:

> I have lately been reading, certainly with great interest, the sermons of John Henry Newman; and I trust they are likely to do great good, by placing in so strong a light as they do the indispensableness of an orthodox belief, the importance of sacraments as the main channels of Christian privileges, and the powers, gifts, and offices of Christian ministers derived by apostolic succession—the insufficiency of personal piety without Catholic brotherhood—the sense that we are all members of one body, and subjects of one kingdom of Christ—the danger of a constant craving for religious excitement, and the fatal mistake of trusting in any devotional thoughts and feelings, which are not immediately put into action, and do not shine through the goings-on of our daily life. But then these exalted views are often supported, as I think, by unfair reasonings; and are connected with other notions which appear to me superstitious, unwarranted by any fair interpretation of Scripture, and containing the germs of Popish errors. [*ML*(1874) 137–38]

Well acquainted with her father's theology and deeply interested in questions of religious doctrine, Sara found herself being pulled away from fairy tales and selfless editorial work and into the world of contemporary theological debate. Throughout the spring and summer of 1837, her attention was focused almost exclusively on the work of Newman and Coleridge.[14] This change of emphasis marked not only a shifting of interests (from children's literature to theology) but also a shifting sense of her own talents as writer and thinker.

Passages throughout Sara's letters from this period attest to a growing intellectual restlessness. Soon after the publication of *Phantasmion* in early summer, she commented upon the requirements for successful authorship:

> It requires no great *face* to publish nowadays; it is not stepping upon a stage where the eyes of an audience are upon you—but entering a crowd, where you must be very tall, strong, and striking, indeed, to obtain the slightest attention. In these days, too, to print a Fairy Tale is the very way to be *not read,* but shoved aside with contempt. I wish, however, I were only as sure that *my* fairy tale is worth printing, as I am that works of this class are wholesome food, by way of variety, for the childish mind. It is curious that on this point Sir Walter Scott, and Charles Lamb, my father, my Uncle Southey, and Mr. Wordsworth, were all agreed. [ML(1874) 136–37]

Citing the authority of her Romantic forefathers, Sara maintained that the fairy tale is indeed "wholesome food" for the "childish mind," however often it is "shoved aside with contempt" by the public. Moreover, to publish such works is entirely in keeping with female modesty, as it is "the very way to be *not read.*" Yet the passage itself brims with anger and resentment; so much so that "be[ing] very tall, strong, and striking" emerges in spite of itself as the desired end and clearly suggests that Sara was not completely satisfied with her status as the anonymous author of children's books or as the unacknowledged laborer behind her father's new editions. Perhaps she realized that *Phantasmion* was, beneath its generic trappings, itself a type of theology easily translatable into a more respected discourse.

Phantasmion was conceived and written during a period of Sara's most intense illness. It was not, however, as she put it, merely a "recumbent amusement" to occupy her mind and entertain her children. Packed with supernatural machinery, it chronicles the adventures of a young hero from boyhood to marriage, emphasizing in the process the dreariness and death inherent in the real world and the love and beauty attainable though the imaginative transformation of nature. But however much a "wondertale"—that is, a tale detached from its original, ritualistic function and resituated in "the free air of artistic creation"[15]—Sara's story does enact the religious values important to its author. Years later, in a poem written in her personal copy of *Phantasmion,* she described the book's purpose:

> Go, little book, and sing of love and beauty,
> To tempt the worldling into fairy-land;
> Tell him that airy dreams are sacred duty,
> Bring better wealth than aught his toils command,—
>   Toils fraught with mickle harm.

> But if thou meet some spirit high and tender,
> On blessed works and noblest love intent,
> Tell him that airy dreams of nature's splendor,
> With graver thoughts and hallowed musings blent,
>   Prove no too earthly charm.
>
> [ML(1874) 136]

As the poem suggests, Sara considered her fairy tale an "airy dream" halfway between the "mickle" house of life and the "blessed works" of the hereafter. In other words, she championed the imagination as a faculty capable of divine insight, an idea just as important to John Henry Newman as it was to Wordsworth and Coleridge.[16] As she explained to Derwent, "If you ask me . . . what advantage a young person could possibly derive from such a tissue of unrealities [that is, her fairy tale], I should say that every work of fancy in its degree, and according to the merit of its execution, feeds and expands the mind; whenever the poetical beauty of things is vividly displayed, truth is exhibited, and thus the imagination of the youthful reader is stimulated to find truth for itself" (Letter [16 Aug 1837]).

When *Phantasmion* appeared in June 1837, it met with mixed reviews. Although Hartley was quick to praise his sister's work ("[it] sets her above all female writers of the age—except Joanna Baillie") and defend it ("I have been a little mortified at the dulness of some folks with regard to Phantasmion"), Derwent felt no such compunction (*HC Letters* 264). He complained of the "disproportionateness of the machinery to the events and people in the tale," the "want of unity in the whole," and lastly the "want of moral" (Letter: SC to DC [16 Aug 1837]). Fortunately for Sara, Derwent's bold criticisms were the worst she had to face. The *Quarterly Review,* honoring Henry Nelson Coleridge's friendship with J. G. Lockhart, treated the work kindly: "'Phantasmion' is not a poem, but it is poetry from beginning to end, and has many poems within it. It is one of a race that has particularly suffered under the assaults of political economy and useful knowledge;—a Fairy Tale, the last, we suppose, that will ever be written in England, and unique in its kind. It is neither German nor French. It is what it is—pure as crystal in diction, tinted like an opal with the hues of an everspringing sunlit fancy" (*Quarterly Review* [Sept 1840], p. 132). As the last of a dying genre, *Phantasmion* is here made to represent a spiritual purity and literary innocence woefully undervalued in an age of utilitarian didacticism. On the whole, however, as Leslie Griggs noted, "*Phantasmion* was rather indifferently received, nor has it ever been much read" (120).

The fairy tale's "indifferent" reception followed predictably from its genre and its anonymity. To console herself Sara needed only to remember that she did not want the merely superficial attention she could have attracted by putting her name on the title page, the "great face" mentioned earlier. Protestations to the contrary, she wanted to be "very tall, strong, and striking"—to write, in other words, something that would immediately be perceived as intellectually substantial. Thus, she shortly abandoned all thoughts of writing more children's literature and set about trying to reconcile her understanding of the imagination to Tractarian theology. The more Sara read, however, the less such a reconciliation seemed possible. "I like the writings of Dodsworth, Keble, and Newman," she told Henry, "on the Unity of the Church, Catholic brotherhood, ordinances, the Ministry, in short all their main general High Church Scheme. What I dislike are the jutties, friezes, cornices, emblazonries, coigns of vantage and various flourishes which they introduce into or dispose around their firm and symmetrical edifice" (Letter [20 Sept 1837]).

Sara quickly realized, however, that those offensive accoutrements were deeply rooted in the structure of the whole. Writing to Henry in September 1837, she explained,

> It seems to be a point with the Oxford writers, either for good or evil, very much to represent . . . men, as the *passive* unco-operating subject (or rather, in one sense, *object*) of divine operation. They are jealous of holding up, or dwelling much upon, grace as an *influence* on the conscious spirit, a stimulator and co-agent of the human will, or enlightener of the human intellect. That view, they think, is insufficient, leads to an inadequate notion of Christian ordinances, and of our Christian condition, and causes a confusion between God's general dealings with the human race, or His subordinate workings with Christians, and His special communications to the members of the new covenant. "Salvation" is to be considered (exclusively) "as God's work in the soul." But whether it be not just as much God's work if carried on with the instrumentality of those faculties which He originally conferred, may be a question. [ML(1874) 143]

By making men into "*passive* unco-operating subject[s]," the Oxford theologians chose to ignore the social politics of religion and to teach the Gospel as "blind servants" convey unseen "messages":

> Newman and his fellow-laborers in the Oxonian vineyard are wont to contend that preachers are bound to preach the Gospel, as a blind servant is bound to deliver a message about things which he can never see—as a carrier-pigeon, to convey a letter the contents of which it can not understand. They are not to preach for the sake of saving souls, nor to select and compose from the Gospel in order to produce a good effect, nor to grieve if the Gospel is the savor of death to those who will not hear. In short, it would be presumption and rationalism in them to suppose that their

intellect or zeal was even to be the medium through which God's purposes were to be effected. What God's purposes *are* in commanding the Gospel to be preached, and sending His Only Son into the world, they maintain that we can not guess. [*ML*(1874) 145]

Unlike Newman, Sara was interested in the "practical results" of the Anglican Church. Elitist mysticism of the Oxford variety denied man his innate mental power, for it exacerbated the political rifts that Sara felt religion should attempt to reconcile. Newman's antirationalism, she feared, could only have disastrous consequences.

For the present, Sara's disquisitions on Oxford Movement theology were limited to long, densely written letters. Without other alternatives and encouraged by the informality of epistolary style, she filled sheet after sheet with her analyses—often to the irritation of her correspondents. Both Derwent and Henry complained with some frequency of her abstruse communications. Derwent thought they were "too long and a waste of time"; he preferred more wit, more news, and less theology (Griggs 122). Henry felt as well that Sara let herself be carried away by her "musings"; time and again, he pleaded for more "news of wife and children" and less "discourse on taste and criticism" (Letter: HNC to SC [15 Sept 1834]). Because he traveled for weeks on end, he also hoped for "special details" to compensate for his absence: "My *heart* feeds on the details of Sara's health & bodily sensations," he explained; "I cannot brook any abridgement of these." Apparently unwilling or unable to indulge her husband's desire, Sara failed to change her letter-writing habits. As a result, Henry could do nothing but acknowledge defeat: "Each letter I receive from you makes me feel totally unworthy of you; I can never refine myself up to your pitch of intellectual & spiritual purity & sweetness" (Letter [24 Sept 1835]).

Although Sara would not begin her formal essay on Newman and Coleridge until December 1838 (an essay later published as an appendix to the 1843 *Aids to Reflection*), by September 1837 she had arrived at her primary objection to Newman's "scheme" and continued to discuss the matter in her letters: "he opposes Faith to Reason, as if there could be any right Faith without Reason. . . . Newman's scheme is a house divided against itself and contains the materials of its refutation within" (Letter: SC to HNC [26 Sept 1837]). Sara's "Essay on Rationalism" would be an extended meditation (some two hundred printed pages) on Newman's "house divided" and a vigorous defense of Coleridgean "Reason." It would also be her first acknowledged publication and the first time she wrote publicly in her own discursive voice, a voice whose discovery was akin to self-affirmation:

I feel the strongest bent for theological topics; and it seems to myself that I should want neither ingenuity in illustration, nor clearness of conception, to a certain extent; but then I am utterly deficient in learning and knowledge. I feel the most complete sympathy with my father in his account of his literary difficulties. Whatever subject I commence, I feel discontent unless I could pursue it in every direction to the farthest bounds of thought, and then, when some scheme is to be executed, my energies are paralyzed with the very notion of the indefinite vastness which I long to fill. This was the reason that my father wrote by snatches. He could not bear to complete incompletely, which every body else does. [ML(1874) 148]

Religious philosophy sparked Sara's interest and her pride. Hardly "deficient in learning and knowledge," she was actually just beginning to reassess her talent and potential. Her "most complete sympathy" with Coleridge worked both to humanize him, to bring him down from the heights of genius, and to intellectualize her, to elevate her mind above the pedestrian duties required of the "proper lady." Discovering her father within herself was a joyful, liberating experience, even if she did share his weakness—his inability "to complete incompletely." Several years earlier, Sara had confided to Henry, "When I have finished a sentence . . . I often laugh inwardly at the filial likeness of manner and aim" (Letter [4 Sept 1834]). Yet the satisfying of her intellectual desires was no laughing matter: "the indefinite vastness" which she "long[ed] to fill" was at once the void of self-doubt and the possibility of self-fulfillment.

However unconvinced of the need to exhibit her "filial likeness" in print, Sara continued writing "practice" essays intended only for circulation among her correspondents. In November 1837, she wrote a short piece on the "idea of the British Constitution," which she sent an old Hampstead neighbor, Mrs. Henry Jones, with whom she had been debating political issues for some years.[17] In that essay, Sara considers the dangers of public opinion and the need for a government controlled by a minority of the nation's most capable leaders. She argues against an obscure pamphlet by John James Park and for a decidedly Coleridgean understanding of government by "clerisy."[18] Unlike her earlier essay on Wordsworth, where she evidenced enthusiasm for a social recognition of spiritual equality, Sara's essay on the Constitution articulates a fear that real democracy will precipitate social and political disaster; for while all men are spiritually equal, all men are not equally spiritual—some are indeed more "reasonable" than others.

The opening paragraph of the essay distinguishes between two sorts of public opinion—informed and uninformed. Public opinion is not "just and wise" simply "by virtue of its being public"; on the contrary, it represents by definition only "the average understandings and morals of the community." As such, it can hardly be trusted with the responsibility to govern the entire nation, for the "opinions of the majority at all times and on all subjects . . . cannot be identified with the collective wisdom of the age." But once public opinion is informed and molded by the insights of "the gifted few," it can then be said to have attained a functional wisdom. Eventually, "'the majority *will* be in the right,'" not simply because of numerical advantage, as Harriet Martineau blithely declared, but because "in course of time the opinions of the wisest . . . are proved by experience and successive accessions of suffrages from competent judges." In other words, democracy is functional because "public opinion is in fact the adoption of *private* opinion by the public." Thus, Sara maintains that the "public opinion of *this* country, on *particular points,* in this *age of the world* is perfectly just and enlightened" as the result of guidance by the intellectually elite, by those whose "reasoning power" enables them to direct spiritual truths into political processes.

America supplies Sara with the prime example of degenerate democracy, and Harriet Martineau with the prime representative of a deluded intelligentsia favoring democratic reform. In fact, Sara's essay is less a meditation on Park and Coleridge than it is a Coleridgean response to Martineau's 1837 travelogue and treatise, *Society in America.* There, in addition to declaring "the majority *will* be in the right," Martineau argues that democracy, while "fall[ing] far below [its] principles," has nevertheless "realised many things for which the rest of the civilised world is still struggling."[19] Sara disagreed, and using evidence gleaned from accounts by Basil Hall, Thomas Hamilton, Alexis de Tocqueville, and Fanny Trollope, she maintains that in the United States "the will of the majority is too much felt for the welfare of the majority."[20] In her opinion, the American government is little more than a machine: its leaders work only to "obey a popular will, like the index of a clock worked by a pendulum."

The government of Great Britain, on the other hand, works by the suggestions of a "wise minority," who consider "the interests of the people . . . rather than their blind wishes." The British Constitution, Sara argues, is based not on a pragmatic system of checks and balances but "according to an idea of perfection (never in this world to e more than partially realized)—an idea existing equally in the minds of all our countrymen, but more distinctly and effectively developed in those which are aided by an acute and powerful intellect, improved to the highest point by education, study, and reflective leisure." Echoing her father on the "idea" of the Constitution ("the most real of all realities," as he put it), Sara begins with a philosophical principle, "an idea of perfection," which is understood by and shared among the clerisy, the "wise minority," who then communicate its tenets to the waiting populace. This mode of government, she argues, is the more responsible democracy, though admittedly not the more "popular."

Both father and daughter agreed that the "old venerable idea of the British Constitution" (Sara's phrase) was venerable not only because it represented a purified philosophical abstraction made real, but also because it brought together the church and state in a mutually supportive relationship. Coleridge's

Mrs. S. T. Coleridge by Matilda Betham, 1809. From an engraving in the possession of the Harry Ransom Humanities Research Center, The University of Texas at Austin

Sara Coleridge by Matilda Betham, 1809. From an engraving in the possession of the Harry Ransom Humanities Research Center, The University of Texas at Austin

Derwent Coleridge by Edward Nash, 1820. From a pencil drawing in the possession of the Harry Ransom Humanities Research Center, The University of Texas at Austin

Robert Southey by Henry Edridge, 1804. National Portrait Gallery, London

Sara Coleridge and Edith May Southey by Edward Nash, 1820. National Portrait Gallery, London

S. T. Coleridge by William Allston, 1814. National Portrait Gallery, London

Sara Coleridge by Charlotte Jones, 1827. From the frontispiece of Edith Coleridge, *Memoir and Letters of Sara Coleridge,* 1873

Sara Coleridge by George Richmond, 1845. From a drawing in the possession of the Harry Ransom Humanities Research Center, The University of Texas at Austin

Edith Coleridge by George
Richmond, 1850. From a
drawing in the possession of the
Harry Ransom Humanities
Research Center, The University
of Texas at Austin

Herbert Coleridge by George
Richmond, 1848. From a
drawing in the possession of the
Harry Ransom Humanities
Research Center, The University
of Texas at Austin

S. T. Coleridge by J. Kayser, 1833. From a copy of a pencil drawing in the possession of the Harry Ransom Humanities Research Center, The University of Texas at Austin. The original is in the possession of Mrs. A. H. B. Coleridge.

last published work, *On the Constitution of the Church and State* (1830), had argued for precisely such a relationship: "I feel very strongly persuaded that an endowed Church, maintaining a body of Catholic doctrine and a State in connection with that Church, are the greatest of public blessings, and it seems to me that the general influence of property and hereditary rank, as well as that which they have hitherto exerted in the national councils has formed a guarantee, to a *certain extent,* for the predominance of talent, intellect, and wisdom— excellence in every department of mind and morals" (*C&S[CC]* 36). Reinforced by property, rank, and God the Father, the British political system stabilizes the vicissitudes of popular opinion even as it centralizes moral and mental excellence. Its voice is the voice of British culture, and it institutionalizes an entire intellectual and religious tradition. But the voice is also Samuel Taylor Coleridge's being defended and maintained by a daughter apprehensive about her father's "popularity." Not nearly as acclaimed as his collaborator Wordsworth, Coleridge needed the stability derived from an assured position among the clerisy: he needed, in short, to occupy the niche defined by his own system. For reasons of her own, Sara labored to make this a possibility.

As she nursed her father's reputation back to health, Sara began to see that the establishment of Coleridge's genius would bring about much needed "cures" for a variety of illnesses. Not only would it serve to answer De Quincey's charges of overindulgence and familial irresponsibility ("eccentric genius" was an accepted oxymoron capable of explaining away even the grossest of indelicacies); it would also alleviate Sara's own nagging doubts about her father's paternal neglect: it would become the unavoidable result of an irreproachable cause. Once satisfied with his status as both parent and pundit, she could then offer this "cured" Coleridge as a proper remedy for the social ills of the 1830s, the necessary alternative to Martineau's dangerous republicanism and Newman's "blind" mysticism. Thus, to remake the Coleridgean genius would be nothing less than to remake the patriarchy, to absolve it of sin and reconceive it in its ideal form—paternally responsible, spiritually reasonable, politically judicious. Such a move would validate those institutions to which Sara had pledged her faith as it confirmed the spiritual models on which they were designed. More important, remaking the Coleridgean genius would afford Sara herself the opportunity for intellectual labors normally denied "clever" women. It would cure her of a debilitating marginality by providing an acceptable rationale for her transgressions. Sara had discovered a way to violate and valorize simultaneously, to be both invalid and nurse, both editor and author.

IV

During the spring of 1838, Sara assisted with proof sheets of the third volume of the *Literary Remains,* prepared a new edition of *On the Constitution of* the Church and State, and continued to study the contemporary religious debates. Joanna Baillie's most recent work, *A View of the general Tenor of the New Testament,* Sara thought to contain a "spurious liberality, incompatible with earnestness in religion and a due reverence for truth" (Letter: SC to Mrs. Henry Jones [Jan? 1838]). Nor was she pleased with James Gillman's one-volume biography, *The Life and Letters of S. T. Coleridge,* which appeared in March. Although she wrote Mrs. Gillman that the Coleridge family was "deeply cheered and pleased to think that such a record . . . will exist for the world" (*ML*[1874] 156), Sara expressed herself more honestly to Emily Trevenen: "A surer way to blur the bright face of his newly bought fame and credit through my father's name [Gillman] could hardly have hit upon than to bring out this absurd hodge podge of stale and vapid ingredients, just to shew how long an unwise man may live with a wise one without catching any of his wisdom" (Letter [9 April 1838]). With increasing frustration, Sara found that contemporary portraits of her father were suiting her less and less. No one, it seemed, properly understood the real Coleridge. Not even Henry: "I rather wish," she chided, "you had not used that vague High Church cant phrase of abuse *rationalized.* . . . It is true my father says 'not to seek to make the mysteries of faith what the world calls rational'—but *what the world calls rational* is a definite phrase: *rationalized* is not so" (Letter [8 Oct 1838]).

Sara's "Coleridge," however, was not the flesh and blood father she had known better and more intimately than had other commentators. In fact, she could make little claim to having known him at all, and confessed as much to her old friend Mary Stanger: "I suffered much in parting with my beloved father, but, unfortunately, I had been so little in his society during my life, being separated from him by illness during two or three years of our residence at Hampstead, that his departure did not make so great a difference to my heart as it would have done otherwise. And so accustomed had I been to commune with him in his books, more than face to face, that even now I never feel, while I peruse his sayings, chiefly on religious subjects, as if he were no more of this world" (Letter: SC to Mrs. Joshua Stranger [16 Jan 1838]). The "Coleridge" she knew and cared for was the author of *Lay Sermons, Aids to Reflection,* and *On the Constitution of the Church and State;* he was not the dissolute poet or the irresponsible father, but rather the soaring metaphysician whose immethodical and miscellaneous corpus testified less to human frailty than to a powerful otherworldly vision. For Sara, he had lost his human features and become the disembodied voice of fragmentary texts desperately in need of filial attention.

As her interest in and knowledge of theology deepened, Sara found herself having to justify her "hobby"—particularly to other women. In letters to Arabella Brooke, Sara played the "desultory" novice: "However, I speak in ignorance [of Thomas Arnold's *History of Rome*]: politics and history are subjects in which I have less of my desultory feminine sort of information than some others which seem rather more within my compass. Divinity may be as wide a field as politics; but it is not so far out of a woman's way, and you derive more benefit from partial and short excursions into it. I should say the same in regard to poetry, natural history in all its branches, and even metaphysics—the study of which, when judiciously pursued, I can not but think highly interesting and useful, and in no respect injurious" (*ML*[1874] 160). Neither divinity nor metaphysics, however, were the usual stuff of letters to friends, and Sara had to explain to Louisa Plummer, among them, the advantages of a "serious" correspondence: "[Letter-writing] is a method of visiting our friends in their absence, and one which has some advantages peculiar to itself; for persons who have any seriousness of character at all endeavor to put the letter part of their mind upon paper; and letter-writing is one of the many calls which life affords to put our minds in order, the salutary effect of which is obvious" (*ML*[1874] 159). To her husband, Sara would also confess that her "seriousness of character" had recently intensified to such a degree that old pleasures suddenly seemed inadequate: "What a strange, superficial thing is the ordinary way of reading a book. . . . I more and more grudge to bestow time on the literature of the day" (Letter [6 Oct 1838]). "Ordinary" reading, presumably for amusement rather than education, could no longer compete, she implies, with the serious study of serious subjects.

Disclaimers to the contrary, Sara did maintain an interest in "the literature of the day." Moreover, she reserved her special attention for works by women: "Mrs. Howitt writes a rough ballad pretty well. But there is a vulgarity about her, and an over solemnity and pomposity about Miss Barrett, an over sentimentality about Miss Landon, and too much of both in Mrs. Hemans" (Letter: SC to HNC [3 Oct 1838]). Harriet Martineau fared considerably better despite her "overpowering" politics: "Miss Martineau's 'Retrospect of Western Travel' I have read and enjoyed. It takes you through outdoor scenes, and though the politics are overpowering now and then, it freshens you up by wanderings amid woods and rivers, and over mountain brows, and among tumbling waterfalls. I think Miss Martineau made one more at home with Niagara than any other of the American travellers. She gives one a most lively *waterfallish* feeling, introduces one not only to the huge mass of running water, but to the details of the environs, the wood in which the stream runs away, etc." (Letter: SC to ET [21 April 1838]). Sara's highest accolades, however, were reserved for Jane Austen, although one suspects that her superiority over Martineau was largely a matter of genre: "Hers [Austen's] is almost the only literary line in which women are not only unsurpassed by men, but in which they have done that which women alone can do to perfection. Miss Austen's peculiarly feminine genius gives an especial charm and value to her writings" (Letter: SC to ET [24 Jan 1838]).

Sara's own "feminine genius" eschewed the literary for the metaphysical, and her attempts to read the theology of her father against that of Newman continued. In January 1839, she responded to a pamphlet by Matthew Plummer, the husband of her friend Louisa, with a detailed assessment of the Oxford "party":

I must candidly confess that I do not follow your husband on the Oxford road so far as he seems to have proceeded. On some subjects, specially handled by Newman and his school, my judgment is suspended. On some points I think the Apostolicals quite right, on others clearly unscriptural and unreasonable, willfully and ostentatiously maintaining positions which, if carried out to their full length, would overthrow the foundations of all religion. I consider the party as having done great service in the religious world, and that in various ways; sometimes by bringing forward what is wholly and absolutely true; sometimes by promoting discussion on points in which I believe their own views to be partly erroneous; sometimes by exposing gross deficiencies in doctrine in the religion of the day; sometimes by keenly detecting the self-flatteries and practical mistakes of religionists. But worst of them, in my opinion, is that they are, one and all, *party men;* and just so far as we become absorbed in a party, just so far are we in danger of parting with honesty and good sense. . . . Such is human nature, that as soon as ever men league together, even for the purest and most exalted objects, their carnal leaven begins to ferment. Insensibly their aims take a less spiritual character, and their means are proportionately vulgarized and debased. . . . Like the Evangelicals, whom they so often condemn on this very point, they use a characteristic phraseology; they have their badges and party marks; they lay great stress on trifling external matters; they have a stock of arguments and topics in common. No sooner has Newman blown the Gospel blast, than it is repeated by Pusey, and Pusey is re-echoed from Leeds. Keble privately persuades Froude, Froude spouts the doctrines of Keble to Newman, and Newman publishes them as "Froude's Remains." Now it seems to me that under these circumstances truth has not quite a fair chance. [ML(1874) 166–67][21]

The danger of party theology, Sara argued, was that the individual's search for truth entwines itself around and becomes inextricable from the party's need for public approval: "A man has hardly time to *reflect on his own reflections,* and ask himself, in the stillness of his heart, whether the views he has put forth are strictly the truth, and nothing more or less than the truth; if, the moment they have parted from him, they are eagerly embraced by a set of prepossessed partisans, who assure him and all the rest of the world that they are thoroughly excellent. (How many truly great men have modified their views after publication, and in subsequent works have written in a somewhat altered strain?)" Reflecting on reflections is a distinctly Coleridgean enterprise, and Sara's closing question invokes its own response: "At least one—S. T. Coleridge." Her father's transition from radical poet to conservative theologian, from Unitarian Democrat to Anglican Tory, was to be explained, in other words, along with the supposed plagiarisms and the fragmentary remains, as the inconsistent results of a very consistent effort—a searching after truth by a man whose goals were always greater than his accomplishments, but whose ideals were never compromised by "party" politics.[22]

Sara's enthusiasm for her various Coleridgean projects and her interest in the ongoing theological debates kept her mentally and physically stronger than she had been in some time. Although she suffered three miscarriages between 1836 and 1839, Sara did not succumb to nervous illness or hysteria—perhaps because of a new "power" derived from intellectualizing illness. To Arabella Brooke, she explained,

> It is painful to be unable to understand one's suffering, to translate it into an intelligible language, and bring it distinctly before the mind's eye. But it is already a sign that we are no longer wholly subdued by its power when we can analyze it, and make this very indefiniteness an object of contemplation. This evinces a degree of mastery over that which has of late been a tyrant. And if "to be weak is miserable" (oh, how often have I thanked Milton for that line!), to exercise any kind of power, or have any kind of strength, is so far an abatement of misery. To be sure, the explanation which my father gives of this mental fact, the uneasiness felt at the *unintelligibility* of an affection, when we can not tell whence it arises nor whither it tends, is not a little abstruse, and what is popularly called transcendental. "There is always a consolatory feeling that accompanies the sense of a proportion between antecedents and consequents. It is eternity revealing itself in the form of time." [ML(1874) 172]

The "'consolatory feeling'" that results from the attempt "to understand one's suffering" implicates Coleridge directly in his daughter's successful (if irregular) "mastery" of illness. Yet the letter itself is not a happy one, and Sara confesses to being "cross and splenetic." The reason, she implies, stems from her own frustrated attempts at composition: "Dear me! some people *think* more over the first page of an essay than others do while they write a volume. Thinking too much, and trying to dive deeper and deeper into every subject that presents itself, is rather an obstacle to much writing. It drags the wheels of composition; for before a book can be written, there is a great deal to be *done*: contemplation is not the whole business. I am convinced that the Cherubim do not write books, much less publish them, or make bargains with booksellers, or submit to the ordeal of disgusting puffery and silly censure. I am convinced they do nothing but think." Hard at work on her "rationalism essay," Sara was having difficulty translating her religious opinions into an acceptable form. But as the reference to "the Cherubim" makes clear, she was not above taking her frustrations out upon the mercantile world of booksellers and reviewers. Like her father, Sara preferred to think of herself as superior to the commercial details of publishing. Yet unlike her father, Sara had to answer to the cultural prohibitions against female authorship: the "angel in the house" was no more expected to write an essay on rationalism than her heavenly counterparts.

Sara worked on her essay for much of 1839, writing and rewriting draft after draft. In September, Henry left London for a two-month tour of France, and the children were sent to Felixstone with their nurse. Alone with her mother at 10 Chester Place, Sara found her work more difficult than ever: "I want to shew the whole subject in all its bearings at once; no one thing seems complete unless all its dependencies are exhibited, and thus while I write a single sentence, ten others are dunning me and demanding to be written" (Letter: SC to HNC [10 Sept 1839]). Encouraged by Derwent's recent publication, *The Scriptural Character of the English Church* (1839), which she agreed with but thought without "power," Sara persisted despite her "tumultuous" ideas and "immethodical" execution. "I am," she told a friend, "an obstinate creature on religious topics. I scarce ever agree with any commentator for five minutes together" (Letter: SC to Mrs. Henry Jones [1839?]).

Sara's intellectual activities abated somewhat during the spring and summer of 1840, although for reasons that had little to do with lack of theological "obstina[cy]." In early January, she had found herself pregnant for the seventh time in ten years, and in July she gave birth to a girl who lived little more than a week. Thirty-seven years old and in delicate health, Sara suffered through a predictably unpleasant pregnancy. The last three months of her term were spent "weak and irritable," and for the first time since her marriage, Sara allowed her correspondence to dwindle to a fraction of its normal volume. When Bertha Fanny Coleridge died on July 24, both parents were affected greatly—although not equally:

> Our loss, indeed, has been a great disappointment, and even a sorrow; for, strange as it may seem, these little speechless creatures, with their wandering, unspeaking eyes, so twine themselves around a parent's heart from the hour of their birth. Henry suffered more than I could have imagined, and I was sorry to see him watch the poor babe so closely, when it was plain that the little darling was not for this world, and that all our visions of a "dark-eyed Bertha," a third joy and comfort of the remainder of our own pilgrimage, must be exchanged for better hopes, and thoughts more entirely

accordant with such a religious frame of mind as it is our best interest to attain. [ML(1874) 178]

While Sara resumed her study of those "better hopes" almost immediately— reading Newman's *Lectures on the Prophetical Office of the Church* (1837) and Dugald Stewart's *Dissertation* (1815–21)—a grief-stricken Henry departed for a month in France. Shortly after his return Sara sent him a consoling letter:

> We ought, indeed, my beloved husband, to be conscious of our blessings, for we are better off than all below us, perhaps than almost all above us. The great art in life, especially for persons of our age, who are leaving the value of youth behind us, just lingering still perhaps in the latter stage of it, . . . is to cultivate the love of doing good and promoting the interests of others, avoiding at the same time the error of those who make a worldly business and a matter of pride of pursuits which originated in pure inten- tions, and bustle away in this secular religious path, with as little real thought of the high prize at which they should aim, and as little growth in mammon more directly. Any thing rather than undergo the mental labor of real self-examination, of the study, not of individual self, but of the charac- ters of our highest being which we share with all men. For one man that *thinks,* with a view to practical excellence, we may find fifty who are ready to *act* on what they call their own thoughts, but which they have uncon- sciously received from others. [ML(1874) 180]

The quiet confidence of this passage, its controlled tone and carefully delineated position, had been ten years in the making. Illness, theology, and the cultural restrictions of her sex had taught Sara the "great art" by which "worldly busi- ness" was condemned in favor of "the mental labor of real self-examination." The "real self," however, was not the physical individual but "the characters of our highest being which we share with all men," characters which, once mas- tered, allowed the "think[er]" to exert a worldly influence—a "practical excel- lence"—even while eschewing worldly "act[ion]." "The great art in life," Sara found, was to have those who "*act* on what they call their own thoughts" act instead on what she knew to be her own.

Sara soon needed all the confidence and control her "great art" could gener- ate. Henry, although never robust, had long been healthier than his wife; but in January 1841 he fell ill and remained so throughout most of the spring. No longer able to afford the luxury of her own extended invalidism, Sara had to assume many of her husband's familial responsibilities. She was, however, by no means overburdened: Herbert had enrolled at Eton, and there were, after all, four servants. Nevertheless, Sara was forced to confront a new domestic situa- tion and to consider for the first time the possibility of Henry's death. He was the one who now needed the expensive medical care, while she was the one who had to pay the bills.

In September, Henry had recovered enough to allow husband and wife a ten-day excursion to Belgium. Sara, never having traveled to Europe, proved an indefatigible tourist and a keen student of art and architecture. She was pleased with the Memlings and Van Eycks at Bruges and impressed by the cathedrals at Antwerp and Ghent—but she was overwhelmed by the Rubenses at the Antwerp museum. His "Descent from the Cross," she wrote to Hartley, was "the most *beautiful* painting I have ever seen," and his "Christ Crucified . . . the most moving passionate picture I ever beheld. It makes the Van Dykes beside appear cold, prim, passionless" (Letter [3 Oct 1841]). To Emily Trevenen, however, Sara voiced the obligatory qualification: "I do not maintain, deep as is my admiration of Rubens, that his pictures thoroughly satisfy a religious mood of mind. They are somewhat over-bold; they almost unhallow the subject by bringing it so home, and exciting such strong earthly passion in connection with it" (ML[1874] 185). Having rejected the "cold, prim, [and] passionless," Sara had only to insure that the powerful sensuality of Rubens not compromise his religious subjects by awakening in her an overly "earthly" response, an "over-bold," "unhallow[ed]" appreciation for voluptuous beauty.

The beauty of Rubens notwithstanding, Sara's "religious mood of mind" remained preoccupied by matters relating to her husband's health, for soon after their return from Europe, Henry fell ill once again. Although she found time to continue her reading and writing—to scrutinize Newman's *Tract 90* and to begin a correspondence with F. D. Maurice—Sara's fears about Henry's worsening health gradually dampened her enthusiasm for study. In May 1842, those fears were confirmed when Henry suffered a major collapse. The disease was evidently a type of spinal paralysis, and within weeks he was hopelessly bedridden.

Henry's illness incapacitated his body but not his mind. Complaining of general "weakness" and poor digestion, he was confined to bed and given opium for the discomfort. All of his legal responsibilities were relinquished, and he was limited, even on his good days, to working on one or another of his Coleridge projects.[23] Despite the efforts of the eminent Dr. Benjamin Brodie, who prescribed the opium and administered the leeches, Henry fast became a helpless invalid, a pitiful image of Sara's own previous struggles with illness and depression and a sad reminder of a marriage marred by sickness and adversity. Speaking of her husband in late 1842, she confessed to a friend, "Bodily weakness and disorder have been the great drawbacks, ever since we met twenty years ago, to our happiness in each other" (ML[1874] 189).

By January 1843, it was clear that Henry would not live much longer. He was subsisting on little more than brandy and opium and was frequently delirious.[24] On the seventeenth Sara began a diary to record her husband's final days. Her second entry reads: "Henry subdued the attack of phlegm in the morning better than yesterday by the raised position, & increased anodyne— But at nine o'clock he had strange *dying* sensations—languor yet "not languor" faintness & sense of inaction. He took brandy & water twice. After this the feeling of faintness went off—but he was very strange in his manner—stared vacantly and talked—not with positive incoherency but with a disproportion- ateness & wildly. Said he had been in a gang of robbers. Asked me if I could ever suffer him to be confined with madmen. That would be so dreadful [he] said" (Diary [18 Jan 1843]). From Sara's perspective, Henry's "strange . . . manner" evidenced less a "positive incoherency" than an excited "disproportionateness," but for Henry such behavior was disturbing enough to become a focal point for his increasing anxieties. Incapable of voicing religious doubt, of directly chal- lenging the idea of an afterlife, Henry used the image of madness—"confine- ment with madmen"—to express multiple fears: irrationality, imprisonment, and isolation conflate into a general powerlessness equivalent to death itself.

Henry's delirium increased with his suffering, and a week later Sara con- fessed that she had "done all a wife can do": his behavior was "heartrending to witness" (Diary [25 Jan 1843]). On January 26, she recorded her last entry: "This day at 10 minutes to one o'clock my most beloved and honored husband breathed his last—James & I sitting beside his bed. . . . Yesterday evening a violent flush came over him. . . . He seemed sleeping & unconscious but breathing hard. I came in and read a few prayers by his bed & he joined in them a little, but more in the Lord's prayer. Those were the last words of sense I heard him utter." The Father's hallowed name, Henry's "last words of sense," and the senseless ravings that followed, Henry's actual last words, marked the bound- aries of sickness and health against which Sara's own discourses were mea- sured.[25] One was the voice of law, indisputable and absolute; the other was the babel of suffering, incoherent and illegitimate. Henry's death freed Sara from the tyranny of both.

"The Business of Life"
Public Venerations, Private Redemptions

Enough evidence has been adduced to show that Sara Coleridge was not an impressionistic critic or an undisciplined thinker. [But] her limitations are pretty clear. She was so thoroughly a devotee of the romantics that she sometimes underestimated the poetry of her contemporaries. Her view of life was partly moulded by Victorian morality, and a feminine bias often interferes with her judgement. More than all this, her critical comments are too casual to be fitted into a system. Reading and criticizing the literary productions of her day was her diversion. . . . Her fault was understatement, not exaggeration.

E. L. Griggs, Coleridge Fille

Mr. Wordsworth was never in love, properly speaking. I have heard him boast of it, in [the] presence of his wife, who smiled angelically, delighted that her husband should be so superior to common men. This superiority, however, entails a certain deficiency. He cannot sympathize with a certain class of feelings in consequence—he cannot realize them. He is always upon stilts when he enters these subjects. He stalks along with a portentous stride & then stamps his great wooden foot down, in the clumsiest manner imaginable. That sonnet among the Duddon ones, about crossing the brook, attempts to describe loverish feelings—but even that is forced and sexagenarian—The loves are brought in to clap their wings from a neighbouring rock. At what shop did he buy those ready-made Cupids?

Sara Coleridge, "Placing 'Laodamia'"

Henry was buried on February 2, 1843, and although Sara maintained at the time that all her "earthly happiness" was buried with him, she did not immediately succumb to debilitating illness or depression (Diary [Feb 2 1843]). A "violent cold" caught during the last days of her husband's illness kept her quiet and at home, and for the sake of propriety she abandoned her correspondence until the period of mourning had officially passed (*ML*[1874] 192–93). But Sara was by no means idle. Since Henry's collapse in May 1842, she had assumed an increasing responsibility for both the family finances and the Coleridge estate. By the following February, she was in full control, but sadly lacking in the knowledge necessary to manage her tasks well. As exasperated letters to John Taylor Coleridge make clear, Sara tried throughout the late winter and early spring to untangle her husband's affairs: she made detailed estimates of income and expenses; she wrestled with the annual tax forms; and she applied directly to relatives for financial assistance. John Taylor graciously agreed to assume the cost of daughter Edith's education (her various tutors' fees, in other words), while his brother Edward provided for Sara's son Herbert at Eton. Nevertheless, for the residents of 10 Chester Place, money had become a matter of some concern, and additional income from the sales of Coleridge's works would have been greatly appreciated.

Unfortunately, Henry's deathbed negotiations with William Pickering had failed; the publisher adamantly refused to relinquish his rights to the Coleridge material or to alter the terms of the original agreement, although he did promise to be more punctual with his payments and less negligent in keeping records. Irate about Pickering's careless ways (*"I could kill him!"* she wrote to her brother-in-law), Sara continued to encourage Edward Moxon throughout the spring of 1843, hoping either that Pickering would agree to split the works between the two publishers or that Moxon's increasingly generous offers would shame Pickering into decreasing his percentage of the profit (Letter [11 Mar 1843]). For his part, Pickering had been disappointed by the slow sales of the *Literary Remains* and was unconvinced of the advantage of flooding the market with other Coleridge volumes. While he agreed with Sara that the *Biographia Literaria* should be reissued and that a single volume of poems might sell more quickly than would another reprint of the three-volume *Poetical Works,* he was not enthusiastic about the new edition of the *Aids to Reflection* or by the prospect of reissuing the other less popular prose works (Letter: SC to JTC [Apr? 1843]). Sara, on the other hand, was pleased about the forthcoming *Aids* and was already anticipating new editions of both *The Friend* and the *Literary Remains,* in addition to a second edition of the *Biographia,* on which she was already at work. Pickering, however, remained implacable, and the negotiations continued.

To prepare for her introduction to the new *Biographia,* Sara began reading Schelling during the spring of 1843. Three years before, J. F. Ferrier had written a damning account of Coleridge's plagiarisms, so damning in fact that its scholarly assessments made De Quincey's earlier accusations seem cordial and uninformed.[1] As a result, Sara and Henry had decided that the new *Biographia* must include a complete refutation of the charges and must explain fully the extent of Coleridge's "borrowings" from the German philosopher. With her two-hundred-page "Essay on Rationalism" currently at the printers, Sara was feeling confident about her intellectual abilities, and although deeply upset about Henry's death, she derived some consolation from her solitary labor: "My spirits are much better while I remain shut up in my own room than when I attempt in any way to return to society. . . . Wrapped up at home in my own voluntary musings, I have the power of producing a comfortable state of feeling for myself—in which I am partly out of this world. To return to the world without him, who so long brightened it to me, is full of depression and sadness" (Letter: SC to ET [Mar? 1843]). The pleasures of isolation would not last. Sara had long been aware that her "voluntary musings" had "the power of producing a comfortable state of feeling" capable of shielding her from the unpleasantries of "this world." Time and again she had used illness as a retreat from familial duty and as an excuse for intellectual labor. But it was only after Henry's death that Sara was free to explore the "world" on her own and to discover its pleasures for herself.

In early May, having finished the proofs of the forthcoming *Aids to Reflection* and evidently tired of being "shut up in [her] own room," Sara accepted an invitation to visit Mrs. Thomas Ferrar at Broadstairs. Grateful for the offer, Sara wanted to make it clear nonetheless that she had yet to recover from her "great sorrow" and so would hardly be the most cheerful of companions. "Sorrow makes us very egotistic, and, to those that understand not the house of mourning, very tedious and commonplace. But to those who are feeling deeply, or sympathizing with those who feel, the sense of *reality* in the oft-expressed sentiment lends it freshness and force" (ML[1874] 200). The "*reality*" of sorrow proved incapable of diminishing the freedoms of widowhood, and Sara enjoyed herself immensely at Broadstairs. So much so, in fact, that upon her return to London she immediately made plans for another trip later in the summer. The "house of mourning," it seemed, could indeed provide unexpected consolations.

Sara spent the first three weeks of September at Margate, and then after ten days at Tunbridge Wells with the Thomas Erskines, she decided to extend her trip another full month by going on to Eton. In mid-October, she wrote Mrs. Henry Jones about the excursion and her new sense of "cheerfulness":

It is good for me to be here [at Eton]. I can not withdraw myself from the world; I must live on in this outward scene (though it continually seems most strange to my feelings that I should yet be mixed up in it, and Henry *gone from* it forever). . . . Ever since my widowhood I have *cultivated cheerfulness* as I never did before. During my time of union I possessed *happiness;* mere *cheerfulness* I looked upon as a weed, the natural wild produce of the soil, which *must* spring up of itself. Now I crave to see fine works of art, or the still more mind-occupying displays of nature. I try to take an interest in the concerns of my friends, to enter into the controversies of the day, to become intimate with the mood of mind and character of various persons. . . . All this with an earnestness unfelt in former times. To a certain extent I find my account this; my mind is restless, and rather full of desultory activity than, what is far better, concentrated energy; but it does not stagnate. I do not brood miserably over my loss, or sink into an aimless, inert despondency; I have even an upper stratum of cheerfulness in my mind, more fixed than in my happy married days, but then it is only an upper stratum; beneath it, unmoved and unmodified, is the sense of my loss. [*ML*(1874) 206–07]

Sara's distinction between her married "happiness" and her present "cheerfulness" was carefully drawn so as not to suggest irreverence for the dead. Nevertheless, it had to explain a new mental and physical "restless[ness]," a desire to engage art, nature, and other human beings "with an earnestness unfelt in former times." Obviously, Sara needed to account for two facts that family and friends would have found somewhat unusual: first, that in the eight months following her husband's death, she had traveled almost as much as she had in the preceding thirteen years; and second, that she was suddenly more active, more interested, more engaged in the "outward scene" than she had ever been while Henry was alive. However "unmoved and unmodified" Sara's "sense of loss," there was no denying that an "upper stratum of cheerfulness" had effectively obscured her deeper sorrow.

Consequently, at the bottom of her letter to Mrs. Jones, Sara affixed the same explanation she had earlier sent to Mrs. Ferrar: "Excuse the egotism of this letter. Sorrow makes one egotistical." The situations, however, were now completely reversed. Whereas before Sara had been explaining what she feared might be taken as a "tedious and commonplace" bereavement, a self-indulgent and antisocial sadness, here she was trying to justify her "restless" good cheer and *lack* of self-consuming despair. In both cases, her grief becomes responsible for an unnatural and unfeminine "egotism" that necessitates apology: whether in private sorrow or public cheer, women were to maintain a selfless identity, living in and through husband and progeny. Paradoxically, Sara's apologies signal nothing less than the beginning of her happiest and most productive years, years during which she would gradually realize how unnecessary such apologies were.

Sara did not, of course, have to apologize for working on behalf of her father; and throughout the spring and summer she continued her reading of German philosophy. "Schelling," she admitted to John Taylor Coleridge, "is not to be read in an afternoon": "I might as well attempt to run up a river, the water up to my waist, as to run through Schelling" (Letter [June? 1843]). She also began planning a single volume of her father's poems, for negotiations with Pickering had reached a more or less satisfactory conclusion by late May. Even though she thought "his dawdling ways . . . a contrast to those of Mr. Moxon," Sara decided to leave Pickering in charge rather than divide the account (Letter: SC to JTC [19 May 1843]). Both she and her father's official executor, Joseph Henry Green, were hoping that the old publisher would change his careless habits.[2]

The early summer saw the publication of the fifth edition of *Aids of Reflection,* the second volume of which included Sara's lengthy essay "On Rationalism." Although she had worked for several years on the project, Sara would not admit to any optimism about its reception. To her cousin, she wrote,

> As to my own production (*much as I admire it myself!*), I do not expect that it will be admired by any one else. It makes larger demands on the attention of readers than I, with my powers, have perhaps any right to make or can repay. Even if the thinking were sound or important, the arrangement is bad. If bad arrangement in S. T. C. is injurious to readability, in S. C. it will be destructive. Moreover, I have made to myself *no friends.* A follower out of the principles of S. T. C. myself, whithersoever they lead me, because they seem to me the *very truth,* I can not join hands with any of his half or quarter disciples. I praise and admire and applaud all the combatants on the theological arena, even the hearty opponents of my father, but I can not entirely agree with any one of them. . . . Yet I should never regret the time spent on this little composition, though I should be rather out of pocket and not into reputation by it, as will certainly be the case; for it has sometimes brought one part of my mind into activity, when the other part, if active, could only have been alive to anguish; and it has given me a more animated intercourse with some great minds now passed from our nether sphere than I could have had from merely reading their thoughts, without thinking them over again myself. [*ML*(1874) 202]

Sara's self-effacing judgments about her "little composition" fail to hide an understandable anxiety about the essay's reception. But even as she faults her work, as she admits its "bad arrangement," she calls attention to the illustrious tradition of which it is a part. Like her father, Sara cares little for felicitous prose; she is committed instead to the "*very truth*" of philosophic "principles." Also like her father, she has "*no friends*"; she stands alone in the "theological arena," contemptuous of the party politics bonding other writers. But unlike his other "disciples," she is brave enough to follow her father's principles "whithersoever they lead." Moreover, the quest is therapeutic: "animated intercourse with . . .

great minds" forces her own mind "into activity" and prevents a debilitating and solipsistic "anguish."

Not all of Sara's readers came away from the essay agreeing with the censures of its author. Even the Eton Coleridges, for example, were impressed by Sara's learning, although they did voice concern that such compositions might detract from domestic duties. Hartley, on the other hand, registered no such reservations: "Dear Sara's treatise on Rationalism is a wonder. I say not a wonder of a woman's work—where lives the man that could have written it? None in Great Britain since our Father died. Poor Henry was perfectly right in saying that she inherited more of her father, than either of us [her brothers]; and that not only in the amount but in the quality of her powers" (*HC Letters* 267).[3] Delighted by Hartley's praise, Sara was pleased as well by Pickering's report that the volumes were selling briskly and by John Duke Coleridge's claim to have heard the essay being discussed by William Ward at Oxford. Sara was also pleased and excited by her response from F. D. Maurice. Another avowed "disciple" of Coleridge, Maurice had for several months been writing her voluminous letters on the fine points of theological doctrine, letters that addressed Sara as an intellectual equal and encouraged her interest in religious philosophy. The publication of the essay "On Rationalism" fueled their debate: her letters frequently ran to over twenty pages, his to over forty.

F. D. Maurice was one of the most important British theologians of the nineteenth century. Although misunderstood in his own day, he has had, according to B. M. G. Reardon, a "pervasive and persistent influence" on the social policies of the Christian church.[4] With Charles Kingsley and C. M. Ludlow, Maurice founded the Christian Social, or Broad, Church movement of the late 1840s. Maurice argued that theological reform was an efficient means by which to avert political revolution and that the competition resulting from laissez-faire economic policies could be alleviated by a return to the more Christian values of cooperation and charity. The Broad Church movement, in Reardon's words, "took the first step in a direction which Christian social concern has since generally pursued" (257).

F. D. Maurice and Sara Coleridge were both convinced that S. T. Coleridge was a "practical" philosopher whose teachings had immediate applicability to the social unrest of the 1840s; and they shared his love of unity and distrust of partisanship. They disagreed, however, about almost everything else. A founding member of the famous Apostles' Club, Maurice had there defended Coleridge and Wordsworth against attacks by proponents of utilitarianism. After leaving Cambridge, he and his fellow apostle John Sterling continued their defense as members of the London Debating Society, where they debated, among others, John Stuart Mill. Maurice's first important theological work, *The Kingdom of Christ* (1838), was, as critics quickly pointed out, heavily indebted to

Coleridgean principles, and the second edition (1842) appeared with a new and generous acknowledgment of the debt. But Maurice took Coleridge farther along the road to mysticism than Sara could tolerate. Her essay "On Rationalism" had stressed the importance of the understanding to her father's theology and had attempted in the process to counter the elitism of the Oxford Movement by suggesting a pathway to spiritual fulfillment open to all mankind. "I shall endeavour to show," she had written,

> that the soul of man cannot properly become religious, or possessed of a true and living faith, or be spiritually influenced and changed from evil to good, without the concurrence of the understanding in every stage of the process; that this process cannot even be commenced by the affection, independently of the intellectual faculty; that to prove the possibility of such an antecedence, were it provable, would in no way tend to uphold and fortify the doctrine of grace; and that conversely, that in proving the necessity of divine grace in the work of religion, we go not one step towards proving that the subordinate and ministrative agency of the understanding is not necessary too. [Aids(1843) 2:242–43]

On one hand, she felt that Maurice was indiscriminate in his celebration of reason; on the other, that he was too quick to differentiate between "personal" and "subjective" religion (Letter: SC to F. D. Maurice [21 Nov 1843]). But regardless of their differences, the correspondence continued, and by mid-1843, F. D. Maurice and Sara Coleridge had transformed a commonplace exchange into a warm and lasting intellectual friendship.[5]

Although Maurice's encouragement was massively important both to Sara's growing self-confidence and to her increasing theological expertise, his was not the mind that intrigued her most in the years following Henry's death. That privilege belonged to Thomas Carlyle. While visiting the Farrers at Broadstairs in May, Sara had been introduced to the writings of Carlyle and was struck immediately by his similarity to Coleridge. Busy with other matters over the summer, including the preparation of a new volume of her father's poetry, she was not able to begin her study of the Scotsman until August, but once begun she read his Past and Present (1843), History of the French Revolution (1837), and On Heroes, Hero-Worship, and the Heroic in History (1841) in rapid succession. In the middle of Past and Present, she wrote to her cousin, "Newman, Carlyle, and Tennyson are perhaps the most striking writers, with Dickens in the novel line, . . . now before the public" (Letter: SC to JTC [25 Aug 1843]). Six days later, she wrote back, "I am reading Carlyle's 'Fr. Revolution'. . . . The Practical sameness of the teaching of Carlyle with that of Pusey and Newman . . . with Coleridge at the bottom of all, is to me very striking" (Letter [31 Aug 1843]). Six days after that, she wrote again, "Carlyle's "Hero-Worship" trembled in my hand like a culprit before a judge; and as the book is very full of paradoxes, and has some questionable matter in it, this shaking seemed rather symbolical. But, oh! it is a book fit rather to shake (take it all in all) than to be shaken. It is very full of noble sentiments and wise reflections, and throws out many a suggestion which will not waste itself like a blast blown in a wilderness, but will surely rouse many a heart and mind to a right, Christian-like way of acting and of dealing with the gifted and godlike in man and of men" (*ML*[1874] 204). Normally an exacting judge of literary "culprit[s]," Sara here confesses to having herself been "shaken" by Carlyle's "noble sentiments and wise reflections." Regardless of its "paradoxes" and "questionable matter," *Hero-Worship* was notable, she felt, because it "will not waste itself . . . but will surely rouse many a heart and mind." It would, in other words, encourage the appreciation of previously ignored intellectual "heroes" by demonstrating the "right . . . way . . . of dealing with the gifted and godlike in man and of men."

Thus, Sara was herself "rouse[d]" for a number of reasons. First, she would have been gratified by Carlyle's approving references to her father. In "The Hero as Priest," Coleridge is quoted on the subject of religious faith; and in "The Hero as King," he is cited again in support of Carlyle's doctrine of individual fulfillment.[6] More important, however, Sara recognized Carlyle as a prophet in the Coleridgean tradition, a nonpartisan philosopher with a pronounced social and religious responsibility unaffected by popular cant. But more important still was the centrality of Carlyle's subject matter to her own filial tasks. Coleridge was her "hero," and her intention was to demonstrate to her contemporaries why he should be worshiped. Carlyle gave Sara an extended argument supporting precisely the kind of activity in which she was engaged; he explained how she could "deal with the gifted and godlike in man and of men"—in particular, how she could use his theory of "veneration" to excuse her father's personal flaws while arguing for both his philosophical greatness and his political relevance.

When Sara arrived at Eton in October 1843, Carlyle was uppermost in her mind. "[R]estless," "cheerful," and eager "to enter into the controversies of the day," she saw to it that his writings came up as a topic for discussion and that her own feelings about his merit were known (*ML*[1874] 206–07). Generally more conservative than her London circle, the Edward Coleridges and their friends were predictably reserved in their admiration for Carlyle's works, and soon Sara reported back to her mother that there had been "a controversy about Carlyle betwixt the gentlemen and me" (Letter [25 Oct 1843]). Delighted by the exchange and impressed by one of the gentlemen in particular—an assistant master at Eton, Charles John Abraham[7]—Sara resolved to clarify her position by committing her arguments to paper. Once back in London, she followed through with her resolution and composed a fifteen-page essay, "Reply to the Strictures of Three Gentlemen upon Carlyle," copies of which she sent to Edward Coleridge, Edward Balston, and Charles John Abraham.[8]

II

Sara's essay focuses on Carlyle's 1841 collection of lectures, *On Heroes, Hero-Worship, and the Heroic in History,* and defends his concept of "veneration," an idea that justifies intellectual nonpartisanship as it celebrates the intellectual as a political and religious hero.[9] Recognizing Carlyle's dislike of organized religion, that "system of empty forms, dead conventionalisms, and lifeless ceremonies," Sara rightly insists that this dislike is counterbalanced by a strong belief in a "living and life-exciting principle" which informs all religions at least in part: "This principle, which he sets up as the 'work of God,' against the artefacts of men—vain substitutes for genuine gifts from on high—he maintains to be 'Veneration'—the principle or feeling which leads men to bow down before the image of God in the soul of man" (*ML*[1874] 358). The "image of God," Sara argues, is reproduced "in the soul of man" through a kind of "mental power," which—because it originates with God—is necessarily benevolent and therefore deserving of worship. Similar to Coleridge's "reason," which he had described as "the Source and Substance of Truth above Sense" (*Aids*[1825] 242), Carlyle's "mental power" leads its worshipers away from "the dominion of sense and the despotism of moral evil" on a salutary journey to spiritual fulfillment.

Defending Carlyle's approval of the veneration of Voltaire, Sara complicates the notion of hero-worship by insisting that its value depends just as much upon the complex historical situation in which both hero and worshipers take part as it does upon the intellectual power of the hero in question. Voltaire was celebrated by the French because at a particular time in history he answered the needs of his countrymen by exhibiting a power worthy of their respect, thus saving them from "groveling along in utter worldliness." While his skepticism was objectionable and his character flawed, Voltaire nevertheless evinced an inner strength that communicated itself to his society as "a redeeming spirit." What Carlyle has argued, Sara maintains, is not that the intellectual should be exalted above the moral, but that "*natural gifts*" of individual men exalt God more effectively than "the vain shows and semblances which commonly pass for religion in the world":

> Poor and needy, indeed, must that people be who have no better object of
> such a feeling than Voltaire. Our author means only to affirm that French-
> men were better employed in "worshiping" him even for supposititious
> merits than in . . . pursuing each his own narrow, selfish path, without a

thought or a care beyond the gratification of the senses. Here is no intention to set the intellectual above the moral, or to substitute the one for the other, but to insist on the superiority of *natural gifts,* as means of bettering the souls of men, to the vain shows and semblances which commonly pass for religion in the world. [*ML*(1874) 359]

Even more so than F. D. Maurice, whose "personal religion" restored the "experience of God" to the individual and downplayed the mediating role of the church, Carlyle stressed that God's "*natural gifts*" as embodied in man are divinely bestowed for the greater good of mankind. Thus, the central objection to *Hero-Worship* made by its detractors—"that [Carlyle] sets up mere intellect as the ultimate object of esteem and admiration, and represents a man as truly great and worthy of all honor purely on the score of intellectual gifts"—fails to consider, in Sara's opinion, the author's overriding concern with historical circumstance.

Heroes deserve respect, Sara argues, not because they are intellectually superior but because they are individuals "whose powers have been employed by God's will and their own, for good and noble purposes on a large scale, chiefly for the purpose of leading men, directly or indirectly, from earth to heaven, from the human to the divine" (*ML*[1874] 361). Like the Christian philosopher she defined and celebrated in her essay on Wordsworth's poem "Lines Left on a Yew-tree Seat," and very similar to the elite members of her father's "clerisy," Carlyle's heroes acknowledge their duty as leaders: "Carlyle's heroes are all men who have striven for truth and justice, and for the emancipation of their fellow-mortals. He represents them as having been misunderstood by the masses of mankind, in the midst of all their effectivity and *ultimate* influence, simply because the masses of mankind are not themselves sufficiently wise and good and perspicacious to understand and sympathize with those who are so in an eminent degree" (*ML*[1874] 362). Sara is not willing, however, to bestow upon Carlyle her unqualified praise. The passage above is followed immediately by a crucial reservation: "There is *some* originality in Carlyle's opinions; but he seems to me to be more original in manner than in matter: the force and feeling with which he brings out his views are more *remarkable* than the views themselves." Although never mentioned, Coleridge's presence in both passages is unmistakable. By defining the hero as one "misunderstood by the masses of mankind," Sara places her father squarely in the tradition established by Carlyle, as she confirms the necessity of her own editorial projects. She then immediately undercuts the authority of that tradition by establishing it within an older tradition whose invisibility both provides the basis for and serves as an example of Carlyle's more recent doctrine. From Carlyle's perspective, then, Coleridge is merely another hero awaiting recognition; but from Sara's point of view, her father is the Ur-hero whose unacknowledged influence generated the tradition of which both Carlyle and his "heroes" are a part. To resurrect Coleridge would be at once to redefine contemporary intellectual history and to stabilize contemporary political unrest.

The remainder of Sara's essay concerns itself with the character of Mirabeau, who, like Voltaire and Coleridge, was open to charges of personal misconduct. Again Sara emphasizes that heroism has to be considered from the larger historical perspective:

> Whatever Mirabeau's private character may have been before God, yet as far as he was a powerful and conspicuous agent in carrying forward the work of the French Revolution, Carlyle was justified, as it seems to me, in setting him forth as an object of interest, and even of admiration, proportioned to the amount and rareness of the gifts which rendered him a potent instrument in the hands of Providence for a particular purpose; and this he might have done without calling evil good, or good evil. [ML(1874) 363]

A comparison to Byron makes her point well. Byron's heroes have "no higher merits than gallantry and courage," whereas Mirabeau, like his father before him, was possessed "of a philanthropic spirit, high disinterested aims, and a zeal to serve his country." In discussing Mirabeau, Sara argues, Carlyle has not "exalted him as a *man,* still less as a subject of the *Prince of Life,* but as an actor in a great historical drama." Carlyle's actual subject is the French Revolution, not the character of Mirabeau: "Carlyle is a satirist," she concludes, "but he is not given to satirize individuals, or even parties of men. The object of his satire, as it appears to me, is the weakness and wickedness of *mankind*—systems of belief, not bodies of believers" (ML[1874] 366). Such an emphasis—on the "historical drama" rather than the individual "character"—displaces the private man for his public counterpart, and Sara recognized that it was precisely the strategy by which to confront and disclaim Coleridge's well-known personal shortcomings. Moreover, the translation of "history" into "drama" and "Mirabeau" into "character" serves to familiarize patriarchal history by resituating it within literary conventions, conventions that empower a female commentator by extending her expertise from the narrowly "artistic" to the broadly "cultural."

From Carlyle, Sara learned a healthy disrespect for "systems of belief," but she also learned how to compensate for her new iconoclasm by redefining her understanding of the role of the intellectual in society. Carlyle's concept of veneration originated in a mistrust of worldly institutions and accommodated the irregularities of private life, but it also celebrated public virtues and promised power (of a decidedly orthodox, Christian variety) to both hero and worshiper alike. The hero assumes the immortality of historical influence, living beyond his own time as a benevolent force capable of bringing about spiritual change, while the worshiper recognizes divinity incarnate and is redeemed "from groveling along in utter worldliness." Both stand to profit from the activity of the other without compromising their Christian values. Thus, if Sara could justify the ways of Coleridge to her contemporaries, then she would participate in and be redeemed by his intellectual and historical influence—all without compromising her selfless, "feminine" ideals.

The process of paternal veneration and filial redemption was, of course, well under way by the time Sara wrote her essay on Carlyle in November 1843. But the essay marks a crucial point in her ongoing redefinition of the intellectual as social hero, an attempt that had begun ten years before with her essay on Wordsworth's "Lines Left on a Yew-tree Seat" and one that would culminate with her two greatest editorial achievements—the 1847 edition of the *Biographia Literaria* and the 1850 edition of *Essays on His Own Times*.

Her essay on Wordsworth had situated the poet in society as a special kind of philosopher speaking special kinds of truths.[10] It had established the primacy of religious principles to artistic expression and had insisted upon the poet's duty to enlighten as well as please his readers. More important, it had argued against an elitist, overly rationalistic, worldly "understanding" of poetry and for an appreciation grounded in spiritual democracy and imaginative freedom. Palpable throughout was the presence of Coleridge as *the* philosophical authority whose thought illuminated the poetry of his collaborator. Paradoxically, however, it was this authority that Sara had to subvert in order to speak for its defense; as a female commentator, she needed first to establish a position that allowed for its own possibility. Therefore, she had argued that a "reader . . . may sometimes read aright . . . from resigning [her]self completely to the will of [her] author," redefining in the process of her argument Coleridge's own insistence on the need for an elite audience.

Written three years later, Sara's essay on the British Constitution had developed the same concerns from an expressly political perspective.[11] It had situated the philosopher in government as a member of an elite body of unofficial rulers—the clerisy. It had established the primacy of religious principles to the concept of state rule and had insisted upon the cleric's duty to communicate those principles to the people. In addition, it had argued against an unprincipled American democracy and for a British aristocracy that was more efficiently and less dangerously democratic. Echoing the words of her father, Sara had supported the British Constitution so as to guarantee that the "voice [of truth would be] heard, not drowned by the clamours of the errant." Faith in that voice of truth was the necessary act of submission that legitimized Sara's own voice, for unlike Harriet Martineau—the essay's bête noire—Sara could not bring herself to violate the codes of female decorum except by ruse.

Sara's essay on Carlyle continued her exploration of the role of the intellectual in society by situating the cleric in history as a remembered hero who continues to assert his power and influence over subsequent generations. It established the primacy of religious principles to historical understanding and insisted upon the hero's ability to redeem and be redeemed through the act of veneration. Moreover, the essay argued against a limited assessment of personal character and for a more extensive appraisal of the hero as a political force, as an actor in the larger historical "drama." As was the case in her earlier essays, Coleridge's presence is evident throughout as that hero who, like Voltaire and Mirabeau, should be venerated regardless of personal shortcomings. Significantly, Sara's defense of Carlyle reenacts the very process under discussion and redeems her voice from a fated silence.

All three essays, then, attempt a definition of the intellectual in society, and with each essay the boundaries of individual stature and power increase. The essay on Wordsworth considers the poet as philosopher; the essay on the British Constitution considers the philosopher as cleric; and the essay on Carlyle considers the cleric as hero. At the level of hero, the intellectual has reached his apogee: he is venerated as a philosophically astute leader of men who is as important to the future as he was to the past. Together, his life and works speak to all mankind, communicating truths of divine origin and offering redemption to all who can recognize "the image of God in the soul of man."

No less important, the three essays also expand the role of the intellectual consumer, for concomitant with the evolution from poet to hero is a similar evolution from reader to worshiper, from observer to critic. As the role of the intellectual becomes greater and greater, the responsibilities of his readers increase proportionally. The submission which in the first essay applies only to the "will of [the] author" and promises only a way to "read aright" evolves by the third essay into the "veneration" that leads "from earth to heaven, from the human to the divine." The stronger the faith of the disciple, the greater the reward.

For Sara, the reward was in the writing, and the authority she borrowed from her "heroes" enabled her to justify the transgression her authorship entailed. Thus, writing itself became an act of redemption which saved her from the mundane realities of Victorian womanhood as it realized the spiritual freedom promised by Christianity. Legitimizing her heroes rhetorically involved at once their veneration and her own: the passive reader yields to the active disciple, commentator, and critic. For Sara, submission was proving an increasingly effective form of mastery.

III

The three and a half years following Sara's essay on Carlyle were devoted to her edition of the *Biographia Literaria* (1847). A scrupulous researcher, she took painstaking care with the text, investigating her father's sources, checking his notebooks and marginalia, and writing detailed explanatory notes to all potentially troublesome passages. So thorough was her editorial practice that subsequent editors of the *Biographia* have been careful to acknowledge their gratitude. James Engell and W. Jackson Bate, for example, the editors of volume 7 of the *Collected Works* (1983), single out Sara for special attention: "Our debt to the work of Sara Coleridge," they admit, "is particularly heavy" (*BL[CC]* 1:xvii). Even so, Norman Fruman, in reviewing Engell and Bate's volume, maintains that "Sara Coleridge's intelligence, energy, learning, and above all her willingness to lay damaging materials clearly before the reader, have . . . never received anything like the praise they deserve."[12] He argues as well that while modern editors have appreciated Sara's detailed commentary, they have failed to recognize that her 1847 text is a more reliable copy-text than that provided by the original 1817 edition. According to Fruman, she had access to and made use of the author's own corrections, deleting unwanted irregularities and revising key passages. Although quick to acknowledge Sara's achievement, however, modern editors generally, Fruman among them, have consistently ignored her other major contributions to the 1847 *Biographia*—her introduction. The 180-page defense of her father's moral character and literary accomplishments is a carefully orchestrated and convincingly written portrayal of Coleridge as the intellectual "hero" so desperately needed by the Victorian public. It is, as a result, a crucial event in the history of Coleridge scholarship.

Sara began working on the introduction during the fall of 1844. She had recovered from a slight illness that winter and had traveled again to Broadstairs and Eton in late summer. Her "cheerfulness" remained undampened, and her routine was, if anything, socially busier and intellectually more committed than ever before. To her cousin Frank, for instance, she defended the literary "*business of life*":

> I quite agree with you . . . that no intellectual undertakings are worthy of a wise man that are not directed to a *practical aim,* and that have no bearing on the *business of life.* But what ought our *practical* aims to be?—what is the *business of life?* I think we cannot answer these questions properly without admitting that mental cultivation and the exercise of the powers of thought are indispensable to the formation of sound *practical* aims, and to the doing the *business of life* well. . . . Not only is it necessary . . . that there should be a class who make literature the business of their lives, but that every individual according to his capacity and opportunity should cultivate his intellectual powers. . . . One large part of the *business of life* for my sex is to educate yours. [Letter (1 Feb 1844)]

With her husband dead and her children no longer a burden, Sara's "business of life" was very much "directed to a *practical aim*" outside her immediate family.

She had committed herself to editing one of her father's most important literary works, and with that project she assumed the responsibility to "educate" her contemporaries about one of their intellectual "heroes." As a representative of a "class who make literature the business of their lives"—a class, in other words, whose responsibility it was to create and maintain a literary "tradition"—she marketed inherited cultural values as much-needed social remedies. Her letter makes clear, however, that that responsibility was conceived of as an extension of maternal duty: her own "powers of thought" would be devoted to helping others "cultivate [their] intellectual powers." Thus, as she edited her father's *Biographia Literaria,* literally and figuratively rewriting his literary life and her own patrimony, Sara adopted the guise of the nurturing mother—selfless, committed, and preeminently powerful; for her "children" now were hardly those of the nursery: her father had a sprawling corpus of some twenty volumes, and his readership included the most influential members of the mid-nineteenth-century reading public.

Intellectual responsibility was an issue of extreme importance for Carlyle, and his influence on Sara's preparation of the *Biographia* was no doubt enhanced by their acquaintanceship. They met at a party at St. Mark's College in July 1844, and Sara was immediately impressed by the famous author: "He is as like what he writes as flesh and blood can well be in a book. In appearance he is both striking and pleasing, more so than in his pictures, . . . because they do not fully give the brightness and delicacy of his face, nor his light, refined figure, nor the look that overspreads his countenance during his hearty laugh. His refinement, however, is that of thought and intellectual cultivation, not of social aristocratic training: he looks like a Scotch Gardener turned into man of letters by native genius" (Letter: SC to JTC [July? 1844]). However admiring of his works, Sara was not one to give her "Scotch Gardener" an easy time. Months later she wrote to her friend Aubrey de Vere:[13]

> Carlyle, I think, too much depreciates money as an instrument. I battled with him a little on this point when I saw him last. He is always smiling and good-natured when I contradict him, perhaps because he sees that I admire him all the while. I fought in defense of the Mammonites, and brought him at least to own that the laborer is worthy of his hire. Now this contains the pith of the whole matter. The man who devotes himself to gain riches deserves to have riches, . . . and if he strives for riches to spend them nobly or kindly, then he deserves to have the luxury of *that sort* of doing good. . . . But Carlyle seems angry because the Burns or the Johnson or the Milton has not the same honors, . . . as millionaires and fashionists; because the whole world—unphilosophical and unpoetical as the main part of it is—does not fall down and worship them. . . . This is overbear-

ing and unfair. Let him teach the world to be philosophical and poetical as fast as he can; but till it is so, let him not grudge it the rattles and sugar-plums and hobby-horses of its infancy. [ML(1874) 278–79]

Having labored long and hard in the margins of the literary world, Sara had come to realize that there were many ways "of doing good," that intellectual riches were not the only means to an end, and that even the most altruistic of contemporary philosophers could be "overbearing and unfair."[14] Because she considered herself representative of an entire class whose duty it was to "culti-vate" the public mind, to market literary culture as an indispensable national commodity, she felt no compunction about "[fighting] in defense of the Mam-monites." Revenues from the sale of her father's works had been, after all, an important motivation behind her ongoing editorial projects. Regardless of their differences, however, it was Carlyle's doctrine of hero-worship, of the intellec-tual's social, political, and religious power, that provided the model for Sara's most effective tribute to her father. For unlike Carlyle, whose paternalistic predilections only alienated the public he was trying to reform, Sara was com-fortable with and could accommodate the world's "infancy": she could teach hero-worship rather than sermonize about it.

Sara's introduction to the 1847 *Biographia Literaria* is divided into three sections. Each section is both a separate, freestanding essay and a fragment of a larger, tripartite argument. The first section, "Mr. Coleridge's Obligations to Schelling," confronts and explains Coleridge's "plagiarisms"; the second sec-tion, "Mr. Coleridge's Religious Opinions," maps his relationships to Kant and Luther as it illuminates his difference from J. H. Newman and the Oxford Movement; and the third section, "Mr. Coleridge's 'Remarks on the Present Mode of conducting Public Journals,'" exposes the party politics behind his poor critical reception. Together, the three essays enact a complex apotheosis: they transform an admittedly imperfect human being into an almost perfect intellectual hero. They subordinate unavoidable character flaws and imme-thodical literary remains to philosophical principles and religious integrity, explaining in the process exactly how one should best approach and profit from the enigmatic eccentricities of the *Biographia Literaria*.

The first essay, on Coleridge's debts to Schelling, is more than a direct and honest answer to J. F. Ferrier's charges of plagiarism; it is a carefully orches-trated exploration of Coleridge as both flawed human being and questing philosopher. The argument begins with the question of intention: do the pas-sages from Schelling *have* to be discussed as "conscious intentional plagiarism"? Ferrier had maintained that her father "'defrauded' Schelling of his due," first by making "no adequate acknowledgements of obligation," and then by "affirm-[ing] that he had in some sort anticipated the system which he proposed to teach." But "defrauding," Sara argues, is clearly a matter of intention: "No man can properly be said to 'defraud' another, nor ought to be so spoken of, who has not a fraudulent 'intention'" (*BL*[1847] 1:vii). Those familiar with her father's "literary habits," she maintains, would recognize that "the passages from Schelling, which he wove into his work, were not transcribed *for the occasion,* but merely transferred from his note-book into the text, some of them, in all likelihood, not even from his note-book immediately, but from recollection of its contents" (viii). Extending the position of J. C. Hare, who had defended Coleridge in 1835 from De Quincey's accusations, and anticipating the argument of Thomas McFarland, who has written the most convincing modern defense, Sara explains her father's plagiarisms as the unfortunate result of an eccentric method of composition, of a careless inattention to "fact" that overlooked matters of individual "ownership" in favor of collective enlightenment.[15]

According to Sara, the word-for-word "borrowings" indicate not that Coleridge stole outright but that he was perfectly oblivious of the debt: he "repeated the *very words* of Schelling, and in so doing made it an easy task for the German to reclaim his own, or for the dullest wight that could read his books to give it back again" (xii). Such full-scale appropriation makes it difficult to attribute guile to the perpetrator, for Coleridge never attempted to make the material his own by artfully rewriting it. "It is not easy to see," Sara argues, "how *that which is borrowed* can ever, strictly speaking, become the property of the borrower, so as to cease to be that of the original possessor" (xi). In her analysis, Coleridge becomes not a thief but a willful debtor, "'a divine ventriloquist, not caring from whose mouth the sounds are supposed to proceed, if only the words are audible and intelligible'" (xiv). He gained no "reputation as a metaphysical discoverer," but instead represented himself as "an introducer of German metaphysics . . . a man of original genius, who had spoiled his own genius by devoting himself to the lucubrations of foreigners" (xv). The education of his countrymen, she argues, was more important to Coleridge than his personal "reputation."

Demanding that critics consider his life in conjunction with his ideas, Sara maintains that her father was too "intent upon the pursuit and enunciation of truth" to attend to questions of ownership: "If he was not always sufficiently considerate of other men's property, he was profuse of his own; and, in truth, such was his temper in regard to all *property* . . . he did not enough regard or value it whether for himself or his neighbour" (xviii). This, she admits, was a fault, a "want of proportion in the faculties of the mind" which precluded the possibility of successful publications. In short, Coleridge was a dedicated metaphysician oblivious to worldly responsibilities: "He loved to go forward, expounding and ennobling the soul of his teaching, and hated the trouble of turning back to look after its body" (xix). The victim of a "nerveless languor, which . . . rendered all exercises difficult to him except of thought and imagination," Coleridge reproduced his "illness" textually:

> The *Biographia Literaria* he composed at that period of his life when his health was most deranged, and his mind most subject to the influence of bodily disorder. It bears marks of this throughout, for it is even less methodical in its arrangement than any of his other works. Up to a certain point the author pursues his plan of writing his literary life, but, in no long time his "slack hand" abandons its grasp of the subject, and the book is filled out to a certain size, with such miscellaneous contents of his desk as seem least remote from it. To say, with the writer in *Blackwood* [Ferrier], that he stopped short in the process of unfolding a theory of the imagination, merely because he had come to the end of all that Schelling had taught . . . is to place the matter in a perfectly false light; he broke down in the prosecution of his whole scheme, the regular history of his literary life and opinions, . . . because his energies for regular composition in any line were deserting him, at least for a time. [xxi]

"Subject to the influence of bodily disorder," Coleridge's mind composed a work as "[im]methodical" as his health was "deranged." Less plagiarist than invalid, he failed to produce "the regular history of his literary life" not because he had run out of passages from Schelling but because "his energies for regular composition" were depleted. The reader, Sara argues, can effect a mutual cure by "meet[ing] the author half way," for "the chief use and aim of writings of such a character" is therapeutic— "to excite the reader to think,—to draw out of his mind a native flame rather than make it bright for a moment by the reflection of alien fires" (xx).[16] Herself in the process of restoring her father's text to a readable health, Sara extends the act of restoration to include her contemporaries, who are to approach Coleridge's work as participants in an ongoing process of educational, and hence social, reform.

Having answered Ferrier's charges of plagiarism, Sara turns to his second accusation—that her father had unlawfully claimed to have anticipated "'the main and fundamental ideas' of Schelling's system" (xxiii). Her refutation begins by locating both Coleridge and Schelling within the same Kantian tradition and by insisting that their intellectual powers were equivalent. She then argues that given their similar historical conditions they could easily have come to the same conclusions at approximately the same time. More important, she maintains that her father was less interested in receiving credit for originality than in having "'the honour of rendering [German philosophy] intelligible to his countrymen'" (xxvii). Reiterating her belief that Coleridge was always more concerned with truth than with his own popularity, Sara effectively distances him from charges of duplicity by granting him both spiritual vision and worldly altruism.

Sara's strategy is aided considerably by her return at the essay's close to the issue of her father's intellectual and moral flaws. Chief among his intellectual deficiencies, she observes, was a certain inability to retain facts and a corresponding predilection for abstraction: "Matter of fact, as such, laid no hold upon his mind; of all he heard and saw, he readily caught and well retained the spirit, but the *letter* escaped him; he seemed incapable of paying due regard to it" (xl). Significantly, this weakness was intimately bound to his greatest strength: "His power of abstracting and referring to universal principles often rendered him unconscious of incorrectness of statement." Similarly, Coleridge's moral constitution was flawed by an irresolute will, a mental paralysis that impeded the dutiful exercising of his genius. But here too his deficiency resulted directly from a corresponding virtue, from the greatness of his heart and the depth of his feeling: "His heart was as warm as his intellectual being was lifesome and active, nay it was from warmth of heart and keenness of feeling that his imagination derived its glow and vivacity" (xlv). Because his feelings operated with such intensity, his mind was frequently overwhelmed and his will paralyzed.

In one sense certainly, the figure who emerges at the conclusion of Sara's essay is, like the text of the *Biographia* itself, deeply humanized. Although his genius is never denied—to the contrary, Coleridge the philosopher is present throughout—that genius functions as a part of a larger personality irreparably flawed by a host of human deficiencies. Making no attempt to obscure her father's faults or the irregularities of his writings, Sara paints a portrait of the artist as an intellectual invalid very much in need of the understanding and compassion of his readers. At the same time, however, this historicized Coleridge is not meant to play the leading role in her argument; he is introduced in all his particularity only to be displaced in favor of his philosophic counterpart—Coleridge the metaphysician devoutly attendant upon distant truths. Just as all his flaws are subservient to greater virtues, so his "humanity" is established in order to be replaced by a metaphysical vision glimmering through his "immethodical" text. Coleridge's readers become active participants in a multiple redemption as Sara remains in the background orchestrating an elaborate redefinition of Carlyle's venerated hero. Whereas Carlyle ignores personal irregularities as irrelevant to intellectual, political, or moral power, Sara traces their interconnections, unafraid of admitting the former as long as she is ultimately assured of establishing the latter.

The second section of Sara's introduction, "On Mr. Coleridge's Religious Opinions," continues the process of veneration by defending Coleridge from contemporary critics as it clarifies his position vis-à-vis his theological fore-fathers. Reacting to a recent article in the *Christian Miscellany,* "Contributions of S. T. Coleridge to the Revival of Catholic Truths,"[17] Sara contends that Coleridge has been maligned by critics "far too prone to discredit a man's opinions at second-hand by tracing them to some averred evil source in his character, or perverting influence in the circumstances of his life" (xlix–l). After refuting the charge that her father's powers as a theologian were impaired by "'his profession of literature, his having edited a newspaper, and his having been engaged in a course of heretical and schismatical teaching,'" Sara maintains that it was his intellectual independence that caused the misrepresentation: "It was the natural consequence of his having no predilection for any sect or party that parties and party organs have either neglected or striven against him" (lxii). While he strove "to examine the truth of modes of thought in general," his opponents "assum[ed] the truth of certain modes of thought [as] the ground of their existence as parties." Thus, unlike many of Carlyle's heroes, Coleridge found that his quest for truth offended the beliefs upheld by those who had most to gain from his inquiries.

Coleridge's marginal status in contemporary debates resulted predictably from his originality, and, according to his daughter, he was victimized by party politics of some complexity. Those representing "the dry land of negative Protestantism" saw him as a dangerous innovator halfway to Romanism; those of High Church persuasion saw his unripe Anglo-Catholicism as little more than a helpful beginning along a well-established route. Trapped between warring sects, Coleridge's contributions were fated to be misunderstood by both, for neither party could recognize or appreciate that his real task was to explain "the universal ideas of Christianity . . . according to modern philosophy" (lxxii).

In order to explore the relationship between her father's "modern philosophy" and his Christian beliefs—or, more accurately, the interdependence between his doctrines of reason and faith—Sara presents a genealogical argument. She identifies the two thinkers who most influenced her father—Luther and Kant—and argues that Coleridge's unpopularity stems first from a critical misunderstanding of his intellectual ancestors and then from an inability to grasp how Coleridge succeeded in resolving the doctrines of both men into one system. "My Father's affectionate respect for Luther," Sara writes, "is enough to alienate him from the High Anglican party, and his admiration of Kant enough to bring him into suspicion with the anti-philosophic part of the religious world" (xciii).

Sara's task, like her father's, becomes one of reconciliation: in order to demonstrate how Coleridge conflated philosophy and religion to the benefit of both, she must uncover the fundamental similarities shared by disparate positions. Thus, she first reconciles the two opposing religious factions—High Church and Low Anglican—by arguing that Luther and Newman are in substantive agreement on the question of justification.[18] She then turns to Kant, whose philosophical system, she explains, provides the means by which her father united faith and reason and so saved the former from descent into dogmatic mysticism. In the same way that Coleridge mediates between the High and Low Anglicans, he unites philosophical speculation to theological doctrine, combining two separate areas of inquiry into one mutually beneficial quest for truth.

Having established and explored the ties that link Coleridge with Luther and Kant, Sara concludes with a predictable but effective discussion of Coleridge as an independent "reformer" within an established tradition. Like both of his German heroes, Coleridge dedicated his efforts to "free[ing] the minds of Christians from the schemes of doctrine, which seemed to him . . . derogatory to God and injurious to man" (cxlviii). He was not, then, as his detractors have claimed, an ineffectual thinker "given to contemplation rather than to action." On the contrary, his entire system—like Kant's and Luther's—has a "'moral origin'" which mandates a "practical" responsibility: "All the poetry, all the poetical criticism which my Father produced, has a practical end; for poetry is a visible creation the final aim of which is to benefit man by means of delight. As for his moral and religious writings, if practical wisdom is not in them, they are empty indeed, for their whole aim is practical usefulness—the regulation of action, the actions of the heart and mind with their appropriate manifestations—the furtherance of man's well being here and hereafter" (clv–clvi). No *"mere intellectualist,"* Coleridge has been victimized, Sara argues, by critics who fail to realize that personal (and stylistic) flaws were counterbalanced by a "practical" concern with the moral betterment of his fellowman. In the same way that in the previous essay she had argued that Coleridge's readers were meant to participate actively in the re-creative process, Sara emphasizes here that that mutually beneficial interaction was conceived as part of a larger socially and spiritually redemptive plan.

By establishing her father's connections to his intellectual forebears, Sara legitimizes his endeavors as she explains his unpopularity. She outlines his lineage to argue first that he had rethought old positions and constructed from them a new system of considerable significance; and second that both the tenor of his works and his position in society are directly analogous to those of his own heroes—men already accepted as intellects of great stature. Engineering an implicit substitution, Sara forges his destiny as the maligned and misunderstood genius, selfless and heroic, who patiently awaits not his own veneration but the redemption of his countrymen.

The last essay from the introduction, "Mr. Coleridge's 'Remarks on the present Mode of conducting Public Journals,'" completes the redefinition of hero begun by the first two. Ostensibly, the essay seeks to justify Sara's removal of a passage "containing *personal* remarks" about Francis Jeffrey from the new edition. Soon, however, the argument moves from a general discussion of the partisan politics of literary journals, through an account of Coleridge's most misguided reviewers, to a persuasive celebration of Coleridge as an intellectual martyr. From beginning to end, Coleridge's personal shortcomings are carefully balanced by a noble Christian altruism that far surpasses the petty selfishness of his opponents. Thus, Sara transforms the issue of critical reception from a potentially selfish concern with popularity (her father was never worried about his "fame" per se) into a heroic preoccupation with the ways in which religious philosophy can affect "the poetic mind of the community" for its collective betterment (clx–clxi).

Sara argues that as "servants of the public in general," both reviewers and journals have a "duty" to do more than "make public taste in literature subservient to their own purposes as members of a party." Unfortunately, such duty was neglected by the early critics of Coleridge, who, like William Hazlitt, "scanned narrowly" in order to "abuse scientifically." For Sara, Hazlitt represents the quintessence of journalistic inequity. His vilifying reviews were focused exclusively on the "attributes of the *man*," while ignoring the substance of his work. Reviewers like Hazlitt "declaim upon virtue and vice, wisdom and folly . . . without any earnest feeling or belief [of their own]"; they are "out of the domain of conscience altogether" (clxx).

It is "against this system," Sara writes, that "the *Biographia Literaria* . . . protest[s], a protest to which private feeling has given a piquancy, but which in the main it has not corrupted or falsified" (clxxi). Coleridge exposed "what he held to be wrong methods of acting on the mind" and "would not have given way to indignation . . . if he had not believed his cause to be the cause of the public also." He had been reviewed "in a way not to expose his errors but to prevent people from attending to him at all; not to make him understood but to stamp upon him the character of hopeless unintelligibility." If in the *Biographia* Coleridge's writing occasionally seems petulant, extravagant, or overdefensive, readers must recognize, Sara insists, the harsh treatment that fueled his resentment.

After considering Hazlitt's charges and her father's responses, Sara concludes with a quotation from *Aids to Reflection,* a passage "'on the keen and poisoned shafts of the tongue'" that is, as she puts it, most "applicable to the subject that has been discussed":

> The slanders, perchance, may not be altogether forged or untrue; they may
> be implements, not the inventions, of malice. But they do not on this

account escape the guilt of detraction. Rather it is characteristic of the evil spirit in question to work by the advantage of real faults; but these stretched and aggravated to the utmost. It is not expressible how deep a wound a tongue sharpened to the work will give, with no noise and a very little word. This is the true white gunpowder, which the dreaming projectors of silent mischiefs and insensible poisons sought for in the laboratories of art and nature, in a world of good; but which was to be found in its most destructive form, "in the World of Evil, the Tongue." [*Aids*(1843) 1:78]

Reduced by synecdoche to the malicious "tongue," the "evil spirit" of slander becomes a common human propensity attributable to Coleridge as well as to his detractors, and in that sense the passage assumes a kind of humility. At the same time, however, the voice is, like much of *Aids to Reflection,* more prophetic and biblical than characteristically Coleridgean or even specifically "human"—it speaks an all-inclusive Truth above and beyond the individual author and his individual readers. This paradoxically aggrandizing self-effacement is reaffirmed by a return to the first paragraph of the aphorism which identifies its intended audience as those who "have attained a self-pleasing pitch of civility or formal religion . . . [and] make their own size the model and rule to examine all by." Coleridge is criticizing those who possess small-minded interpretive certainty while he himself speaks with the assurance of universal vision. Importantly, this vision embraces human fallibility, original sin, and earthly suffering. In other words, Coleridge makes himself a part of the human situation only to stand above it as an authoritative commentator. Thus, his passage enacts precisely the same process being orchestrated by the larger argument in which it appears: Coleridge the man is subsumed by the Truth he speaks. In that last paragraph, father and daughter strike the same note simultaneously.

Taken together, then, Sara's three essays are more than a protracted vindication of Coleridge's life and work; they enact a complex apotheosis of a flawed man into an intellectual hero by first presenting what he was, by then arguing for what he did, and by finally lamenting what he was made into. The first essay establishes Coleridge's humanity, the second maps out his contributions, and the third engineers his martyrdom. In the opening section, Coleridge's humanity transforms plagiarism into an unusual mode of composition. Faults are emphasized only to be subordinated to greater virtues as lack of concern for details is balanced by an obsession with "principles." Thus, the historical self exists to be displaced by the inquiring philosopher. In the second essay, Coleridge's contributions are seen as effecting a reconciliation between religion and philosophy. Like his heroes Luther and Kant (whom he implicitly surpasses), Coleridge is a statesman devoted to no party but speaking for all. His intellectual integrity hinges upon his nonallegiance to worldly sects, but his deep faith in spiritual freedom mandates a "practical" direction for even his most abstruse works: he is unworldly but still a man of action, not just a philosopher but a cleric attempting to use his gifts for the benefit of the people. In the third essay, the process completes itself as the cleric is betrayed by his friends and rejected by his contemporaries; he becomes an unacknowledged hero in a spiteful and inattentive world. The entire introduction then concludes with an apotheosis that is both actual and prophetic: Coleridge's martyrdom has already occurred, but his resurrection is still in progress.

IV

Sara's labors on behalf of her father were both a duty and an exorcism. She labored for Coleridge because he was her father and because his works needed and deserved her assistance. But she also labored for herself, for a "self" not submissive and patronized but one newly "restless," "cheerful," and engaged "in the controversies of the day." Thus, filial duty of the kind required by her father inadvertently encouraged an "egotism" that Sara felt compelled to explain and for which she repeatedly apologized. During the early months of her project, for example, soon after the death of her mother in September 1845, Sara hesitantly expressed a growing pride in her accomplishments: "I am not, however, brooding over my grief from want of employment. I am just now, *absurdly* busy. I have to edit my father's fragmentary work, the 'Biographia Literaria'. . . . The trouble I take is so ridiculously disproportioned to any effect that can be produced, and we so apt to measure our importance by the efforts we make, rather than the good we do, that I am obliged to keep reminding myself of this very truth, in order not to become a mighty person in my own eyes, while I remain as small as ever in the eyes of every one else" (*ML*[1874] 242). Editing was a selfless activity fully in keeping with early-nineteenth-century strictures against female assertiveness, but the editorial labors necessitated by Coleridge's abstruse and immethodical works were so demanding that Sara was tempted "to become a mighty person in [her] own eyes" even without the public recognition that measured more accurately the social value of her efforts. As the dissatisfaction in the passage suggests, Sara was in the process of redefining her ideas about female authorship and "feminine" propriety; given the "trouble" taken, she had no real desire to "remain as small as ever in the eyes of every one else." Editing the *Biographia* thus provided the perfect opportunity to test a "restless" intellectual enthusiasm against the restrictive demands of her society.

By the time the *Biographia Literaria* appeared in the spring of 1847, Sara had become accustomed and committed to her "unwomanly" activities. When John Taylor Coleridge criticized her introduction as "arrogant" and "immodest," she quickly retorted, "If I was justified in attempting to defend my Father's opinions at all, what could have been the use of perpetually interspersing modest *phrases,* which after all mean very little—for the arrogance—if such there be—counts in doing the thing at all—not in doing it, as I have done it, plainly and straight forwardly" (Letter [April? 1847]). Several months later, Sara explained herself again to Aubrey de Vere in a remarkable passage that bears quoting in full:

I had a very interesting talk last night with Mr. H[enry] T[aylor], who is looking remarkably well. He put in a strong light the unattractiveness of intellectual ladies to gentlemen, even those who are themselves on the intellectual side of the world—men of genius, men of learning and letters. I could have said, in reply, that while women are young, where there is a pretty face, it covers a multitude of sins, even intellectuality; where there is not that grand desideratum to young marrying men, a love of books does not make the matter much worse in one way, and does make it decidedly better in the other: that when youth is past, a certain number of persons are bound to us, in the midst of all our plainness and pedantry; these old friends and lovers cleave to us for something underneath *all that,* not only below the region of good looks, skin, lip, and eye, but even far deeper down than intellect, for our individual, moral, personal being, which shall endure when we shall be where all will see as angels ken: that as for the *world of gentlemen at large*—that world which a *young* lady desires, in an indefinite, infinite way, to charm and smite—we that are no longer young pass into a new, old-womanish, tough state of mind; to *please* them is not so much the aim as to set them to rights, lay down the law to them, convict them of their errors, pretenses, superficialities, etc., etc.; in short, tell them a *bit of our mind.* . . . . Intellectualism, if it be not wrong in itself, will not be abandoned by us to please the gentlemen. [*ML*(1874) 319][19]

Sara had indeed adopted "a new, old-womanish, tough state of mind," and no longer, it seemed, would she suffer male "errors, pretensions, superficialities, etc." in silence. Freed from the youthful illusions of the power of female beauty "to charm and smite," she enjoyed a new "intellectualism" that recognized the right of women to "lay down the law" rather than cringe before it. "Pleasing the gentlemen" with "modest phrases" ran counter to the "plainness and pedantry" of a forty-five-year-old widow who managed her own household, her own finances, and her own publications without assistance from or dependence on male expertise. Begun in filial duty, Sara's labors on the *Biographia* had fostered filial freedom.

Yet even at her most strident, Sara would never claim equality for women or support progressive, "Whiggish" reforms. She clung fiercely to inherited notions of "masculine" and "feminine" that gave men physical, intellectual, and psychological superiority over women—at least nominally. To Mary Stanger, for instance, she explained the advantages of "diffident, feminine, and submissive . . . habits":

> Young ladies who take upon them to oppose the usages of society, which, as I fully believe, are the safeguards of female honor and happiness, and supporters of their influence over the stronger and wiser sex, and have arisen gradually out of the growing wisdom of mankind, as they increase in civilization and cultivation, are generally found to possess, I think, more self-confidence than thorough good sense, intellect, and genius. Certainly all the women of first-rate genius that I know have been, and are, diffident, feminine, and submissive in habits and temper. For none can govern so well as those who know how to obey, or can teach so effectively as those who have been docile learners. [ML(1874) 375]

In the same way that for Sara the confinements of marriage had yielded to the freedoms of widowhood, so her own "first-rate genius" had arisen from an unquestioned faith in a "feminine" ideal. She accepted "the stronger and wiser sex" as a biological, philosophical, and cultural given; but she used female subservience only as far as it guaranteed an "influence" over her superiors. As she explains it, women should cultivate "diffident, feminine, and submissive . . . habits" in order to acquire "thorough good sense, intellect, and genius." Once educated, they are then free to assume their proper function: they "govern" and "teach."

Sara's concern with the strategies by which "women of first-rate genius" asserted themselves and influenced others is evident as well in a short essay on Wordsworth's poem "Laodamia." Written specifically for Aubrey de Vere in early 1847, Sara's essay—"Reasons for Not Placing 'Laodamia' in the First Rank of Wordsworthian Poetry"—is an informal diatribe against vulgar representations of women. Although she was genuinely fond of Wordsworth (the 1847 *Biographia* was dedicated to him by his "Child in heart and faithful Friend"), he was hardly exempt from her criticisms; in fact, her critique of "Laodamia" numbers among her harshest both in tone and argumentation. Attacked on personal, poetic, and philosophic grounds, Wordsworth is made into an insensitive egotist whose understanding of women was "deficient" at best.

Sara's ire could have resulted in part from Wordsworth's palpable suspicion of the merits of her editorial activity. Writing to Edward Quillinan on March 9, 1840, he complained, "I cannot altogether forgive dear Sara Coleridge being such a monopolist of your conversation in Dora's presence. It was to say the least indelicate; but bluestockingism is sadly at enmity with true refinement of mind" (*W Letters* 7:241). In early November 1846, he wrote Isabella Fenwick, "You have seen, I understand, not a little of Sara Coleridge. I rather tremble for the Notice she is engaged in giving of her Father's life. Her opportunities of knowing anything about him were too small for such an Employment, which would be very difficult to manage for any one, nor could her judgement be free from bias unfavourable to truth" (7:813). Several months later, he explained himself again: "Sara Coleridge is about to publish a new Edition of her Father's Literary Biography, which she asked permission to dedicate to me; which I could not refuse, though [the] Book contains many things not at all to my taste as far as I am individually concerned" (7:833). Considering the "enmity" Wordsworth perceived between "bluestockingism" and "true refinement of the mind," the lack of faith he had in Sara's "knowing anything" about her father or his works, and the reluctance he felt about associating his name with the new edition of the *Biographia*, it is entirely possible that Sara knew of his displeasure. Writing to Henry Crabb Robinson in 1849, for instance, Mary Wordsworth made no attempt at indirection: "I do wish poor dear indefatigable Sara would let her Father's character rest. Surely that great spirit has left sufficient to gratify the craving for literary fame in any one, without that dear Creature worrying her brain in her endeavours to increase, or justify it—which with all her pains she will never accomplish" (7:889). The smug superiority about Sara's unavoidable failure as editor and Coleridgean proselytizer speaks volumes about the status both of women writers and intellectuals in nineteenth-century Britain and of Coleridge's reputation at Rydal Mount during Wordsworth's later years.

Opening her essay with misleading humility, Sara admits "how inferiour are [her] powers . . . in the evolution and defence of critical doctrines and theories." She soon claims, however, an alternative strength: she possesses "feelings,—perceptions not yet awakened in [others]"—which may be more appropriate "material of judgment on this subject." Then, without unnecessary introduction, she sets forth her first point: "There is a great want of *feeling*, of *tenderness* and *delicacy*, of *truthfulness* in the representation of Laodamia herself." Laodamia's speeches are as "unrefined in tone" as they are "pompous and inflated in manner," a paradox exacerbated by the poet, who "makes a commentary on her feelings, which, if just, would render her utterly unworthy of that deep sympathy and compassion, which yet he claims as her due." "What wife who *deeply loved* a husband," Sara asks, "was ever subdued to those inferiour feelings? Even when they become excited, affection, which is so unspeakably deeper and stronger, would absorb and merge them."

As her question makes clear, Sara is insisting that a distinction be made between "inferiour" and "superiour" feelings, between vulgar "passion" on the one hand and genuine "affection" on the other. Wordsworth errs by portraying the former and neglecting the latter. He fails to see that "feelings" do not belong to "mere sense" alone but can become the vehicle for a higher, more spiritual desire. In the same way that Sara's own feelings provide her with both an emotional response and an interpretive standard—"material of judgment"—so should Laodamia's feelings be represented as partaking in a greater truth. Once a woman becomes "a devoted and deeply loving wife," Sara argues, all "inferiour" feelings are subsumed by a more spiritual "affection," and that affection is not passive and helpless but active, assertive, and influential.

According to Sara, Wordsworth's portrait of Laodamia was not drawn "from *very nature*," not "by the light of the sun in heaven, [n]or by the real moonlight, with all its purity and freshness," but by the "beams of a purple-tinted lamp in his study—a lamp gaudily coloured but dimmed with particles of smoke and fumes of the candle." The "coarseness in the leading conception of 'Laodamia' " results from an unnatural desire "to separate off the sensuous from our humanity, to draw so sharp a line between the outward and visible and the inward": "sense . . . thus severed and divorced from our higher being [becomes] . . . a low thing." Wordsworth was capable of such misrepresentation, Sara concludes, because he himself "was never *in love*, properly speaking":

> Mr. Wordsworth was never *in love*, properly speaking. I have heard him boast of it, in [the] presence of his wife, who smiled angelically, delighted that her husband should be so superior to common men. This superiority, however, entails a certain deficiency. He cannot sympathize with a certain class of feelings in consequence—he cannot realize them. He is always upon stilts when he enters these subjects. He stalks along with a portentous stride & then stamps his great wooden foot down, in the clumsiest manner imaginable. That sonnet among the Duddon ones, about crossing the brook, attempts to describe *loverish* feelings—but even that is forced and sexagenarian—The loves are brought in to clap their wings from a neighboring rock. At what shop did he buy those ready-made Cupids?

"More pompous than truly elevated," Wordsworth's poem exudes an anachronistic grandeur uninformed by spiritual or philosophic depth. It fails to make needed distinctions between levels of "feeling" and so misrepresents the "nature" of woman. The implied answer to Sara's closing question—"Are we in the humour for it?"—is an unequivocal no! For without a spiritual dimension, without the means of transcending the commonplace and the inferior, women are entrapped within an oppressive social system incapable of justifying itself. Once the spirit redeems the flesh, however, submission bespeaks a power whose authority is borrowed but no less real to those who exercise it. So considered, what might appear to be Victorian prudishness on Sara's part becomes a complex strategy for acquiring and maintaining a marginally effective literary, social, and political influence.

Given her recently acquired "tough state of mind" and the advent of a new series of financial difficulties, it was not surprising that in January 1848 Sara turned to writing reviews in order to supplement her income. A letter of inquiry to Henry's old friend and current editor of the *Quarterly Review,* John Gibson Lockhart, resulted in her being assigned Tennyson's latest work, *The Princess.* The task was an enjoyable one, for Sara was well acquainted with his poetry and with the ongoing critical debate over his "genius." She knew, for instance, that *The Princess* was intended to be that great long poem that would finally and decisively solidify the poet's reputation.[20] Unfortunately, as Sara soon realized, *The Princess* would prove incapable of solidifying anything; for although its handling of the "woman question" assured contemporary interest, its poetical "incongruities" were left unredeemed.[21]

Sara's essay begins with a lengthy debate as to when the "poetical faculty" reaches the height of its power. Taking issue with Henry Taylor's *Notes from Life,* she argues from the outset that this "faculty," that "peculiar character of the imagination, modified by individual temperament [and] distinct in idea from all other powers," reaches its zenith in youth or early middle age, not in later middle age as Taylor had maintained. Cataloguing an impressive number of examples, she makes her point only to drop the argument precisely when its obvious relevance to the debate over Tennyson's reputation would seem to demand a coup de grace. Stating only that "this inquiry into the relation between poetic products and the age of their producers not improperly introduces a brief notice of a new work," Sara proceeds immediately to the relationship between the schools of "Sensation" and "Reflection" before moving to *The Princess* itself. This subtle evasion of the unavoidable conclusion—that the poet had already achieved his best work—indirectly questions the probability of Tennyson's long-hoped-for maturation as it grants the possibility that the poet may yet live up to his reputation.

Sara's tactful hesitancy speaks of vested interests, for as one of Coleridge's literary heirs, Tennyson was still capable of doing his tradition a disservice. Believing that portions of her father's poetry occupied a crucial mediating position between the moral reflections of Wordsworth and the lush sensationalism of Shelley and Keats, Sara argues that Tennyson takes his place in a tradition begun by Coleridge but not necessarily endorsed by him. She praises the centered "moral thinking" that characterizes the poetry of Wordsworth and Coleridge, while deploring its loss in that of their successors:

> By comparing the "Skylark" of Shelley with Mr. Wordsworth's two poems on the same bird, <and Keats's "Ode to a Nightingale" with Coleridge's "Nightingale. A Conversation Poem,"> the reader will perceive the characteristic difference which we desire to point out; in the elder poems, though outward nature is presented and the senses are called in aid of the poet, yet moral thinking forms the centre of the piece; and in the latter,

vivid paintings, fine expression, and melody of verse are devoted to the illustration of natural feeling, which, though modified by its co-existence with the spiritual and rational, has its seat in a lower part of the soul.[22]

Thus, Sara praises Tennyson's beauties and recognizes his genius only to spend most of her review criticizing his excesses. One of the final charges she makes against both *The Princess* and its author is identical to that made previously against both "Laodamia" and Wordsworth: "absence of refinement and failure of dignity and decorum." By contrast, the most Coleridgean portions of the poem, the individual songs, are salvaged and used to argue a most arguable point—that Tennyson's talents are of the lyric rather than epic variety.

Sara's reactions to *The Princess* were not all negative, nor were her father's standards the only ones she applied. She responded favorably to Tennyson's denouement, agreeing completely with his solution to the "woman question." Like the poet, Sara was disturbed by the rise of radical feminism so much a part of the Owenist and Saint Simonian movements. Thus, Princess Ida's fall from antagonistic self-sufficiency to a loving and wiser subservience reinforced Sara's belief in women's spiritual and intellectual freedom, at the same time it left her faith in family, church, and state unassailed. As Tennyson's hero expresses it,

> The woman is not undevelopt man,
> But diverse: could we make her as the man,
> Sweet love were slain, whose dearest bond is this,
> Not like to like, but like in difference.
> Yet in the long years liker must they grow—
> The man be more of woman, she of man;
> He gain in sweetness and in moral height,
> Nor lose the wrestling thews that throw the world;
> She mental breadth, for fail in childward care:
> More as the double-natured Poet each—
> Till at the last she set herself to man,
> Like perfect music unto noble words.

"Woman," Sara reiterates, "is no duplicate of man, but the complement of his being . . . her sphere of action is not commensurate or parallel with his, but lies within it, sending its soft influence throughout his wider range." As she had maintained earlier in both her essay on "Laodamia" and her letters to Aubrey de Vere and John Taylor Coleridge, female submissiveness by no means necessitated female servitude. However different woman's "sphere of action," it was nevertheless capable of making "its soft influence" felt, a point proved by Sara's own act of authorship.[23]

In her concluding assessment, Sara finds *The Princess* a "disappointment," a "lively" but uneven work, unable in the end to overcome its "incongruous" design: "The second title of this lively performance points out its principal defect . . . it is a medley, and, we must think, a somewhat incongruous one. The fearless intermixture of modes and phrases of all ages, past and present, is a resource better fitted for a brief *jeu d'esprit* than for a work of this compass—but that is not the worst. The main web of the tale is a gossamer fabric, and can ill sustain the heavy embroidery raised upon it: the low key at which it is pitched indisposes the mind for the higher strains to which the piece changes." Sara here voices what has since become the major complaint against Tennyson's poem. As Christopher Ricks has reiterated, "The tone, the story, the outcome are at once earnest and flippant, and the crucial question—'What's to be done?'—is left where it was found."[24] But Sara made her judgments without an assuring overview of Tennyson's future accomplishments, without having read the extended elegy which in 1850 would secure the poet's reputation once and for all. And significantly, she read a poem substantially different from the one we now know. As was his way, Tennyson revised *The Princess* in response to his reviewer's objections, and chiefly—as John Jump has affirmed—"with a view to reducing incongruity."[25] Refusing to let the incongruities of the whole dampen the beauty of its parts, Sara chose to end her essay to citing two of Tennyson's finest lyrics: "Tears, idle tears" and "Come down, O maid." Such a gesture at once recognizes the poet's strength as it alludes to the heritage so important to both the poem and its reviewer.

When Sara's review appeared in March 1848, it was not as she had originally written it. John Gibson Lockhart, dictating editorial policy in the manner of the day, deleted many of the favorable references to Tennyson, often inserting acerbic comments of his own. Sara was particularly displeased with the phrase he used to describe Princess Ida—"Buckland in petticoats"—and she complained to her sister-in-law: "In the latter half of the review sundry lines and expressions were introduced, as 'Buckland in petticoats'—all tending to disrespect" (Letter: SC to Mrs. DC [Sept 1848]). Similarly, although with more consistency and rigor, he deleted every reference to Keats in the thirty-three-page manuscript, amounting to—as Sara later estimated—about a third of the whole. Lockhart explained, "As to the omissions of Keats & so forth. There is still extant the old reviewer of both Keats & the original Tennyson in the *QR*. He was very wroth with me for allowing John Sterling to praise Tennyson's 2nd publication and he will not like this dose of Tennyson—but he c[oul]d not swallow laudations of Keats at the same time. I believe he was also the old hand upon Shelley—if so, the worse will his digestion prove" (Letter: JGL to SC [Mar 1848]). Sara was disappointed but not surprised. Well aware of J. W. Croker's identity as that "extant reviewer," she recognized the literary politics at play and the futility of any protest on her part.[26] Moreover, she was already halfway through another review (of Alexander Dyce's and George Darley's new editions of Beaumont and Fletcher) and hardly wanted to jeopardize her ties to the *Quarterly*.

The Chartist uprising in April and Sara's subsequent escape to Eton disrupted but did not deter the completion of her essay on Beaumont and Fletcher. As submitted to the *Quarterly*, the manuscript ran to over ninety pages, and Lockhart was horrified: "I am very sorry to say," he wrote, "that the paper as presented will fill 99 pages of the QR. This will never do" (Letter: JGL to SC [22 July 1848]). When it appeared in September, Sara's review filled only twenty-three pages; it had been cut to less than a third of the original.[27] Nevertheless, it was a knowledgeable and detailed assessment of both the plays and their editors, and it earned her a much-needed £ 30.

Financial rewards notwithstanding, Sara had no intention of making a career in journalism. She disliked Lockhart's editorial policies and loathed the party politics of which he was a part. Several years earlier, for example, she had written to Hartley, "It is remarkable how strong the Quarterly is in dealing with *matter of fact*—various as the writers in it must be—they always shine in that department;—in abstract reasoning this review is not great; & in aesthetics it is generally poor enough. Its poetical criticism is sometimes below contempt—arbitrary, vague, without the slightest attempt at principle, and in a sneering contemptuous spirit. Its treatment of Keats & Tennyson was ultra-Zoilian" (Letter [20 Jan 1845]). "There is much attendant on reviewing that is not to my taste," she explained to her sister-in-law; "I can well understand my father's abjuration of the business" (Letter: SC to Mrs. DC [3 Dec 1848]). Thus, when in September Pickering suggested the possibility of publishing several new Coleridge volumes, Sara leapt at the opportunity and immediately began preparations for reissuing the *Confessions of an Inquiring Spirit* and the *Literary Remains*. The latter, however, Pickering had no intention of publishing as an expensive four-volume set, and so Sara decided to limit the new edition exclusively to her father's literary criticism. The result was a two-volume work she entitled *Notes upon Shakespeare*. Although she did include some new material, the projects were relatively uncomplicated, and by early 1849 both editions were available from booksellers.

But by early 1849 neither *Confessions of an Inquiring Spirit* nor *Notes upon Shakespeare* was uppermost in Sara's mind. On January 6, Hartley died suddenly at Nab Cottage, and Sara was greatly shaken. Just before learning of his death, Sara had described her apprehensions to Isabella Fenwick: "His illness has brought up strongly before my mind all my past early life in connection with my dear brother. I feel now more than I had done before how strong the tie is that binds me to him. Scarce any death would make me anticipate my own with such vividness as would his. Children and parents belong each to a different generation; but a brother, a few years older, who has never suffered from any malady—in him I should seem in some sort to die myself" (ML[1874] 369). Several weeks later she confided to John Taylor Coleridge, "This most unexpected death of my brother is a spiritual benefit to me. Nothing has ever so shaken my hold upon earth. Our long separation made me dwell the more earnestly on thoughts of a reunion with him, and the whole of my early life is so connected with him, he was in my girlhood so deep a source a pride and pleasure, and at the same time the cause of such keen anguish and searching anxiety, that his departure brings my own before me more vividly and with more of reality than any other death ever has done" (ML[1874] 372). Sara's introduction to her father's literary life had demonstrated how his otherworldly metaphysics could be used to redeem his personal flaws and to argue for his status as hero. Similarly, Sara's essays on Wordsworth and Tennyson had demonstrated how her otherworldly femininity could be used to redeem her own inescapable weakness—a sexually defined inferiority—by providing an "influence" that justified her role as literary commentator. In both cases, otherworldly ideals redefine historical circumstance so as to insure an individual power employed on behalf of collective betterment. Thus, Hartley's death, a tragedy that for Sara vividly evoked her own end and dramatically shook her "hold upon earth," did not signal the death of her intellectual "restlessness." Although it did in fact mark the beginning of a physical decline that would last three years and would end in death, Sara's shock in January 1849 and her increasing preoccupation with spiritual concerns only strengthened her earthly resolve.

CHAPTER SIX

"Putting in Order a Literary House"
Last Rites and First Memories

Much of it was not self-sacrifice, but self-realization. She found her father, in those blurred pages, as she had not found him in the flesh; and she found that he was herself. She did not copy him, she insisted; she was him. Often she continued his thoughts as if they had been her own. . . . Yet though she spent half her time in reflecting that vanished radiance, the other half was spent in the light of common day.

Virginia Woolf, "Sara Coleridge"

It is politic to tell our own story, for if we do not, it will surely be told for us, and always a degree more disadvantageously than the truth warrants.

Sara Coleridge, Letter to J. T. Coleridge

In the early weeks of 1849, Sara decided that she wanted Derwent to do for Hartley what she wished John Taylor Coleridge had done for her husband—a memoir. Only two days after learning of Hartley's death, she wrote Derwent to explain her sorrow at not being able to attend the funeral, and then added, "About his poems. They ought to be collected, and in better days—if not immediately—we may be able to have them printed and published too. . . . The fragment of Prometheus I always admired much" (Letter [10 Jan 1849]).[1] Urging her brother to remember their cousin's failed promises, she counseled prompt action, and within a week they were both collecting manuscripts and making preparations. If she organized and edited the poems, then Derwent would write the memoir. It was for Sara an effort as predictable as asking for a lock of Hartley's hair, an attempt to memorialize her brother, to do for him what he was unable to do for himself by editing a neat and orderly selection of a literary life gone inexplicably awry. Like all of her editorial projects, it was an attempt to put the Coleridgean house in order, to systematize the fragmentary remains of a decidedly immethodical family.

Not all of Sara's correspondents, however, thought her brother's memoir a worthy project. Neither the Wordsworths nor the John Taylor Coleridges, for example, felt that Hartley's accomplishments warranted the telling of his sad and often pathetic failures: habitual intemperance and chronic irresponsibility were hardly traits to be celebrated. Nevertheless, Sara persisted, maintaining that the merits of Hartley's writings would redeem his errant ways. As in the case of her father, human frailty was undeniable but ultimately unimportant. To her cousin, she explained,

> A sensitiveness about any exposure of private matters to the public . . . I can not *now* quite sympathize [with]. A good deal of thought upon the subject, through a good deal of experience, has brought me to think that a serious, anxious concern on such points is hardly worth while. If we could but overhear all that people say of us, . . . I believe it would cure a good deal of this anxiety, by showing us how vain it is to aim at keeping ourselves out of the reach of observation; that it is but an ostrich-like business of hiding one's head in the sand. . . . It is politic to tell our own story, for if we do not, it will surely be told for us, and always a degree more disadvantageously than truth warrants. The *desire* to be the object of public attention is weak, but excessive dread of it is but a form of vanity and over-self-contemplativeness. . . . If a strain of thought is beautiful and interesting in itself, I would not generally withdraw it from a collection of poems about to be published because it touches on private affairs. I remember the time when I felt otherwise; but now I can not help thinking that we should so order our lives, and also our feelings and expectations, that we may be as far as possible independent of the opinions and judgments of our fellow men; and that whatever is the truth on a subject of any sort of interest can very seldom in the long run be effectively or beneficially concealed. [ML (1874) 372–73][2]

Rejecting as an editorial criterion the honored Victorian distinction between public and private, Sara recognized the need to make herself "as far as possible independent of the opinions and judgment of [her] fellow men." The whims of public morality were to be discarded in favor of "truth[ful]" self-expression: "it is politic," she argues, "to tell our own story" rather than play the "ostrich . . . hiding one's head in the sand." To be properly "independent" thus necessitated not a retreat from the public arena but a mastery over it, a complete disclosure through which the private and the public selves conflated into a spiritually minded "order" neither desirous nor fearful of "public attention." Paradoxically, such a mastery could be achieved only by participation in that which was to be transcended—in other words, by publicly expressing private "truth," by "tell[ing] our own story."

Sara's "own story," however, was still very much a part of her father's, for unlike Hartley, who enjoyed all the benefits of male privilege, she had never been encouraged to compose, much less publish, expressly for her own personal and intellectual satisfaction. Rhetorical and logical skills had been sharpened in letters and informal essays and then tested in introductions and appendices affixed to and legitimized by her father's works. Such commentary always defended against a prior attack or clarified an earlier misunderstanding: authority was not assumed but borrowed, and never would she admit to writing publicly for her own pleasure or at her own instigation. Even her reviews in the *Quarterly* were written first and foremost for financial reasons—and of course published anonymously.

Regardless, then, of Sara's "new, old-womanish, tough state of mind," she still very much needed Coleridge's fragmentary remains as a *raison d'écrire,* as the occasion for and the justification of her authorship. This dependence upon a precedent authority, however, by no means involved only self-effacement; for if self-effacing when compared to standard male authorial practice, Sara's discursive strategies were also self-aggrandizing when considered in the context of strictures against female intellectuals. Sara had learned how to use her avowed subservience to male authority for her own purposes; she had transformed the public veneration of her father into a private redemption and so had in effect coauthored his "story" as he had her own. By 1849, however, coauthorship of that variety was less attractive than it once had seemed, and Sara was considering new ways to "tell [her] own story."

Thus, although busy with the first two volumes of Macaulay's *History of England* and exasperated by constant social engagements, Sara made plans during the spring for what she hoped would be the last project in her ongoing attempt to establish Coleridge as the premier Victorian "hero." Devised while vacationing at Margate (a May visit during which she read Carlyle's *Latter-Day Pamphlets* and mulled over the worsening plight of the Irish), Sara's proposed edition was to collect all of Coleridge's political writings, all of his long-forgotten contributions to the *Morning Post* and the *Courier,* and thereby demonstrate both his moral seriousness and his worldly altruism. Resuming her argument precisely where the introduction to the 1847 *Biographia* left off, Sara intended to reinforce the image of her father as a "practical" thinker committed to social betterment. To John Taylor Coleridge, she explained her motivations: "The deepest reason why I have been anxious to do it relates to my father's moral, not his intellectual reputation. I think it will show, first, that he *did labor* before he fell into paralyzing ill-health, and contributed far more to the *Morning Post* than any one would dream from [Daniel] Stuart's representation; and, secondly, I believe it will show his political course to have been characterized by honesty, strong feeling for his country, especially the poor, and a sagacity almost prophetic" (*ML*[1874] 389).[3] With the revolutions of 1848 fresh in her mind and Carlyle's moral exhortations still ringing in her ears, Sara knew that in order to complete the process of veneration begun in the *Biographia* and cure the "paralyz[ed]" metaphysician of his reputed indolence, she would have to prove Coleridge's "practicality" by publishing material that directly engaged the political scene. His writings for the *Morning Post* (1798–1803) and the *Courier* (1804–18) sufficed admirably by focusing on three topics still very much of interest to the mid-Victorians: the French Revolution and its aftermath; the Irish and their mismanagement; and the United States and its democratic "experiment."

Sara worked on the collection, which she entitled *Essays on His Own Times,* for a full year and a half, from June 1849 to October 1850. In terms of labor, it was, as she had described the *Biographia,* "a filial phenomenon," for besides having to wade through piles of old newspapers, she had to be extremely careful about questions of attribution.[4] Although Coleridge did keep a file of signed clippings, it was by no means complete, and many of his articles were anonymous. As a result, Sara's first task was to collect a complete run of the newspapers published during her father's tenure as journalist. She then had to scrutinize hundreds of essays to determine whether or not their content or style was characteristically Coleridgean. "I am grown a great adept," she wrote, "in discovering the ownership of styles. I fastened on a passage as being certainly my father's and shewed the article which contained it to be undoubtedly his. After, I found that the passage was quoted from another political piece of my father's. As clergymen preach their sermons over and over again, so my father sometimes reproduced his newspaper pieces of some years back" (Griggs 161).[5] It was, as she put it, a project of "painstaking and jog-trot drudgery":

> I am beleaguered with piles of the *Morning Post* of near fifty years since, and with *Couriers* above thirty years old. I hope to get away next week [to Herne Bay], but it will be difficult. This is the last editing work, I trust, in which I shall engage that will be very laborious and confining. The mere bodily exertion which it involves is not small; and if I were as *weak* in muscle as I am disordered and uneasy in nerves, I could not get on with my task at all, far less in the exact, complete sort of way in which it is my nature to execute whatever I undertake, as far as my abilities extend (for I am now speaking only of painstaking and jog-trot drudgery). [*ML*(1874) 388]

Sara's "complete sort of way" of fulfilling her "task" has earned the respect of modern scholars. David Erdman, the editor of the *Collected Works* edition of

Essays on His Own Times, recently confirmed Sara's "exact[ing]" standards: "Her recovery of many of [STC's] contributions, her examination of Stuart's 'pieces of bad construing, dictated by resentment,' and her extensive introductory interpretation and extrapolation of her father's political ideas all served to correct the record" (*EOT[CC]* 1:lxiii). As his introduction makes clear, Sara "correct[ed] the record" at precisely the time when Coleridge's political allegiances were in danger of being permanently misconstrued.

"Jog-trot drudgery" aside, Sara's "nerves" had indeed worsened since Hartley's death, and opium threatened once again to become more than an annoying "habit." To Edward Quillinan, she explained and justified her "dependence" upon the drug:

> Want of sleep induced the use of opium, and as is commonly the case, an increased quantity was required, as time went on, to produce the desired effect. I now am wholly sleepless on one night—that on which I take the heavy dose—but quiet, not turning restlessly from side to side. On the next night I sleep heavily, & wake very relaxed and comfortable. A small dose of morphine is necessary before this heavy sleep to prevent me from feeling quite powerless and good for nothing. Now I begin to be very anxious gradually to reduce the morphine—which is at present far too much. But in London—especially on the children's account, there is such constant call for exertion, that it is almost impossible to effect a change which must cause me not only great misery of feeling, but for a time, till the nerves have recovered their tone & natural spring, great incapacity and feelinglessness. You will think I ought to commence the reformation immediately, in spite of everything. But even if I were weaned of the habit & had regained a natural state, this would be far below my present state of strength and comfortable sensations.
>
> I should sleep every night but never sleep soundly; interrupted sleep every night would not sustain me as does the long trance of entire self-forgetfulness which I now have once in 48 hours. I wish to leave off the drug not from present inconvenience or suffering, but from anticipation of some evil effect in [the] future & possible injury to the brain. I do not think however that medical men in general, who talk on the subject, sufficiently consider the injury to the vital parts which must be produced by a continual deficiency of sleep, especially in a frame like mine. I ought to sleep seven hours at least every night, and that soundly. But not half that quantity of sleep will be my portion without morphine. I was saying to Edith last night that my medical attendant who now so regrets my use of morphine, himself brought me to it. By his advice I strove to do without it. I returned from the sea-side having been entirely abstinent for the last week but never sleeping well. He saw me, was alarmed at my appearance,

& himself urged my trying the morphine again. Fifteen drops he pre-
scribed. From that time until this (it was in the summer of 1843) I have
never been able to leave it off. [Letter DCL (1849?)]

Apprehension about some future "injury" notwithstanding, Sara speaks calmly
and forthrightly of a "habit" that she has succeeded in reducing to an unvarying
routine, a routine whose order and stability stressed her own self-control.
Blaming the male medical profession and a constitutional predisposition to
sleeplessness, she argues against the possibility of "reformation" and for a
sympathetic understanding of her situation. Her studied self-justifications sug-
gest, however, that her self-control was largely illusory. That her dependence on
opium began during the summer of 1843 was patently untrue; by 1843, her
habit was already more than a decade old.

Sara's enthusiasm for editorial labor remained high, and she eagerly antici-
pated writing a new essay on her father's politics. When cholera swept through
London that summer, she moved to the shore, taking her newspapers and her
books and hoping for a productive respite from the constant stream of visitors:
"I find it difficult to carry on literary business . . . (and a long task in that way
yet lies before me). . . . Oh! how I do abominate the afternoon calling, to pay or
to receive it! To go out *prepared* to meet our friends is pleasant enough, but in
the afternoon, when one is engaged, their coming is felt as an interruption.
Nothing is so fatiguing" (*ML*[1874] 384). "Literary business" "carr[ied] on," for
Herne Bay quickly solved the problem of frequent interruptions. It also pro-
vided extra time for reading and writing. But worse than unwanted visitors, Sara
discovered, was the latest volume of Clement Carlyon's *Early Years and Late
Reflections* (1836–58): "Of all the narrow-minded petty cavillers that ever took
pen in paw to write about our poor dear be-*pawed* father—that Carlyon is the
narrow-mindedest and pettiest. He has recorded a few things that one must be
obliged to him for—But I cannot turn over the leaves of his silly volume without
getting into a rage" (Letter: SC to Mrs. DC [22–23 Aug 1849)]). Sara's rages
were eased by long "constitutionals." Carefully balancing her mental and phys-
ical labors, she took frequent walks by the sea with her daughter, Edith. It
proved a productive routine, and when Sara returned to London in early
October, her project was well under way.

London, of course, was not always a distraction, and soon after her arrival
back at Chester Place, Sara was delighted to meet for the second time her
brother Derwent's old college friend Thomas Macaulay.[6] Although she did not
consider him equal to Carlyle, Sara respected his achievements and read his
works with some care. His latest publication, however, *The History of England,*
fell below her expectations:

Macaulay's History has had, and is still having, an immense run. It is
certainly a fascinating book; but in some respects, perhaps, too fascinating

and attractive to be thoroughly good as history. Dry matters are skipped, and many important events are rather commented on than narrated. And yet every true history that is to be a useful and faithful record must contain much that is dry and heavy to the common reader. His account of James II makes the profligate, unpatriotic despot Charles II appear like an angel of light; for what can be more hideous in the human character than implacable malice and revenge, deliberate barbarity, and love of human suffering and misery for its own sake? [ML[1874] 387]

Her criticisms notwithstanding, Sara was pleased to spend the evening with Macaulay and was surprised to discover how much he resembled her father:

I met Mr. Macaulay on Tuesday at a very pleasant party at Sir Robert Inglis's. He was a great force, and I saw the likeness (amid great unlikeness) to my father, as I never had seen it before. It is not in the features, which in my father were . . . more vague, but resides very much in the look and expression of the material of the face, the mobility, softness, and sensitiveness of all the flesh. . . . The eyes are quite unlike—even opposite in expression—my father's in-looking and visionary, Macaulay's out-looking and objective. His talk, too, though different as to sentiment and matter, was like a little, in manner, in its labyrinthine multiplicity and multitudinousness; and the tones, so flexible and *sinuous,* as it were, reminded me of the departed eloquence. [ML(1874) 412]

Macaulay's "labyrinthine" eloquence was particularly pleasing to Sara because of his topic: after dinner he declaimed at length on the difference between the "practical" and "literary" genius, precisely the distinction she was trying to redefine as it related to Coleridge—in her eyes a "practical" philosopher. Macaulay, however, was quick to elevate the literary mind over its more worldly counterpart, a hierarchical move Sara was reluctant to accept (Diary [14 Nov 1849]).

If Sara was less willing to criticize the "practical" than was Macaulay, that hesitancy was largely attributable to the influence of Aubrey de Vere. Although de Vere supported High Church theology and frequently disagreed with Sara on religious issues, he was also Irish and politically committed to alleviating the Irish misery. Ireland was, in 1849, recovering from the great potato famine of 1845–46, a famine that had decimated its economy and reduced its population by a quarter. The political controversies were still raging over England's management of the affair, for the opposition parties in both England and Ireland were justifiably irate that the richest government in the world had let its own people die rather than enforce economic sanctions against the exportation of meat and grain.[7] In addition to his book *English Misrule and Irish Misdeeds* (1848), de Vere had published numerous articles on "the Irish question" and had strongly influenced Sara's political opinions, a debt she would soon acknowledge in her introduction to *Essays on His Own Times*. She was particularly impressed with his "Nine Letters," a series of essays written for the *Morning Chronicle* during the spring of 1849, and with "Colonization," a lengthy article that appeared in the *Edinburgh Review* (91 [Jan 1850]: 1–62). No less important, he had been a kindred literary spirit with whom she could discuss contemporary poetry as well as theology and politics.[8]

Sara's relationship with de Vere, however, was not exclusively intellectual: since 1845 he had been a tireless correspondent, a frequent visitor, and a very close friend. Had her temperament been different, he might have also become her lover, to judge from one of her poems of the period. "Dream Love" explains her feelings:

> The union of thy heart and mine,
> Ah yes! I know 'tis all a dream:
> For I am dark, in life's decline—
> Round thee the noon-day splendours beam:
> But let this fair tho' flickering gleam
> Of fancied love one moment shine;
> Thou mayst afford at least to seem
> For one brief moment to be mine.
>
> Haste not at once to break the spell—
> Before thee is the long long day
> With gayer hearts than mine to dwell,
> In laughing meads far off to stray:
> One little hour beside me stay,
> And let the conscious dream go on;
> E'en now the tears are on their way
> To flood my cheeks when thou art gone.
>
> More brightness than is wholly thine
> Will vanish with thy last adieu,
> For whilst I dream that thou art mine
> It seems my youth is with me too;
> My glittering youth thy looks renew,
> That turn'd on me so brightly beam,
> As if from mine fresh light they drew—
> Of light and love is all my dream.
>
> Can dream-light to the soul be dear?
> Ah! who would weep 'mid light of day,
> To see the meteors disappear,

'The cold phosphoric fires decay'?
But when my dream-light fades away
What darkness will my soul invade?—
For sunshine or the moon's mild ray
One mass of cheerless, starless shade.

Fade phantom dream-light, full of strife,
Oh fade before that serious mien,
Which, kind and warm as day and life,
Is e'en as painless death serene.
The storm-clouds 'mid the radiance keen
Of Heav'n's deep vault how lost are they!—
So might I 'mid the azure sheen
Of that pure spirit melt away!

De Vere, twelve years Sara's junior, evoked in her not only a "dream love," an ostensibly Platonic affection at once decorous and lusty, but also a powerful longing for youth and beauty and the opportunity to relive her early adulthood. The "spell" she casts unites the lovers, vanquishes the unhappiness of the present, and fulfills the unfulfilled expectations of her "glittering youth." Elsewhere, she had confessed to de Vere, "You can scarce imagine the change from wife to widow, from being lovingly flattered from morn to night, to a sudden stillness of the voice of praise and approbation and admiration—a comparative dead silence it seems" (*ML*[1874] 402).

The "dead silence" of Sara's widowhood was experienced privately. It was an emotional emptiness that I suspect she rarely admitted to herself, much less to others, although it no doubt contributed to the intellectual "restlessness" that characterized the years immediately after the loss of her husband. As the poem to de Vere makes clear, her desires could be admitted only if immediately denied, displaced by improbability, spiritualism, and death. But Sara's poem is nevertheless a startling admission of affection from one normally so reticent about her feelings. As such, it becomes for her a new kind of self-expression, a verbal acknowledgement of the need to express her desires and dissatisfaction both to herself and others, a need "to tell [her] own story."

II

Sara wrote her introduction to *Essays on His Own Times* during the spring of 1850. Depressed by the deaths of Joanna Baillie in February and William Wordsworth in April, she declined in health and spirits but continued her work. Wordsworth's death, in particular, affected her greatly, but, like her other tragedies, it served to encourage editorial labor:

Still, though relieved and calmed, I feel stunned to think that my dear old friend is no more in this world. It seems as if the present life were passing away, and leaving me for a while behind. The event renews to me all my great irremediable losses. Henry, my mother, Fanny, Hartley, my Uncle and Aunt Southey, my father—in some respects so great a loss, yet in another way less felt than the rest, and more with me still. Indeed, he seems ever at my ear, in his books, for especially his marginalia—speaking not personally to me, and yet in a way so natural to my feelings, that *finds* me so fully, and awakens such a strong echo in my mind and heart, that I seem more intimate with him now than I ever was in my life. This sort of intercourse is the more to me because of the withdrawal of my nearest friends of youth, whom I had known in youth. Still, the heart often sinks, and craves for more immediate stuff of the heart. [*ML*(1874) 435]

Sara's "crav[ings] for more immediate stuff of the heart" found compensation in "intercourse" with her father's writings, with his intellectual spirit, yet it was a less than satisfactory exchange, one made desirable by default, by "the withdrawal of [her] nearest friends of youth." "I feel as if life were passing away from me," Sara admitted to Mrs. Jones; "so many friends of my childhood and youth removed. . . . It seems as if a barrier betwixt me and the grave were cast down" (*ML*[1874] 437).

Sara's spirits were lifted somewhat by the appearance in late summer of two poetic milestones—Wordsworth's *Prelude* and Tennyson's *In Memoriam*. Although Aubrey de Vere "perfectly raved" about *In Memoriam,* calling it "the finest vol[ume] of poetry since Shakespeare," Sara was more impressed by Wordsworth's long "tribute" to her father:

I do feel deeply thankful for the revelation of Wordsworth's *heart* in this poem. Whatever sterner feelings may have succeeded at times to this tenderness and these outpourings of love, it raises him greatly in my mind to find that he was able to give himself thus out to another, during one period of his life—not to absorb all my father's affectionate homage, and to respond no otherwise than by a gracious reception of it. There are many touches, too, of something like softness and modesty and humbleness, which, taken in conjunction with those virtues of his character which are allied to confidence and dignified self-assertion, add much to his character of amiability. To be humble, in *him* was a merit indeed; and this merit did not appear so evidently in his later life as in these earlier manifestations of his mind. [*ML*(1874) 455]

Sara was, of course, especially partial to the older poet because her father was "the friend" to whom *The Prelude* was addressed. "I know how many hearts," she wrote, "will be deeply touched with this tribute to my Father from the great philosophical Poet of the Age" (Letter: SC to EC [3–5 Aug 1850]). Like *The Prelude, In Memoriam* contained "great intensity of feeling," but instead of Wordsworth's "deep thought," she saw in Tennyson "nothing more than a succession of conceits and fancies." "Tennyson fancies his friend in heaven," Sara explained to her daughter, "and summons up all the images of heaven and the Celestial Paradise which he has ever read or dreamed of." "All this mystical symbolic imagery," she declared, is just "too quaint" (Letter [25–26 Aug 1850]).[9]

Sara's own "tribute" to her father appeared during the fall of 1850, and, like Wordsworth's *Prelude,* it documents a spiritual journey from "Love of Nature" to "Love of Man," a journey that attends more to "deep thought" than poetical "fancy." The three volumes of *Essays on His Own Times* were accompanied by a seventy-five-page introduction in which she describes and defends Coleridge as a "patriot and political philosopher." Calmer, less strident, and more self-assured, the essay marks a significant departure from the unrelenting thrust and parry that characterized her earlier tributes. Although Daniel Stuart becomes the straw man whose deluded views of Coleridge's journalistic career Sara sets out to correct,[10] she combines her rebuttal with an astute and persuasive analysis of her father's "steady coherence of thought" and with her own extended account of the contemporary Irish situation. For the first time since she began editing his "immethodical literary remains," Sara used an introduction to express opinions on matters seemingly unrelated to her father's life and work.

Sara's essay begins by stating her larger editorial intentions. The collection, she explains, "will both corroborate former defenses of [Coleridge's] political honesty and establish his claim to the praise of patriotism and zeal on behalf of his fellow countrymen, especially . . . the Poor" (*EOT*[1850] 1:ix). It will also serve "as a vindication of him from contemporary charges affecting his private life and conduct, as that of indolence and practical apathy." And, "it goes far to shew that some portions of his life, when he was supposed to be 'steeped in idleness,' were employed in promoting the good and the true, in sending abroad just views and wholesome sentiments" (xx). Most important, however, the collection will counter accusations of Coleridge's political inconsistency by demonstrating his philosophic rigor: "S. T. Coleridge of 1796–97," Sara argues, "differs from S. T. Coleridge of 1816–17 less in principles and sentiment than in their application. . . . The spirit of his teaching was ever the same amid all the variations and corrections of the letter" (xxiii).

The debate over Coleridge's changing political opinions, sparked by Hazlitt's vituperative critiques in the *Examiner,*[11] focused primarily on the French Revolution. In his youth, Coleridge had, like many of his contemporaries, fervently supported the French cause and just as fervently opposed the English war. By late 1802, however, just after Napoleon claimed the consulship for life and then invaded Switzerland, Coleridge reversed his position; he denounced the Peace of Amiens and advocated war. The question was simply whether Coleridge's reversal had been born of conviction or opportunism.

In order to demonstrate her father's "steady coherency of thought," Sara posits two "undeniable" premises: "First, that in him an understanding strong and perspicacious was united with a temper of spiritual susceptibility; secondly, that he was at all times singularly free, by position, from external bias, having the world of political judgment before him, where to choose, unimpeded by the fetters of favour or the burden of emolument" (xxii–xxiii). The conclusion follows logically: "It may be anticipated that he can have betrayed no other discrepancies in his literary political career than such as are sure to arise, when a man gradually frames his own system of belief, instead of receiving it ready-made on authority" (xxiii). As the Miltonic reference suggests, Coleridge the journalist, like Adam and Eve at the end of *Paradise Lost,* followed his solitary way through a postlapsarian "world of political judgment" at once corrupt and unavoidable, a world inferior to the paradise of abstruse metaphysics but no less necessary. "Unimpeded by the fetters of favour or the burden of emolument," he was free to choose a Godly path, for he too could claim Providence his guide; he too brought a sadder and wiser faith into a fallen world.

Sara also implies that Coleridge, like Milton himself, felt the need to criticize worldly pretense and justify the ways of God to man:

> The cast of my Father's opinions was ever of one kind—ever reflected his personal character and individuality. In 1796–97, he saw in a strong light the evils of a rich hierarchy and entered into Milton's mood on Prelacy: in 1816–17, he was supporting our Episcopal Church with a fervent *Esto perpetua;* but though, at the latter period, he was joined in no bond of sympathy either with Anti-Churchmen or with those Anti-Reformed-Churchmen. . . . he was far from having lost sight of all the ills which flow from prelatical grandeur and clerical domination. He was still preaching against Mammon, still opposing the rich and powerful as much as ever. [xxiv]

What changed, Sara argues, was not her father's principles but the political situation in France, a situation that he judged by the "character and conduct" of its leaders: "The character and conduct of Napoleon Buonaparte, indeed, as they were gradually developed, appear to have been the plant or bridge, where-on Mr. Coleridge and the *Morning Post* crossed over from warm interest in the cause of the French nation to decided Anti-Gallicanism, from earnest demands for peace to vigorous defence of renewed and continued war, with indignant antagonism to the unpatriotic to their measures and doctrines, to firm and serviceable, though unfettered support of Government" (xxviii–xxix).[12] A "great offender against God's law," Napoleon provided Coleridge with a standard by which to judge the changing French government, and under her father's influence, Sara maintains, "the *Morning Post* shewed as discerning a patriotism in opposing the earlier war with France as in advocating the later one" (xxxi).

To confirm her father's authority as divinely sanctioned and to extend it beyond that claimed either by Wordsworth or Milton, Sara concludes her opening discussion by arguing for Coleridge's "gift of political prophecy." "The sagacity of Coleridge," she writes, "is illustrated by the fact of his having distinctly foretold the restoration of the Bourbons" and by his insistence on "the internal stability of the English constitution, and the difference of its condition, in this respect, from that of the continental kingdoms" (xxxii). The latter prophecy was borne out by "the advantageous posture of our island . . . amid the recent revolutions of the European states." England alone, Coleridge had recognized, "was founded . . . on a rock of moral superiority," and according to his daughter, "Not to ascribe the peaceful state of England, in this epoch of change, and her exemption from injurious commotion, to the cause [of moral superiority] is to betray want of faith in a moral Governor of the World" (xxxiii). Speaking for reason, justice, morality, and patriotism, Coleridge is at once philosopher, judge, priest, and statesman—in sum, the hero as prophet.

Himself transfigured by his daughter's essay into a "moral Governor of the World," Coleridge the prophet suddenly disappears from the introduction. After a brief discussion of her father's views on Ireland, Sara begins her own lengthy discussion of the English/Irish situation, a discussion predicated upon allegiance to paternal authority but one without the slightest reference to Coleridge or his opinions. Thus, although her father is the reason for and the presumed subject of her introduction, Sara displaces him as commentator and writes an extended analysis of a contemporary political problem neither he nor his generation could remedy. Paradoxically, this moment of interpretive freedom is situated within and defined by a prior subservience: Sara's displacement of paternal authority is both its subversion and continuation; she speaks independently of her father only by assuming his voice as her own.

England, she argues from the outset, cannot adopt a convenient self-righteousness about its relations to Ireland. Although "the history of a powerful nation is a history of human wickedness" and "England and her governments have not been more selfish and cruel than other nations," the British "ought not to deny the criminality of a system which [they] dare no longer persist in." Tempted into complacency by the Catholic Emancipation and the general "munificence of the present age," it is too easy to forget how "truly murderous" was the English oppression. Yet, Sara argues, that oppression continues: "Those chimeras respecting Celtic original defect and faultiness tend to encourage a system of permissive cruelty . . . which . . . reminds one of the brilliant and accomplished Edmund . . . hasting out of sight of the barbarities about to be committed on the body of his miserable and defenceless parent" (lvii). To recognize the workings of this "system of permissive cruelty" was not for Sara to disavow "the superior virtue of these times and of Great Britain" but only to see "that far as we have advanced beyond other lands and ages so far do we lag behind the standard we ought to attain" (lvii). Sara's "standard" is that dictated by the Christian church, and in subscribing to it, she advocates governmental aid: "A provision for the destitute . . . can hardly be thought to diverge from the great High road of a wise and Christian Policy" (lviii). Thus politicized, Christian charity finds its opposition in the "Malthusian theories of the Poor Law," and Sara exhibits no restraint in agreeing with her former enemy William Hazlitt: "These [Malthusian] theories," she writes, ". . . teach that 'by the laws of God and Nature the Rich have a right to starve the Poor, whenever they, the Poor, cannot maintain themselves'" (lviii).

Christian duty, Sara maintains, translates easily into familial terms: "The State, beheld in the character of its Ideal Sovereign, stands in a parental relation to all its members, and owes them preservative care in return for childlike submission and compliance on their part" (lxi). Because "suffering is not the perfect gauge of faultiness" any more than "the sufferers and the authors of the misery are . . . always identical," government must mediate in order to see "justice" done. "Justice," she argues, "lies at the bottom of the claim made on the resources of the comparatively rich by the Poor Law," and, in keeping with her father's concept of clerisy, that justice can be administered only by those adept in "moral science." If the rich make laws only for the benefit of the rich, laws uninformed by moral vision, then "the Poor will avail themselves on every opportunity, of *their* native power, seated in the bones and muscles, to rise in rebellion against a partial government" (lxiv). Irresponsible parenting, she argues, fosters filial rebellion. Or, to put her final position more succinctly, "childlike submission" to a "moral Governor" guarantees "preservative care," and the result is familial harmony: Ireland and England become "one people."

As Sara's phrasing suggests, her analysis of the "Irish question" allegorizes the family drama in which she herself participates. In the same way that Irish submission to English rule would, according to Sara, relinquish a conflicted nationalism in favor of a harmonious union whose "justice" guarantees freedom as it abolishes autonomy; so her own filial submissiveness to the genius of her father has resulted in the expression of "just" opinions neither exclusively his nor entirely hers:

> In the foregoing sections I have noticed some salient points of my Father's opinions on politics,—indeed to do this was alone my original intent; but

once entered into the stream of such thought I was carried forward almost involuntarily by the current. I went on to imagine what my Father's view would be of subjects which are even now engaging public attention. It has so deeply interested myself thus to bring him down into the present hour,—to fancy him speaking in detail as he would speak were he now alive; and by long dwelling on all that remains of him, his poems of sentiment and of satire, his prose works, his letters of various sorts, his sayings and the reports and remarks of others about him, I have come to feel so unified with him in mind, that I cannot help anticipating a ready pardon for my bold attempt; nay even a sympathy in it from genial readers, and such, or none at all, I think to have for the present publication. [lxxxiv]

Contrary to her "original intent," Sara's "stream of . . . thought" carried her "almost involuntarily" into a discussion of contemporary politics seemingly unrelated to her "Father's opinions." But her thirty-page digression was less an independent foray into uncharted waters than it was an "imagin[ative]" continuation of an already established parental "current." Sara was "so deeply interested" in bringing Coleridge "down into the present hour" and "so unified with him in mind" that her discourse relinquishes its claim to individual authorship and becomes the outward and visible sign of a spiritual and intellectual union between father and daughter, past and present, male and female.

Thus, Sara's "own story," her analysis of contemporary politics, transforms the freedom of expression into the servitude of mimicry so as to transcend both. Like Ireland, which will discover true "justice" only by renouncing rebellion and embracing the "moral" governance of England, so Sara discovers the voice of truth by renouncing authorship and embracing parental authority. The resulting discourse belongs neither to Coleridge nor to his daughter yet somehow to both: it brings the voice of the dead philosopher "down into the present hour," redeeming his reputed indolence and demonstrating his political "sagacity"; it also gives voice to the muted opinions of a woman brought up to believe in the impropriety of female authorship. Coleridge is cured of his unjust reputation; his daughter is cured of her sex. Even so, Sara's presumption necessitates a polite apology: "Genial readers," she concludes, will readily pardon "my bold attempt."

III

When Sara's "bold attempt" appeared during the fall of 1850, she had been aware for almost a year of a tumor in her right breast. Assured repeatedly by her physician, Edward Newton, that there was no cause for alarm, that the tumor was inert and would not increase in size, she maintained her busy schedule and thought little about her condition. But during the fall of 1850, the tumor did grow larger and a new tumor appeared under her arm. Newton prescribed regular walks, Dr. Stuart's tonic pills, and opium mixed with cod liver oil. By the spring of 1851, all assurances to the contrary, the tumor had grown larger still and had begun to hurt. Although daily turns through Regent's Park, occasional concerts at St. Mark's, and the endless stream of visitors and engagements all helped to alleviate her anxiety, Sara had trouble sharing the bustling enthusiasm which seemed to grip London during the spring of the Great Exhibition.

Sara did, however, make the obligatory trip to the Crystal Palace in late May, needing a proper answer, she told Isabella Fenwick, to "the perpetual question, 'Have you seen the great wonder?'" (Letter [25 May 1851]). And she confessed to some excitement: "We staid *four hours,* and I came away far less fatigued than I have often felt after half an hour in the R[oyal] Academy Exhibition." But the Crystal Palace could not alleviate the night sweats, and although Sara enjoyed other diversions—engaging the novelist Anne Marsh in a lengthy discussion about female employment and going with Anna Jameson to hear Mrs. Butler (Fanny Kemble) read *Hamlet*—she was soon glad to escape London for Margate.[13]

At first, however, Margate only encouraged a careful monitoring of her illness. Without the pressing demands of galleys or the distracting social obligations of London, Sara was free to indulge her obsession with the vicissitudes of health. As was always the case when untrammeled by work, her daily ration of opium increased and chronic insomnia set in. For relief she turned to the scenery and to Walter Scott, rereading the novels of her youth and taking long walks with Edith. Although Scott seemed less the master she remembered, *Redgauntlet* and *Peveril,* with smatterings of Leibniz, helped to dissipate her depression. More therapeutic were the walks, twice daily, along the shore or in town to one of the libraries for yet another novel. But the novels soon grew wearisome. Her diary tersely records, "Reading Cabinet Minister by Mrs Gore. Insipid" (Diary [28 June 1851]).[14]

Stimulated perhaps by the scenery or perhaps by Derwent and Mary's tentative plans to visit the Lakes, Sara's thoughts returned to childhood years at Greta Hall. Writing to her sister-in-law she commented on her own inability to walk up and down on "fashionable" terraces and recalled Wordsworth's "contemptuous description of that kind of exercise—when Miss Hutchinson said to his sister, in her usual *my-way exulting* tone—'I never want to go beyond the terrace. Why need you ramble away so far with such a terrace to walk upon'" (Letter [21 June 1851]). Infirm or not, Sara had always been a great rambler, charging over the Grasmere trails with an energy that never failed to surprise new visitors. During her last weeks at Margate she rediscovered that energy and walked along the shore morning and evening in "restored spirits."

By the time the Derwent Coleridges left for the Lakes in mid-July, Sara was already back in London, and although she would have liked to have accompanied them, ill health kept her tethered to 10 Chester Place. Mary's letters provided a degree of compensation, however, and Sara toured vicariously, encouraging and confirming Mary's enthusiasm: "I know not," Sara wrote, "that any combination of earth, water, and sky, woods and fields, hills and pools and streams, could be substantially more beautiful than the vale of Keswick" (Letter [23 July 1851]). Even the "blooming Daturas" in the Botanical Gardens could not touch the beauty of her "native Greta" (Letter [29 July 1851]). As her longing for the Lakes grew more pronounced, she turned to other duties— monitoring the reception of Derwent's *The Poems of Hartley Coleridge,* keeping up with her American correspondents Henry Reed and Ellis Yarnall, and finishing her *almost* comprehensive rereading of Scott.[15]

Finding Sara's worsening condition some cause for alarm but full nonetheless of endless reassurances, Newton, who visited faithfully every fourth or fifth day throughout July, decided on the thirtieth that she should see Sir Benjamin Brodie. Brodie, then the sergeant-surgeon to the queen, had been consulted three times before. Although famous for his surgical skill, and for once having removed a tumor from the scalp of George IV, Brodie on all three occasions had been reluctant to advise an operation.[16] This visit was no exception: "Sir B B. finds the tumour still quiet (though advanced) he did not say it was but that is plain, and no surgical interference at present advisable as my general health is so little affected and there is no pain. He wishes me to [continue] the codliver oil, and do everything to keep up the constitution" (Diary [4 Aug 1851]). Although diary entries from the three previous months indicate that she was acutely aware of the ways in which her "general health" had been "affected," Sara chose to acquiesce to her physicians. Whereas she complained repeatedly of a "discomfort," "soreness," and "tension" in her breast, she rarely if ever used the word "pain"; for pain, evidently, was the one criterion designated to separate the benign from the cancerous. As a result, even though the tumor had already begun to drain, the official position remained "wait and see."

By the end of August even the ever-optimistic Mr. Newton had to reconsider his diagnosis. The patient was weaker, paler, and obviously in greater discomfort than before. Perhaps he noticed too that she seemed less inclined to accept his assurances. But because it was now too late to operate—the swellings were too large and too many—he could only stick resolutely to his original prognosis. Sara noted, "Woke in perspiration. Sent for Mr. Newton. He prescribes quinine, said my pulse & [temperature?] are not amiss. I asked him about removal of the lump. He said they feared in its present state to inoculate the constitution with it by interferring surgically. I cannot quite understand it. It is perhaps vain to say, I wish it had been removed before" (Diary [4 Aug 1851]). Tonic pills and cod liver oil proved a weak line of resistance against the worsening cancer, and with surgery no longer a possibility, doctor and patient found it difficult to keep up appearances. Sara confided to her diary, "He finds little change at present, but I know now more clearly how hopeless my state is—It may be a matter of years—it may be over in a few months" (Diary [26 Aug 1851]).

For the next three weeks Sara had little relief from her "hopeless" situation, and her depression manifested itself as two distinct but related conditions. On one hand, as letters and diary entries attest, she found solace in morbid reflections and resigned pieties; she would chronicle her life's misfortunes and would then profess, in the best tradition of evangelical fatalism, a calm acceptance of "God's will." In late August, for example, she recorded,

> I think much of dear Fanny [Patterson, Sara's sister-in-law]—How ready, even glad, she seemed to depart. . . . much of the feeling was strength & resignation, some part was an indifference to life from her state of sensation. With me disease is more local and confined at present. The cup of earthly pleasure has always been more or less embittered to my taste[,] my bodily weakness, nervous instability and an inefficiency of nervous force & firm elasticity. It was only at certain hours by some conjunction of favourable circumstances that I felt *quite* at ease & strong— released from the body. . . . I feel more as my beloved Henry did in the near prospect of death—but more subdued, I believe, and resigned than he felt. I am four years older, and have had more time to think—have lost far more dear friends—my parents, who, in different ways, were more to me than his to him, my *husband,* Hartley, my Uncle Southey[,] and the friend and Poet Oracle of my childhood & youth, Mr. Wordsworth— removed from this world in which, for my mind they played so great a part—Dora and now Mr. Quillinan[,] known to me for 28 years, sleeping in the Grasmere Churchyard—my dear friend, Lady Palgrave, confined to her couch & suffering severely from what is feared to be [a] cureless inward tumour—my excellent friend Miss Fenwick sinking yearly lower in bodily infirmity. All the sorrow & strangeness about young Derwent causing intense thought on the nature of the human mind & will—These things have disciplined my mind & feelings, and prepared me for the thought of a speedy departure. But keen is the regret at parting from my children. [Diary (28 Aug 1851)]

Faith in the blessings of the hereafter worked to rationalize and displace worldly sufferings, alleviating physical fear with the promise of spiritual reward. But, as the horrors of cancer increased and her doctors' assurances waned, Sara's faith assumed an understandably desperate edge: "When I see the sad state of the tumour I feel heart broken. But I sustain my poor heart & bind it up again by saying—It is only the body—*not the mind*—*not the mind*" (Diary [9 Sept 1851]).

One response, then, to Newton's admission of failure was a calm resignation buttressed by religious beliefs and emotional recollections of childhood. Sara's other response, however, was anything but calm. Like many of her female contemporaries, she suffered from hysteria—violent "fits" as uncontrollable as they were unpredictable. Whereas the first condition epitomized womanly health—a constitutional inclination to meekness and propriety, passivity and resignation—the second enacted the quintessential female disease—irrationality and unrestrained passion.

When Sara could not meet Henry Crabb Robinson on August 27 because of a hysterical fit, and when she threw similar fits repeatedly during the following week, she was acting within a prescribed pattern of behavior common to middle- and upper-class women of the nineteenth century; she was acting in accordance with a "cult of female invalidism" fostered by a social system rigidly patriarchal, defined "scientifically" by a self-interested medical profession, and reinforced time and again by a barrage of popular novels and advertisements (Ehrenreich and English 11–44). Her reaction was also consistent with her lifelong predisposition to infirmity, an ill health encouraged by family and friends and exacerbated by addiction to opium and by a ten-year period of uninterrupted pregnancy. For Sara, as for many of her contemporaries, hysteria represented the logical extreme of a cultural stereotype, a paradoxical state in which the warring facets of the ideal Victorian woman—the pure and the diseased, the angel and the demon—could be present simultaneously.

It is understandable, then, that the trauma of a slow and horrific death should find some relief in hysteria, and that the tension building for over a year should overwhelm the efficient, resolute, in-command Sara who had accomplished so much without swerving from the selfless ideals of Victorian womanhood. It is understandable too that Sara was unable to recognize the connection between her religiously informed stoicism and her raging hysterical fits. She could write dispassionately of the events of the summer, looking back to the idyllic days of June to acknowledge a naive and deluded confidence, but she could not confront the significance of the "hysterical agitation" which now beset her:

I saw while at Margate that the local complaint was changing, but I was sustained by the hope, amid much misgiving, that it would break and come to an end like the glandular swellings which one sees in children. This was a vain hope, though useful while it lasted. I am weakening daily from the drain, and for this there seems *no remedy*. The removal of the tumour surgically in my case is not desirable. . . . I have no shooting pains nor any cough—but appetite fails in spite of cod liver oil, which however seems of some use in keeping me up, and the nervous faintness which I have had today and yesterday is dreadful. . . . I am resigned inwardly and at the *bottom* of *my heart,* though full of hysterical agitation in my poor bodily frame. [Letter: SC to Mrs. Henry Jones (7 Sept 1851)]

She could, however, write more explicitly in her diary: "Oh! this dreadful faintness! If it increases what will become of me. Lady P[algrave &] Miss F[enwick], with all their weakness, do not seem this miserably spiritless. My heart & life seem dying within me" (Diary [8 Sept 1851]). Here, during the worst period of her "nervous hysterical faintness" and fully convinced of being in the midst of her "final decline," Sara searches for the very spiritual certainty she elsewhere so resolutely maintained (Letter: SC to Mrs. DC [3 Sept 1851]). For the second time in forty-nine years she wavered perilously close to a complete breakdown. The dauntless and indefatigable editor, the confident and self-righteous theologian, and the dutiful daughter, wife, and mother now seemed unfamiliar and uncomfortable guises suddenly in need of alteration, of reordering and refitting so as to make sense of a life never before requiring justification. No longer was she simply "Coleridge's daughter," and during her September crisis it suddenly became imperative to discover who in fact she was. It became necessary to unravel the various roles she had adopted and order them as neatly as she had her father's works. This time the "story" would have to be entirely her own.

Consequently, on the same Monday that daughter Edith was sent against her wishes to visit friends at Putney Park, Sara began a project never mentioned in letters or diary, a curious omission for one so fond of discussing projects. Writing specifically to Edith, in two marble-backed copybooks, she began her autobiography.

IV

When Sara was born on December 23, 1802, her father was absent from the family home at Greta Hall. Although letters from the period reveal that domestic relations between the poet and his wife were temporarily improved, Coleridge nevertheless decided to leave Greta Hall on the morning of November 4—with Mrs. Coleridge eight months pregnant—for what was originally intended to be a journey of France. Instead, Coleridge accompanied his friend and benefactor Thomas Wedgwood on a trip to Wales, not returning to Keswick until December 24, the day after Sara's birth. For the dispirited woman dying of breast cancer in 1851, such an absence seemed all too appropriate. Her autobiography begins,

> My Father has entered his marriage with my mother and the births of my three brothers with some particularity in a family Bible, given him, as he also notes, by Joseph Cottle on his marriage; the entry of my birth is in my dear Mother's hand-writing, and this seems like an omen of our life-long separation, for I was never with him for more than a few weeks at a time. He lived not much more, indeed, with his other children, but most of their infancy passed under his eye. Alas! more than any of them I inherited that uneasy health of his, which kept us apart. But I did not mean to begin with "alas!" so soon, or so early to advert to the great misfortune of both our lives—want of bodily vigour adequate to the ordinary demands of life even under favourable circumstances.[17]

Here, in one revealing paragraph, crowd many of the issues centrally important to Sara Coleridge's life and work. In 1851, as in 1802, the "family Bible" represented both the Book of the Father and the father's book, conveniently superimposing one privileged institution over another. Absent from it was not Sara's name, which had been dutifully transcribed by her mother soon after her birth, but the legitimizing "hand" of her father, which alone could give that name its proper status. While the names of her brothers—Hartley, Berkeley, and Derwent—were officially recorded with "some particularity,"[18] and thereby claimed by a sanctioned and sanctioning patriarchy, her name is symbolically orphaned, inscribed by an authority not genuine but borrowed. The tone of the passage is resigned, sorrowful, with just an edge of bitterness: "most of *their* infancy passed under his eye." Then, in the lamentations which close the paragraph, a reversal is engineered and a rationale put forth. The separation was caused not by indifference, as the inscription suggests, but by similarity. "More than any of them," she "inherited" her father's "great misfortune"—a "want of bodily vigour." Appearances to the contrary, unity is achieved through mutual infirmity, and the "Alas" which seems to echo with unrestrained grief assumes upon repetition a stoic pride.

The bonding that occurs between father and daughter in the closing sentences of the paragraph offers an interpretation that shields the ailing writer from potentially uncomfortable symbolism. The irregularity of inscription suggests, as Sara notes, "an omen" of a "life-long separation," but quite obviously it also proclaims her marginal status as woman. Endorsed by a female hand, she inherits not the world of her father but that of her mother, and—conversely—her estrangement from him is also her estrangement from a world of freedom and opportunity. That this estrangement should be linguistically mandated, a consequence of her "dear Mother's hand-writing," appropriately reveals the dilemma of the intellectual woman brought up to believe her writings were of no marketable value.

Ironically, Greta Hall during the first decades of the nineteenth century had been one of the most intellectually stimulating environments in all of England. But however stimulating, that environment was hardly enlightened—at least in its attitude toward women. As an 1815 letter from Wordsworth to Thomas Poole implies, the professional options open to Sara (at that time a girl of twelve) were as clear as they were constraining: "Sara has made great progress in Italian under her mother; and is learning French and Latin. She is also instructed in music by Miss Barker, a friend of Southey's, who is their neighbour; so that should it be *necessary* she will be well fitted to become a Governess in a nobleman's or a gentleman's family, in course of time; she is remarkably clever; and her musical Teacher says that her progress is truly astonishing. Her health unfortunately is but delicate" (*W Letters* 3:209–10). Having just finished discussing the career choices of Sara's brothers, both of whom were soon to attend the universities, Wordsworth makes clear that education for women was no more than a temporary luxury which—given a situation of economic necessity—could provide the fortuitous solution. The phrase "should it be *necessary*" translates readily into "should she not marry," for marriage was at that time a woman's most acceptable mode of employment. Faced with a failure to procure a husband and gifted with a modicum of intelligence, Sara could seek work as a governess, a substitute mother for a substitute family. In either case, her education, then progressing rapidly under Uncle Southey's tutelage, would contribute only to the raising of children and certainly not to the production of any kind of marketable writing.

Whether intended or not, then, the opening paragraph from the 1851 memoir asks that the "life-long separation" between father and daughter be seen in terms of, among other things, sexual difference. The absent father is both the eccentric poet comfortably installed at Highgate and the patriarchal endorsement never a possibility; he is both the author and the authority, both the biological father and the law. While the physical distance between them could easily have been overcome, the sexual difference was an unbreachable gulf enforced fervently by family, church, and state. So disenfranchised from the beginning, Sara might have measured the inequities within her own narrative, stopping to reflect upon the difference between the maternal and paternal inscriptions and perhaps seeing there an apt emblem for her own marginal career as woman of letters. Still more reflective, she might have considered the obvious irony—that the greater part of her public labors had been spent verifying, legitimizing, and defending the words of her father, which, from the outset (and regardless of the charges of plagiarism), maintained a greater credibility than her own. Yet such reflection was simply not a possibility, for her identity was forged by the very institutions which constrained her, and from her perspective those constraints were not her bondage but her liberation and her blessing. Thus it is not surprising that the "want of bodily vigour" which explains the "life-long separation" also becomes a valued legacy bonding father and daughter through shared adversity. Resignation is, after all, a Christian virtue, and Sara, like her father, depended heavily on a theology that accommodated and justified human frailty.

As the autobiography continues, the issue of health, both physical and psychological, emerges as a dominant theme and reveals substantially more than the author perhaps intended. One of Sara's first and most vivid memories of her childhood at Greta Hall concerns a traumatic accident which occurred in the spring of 1805:

> Something happened to me, when I was two years old, which was so striking as to leave an indelible trace on my memory. I fancy I can even now recall, though it *may* be but the echo or reflection of past remembrances, my coming dripping up the Forge Field, after having fallen into the river between the rails of the high wooden bridge that crossed the Greta, which flowed behind Greta Hall Hill. The maid had my baby cousin Edith, 16 months younger than I, in her arms; I was rushing away from Derwent, who was fond of playing the elder brother, on the strength of his two years' seniority, when he was trying in some way to control me, and, in my hurry, slipped from the bridge into the current. Luckily for me, young Richardson was still at work in his father's forge. He doffed his coat and rescued me from the water. I had fallen from a considerable height, but the strong current of the Greta received me safely.

With Coleridge off at Malta characteristically negligent about his correspondence, the two households—the Wordsworths at Dove Cottage and the Coleridges and Southeys at Greta Hall—had drawn closer together, both eager to share the latest news from Coleridge and the most recent events in the lives of their children. Understandably, Sara's accident was much discussed. Dorothy Wordsworth, commenting to Lady Beaumont, observed, "It is almost miraculous that she was not dashed to pieces," for the bridge was "very high above the Stream, and the water was low" (*W Letters* 1:599). But the "almost miraculous" escape was not completely without repercussions. While Wordsworth's sister simply noted that "little Darling Sara" has "never been *perfectly* well since," some forty-five years later the victim herself provided a more detailed account: "I was put between blankets on my return to the house; but my constitution had received a shock, and I became tender and delicate, having before been a thriving child, & called by my Uncle 'fat Sall.' As an infant I had been nervous

& insomnolent. My mother has often told me how seldom I would sleep in the cradle—how I required to be in her arms before I could settle into sound sleep. This weakness has accompanied me through life." Seeking to escape from a brother's domineering "strength" and "control," Sara fell from the bridge into a lifelong "weakness" that combined constitutional "delicacy" with an already "nervous" temperament. The resulting condition was both physical and psychological, a state of mind as well as a predisposition of the body. Furthermore, this condition provided the struggling autobiographer with the crucial link to the absent authority she so desperately sought, an authority capable of justifying selfless duty and explaining away suspicions of wasted talent. Thus, to focus on the issue of health in the autobiography is to trace the emergence of a self-understanding defined within a recoverable pattern of familial relationships, a complex network of tensions among three unusual families.

After anecdotes of young Derwent and Hartley, an account of Aunts Martha and Elizabeth Fricker, and an extended description of Greta Hall, Sara turns to a November 1809 visit to Allan Bank, where the Wordsworths had settled in May 1808. Her candid discussion of the experience interweaves adult anxieties and childhood fears, attempting to ease recurrent doubts but succeeding only in raising further questions. The narrative follows the sequence of memory and opens with a recollection of the young Dora: "Allan Bank is large house on a hill overlooking Easedale on one side and Grasmere Lake on the other. Dorothy, Mr. Wordsworth's only daughter, was at this time very picturesque in her appearance with her long thick yellow locks, which were never cut, but curled with papers, a thing which seems much out of keeping with the poetic simplicity of the household. I remember being asked by my Father and Miss Wordsworth, the Poet's sister, if I did not think her very pretty. No, said I, bluntly; for which I [met a] rebuff which made me feel as if I was a culprit." The paragraph ends here without comment upon the obvious tension between father and daughter over the standards of girlish beauty, or upon the guilt precipitated by a harsh response to an honest, if rude, answer. Instead, a new paragraph begins redefining the problem in slightly different terms: "My Father's wish it was to have me for a month with him at Grasmere, where he was domesticated with the Wordsworths. He insisted on it that I became rosier and hardier during my absence from Mamma. She did not much like to part with me, and I think my Father's motive at bottom must have been a wish to fasten my affections on him." No longer a matter simply of competing with Dora or being unfairly rebuked for an honest opinion, Sara here recognizes her position as one caught between warring parents. Indeed, Coleridge's precipitant marriage, an unfortunate consequence of his ill-fated Pantisocracy scheme, had begun to crumble well before Sara's birth, and she could hardly have been immune to the repeated flare-ups of ill will or unaffected by Coleridge's almost constant absence from his supposed home at Greta Hall. Here, her parents' ostensible concern is for her health; and by extension that concern becomes part of a larger debate over the proper mode of raising a young girl. Coleridge sides with the Wordsworths, his wife with the Southeys.

The differences between Greta Hall and Allan Bank were, of course, part of and greatly complicated by the marital turbulence of the Coleridges. Mrs. Coleridge's plainspoken concern for the welfare of her family irritated the eccentric poet then trying desperately to save his latest venture, *The Friend,* from impending disaster. Also a problem was Coleridge's continued infatuation with Sara Hutchinson, his present amanuensis and Wordsworth's sister-in-law.[19] As his daughter's account of the 1809 visit demonstrates, Sara had good reason to perceive herself as an unintended victim:

> I have no doubt there was much enjoyment in my young life at that time but some of my recollections are tinged with pain. I think my dear Father was anxious that I should learn to love him and the Wordsworths & their children, and not cling so exclusively to my mother and all around me at home. He was therefore much annoyed when on my mother's coming to Allan Bank I flew to her, and wished not to be separated from her any more. I remember his showing displeasure with me, and accusing me of want of affection. I could not understand why. The young Wordsworths came in and caressed him. I sate benumbed; for truly nothing does so freeze affection as the breath of Jealousy. The sense that you have done very wrong, or at least given great offence, you know not how or why—that you are dunned for some payment of love and feeling which you know not how to produce or to demonstrate on a sudden—chills the heart & fills it with perplexity and bitterness. My Father reproached me & contrasted my coldness with the childish caresses of the little Wordsworths—who felt but lightly, and easily adopted any ways of affection that were required with lively but not deep feeling. I slunk away & hid myself in the wood behind the house.

By accusing his daughter of "want of affection," the displeased Coleridge effectively paralyzed her ability to express emotion and forced her loyalties into an either/or stalemate. Of equal importance, his reproaches expand the issue of health into its psychological dimension by insisting on a "natural" demonstrativeness that ran contrary to his daughter's inclinations and again pitted Allan Bank against Greta Hall, husband against wife, and Sara against the young Wordsworths. Caught in the middle, the victim faced a choice not only between parents but also between differing ideals of woman-as-young-girl, between alternate versions of "daughter." The arguments about health were thus subsumed by a larger question of what it meant to be a woman; and, as a mere child, Sara's only answer was mute confusion.

The reminiscing writer, however, had more freedom in 1851 than she did in 1809. Perhaps expecting that poor health and opium would prevent the completion of her autobiography as they had conspired to destroy many of her other projects,[20] Sara openly criticizes the Wordsworths' "rough & rustic . . . management of children" and confesses to having "suffered a [great] deal of 'miserality' at Grasmere." Ostensible gestures of intimacy—"Our dear friends, the Wordsworths"—are undercut with details of "the untidy tenancy . . . the horrid smoke . . . the dirt, the irregular Scotchy ways, . . . [and] the children, who were chid & chuffed freely enough, yet far from kept in good order." She also complicates the perspective on her role as contested child by suggesting that she was caught not only in an either/or stalemate between husband and wife but also in a three-way struggle among Coleridge's, Southey's, and Wordsworth's differing ideas of femininity, ideas which informed their taste in female apparel. Coleridge, for example, disliked brightly colored clothes or that which aspired to finery, preferring simple white frocks: "He much liked everything feminine and domestic, pretty and becoming, but *not* fine ladyish." Southey, on the other hand, "was all for gay bright cheerful colours, & even declared he had a taste for the *grand*." Wordsworth, meanwhile, "loved all that was rich and picturesque, light & free in clothing. A deep Prussian blue or purple was one of his favourite colours." As opposed to Coleridge, "he wished that white dresses were banished. . . . White dresses he thought cold—a blot and disharmony in any picture in door or out door."

Regardless of Southey's or Wordsworth's opinions, Sara clearly accepted Coleridge's preferences; she writes, "My Father admired white clothing, because he looked at [it] in reference to woman as expressive of her delicacy & purity, not merely as a component part of a general picture." Of the three, then, Coleridge alone employed a taste bolstered by philosophic certainties. Not simply a personal predilection or an aesthetic judgment, his favoring of simple, white attire was meant to reinforce an ideal of womanhood, an irrepressible spiritual "purity" part of but greater than its physical manifestation. Thus, for Sara, accepting her father's preferences became synonymous with making a philosophical choice about the nature of woman.

As Sara emphasizes, she and Wordsworth's daughter Dora must have made a "curious contrast." Dora, "with her wild eyes, impetuous movements, and fine long floating yellow hair," was a fitting exemplum of her father's tastes and of the "natural wildness" that Dorothy found sadly wanting in Coleridge's daughter.[21] Sara, with "timid large blue eyes[,] slender form[,] & little fair delicate face muffled up in lace border & muslin," was Coleridge's "purity" incarnate, a fragile innocence that embraced worldly weakness on its way to a more powerful spirituality. The complementarity, Sara suggests, was striking. Coleridge himself remarked, "Little Dorothy and Sara make a most amusing Contrast—S. so lady-fairy-like, & Dorothy sic a wild one; but so pretty, especially when she is naughty" (*CL* 3:122). Dora embodies an unrestrained physicality, a "natural" freedom of movement which liberates the child from social decorum but which also encourages—as the autobiography repeatedly implies—a descent into slovenliness and unrefinement. Sara, on the other hand, renounces the body and indulges its weakness in order to partake of a higher essence. Whereas the one finds earthly health at the expense of the spiritual, the other finds spiritual health at the expense of the earthly.

It is important to remember that Sara's account is retrospective and necessarily strategic. Earlier descriptions of Coleridge's displeasure with his daughter's lack of demonstrativeness, occurrences which obviously continued to cause her unease, are, in the course of the autobiography, subsumed and explained by repeated references to her weak health. The infirmities which separated father and daughter geographically—he at Highgate, she at Greta Hall—also served, she suggests, to separate them emotionally, encouraging passive solitude and prohibiting genuine communication. But even that separation could be overcome by an interpretive act which used hindsight to transform the cause of estrangement into its cure. Only in retrospect could Sara recognize (and deploy) mutual weakness as a means in service of a greater end. Since her father's death in 1834, she had learned that the same obsessive accounts of fluctuating bowels and torturing drug dependence that filled her diaries were also to be found throughout his notebooks and letters. She also came to see that they shared a mental and emotional predisposition to infirmity far more binding than mere bodily aches and pains. Thus, at the close of the opening section of the autobiography, she ponders her objectives and questions the relationship between her "childish experience" and her "maturer self": "Such are the chief *historical* events of my little life, up to nine years of age. But can I in any degree trace what being I was then—what relation my then being held to my maturer self? Can I draw any useful reflection from my childish experience, or found any useful maxim upon it?" She then immediately returns—as if in answer—to her health, to Grasmere, and to her father:

I remember well that nervous sensitiveness and morbid imaginativeness had set in with me very early. During my Grasmere visit I used to feel frightened at night, on account of the darkness. I then was a stranger to the whole host of night-agitators. . . . And yet I was terrified in the dark, and used to think of lions. . . . My next bugbear was the Ghost in Hamlet. Then the picture of Death at Hellgate in an old edition of Par[adise]

Lost . . . last & worst came my Uncle Southey's ballad horrors, above all the Old Woman of Berkeley. Oh the agonies I have endured between nine & twelve at night. . . . I dare not, even now, rehearse these particulars for fear of calling up some of the old feeling, which indeed I have never in my life been quite free from. What made the matter worse was that . . . it could not be understood by the inexperienced. . . . My Uncle S[outhey] laughed. . . . Even mama scolded me. . . . But my Father understood the case better. He insisted that a lighted candle should be left in my room. . . . From that time forth my sufferings ceased. I believe they would have destroyed my health had they continued.

Here, the bodily—"nervous sensitiveness"—and the psychological—"morbid imaginativeness"—are traced back to the conflated in "the old feeling," a primordial fear which appeared to the young Sara in various guises, as "the Ghost in Hamlet," "the picture of Death" from *Paradise Lost,* and most forcefully as Southey's "Old Woman of Berkeley."[22] This (dis)ease, the Ur-infirmity at the root of all others, was understood by no one except her father, and it is through this uncommon bond that we are to perceive and evaluate their relationship. "The old feeling" was not a single experience or even a predisposition of character but rather a psycho-philosophical given seen by Sara as a religious first-principle, a sensitivity to be sure, but a sensitivity to the unchanging spiritual condition of man—call it original sin, natural depravity, or congenital Coleridgean guilt. Ill health, thus linked to "the old feeling," becomes the sign of spiritual strength, insight, and piety—a tacit acknowledgment both of worldly imperfection and otherworldly aspiration.

The "Alas" with which the autobiography began echoes here to bring the narrative around full circle, as the "lighted candle" that Coleridge leaves his daughter illuminates both child and adult. For the six-year-old girl, the taper dispels night fears and calms her immediate anxieties; for the forty-eight-year-old woman, it enlightens a lifetime of frustrations, explaining away parental neglect, male/female inequities, and, above all, the nagging feeling that natural talent had been wasted in the service of others. For one, the light is a physical comfort, for the other a spiritual justification. In both cases, paternal intervention rectifies and redeems a filial lack.

But if her father's religious philosophy provided a convenient interpretive frame within which to order and evaluate life's misfortunes, it fails to hide both the girl's anxiety at being caught between warring parents and her confusion at confronting three separate ideals of female beauty. Nor can it explain the woman's desperate need to remain the dutiful daughter, a daughter determined to pave over the jarring memories of her youth with a smoothing retrospective vision that subsumes all dissatisfactions into an Ur-infirmity ultimately redeemed by faith. Thus, to measure the distance between the experience and the interpretation, between the little girl and the dying woman, is to trace the process of an education and the events of a lifetime. It is also to recognize two important points about the autobiography: first, that the success of Sara's narrative strategy is contingent upon the degree to which she can reconcile childhood unhappiness to adult resignation; and second, that that reconciliation is less between the child and the adult than it is between their very different images of Coleridge the father. For the child, he is a palpable presence, a source of emotional pain and confusion, an authority quite real but not yet understood. For the adult, he is the disembodied law, the source of emotional, intellectual, and spiritual salvation, the authority no longer of flesh and blood but that of patriarchal idealism, the Father as manifested by Family, Church, and State. Thus, the tension between the girl's "father" and the woman's "Father" is nothing less than a tension between the anguish of doubt and the security of faith. Sara's autobiography, like her life itself, was an attempt to reconcile the experience of the one to the vision of the other.

But the autobiography was never completed. It ends abruptly after only the first of what was intended to be eight separate sections. Each section, as Sara confided to Edith, was to conclude with an appropriate "Moral or Reflection, . . . some maxim which [that section] specifically illustrated, or truth which it exemplified, or warning which it suggested." The autobiographical fragment, however, breaks off in midsentence: "On reviewing my earlier childhood I find the predominant reflection. . . ." There she stops, interrupted perhaps by her own "person . . . from Porlock" sent to dispel the creative vision or, more likely, by the disturbing realization that her "predominant reflection" was anything but predominant, that the little girl and the dying woman could no more be reconciled by "Moral or Reflection" than the unpleasant memories of a negligent parent could be erased by a lifetime of reverence and filial duty.

Sara had worked for seventeen years to cure the Coleridgean corpus of its various ills, to establish her father as a Victorian sage worthy of respect and veneration, and to justify to herself her own allegiance to paternal authority. The autobiography suggests that she was not entirely successful, that the "life-long separation" prophesied by her mother's inscription continued well after Coleridge's death, and that regardless of her assurances to the contrary, regardless of her introductions and appendices and avowed "intercourse" with the mind of her father, Sara's "own story" could not reconcile the life she had led to the ideals she had championed. Several years before writing her autobiography, she had confided to her diary, "It is something to myself to feel that I am putting in order a literary house that otherwise would be open to censure. . . . But when there is not mere carelessness but a positive coldness in regard to what

I have done, I do sometimes feel as if I had been wasting myself a good deal—at least as far as worldly advantage is concerned" (Diary [28 Oct 1848]).

V

Public "coldness" notwithstanding, Sara discovered that her literary house-keeping had become increasingly important to her general well-being. In fact, the autobiography was relinquished not for the obsessive monitoring of a now indisputably fatal illness, but instead for one last attempt to "put the Esteesian House in order" (Letter: SC to DC [28 Sept 1851]). Unconvinced of Derwent's ability to manage the estate, Sara devoted the remaining eight months of her life to three related "chores." First, she wanted to change publishers, specifically to shift the center of operations from William Pickering's establishment to that of Edward Moxon. Henry Nelson Coleridge's deathbed negotiations had been unable to wrest rights away from Pickering, and Sara, now on her own death-bed, wanted very much to succeed where her husband had failed. Edward Moxon, while not an exacting craftsman, was an extremely able businessman, and both Sara and Derwent believed that their father's literary reputation rested upon his continued success in the marketplace. The second chore was to relieve Joseph Henry Green of all legal involvement in the estate. Since Henry's death in 1843, Green had been excluded almost completely from the decision-making process, and Sara wanted to ensure that control of the estate remained in family hands after her death. The third chore, both the most arduous and the most enjoyable, consisted of editing a new edition of Coleridge's poems and arranging the publishing schedule for the next decade.

Negotiations with Pickering and Green were concluded by late December, by which time Sara had been working on her new edition for some two months. Maintaining on one hand that she was too sick for such work and on the other that Moxon himself was not working fast enough to keep up with her, Sara ostensibly divided her "literary exertions" with Derwent, who, according to Sara's plan, would take over the literary estate upon her death (*ML*[1874] 528). Collaboration with Derwent, however, was not without its difficulties, and brother and sister squabbled routinely over matters great and small. Often Sara would capitulate: "I must say I *regret very much* your new arrangement [of STC's poems]. But one or other must yield—therefore have your way. We shall never settle it if we settle and unsettle so often" (Letter: SC to DC [Jan 1852?]). The "new arrangement" was to be chronological, and originally it had been Sara's idea. Derwent, however, persisted in arranging by subject matter and was reluctant to tamper with the *Sibylline Leaves:* "I cannot enter into your scruple about disturbing . . . the 'Sib. Leaves" of 1828," Sara retorted, "because that is so obviously to me—*not designed by STC on any principle*—any internal principle—but dictated by the 3 vol. form" (Letter [24 Jan 1852]). "Students of poetry," she continued, "are beginning more and more to approve the ordering of poems according to date of publication. Now many lovers of Wordsworth are longing for a regular chronological arrangement of his poems."

Sara's capitulations were in part strategic, and she never lost a major debate. She wanted, for example, to omit "Two Round Spaces" from the new collection on the grounds that its attack on Sir James Mackintosh did not show Coleridge in a flattering light. Such an omission, she argued, was based upon "high moral principle" not upon "Drawing Room and School Room popularity" (Letter: SC to DC [17 Jan 1852]). As she well knew, censorship would set a dangerous precedent, and she wanted Derwent to be clear about her rationale. "Coleridge's Poems," she maintained, were not and would never be "a book for the School Room." Nor could his poetry "be just the *very proper* article which is fit for *every* drawing room. . . . [And] I think it can never be *entirely* fit . . . as Southey, Wordsworth, Scott, Rogers. . . . This Coleridge poetry is so *sensuous* and *impassioned* . . . [that] I have never put it into the hands of Edith. Wordsworth and Southey are read aloud to me—not so with Coleridge. I could not well have pored over STC's P. Works with A. de Vere as I did with WW's" (Letter: SC to DC [18 Jan 1852]). Unwilling to censor the "*sensuous* and *impassioned*," Sara nevertheless reveals a pronounced reluctance to share it. Her father's more emotional writings could be enjoyed only in private, in the sanctity of a quiet room where the communication between father and daughter would never be sullied by the routine distractions that had effectively separated them during his lifetime. Reading her father's poetry had perhaps become, like editing, a collaborative experience: "I think myself," she told Derwent, "partially Editor of every work of my Father and this is as it should be" (Letter [7 Apr 1852?]).

As Sara's illness worsened, editorial labors became more and more attractive, welcome relief from the daily suffering. "When D[erwent] comes, I see him *if I can*," she wrote John Taylor Coleridge, for "he plunges at once into Moxon-Pickering-Hartley-STC-ism and such topics which do me good by taking my mind off my uncomfortable *self*" (Letter [19 Nov 1851]). This strategy for evading the "uncomfortable" present was nothing new; in fact, it nicely illustrates a lifelong tendency, an ability to use literary labors as an escape from the distressing realities of daily life. "I am thankful," she confessed several years before, that "I am one of the abstractors and generalizers myself and am rather weary at times of . . . perpetual concretes" (Letter: SC to Mrs. Richard Townsend [nd]). Editing her father's poems was not equivalent to "telling [her] own story," but it was far more attractive than confronting her "uncomfortable self" either in the pages of her own autobiography or in the "perpetual concretes" of a worsening illness.

Thus, it should have come as no surprise to Derwent to learn that the preface to the forthcoming volume, the preface that he had composed at Sara's insistence, was not quite up to snuff. "It is a bonny skeleton," Sara admitted, "but it seemeth to me that the flesh and some of the muscle require a little re-edification" (Letter: SC to DC [23 Jan 1852]). As her "seemeth" implies, Sara was both put off and amused by Derwent's prose: "It strikes me that there is a slight air of—what shall I say—conventionalism—commonplace stiffness—bordering on the vulgar in that expression, '*the responsibility of the Editors is limited* to the exclusion etc.' In editing works of genius a sort of blunt simplicity appears to be the appropriate style. . . . I can see neither policy nor dignity in being so very timid and obsequious before the Public, which never will require aught of the kind, if you don't put it into its noddle." "Style," she reiterated in another letter, "is a nice evanescent sort of thing—a *whole Preface* by your pen would have a different sort of air from mine—a *satin* web, while mine would be plain *Gros de Naples*" (Letter: SC to DC [Jan 1852?]). Although Derwent agreed to make select changes, Sara had something different in mind: "if the Preface is wholly written by you—your style and mine being so different—it will be concluded by all men, under the circumstances, that I am joined with you as co-editor in title page merely out of courtesy and condescension on your part. . . . All I ask is to be allowed to write a small part. . . . This will enable me to sign S.C. with more comfort. Besides, there are some things which I want to express" (Letter: SC to DC [2 Feb 1852]). By the time the preface went to press in late March, it was entirely Sara's composition, and Derwent felt that the division of editorial labor was generally so unequal that Sara's name alone should go on the title page. Sara felt otherwise, and as usual she got her way. Derwent did, however, have the last word. In the Advertisement to the new volume he wrote, "At her earnest request, my name appears with hers on the title-page, but the assistance rendered by me has been, in fact, little more than mechanical. The preface, and the greater part of the notes, are of her composition:—the selection and the arrangement have been determined almost exclusively by her critical judgment." Sixteen years later, in the Advertisement of the 1868 reprint, Derwent was even more forthright: "The work was performed almost entirely by herself. . . . I had no occasion to do more than confirm the conclusions to which she had herself arrived, and sanction the course which she herself adopted."

Unlike her previous introductions and appendixes, Sara's preface was neither defense nor diatribe: it was a direct and commonsensical explanation of editorial procedures. Moreover, it was an essay whose quiet confidence about the literary value of the proffered poems had been fifteen years in the making. The "Coleridge" now before the public was an established man of letters no longer in need of polemics, and Sara had the luxury of assuming merit instead of defining it. Indeed, the "Coleridge" she could now assume was the "Coleridge" she had in fact defined, the "Coleridge" whose reputation would remain relatively constant until the early part of this century, at which point "Coleridge" was remade once again to suit the needs of a fledgling discipline desperately in search of critical forefathers. For Sara, then, that last act of composition signaled the end of an editorial campaign that had successfully transformed a fragmentary and miscellaneous corpus into a respected body of literary and philosophical writings. The flawed Romantic Rebel had become the wise Victorian Sage, and the negligent husband, irresponsible parent, and confirmed plagiarist all were facets of a personality ultimately subordinate to the eccentric and enigmatic "man of genius." But for Sara, product was less important than process; she needed the editorial work, the collaboration, because it was only as an active agent that she could balance the roles of dutiful daughter and engaged intellectual. To accept only the former was to relinquish autonomy and power and to adopt the passivity, the death-in-life of conventional womanhood; to accept only the latter was to violate codes of female propriety and to transgress norms now deeply internalized. Literary labors, then, more so than the goal at which they were directed, provided Sara a much-needed equilibrium, a unique opportunity to define personal desire within societal constraint. A passage from Sara's last letter to Derwent poignantly emphasizes the centrality of her "work": "If the drain does not diminish and I continue to worsen, my work is done. I am much worse today than ever before. . . . I had thought of adding the date of my Father's birth to the Preface. But dear Derwent, I am dying. I feel it" (Letter [May 1852?]). Ironically inscribed within an announcement of her imminent death, the "thought of adding the date of [her] Father's birth to the Preface" constitutes both a last wish and a final command—on one hand, a desire to continue labors that must end and, on the other, a reminder to Derwent that such responsibilities were now his.

CHAPTER SEVEN

Postscript
"Child of Genius"

I define GENIUS, *as originality of intellectual construction: the moral accompaniment, and actuating principle of which consists, perhaps, in the carrying on of the freshness and feelings of childhood into the power of manhood.*

S. T. Coleridge, The Friend

Ne'er was it mine t'unlock rich founts of song,
As thine it was ere Time had done thee wrong:—

Sara Coleridge, *"To my Father"*

When Sara Coleridge died on May 3, 1852, after a long and horrific battle with cancer, the autobiography was only one of many original compositions that remained unfinished. Among the thousands of pages of manuscripts—among the poems and letters, the essays and journals—there was another literary effort still in draft, a single poem addressed specifically to her father:

To my Father, on his lines called
"Work without Hope"

Father, no amaranths e'er shall wreathe my brow.—
Enough that round they grave they flourish now:—
But Love mid' my young locks his roses braided,
And what car'd I for flowr's of deeper bloom?
Those too seem deathless—here they never faded,
But, drench'd and shatter'd dropp'd into the tomb.

Ne'er was it mine t'unlock rich founts of song,
As thine it was ere Time had done thee wrong:—
But ah! how blest I wander'd nigh the stream,

Whilst Love, fond guardian, hover'd o'er me still!
His downy pinions shed the tender gleam
That shone from river wide or scantiest rill.

Now, whether Winter "slumbering dreams of Spring,"
Or, heard far off, his resonant footsteps fling
O'er Autumn's sunburnt cheek a wanner hue,
While droops her heavy garland, here and there,
Nought can for me those golden gleams renew,
The roses of my shattered wreath repair.
Yet Hope still lives and oft, to objects fair
In prospect pointing, bids me still pursue
My humble tasks:—I list—but backward cast
Fain would mine eye discern the Future in the Past.

Offering itself as a corrective to Coleridge's dispirited insistence on his own obscurity ("O ye amaranths! bloom for whom ye may. / For me ye bloom not!"), Sara's poem makes clear that his reputation was revived at the expense of her own. Regardless of her dutiful claims to the contrary, Love's braided roses could not equal the unfading amaranths of worldly success, and her gratitude at "wander[ing] nigh the stream" of poetic achievement fails to hide a wistful regret about wasted talents. Moreover, the third stanza highlights her misgivings by establishing a "Now" in which the writer, presumably close to death, entertains no hope whatsoever for "renew[ed]" visions or "repair[ed]" wreaths. Then, at the moment of despondency, "Hope" is suddenly introduced as the benevolent taskmaster who encourages her "humble" efforts and offers as incentive "objects fair / In prospect." The closing couplet, however, "list[s]" ambiguously not forward to fair objects but "backward" to a "Past" whose hidden "Future" could be either that of her father's long-awaited public recognition or that of Sara's sacrificed talents. Neither, the poem suggests, can be "discern[ed]" independently of the other.

The calculated ambiguity of Sara's poem nicely captures the complexities of a father–daughter relationship few critics have been willing to acknowledge, much less explore in detail. Interestingly, however, Henry Reed, the first commentator to assess Sara Coleridge's life and work, did recognize and attempt to explain the complex interconnections between the celebrated parent and the dutiful daughter. Writing in July 1852, he made bold claims as to the powers of her "genius," yet he was careful to construct a context within which that genius assumed a properly "feminine" character. The first paragraph of his essay bears quoting at length:

This brief and simple record is the announcement of the death of one who may be described not only as a very gifted member of a gifted family, but in genius and acquirements one of the most remarkable women of our own or other times. Such was the modesty of her career of authorship and so little did she solicit public applause, that these words of strong eulogy may surprise many: but the friends who knew her and have studied her mind, her learning, and withal the beautiful feminineness of her character will recognize the praise as faithful and not fanciful. The highest critical authority in England, in an article written about two years since, speaking of the daughter of Coleridge, described her as "the inheritrix of her father's genius and almost rival of his attainments". . . . The daughter's mind resembled the father's in its discursive character and in the well-constituted combination of the poetic and philosophic elements: with no self-considering economy of its strength and resources, it strove not for reputation, but, like the father's, with simple earnestness for the cause of truth in the large circuits of its thoughts in the regions of literature and art—of morals and theology. The genius and learning which, if she had sought for fame, would soon have won it, were expended for the most part in editorial notes and prefaces and in familiar correspondence: and so varied were her writings and so rich in thought and in the accumulation of knowledge, that they may be compared to the conversation and "*marginalia*" of her father—distinguished by such difference as originality gives, and by the transfiguration, as it were, of womanly thought and feeling. [1–2]

The "beautiful feminineness of her character" serves at once to explain and to justify the apparent absence of a "self-considering economy of . . . strength and resources." Sara's mind, according to Reed, "strove not for reputation" but, like her father's, for "the causes of truth." The crucial qualification, however, is that her writings, unlike his, are "distinguished . . . by the transfiguration, as it were, of womanly thought and feeling." Thus, what Reed praises as distinctly "feminine" or "womanly" explains the curious disregard for "fame" and the equally curious dedication (for an avowed "genius") to the work and reputation of another writer and thinker.

The uncomfortable tension lurking beneath Reed's insistence on Sara's "genius" and his admission of her "varied" and fragmentary writings finds partial resolution in the "beautiful feminineness of character" because that "feminine . . . character" was itself largely defined by "duty." Duty becomes the sign of "a high-bred woman" whose "remarkable learning" labors only in the service of her male forebears. "Indeed," Reed writes,

a noticeable peculiarity of the story of her literary labors is that they were prompted, not so much—if at all—by ambition of authorship, as by some form of duty—filial for the most part, or maternal, which led to the publicity of print. . . . It was a career of womanly authorship of surpassing dignity and beauty, disfigured by no mean motive or mannish temper. It was the same spirit which kept her remarkable learning pure from the taint of pedantry for she bore her varied attainments with the ease and grace with which a high-bred woman carries the customary accomplishments of female education. . . . A great charm of all Mrs. Coleridge's writings lies in this: that you recognize not only the processes of a strong and clear-sighted intellect, but the full pulses of a woman's heart; they largely illustrate that unison and harmony of the intellect and moral powers, wherein is to be found, we believe, one of the chief characteristics of genius. [2–3]

Sara's sense of duty—whether "filial for the most part, or maternal"—displaces "ambition" as a motivation for "literary labor" and serves to define a type of "womanly authorship" free from "mean motive" and "mannish temper." The submissiveness of "womanly authorship" to male authority is then attributed to "moral powers," which in turn redefine (and vitiate) Sara's claim to "genius." The literary labors of Mrs. Coleridge," Reed concludes,

during the ten years of her widowed life, were devoted to one pursuit—the completion of what her husband had begun—the editorial care of her father's writings, and the guardianship of his character as a poet, a critic, and most of all, as a Christian philosopher. These labors had a moral impulse in the genial sense of duty to the memory of both her father and her husband. It was fit filial and conjugal work; and intellectually it gave full scope to her genius and learning in following the footsteps of her father. . . . But it was her father's fame, and not her own that was foremost in her thoughts; and it is this that puts her character in such fine contrast with the self-considering temper of common authorship.

Reed equates Sara's moral virtue with her submission to paternal authority, and thus, by his account, her "genius" derives from and is subordinate to that of her father. Without stating it explicitly, then, Reed establishes and maintains a clear line of demarcation between male and female genius. He is quite willing to acknowledge Sara's "genius" as long as his explanation of her "beautiful femi-nineness of character" makes clear her allegiance to male superiority, her "duty to the memory of both her father and her husband." Such "duty" at once derives from and offers the only available evidence of a supposedly preexistent and explicitly feminine "moral impulse." As the crucial factor in the equation, "morality" transforms "duty" into virtue and explains away Sara's irregular corpus as commensurate with her inescapably "feminine character," a character in "fine contrast with the self-considering temper of common authorship." Of course, Reed is not intentionally condescending: on the contrary, his intention is to convince his readers that Sara Coleridge was "in genius and acquirements one of the most remarkable women of [his] own or other times." Nevertheless, the strategy by which he chooses to champion her merits only reinforces her marginality. So afraid is he that Sara's literary labors might compromise her sex that his argument undoes itself; it relegates her "genius" to a subordinate position aligned to but incompatible with its male counterpart, ensuring that her value as editor, author, and intellectual begins and ends with her status as woman.

If Henry Reed's tribute offers a startling example of the pronounced incompatibility existing between "female" and "intellect" in the mid-nineteenth century, then Earl Leslie Griggs's 1940 biography, *Coleridge Fille,* provides an equally important opportunity to see the ways in which that incompatibility lost its immediacy and became an institutionalized predisposition. Writing some ninety years after Reed, Griggs never thought it necessary to discuss Sara's claims to "genius." She was, as he stated matter-of-factly in his preface, a "distinctly minor figure" (vii), and his biography, while scrupulously researched and honestly written, assumes from the outset that Sara's life amounts to little more than an interesting addendum to the life of her illustrious father. Literary history was for Griggs merely an exhaustive accounting of great men and great books, and Coleridge's daughter was valuable to the extent that she offered a new perspective on the established figures of Romantic history. Like Reed, however, Griggs was unable to judge Sara's intellectual merits apart from her "thoroughly feminine personality": "An examination of the large collection of Sara Coleridge's letters, diaries, and miscellaneous writings (many of which are unpublished) reveals not only the picture of a talented and intellectual woman but also the portrait of an attractive and thoroughly feminine personality. The sweet charm and innate goodness of the woman, 'nobly planned,' are, in the long run, fully as impressive as the penetrating intelligence" (vii–viii). The "sweet charm and innate goodness" counterbalance "the penetrating intelligence," thereby feminizing the "talented and intellectual woman" into a nonthreatening stereotype. The crucial phrase is "in the long run," for with it Griggs evokes the test of time and the standards of history as the measures by which Sara's "thoroughly feminine personality" will emerge as equal to her intellectual contributions. In effect, then, Griggs uses "history" to deploy value judgements of which he remains supremely confident—as long as they are distant, externalized, and seemingly objective.

Toward the end of *Coleridge Fille,* Griggs becomes even more forthright about the criteria used to define Sara's life and work as "distinctly minor." Unlike his earlier claims to the contrary, the "feminine" here emerges as unquestionably pejorative, a "bias" that clouds Sara's critical judgment:

Enough evidence has been adduced to show that Sara Coleridge was not an impressionistic critic or an undisciplined thinker. [But] her limitations are pretty clear. She was so thoroughly a devotee of the romantics that she sometimes underestimated the poetry of her contemporaries. Her view of life was partly moulded by Victorian morality, and a feminine bias often interferes with her judgment. More than all this, her critical comments are too casual to be fitted into a system. Reading and criticizing the literary productions of her day was her diversion. [215]

A commitment to Romantic principles and a predilection to Victorian morality conflate into "feminine bias," a specifically engendered and presumably emotional predisposition clearly subordinate to the unbiased logic and objective judgment of more traditional literary figures. Most important of all, according to Griggs, is that Sara's writings are "too casual to be fitted into a system." Missing the crucial irony that Sara spent her life systematizing the fragmentary and miscellaneous remains of her father, Griggs defines her historical value in terms of formalist criteria and subordinates her life and work to an idea of "system" that is the result and not the starting point of the very process in which she was involved. In other words, Sara found her "system" in and through her editorial labors, and Griggs fails to see that flaws of form—fragmentary and miscellaneous writings, for example—are "flaws" only if one begins with normative assumptions about literary "merit," "merit" created by "genius" and recognized by "taste."

Such assumptions, as I have argued, constitute in part the legacy of Romanticism, and the definition of *genius* that Griggs works hard to avoid mentioning in connection with Sara is largely derived from that offered by Coleridge himself in *The Friend*: "I define GENIUS, as originality of intellectual construction: the moral accompaniment, and actuating principle of which consists, perhaps, in the carrying on of the freshness and feelings of childhood into the power of manhood" (*Fr[CC]* 1:419). Coleridge's phrase "originality of intellectual construction" correlates nicely to Griggs's formal system, emphasizing that both critics conceive of genius as assuming a recognizable form within an established tradition. That the "actuating principle" of genius should be defined in terms of "the power of manhood" only serves to remind us that *logic, reason, intellect,* and *system*—not to mention *genius* itself—were all exclusively defined by and in the interests of upper-class, educated, white men. For that reason, women's writings generally, and Sara Coleridge's writings in particular, found themselves at the margins of an entrenched tradition whose defining characteristics precluded nonconformity. Put another way, the process of literary valuation has been, and continues to be, notoriously unreceptive to the politically, ethnically, or sexually disenfranchised. Griggs, of course, would argue otherwise, for the standards of literary merit he upholds cling fiercely to notions of their own disinterestedness. Nevertheless, his brand of historiography aids and abets the very processes that worked to marginalize Sara Coleridge during her lifetime.

The distance between Reed and Griggs measures the time it took for a somewhat off-balance male response to the emergence of women in the literary marketplace to become a stable set of institutionalized prejudices against women intellectuals. The history of professional literary criticism has been synonymous with, as recent commentators Terry Eagleton and Gerald Graff have noted, a search for artistic "truths" verifiable through "objective" methodologies. Threatened by the rise of science and the death of religion, the humanistic disciplines borrowed scientific strategies to assist in the reclamation of religious values reconstituted as the verities of art. While quick to expose this institutional quest as an ideological masquerade, neither Eagleton nor Graff stresses the degree to which such "objectivity" is engendered or how such crucial terms as *genius* and *taste* work against all but the enfranchised few. Sara Coleridge's relative obscurity serves to remind us of the complex process by which Romantic values were sold first to a Victorian public and then to a fledgling profession deeply insecure about its own social and intellectual status. That she should be ignored, that her role as purveyor and mediator of literary and interpretative standards should be undervalued, offers an instructive if unfortunate irony. So successful were her labors that Coleridgean values now comprise the theoretical foundations of the very institution that finds it difficult to recognize such labors as legitimate areas of inquiry. Sara's obscurity, in other words, symbolically marks the ironic end of an all-too-successful editorial project.

The adoption of Romantic values by the institution of literary criticism has had, and continues to have, profound consequences for literary historiography, particularly for feminist historiography. Virginia Woolf, arguably the first theoretically sophisticated feminist critic, provides a case in point. Unlike Griggs, Woolf harbored deep suspicions about history's ongoing claims to objectivity. She saw in Sara Coleridge another of Shakespeare's sisters, another woman whose historical situation denied her the routine freedoms accorded male contemporaries. She saw too that Sara's editorial labors were more than filial duty, more than the virtuous submission to male authority that both Reed and Griggs recognized and admired. "She found her father, in those blurred pages," Woolf wrote, "as she had not found him in the flesh; and she found he was herself. She did not copy him, she insisted; she was him." But the miraculous union Woolf engineers to redeem Sara from the claustrophobic ranks of dutiful daughter, wife, and mother only partially obscures an anxiety about the marginal status of Sara's fragmentary texts. Like Reed and Griggs, Virginia Woolf could not envision a literary history without exclusionary standards derived from unquestioned assumptions about "genius" and "taste." However sympathetic to "the lives of the obscure," Woolf needed to believe in the freedoms afforded by the literary imagination. She could not see, in short, how literary hierarchies reinforced class conflicts and dominant ideologies at the very moment of proclaiming their independence from social and political interest. As a result, Sara Coleridge's role as purveyor of "culture" and "tradition," as one who considered it her "business" to educate her contemporaries in Coleridgean philosophy and politics, went unacknowledged by Woolf. Eager to "think back through [her] mothers" (*Room* 79), Woolf could sympathize with women's oppression, but she was unable to recognize the degree to which the labors of Sara Coleridge and women like her were both intimately involved with the making of literary value and an implicit challenge to the very standards they worked so hard to maintain.

Although Woolf's revisionary double bind is still very much in evidence among feminist historians, recent scholars have become increasingly sensitive to the ways in which literary values are created and deployed in the cultural marketplace. Theoretical innovations have called conventional methods into question, ensuring that the writing of history can no longer assume a naive faith in its ability to recover an objective and verifiable "truth." Because of their oppositional politics, feminist scholars have been quick to argue that both "history" and "literature" are less God-given essences, stable and unchanging verities, than they are discursive terrains over which and within which competing social forces vie for cultural, hence political, ascendancy. Sara Coleridge's life and work, together with the various commentators who have assessed her contributions and established her position in literary history, provide a striking example of this process in motion. Not only do we see how unquestioned assumptions and political prejudices determine, and in fact constitute, the final products—the representations of Sara Coleridge as offered by Reed, Griggs, and Woolf—but we also recognize the degree to which the unresolved tensions and conflicts of the critical moment superimpose themselves upon the unresolved tensions and conflicts of the past. Studying Sara Coleridge, rethinking her contributions and revising her position(s) in literary history, thus becomes less a straightforward recovery of the past than an ongoing exploration of the present, in Adrienne Rich's words, "an act of survival." "Until we can understand the assumptions in which we are drenched," Rich writes, "we cannot know ourselves." To "know" Sara Coleridge is to glimpse momentarily the complexities of nineteenth-century literary production and reception, to appreciate both the adversities and the accomplishments of nineteenth-century women writers, and, perhaps more important still, to come to a better understanding of the literary and critical traditions of which we are a part.

APPENDIX

The Essays of Sara Coleridge

On the Disadvantages Resulting from the Possession of Beauty

The world's a floor, whose swelling heaps retain
The mingled wages of the plowman's toil;
The world's a heap, whose yet unwinnowed grain
Is lodged with chaff, and bury'd in her soil:
All things are mixt, the useful with the vain;
The good with bad, the noble with the vile:
The world's an ark wherein things pure & gross
Present their lossfull gain, & gainful loss,
Where every dram of gold contains a pound of dross.

Quarles [Emblems II, VII].

Beauty! thou active, passive ill!
Which dyst thyself as fast as thou dost kill!
Thou tulip! who thy stock in paint dost waste,
Neither for physic good, nor smell, nor taste.

Cowley ["Beauty"].

It is the remark of a "keen and witty" writer that "hardly shall you meet with a man or woman so aged or illfavoured, but, if you will commend them for comeliness, nay & for youth too, [they] shall take it well." I believe this to be no hyperbole;—of all natural endowments, those of person are perhaps the most generally & the most warmly desired, & great as the influence of Beauty has been at all periods of the world, from the days of Helen even to our own, never, I verily believe, had the Goddess more numerous or more ardent votaries than at the present time. For this is the Age of Taste if not of Reason: we all visit picturesque scenery, scramble up rocks, & brave "the pelting of the pitiless storm" in hunting lakes & waterfalls; we pore over collections of pictures, striving with might & main to admire what ought to be admired and *vice versa;*

we discuss the merits of actors, dancers, & singers with a view to display our own exquisite taste if not profound knowledge of the arts of acting, dancing, & singing; and [we] acquire weak eyes (one of the most fashionable juvenile diseases) by hurrying through an endless succession of novels, poems, & new publications of all sorts; in such an age it is not wonderful that Beauty, the great object of Taste, should be more than ever the theme of admiring eyes & tongues:—our mothers tell us a pretty face was not half so much extolled nor a plain one criticized when they were young as is the case at present. The subject of personal appearance, they complain[,] is perpetually on the carpet, the bad tendency of which is to render beauty daily more & more the object of their daughters' aims and wishes, indeed the engrossing concern of their thoughts & lives. The rage for novel reading too fosters this evil:—it is natural for the young female reader to long for the silken eyelashes & the Grecian features which generally constitute the chief charm of the heroine, and enable her to reign triumphantly in all hearts. And there can be no doubt that the consciousness of exciting pleasure, of chaining attention, of awakening emotions akin to love, & that immediately & without effort, is an exhilarating & almost intoxicating sensation, to some tempers the most seducing of all Earth's painted bribes, the most delicious of all her "grief-engendering joys." But few are the sweets in this world of bitterness that have not their "sour doses";—few the seeming advantages that have not their attendant ills: whether this be true with regard to the one in question, whether Beauty be productive of the most pain or pleasure, benefit or injury to those endowed with it, & whether parents who profess that they are well pleased with their daughter's mediocrity in point of personal attractions and that they desire no "shower of Beauty for their earthly bower" merit all the sportive abuse & ridicule with which they are assailed in a very sprightly morceau on the subject by a pen more wont to excite tears than laughter, that to which we owe "Ellen Fitzarthur" & the "Widow's Tale," is a question I would fain discuss with some gentle reader, who must already have perceived to which side my opinions lean.[1]

I am far from affirming that all who sport the above mentioned sentiment are sincere—some may affect the virtue or the wisdom which they have not—but is the sentiment a just one or no? —does Beauty of person in reality tend to make its possessor estimable & happy? —I say *tend,* for such is the diversity of dispositions that the same circumstances will operate very differently upon

1. Caroline Anne Bowles (1786–1859), poet and second wife of Robert Southey, published *Ellen Fitzarthur: a Metrical Romance* in 1820 and *The Widow's Tale, and Other Poems* in 1822. Her most famous work, and that to which SC refers, was *Chapters on Churchyards* (1829), published first in *Blackwood's* as a serial. The "sprightly morceau," chapter three of the work, satirizes a Mrs. Buckwheat and her two daughters.

different persons,—the brightest smiles of Nature & Fortune fail to bestow contentment on some, their darkest frowns will not wholly impair the cheerfulness of others;—in some soils Vanity will never take root, be it ever so copiously watered. In others it will thrive & luxuriate [in] spite of parching droughts and nipping frosts, surviving the most ungenial and inclement seasons, & only too apt, unless anxiously pruned, to choke up and devour each wholesome herb and beauteous flower. But does the possession of Beauty *tend* to inspire cordial peace into the bosom of its owner? Does cheerfulness, the sunshine of the soul, more willingly irradiate an elegant than a homely tenement? I think not. —like all the other good things of this life[,] personal advantages, I believe, are more craved for when unattainable than enjoyed when possessed. What are the feelings of the flattered belle, of her that is accustomed to be gazed at & raved about, when she examines her admired form & features in the glass? Except on rare occasions she can feel little gratification in the idea that the image before her is surprisingly fair, that she is handsomer than the generality of her young companions; but is she more or less handsome than she was so many years, months, weeks ago? —do the eyes sparkle as brilliantly as when their beams, light flashing out of darkness, were last concentrated & fixed in song or sonnet? —do the ringlets curl as gracefully, does the complexion glow as delicately, as much like the snow on some mountain top faintly blushing with the rays of the morning, as when they were last admired & praised? Has the figure lost none of its Corinthian richness & lightness? —these are the agitating questions on which the fair one's hopes & fears[,] her exultation or disappointment[,] depend, and seldom are they answered entirely to the satisfaction of the anxious querist, who though handsome enough to be vain is not sufficiently so to be contented; for while the scantiest fare will keep vanity alive, the most abundant suffices not to satisfy her ravenous appetite, an appetite which "grows by what it feeds on," whose desires not knowing

> Where next to pitch, ev'n like the boundless Ocean,
> Gain & gain ground & grow more strong by motion.

If the plain woman exhibit *us-que ad nauseam* her one charm of person[,] the beauty bewails her one blemish with as childish & more lamentable folly: it is the solitary fly that spoils her whole box of ointment. One can hardly credit the story of Lady Carteret's dying because Lewis the XIVth pronounced a lady, to whom a noble of his court compared her, handsomer than she; but the thing would scarce have been reported had not fair ladies been often known to take it to heart that others should be accounted more fair:—*felix post Cynaram* is a sentence which few of the she-professors of Beauty, as they have been quaintly termed, can listen to with any tolerable degree of tranquillity & satisfaction.

How wretched that poor girl whose happiness is dependent on the varying though faithful report of her mirror! But are the lovely & elegant alone subject to such grievous thraldom? Have ill favoured damsels no anxieties respecting personal appearance? To be wholly exempt from them, I regret to say, is for women almost impossible:—a freedom from such petty cares is the enviable privilege of the other sex (a privilege however which they sometimes meanly abandon, becoming voluntary slaves to their glass & toilet). But the plain girl, as Miss Burney shews in the character of Eugenia,[2] till her attention is rudely called to the subject, feels no very keen regret concerning her want of beauty:—she views her coarse skin & homely shape & visage in general without a sigh. Any new defeature that she may perceive will cause her some disturbance, but she cannot seek her glass or hang on its report with the anxiety of her beauteous contrast, who beguiled by the Temper Flattery fastens more than half her happiness on that slippery surface,–

> Whose hopes & fears, whose joy & love
> Do all within that *crystal* move.

"To look almost pretty," observes the authoress of Northanger Abbey, "is an acquisition of higher delight to a girl who has been looking plain for the first fifteen years of her life than a beauty from her cradle can ever receive."[3] That this *must* be the case, that it proceeds from a common principle of human nature, all who give the matter a moment's thought will allow,—"*poor* Codrus is made richly fine & cheerfully warm by what *wealthy* Sempronius is ashamed to wear": that it *is* the case on passing their female acquaintance in review before their mind's eye few will hesitate I think to admit. Are the fairest faces in the domestic circle, or even in the gay ball or party, the seldomest clouded with chagrin, disappointment, or even with envy? —to this latter passion indeed I believe beauties are particularly prone. When some new belle, some "earth-treading star," whose charms have been extolled & exaggerated by loud-tongued Fame, (speaking more especially through the mouths of neglected beaux & spiteful old bachelors,) makes her appearance at the country ball, whose heart beats with most anxiety and perturbation, who feels most secretly overjoyed at being *quite disappointed* in the beauty of the new comer, or most desperate at being unable to think or make others think that it falls short of what description led them to suppose? Is it the homely maiden, who, enured to the hardship of being eclipsed, has no fresh mortification to endure, who if she possess good taste & good nature, may derive genuine pleasure from the contemplation of what

---

2. Frances Burney (1752–1840), the celebrated novelist, published *Evelina* in 1778, *Cecilia* in 1782, and *Camilla* in 1796.

3. Jane Austen (1775–1817) was a favorite with SC, who thought her "if not the greatest . . . surely the most faultless of female writers" (Letter: SC to ET [3 Aug 1834]).

Burns gallantly avers to be "Nature's noblest work," a lovely woman, or if she have ever so ill regulated a mind will rather be amused than grieved at seeing the homage she can never hope to obtain transferred from one object to another? —No, I should rather look for such uneasy sensations in the bosom of her showy neighbour who naturally regards the fair stranger in the odious light of an usurping rival.

But we are told by a high authority in more than one place that deformed persons are envious; and that they have strong temptations to envy is indeed too true; absolute deformity, however, that which is out of the common course of Nature, & the absence of Beauty, or even positive plainness, are two very different things, and affect those to whom they belong in a very different manner: the one draws attention, the other escapes it:—I am not prepared to deny that repulsive ugliness is a worse misfortune than striking beauty.

However though I do not believe the unflattered part of the female sex to be the chief, or at any rate, the only enviers[,] I am ready enough to admit that beauty excites almost more envy than any other advantage real or fancied. And is not this very circumstance productive of infinite uneasiness to the envied fair one? Is not "Beauty brought to unworthy wretchedness through envy's snares" as well as by "fortune's freaks unkind"? The writer whose views on the subject I have mentioned as not entirely coinciding with my own seems to think that Nature's favourites are also the favourites of their fellow beings, that the "fair engaging girl"—(Are the fairest girls always the most engaging any more than the gayest flowers always the sweetest?) is the more beloved & cherished at home as well as abroad by reason of her fairness, as if Beauty were warmed & cheered by the reflection of her own radiance even as the earth receives benefit from that refreshing moisture which originally proceeds from her own bosom. Too often, however, the reverse of all this is the case:—the beams of Beauty are fully as apt to scorch & blind as to gladden the sight. The comeliness of one not infrequently becomes the ugliness of another.

> Who marks at Church-time others' symmetry
> Makes all their beauty his deformity.

Who envies it at any time may be said to do the same. Now though envy is undoubtedly a greater torment to the bosom in which it lurks than to that which is the mark of its arrows, yet all will agree that an evil eye, even though it cannot *blast* the object of its glances, has generally the power to do it a considerable degree of mischief. Three fourths of all the ill-natured things that are said in this world are dictated by Envy & by the same fiendish spirit conveyed to the ears of the hapless subject of them, who generally receives more pain from the envy than pleasure from the thing envied, the desirableness of which often exists chiefly in the imagination of the envier. In many families, I believe, the superior beauty of one member has been the source of uneasiness to all parties,—discontent on one side and all its baleful results on both, not to mention other ill consequences which I shall speak of hereafter. Children, I am convinced, derive little pleasure from the notice of a very attractive appearance—the rapturous kiss, the loudly expressed admiration, are oftener troublesome than gratifying to creatures in whom vanity, unless forced by unnatural nurture, is seldom more than a dormant passion. The attention of casual visitors therefore can add little to the happiness of the child—whatever it may do to that of the woman. From her own family beauty will scarcely procure her any superior degree of love or favour: brothers are indifferent to it, sisters apt to regard it with envy rather than with pleasure: —if parents ever evince a partiality for their handsomer offspring I think it is because being spoilt by admiration, or regarded with envy they are less favoured and more blamed by the rest of the household. The same feeling, the same wish to defend them against the attacks or make up to them for the neglect of others, leads them to favour, as they are frequently known to do, their least attractive or most offending children. Through the same feeling, a mother generally loves her sickliest child the best.

Let me not be set down among the enviers if I venture to express my belief that Beauty is rather unfavourable than otherwise to the formation of an estimable & amiable character. General opinion I think runs this way: to Proverbs one may apply what has been said of Language, that "as the embodied and articulated Spirit of the Race, as the growth and emanation of a People, and not the work of any individual Wit or Will, though often inadequate, sometimes deficient, they never are false or delusive."[4] Now the French have two old saws which decidedly support my view of the subject:—*Belle femme mauvaise teste,* and *Les beaux hommes au gibet.* This latter adage the modern annals of Newgate would seem to confirm: —our housebreakers and murderers are now a days depicted in such glowing colours that we are ready to exclaim with Gilderoy's sweetheart[5]

> "Oh! what rair cruelty is this
> To hang sic handsome men!"

Indeed so far from confounding moral with personal deformity[,] the public, influenced perhaps by the Satanic School of Poetry, is now running into the other extreme, and delights in contrasting the ugliness of men's deeds with the comeliness of their persons. Handsome is that [which] most unhandsome does, according to prevailing notions.

But to return:—even the poets in whom one would look for the warmest

4. Compare the end of WW's "Essay, Supplementary to the Preface" (*W Prose* 2:84).
5. Gilderoy (alias Patrick Macgregor) was a famous Scottish highwayman celebrated in Percy's *Reliques* and in a ballad by Thomas Campbell.

advocates of Beauty, the Goddess who so often has inspired their strains, do not always speak of her in the handsomest terms. Cowley compares her to a false coin of which the stamp and colour are good, the metal ill; Quarles treats her with still less ceremony; but, however slightly we may be inclined to think of poetical justice, some attention is surely due to Lord Bacon's maxim, which however is not unqualified, that "very beautiful persons are scarcely ever seen to be otherwise of great virtue, that they prove accomplished but not of great spirit, and study behaviour rather than virtue."[6] We need not go far to seek the cause of this:— "women to whom nature has not been indulgent in good features and colours" feel the necessity of making it up themselves with excellent manners, and though "the beautiful and comely should be careful that so fair a body be not disgraced with unhandsome usages," yet I believe personal graces are oftener relied on as a cover for faults and deficiencies, or a charm to divert attention from them, than as an incentive to add inward to outward excellence. Many fair ones flatter themselves, like Lady Betty Modish,[7] that the woman who has beauty stands in little need of virtue, and repose comfortably in the idea that all the talking in the world cannot "spoil their complexion nor put their hair out of order." Satisfied or absorbed with the contemplation of their outward image[,] they care not to hold up the mirror to their minds. Pretty women may say and do, leave unsaid and undone, not what they like, but certainly much more than less attractive persons: but does such licence tend to make them happier or better? Reason & experience teach the contrary. The children's tale of Bella and Mousterina[,] shewing how the latter made up for want of outward adornments by the acquired ones of her mind, & how the former could find no solid content or happiness till she learnt to depend less on her personal attractions, contains some truth. Certainly if Mousterina be as proud as Bella she has less excuse, inasmuch as she neglects to make use of that "instrument to resist pride and nurse humility" which we are told our every defect and imperfection may and ought to be. With regard to vanity, though it cannot be denied that some ugly women have a most unaccountable share of it, and that any narrow nook or oasis of beauty in the persons of such ladies, which has once been visited by a word or glance of admiration is sometimes prized and displayed with ludicrous impolicy and want of taste, yet I cannot think that in the general way a little beauty is a dangerous thing on the same grounds as a little learning: —mental adornments natural or acquired contain in themselves an antidote to that vanity which the applause that follows them is apt to inspire:—those of person have no such counteracting quality,—a charm they certainly possess to disable the judgement. [T]he same degree of vanity which in a plain woman would be

6. From "Of Beauty" in the *Essays* of Francis Bacon.
7. Lady Betty Modish is the fashionable coquette of Colley Cibber's *The Careless Husband* (1705).

thought ridiculous & disgusting passes uncensured & almost unobserved, by one sex at least, in her whose beauty's brightness blinds or gains her judges. [A]n ounce of it in the former is certainly less excusable than a pound in the latter, but to those who view the scales with an undazzled eye, the proportion, I think, will seldom appear other than this.

Let us suppose the female sex divided into two companies—the one consisting of the plain and *unnoticeable,* the other of the admired and lovely;—let us cast our eyes over the less brilliant group;—here & there we may spy that ineffable absurdity, a vain ugly woman, courting the notice she should seek to shun, her unattractive form and features pointed out to general ridicule by the bravery of glittering ornaments, to which her dull complexion, instead of being set off by them, serves as a foil, or by a singular style of dress, which on a handsome woman would look affected, on her appears absolutely *outré.* Such objects as the one I have described will however be conspicuous for their rarity as well as for their folly:—the greater number, if remarkable at all, will rather be so for their unpretending attire, their natural mien and gestures.

The fairer bevy, from which our eyes shall now no longer be withheld, will contain some damsels who by wondrous art, or a most fortunate natural disposition, can contrive to look unexpectant—unconscious of admiration, can drink the Circean cup of flattery & by some powerful antidote keep the heady liquor from bewildering their brains & eyes and causing them to see their own perfectious double, who both remain sober enough not to fancy themselves any handsomer than they are, i.e. than they seem to the world in general, and are free from the worser part of vanity, an over-value for the frail bauble they possess, and a restless anxiety to preserve or heighten its lustre in the eyes of others. [S]uch bright paragons will doubtless be espied, shining like Cynthia among the lesser stars, but how large a proportion will be found, on a steady view, to abound still more in airs than in graces! —how many of those adorned visages will, to such a sour critic as myself at any rate, be half spoiled by a languishing motion of the eyes or a silly unmeaning unvarying simper, except when it so happens that the interior of the mouth does not correspond in beauty with the external part, in which case Euphrosyne will be resolutely kept at bay lest she should tempt the "ruby gates" to open and disclose—not "pearl portcullis"—but mere human teeth, liable to imperfection, dilapidation and decay![8] If we address the conscious fair ones we shall generally be regaled with syllables gently ejected as if they were too large and coarse & rough hewn for the delicate mouth:—we must listen to dying falls or a sustained falsetto treble key more wearisome to any but spell-bound ears than the roughest intonations breathed forth naturally and without attempt: the desire and consciousness of admiration

8. Euphrosyne, Aglaia, and Thalia, better known as the three Graces or Charities, were the Greek goddesses of beauty and grace who distributed joy and gentleness.

is seen to influence every look and gesture—their very gait betrays it—they mince as they go and put out their feet as if each step were to fall under the cognizance of observing eyes. By nothing are sense & dignity so completely banished from the countenance and demeanour as by vanity, which bids the eyes open not to see but to be seen, and the feet move not so much for the purpose of locomotion as of betraying the fair proportion of an ankle.

Hard is it for an admired woman not to appear and to be vain and affected;— unconscious beauties are I believe rare birds all the world over, even in the wilds of Guisha some centuries ago. Sir Walter Raleigh observed the natural effect of beauty on the mind & manners of a fair Savage, the wife of an Indian Cacique, whom he thus describes: "In all my life I have seldom seen a better favoured woman; she was of good stature, with black eyes, fat of body, of an excellent countenance, her hair almost as long as herself, tied up again in pretty knots, and it seemed she stood not in that awe of her husband as the rest, for she spake and discoursed, and drank among the gentlemen and captains, and was very pleasant, *knowing her own comeliness, and taking great pride therein*." Our traveller's great and fair Mistress would not have allowed her to be very pleasant who betrayed a knowledge of her own comeliness and a great pride therein: though she herself, with all her wisdom and erudition, appears to have been as much influenced by personal vanity as the least of her contemporaries. Sir Walter's handsome brunette, however, seems to have derived some solid advantages from her charms:—where a general feeling of gallantry does not proceed, where "allegiance and fast fealty" are not professed unto "*all* womankind," beauty must indeed be an enviable endowment.

Extravagance in dress and waste of time are also the frequent ill effects of personal beauty. All men are apt to spend most on that object which is the most interesting to them & occupies the most of their thoughts:—the lover of books will pinch himself "black & blue" to add some favourite author to his library:— the painter who scarcely dares indulge in the commonest luxuries of food and clothing will grudge no sum he can by any means command in the furtherance of his art:—and the beauty who pants to repeat and extend her conquests will be strongly tempted to bestow an undue portion of her time and means in outward adornments, in heightening those personal attractions which are her all in all. Oh! the slavery of having a reputation for beauty to keep up! Oh! the constant trouble and anxiety it entails! And then to run the gauntlet of criticism in every company of new faces,—to be sick of that disease, the desire to be thought handsome, which sets everybody at work to examine what the stranger's pretensions are,—

Quali
Sit facie, *forma* quali, pede, dente, capillo.
[Whatever the face, whatever the figure, feet, teeth, and hair.]

Troublesome, however, as the possession of beauty is, few have philosophy enough to resign it without many a struggle,—'tis death to lose what it has been but a careful comfort to possess. The departure of youth summons all mankind from manifold enjoyments; to the fading fair it must in too many cases ring the knell of all that is most prized & cherished. Human beauty, which Taylor pronounces in some respects inferior to that of flowers,[9] is not infrequently impaired by the very anxiety for its preservation: some living breathing lilies would perhaps bloom the longer if they toiled no more to adorn themselves, if they took no more thought for the morrow than those of the field. Alas! trying to look handsome and engaging in the teeth of Nature is as unsatisfactory & feverish a pursuit as *trying* to go to sleep, as trying to win the approach of that false friend which is "still last to come when it is wanted most." And here I must observe that as the best things in corruption are said to be the worst, and the fairest flowers the first to wither & decay, the most exquisitely pretty women in advanced or middle age often become less handsome than those who have had fewer attractions to boast in youth: the most delicate frames are those least fitted to hold out against the "storms of sickness" and the "siege of years." Time's hand, which not unfrequently softens harsh features, and leaves a coarse but hardy figure and complexion at any rate unimpaired, will crush the elegant form, vulgarize and almost obliterate the delicate features by choking them up with flesh or injure their soft symmetry by stealing too large a portion of it, and destroy the loveliest compound of red & white by causing one to predominate unbecomingly over the other.

These remarks however apply only to a certain style of beauty:—*pulchrorum Autumnus pulcher*[10] may be true enough with regard to many; though some rejoice in a comely Autumn who have never known a beauteous Spring, and enjoy greater credit than is due to them for past charms on the stock of their present good looks. However to Beauties of every class the fading season, which sooner or later must arrive, can hardly fail to be one fraught with mortification and despondency, if not with despair:—those who by luck or management have *made their fortunes* before it sets in sometimes transmit their good looks to their children; in this case the passion of vanity which still reigns in their bosoms assumes a less unpleasing form when almost indistinguishably blended with parental love. If there be any parents who shew a decided preference for the handsomest of their family[,] uninfluenced by the feelings I mentioned before, it is perhaps those who having been used to the stimulus of admiration of their younger days still crave for it in one shape or another, and look upon a

9. SC read the sermons of Jeremy Taylor (1613–67), English divine and disciple of William Laud, during the winter of 1825–26.

10. "The autumn of beautiful persons is beautiful" (Plutarch, *Lives,* 2.90). Quoted in Bacon's essay "On Beauty."

plain child as a discredit and a slander to themselves. Those who have never had much beauty to boast in their own persons do not expect it in their children:—it is welcome if it comes but not reckoned upon. It is not always found that either fathers or mothers are most attached to those children of whom they are the fondest;—though it certainly is too often the case. I do not believe that the mere attractiveness of beauty in itself has any influence on the heart of a parent.

Inattention however to the maxim *nimium ne crede colori* has kept numbers single:—many a haughty Miss has cozened herself of a good bargain by rating her charms too dear;—such a damsel, if her constitution withstand the under-mining hostilities of disappointment and discontent, will generally ripen into that much satirized character which is immediately brought before one's mind by the term *old maid;* and of all the various species of that genus none is more to be dreaded than the *has been* beauty, who, eager to satiate her starved but still craving vanity, pours into unwilling ears long legends of love and murder, the features of which, viewed through the mists of time and robed in the shadows of antiquity, assume a bold exaggerated aspect, an air of romance and grandeur, which would render them scarce credible even from lips whose freshness might help to confirm such histories:—meantime her hapless hearers vainly stretch their imaginations to conceive how any other sort of mischief than the ennui they groan under could ever have proceeded from the phiz before them.

> Quo fugit Venus, quive color decens?
> [Where has Venus flown, what color befits her?]

Surely an old woman striving to call up the spirit of her departed charms before the mind's eye of another generation is scarce less worthy of ridicule than she who thinks by aid of art to bring them to life again in her own person.

Another calamity incident to beautiful women is their attracting a swarm of admirers or ephemeral lovers who are sure to cause abundant vexation and perturbation, but from whom, except the gratifying [of] an unworthy vanity, not the shadow of a shade of benefit is to be derived. Rossi has an epigram in which he describes Cupid presenting a mirror to Beauty,[11] when Time has broken the chains he cast around her, and maliciously exclaiming "See how much thy liberty costs thee!" It is indeed her fate to be tormented by the varlet in youth and taunted by him in age. The pretty woman will have more lovers than the plain, but not better ones, either before or after marriage:—

> Beauty, whose conquests still are made
> O'er hearts by *cowards* kept or else betray'd,
> [Cowley, "Beauty"]

11. Giovanni-Gherado de Rossi (1754–1827) wrote *Scherzi poetici e pittorici* (1798), a favorite childhood book of SC's.

owes more than half of her power to novelty, and consequently influences the husband little more than the parent or the brother;—daily experience I think shews that handsome wives are not more cherished than homely ones. Affection creates imaginary charms; time and familiarity dissipate real ones. She who is married for her person chiefly is in one point of view more to be pitied than she who is sought for the sake of her purse:—the latter may remain to keep the party in good humour, while the former soon slips through the fingers of the bargainee.

It is true the "flame of love" sometimes "survives the fuel," but the danger of its decay or extinction cannot but cause disquieting doubts & apprehensions in the bosom of the betrothed, if not of the wedded fair; far more securely blest is she who feels that Time will tend rather to strengthen than to impair her influence. If beauty adds little to the happiness of a wife in her own person still less does it to that of her spouse; the admired Adonis generally makes a careless husband, even though he belongs not to that class of creatures with whom "Sun burn me if I do!" is the most horrible of imprecations. To my thinking, it is only in caprice or in error that Nature ever assigns beauty to a man: that of which delicacy, according to a celebrated writer, is an essential part, can surely be no fitting attribute of the Lords of the Creation.

On a careful survey of the matter in all its bearings I cannot think those parents unwise who deem a conspicuous share of beauty as dangerous an inheritance for a daughter as a tempting fortune of another kind. Even if in the luscious bowl of flattery each drop were not thus "guarded with a thousand stings," could it be drawn from the well & not from the cistern, were it not so quickly drained to the dregs & those dregs so unsavoury, like all earthly sweets it is apt to cloy, & when no longer capable of delighting the palate, to render wholesome food insipid and even distasteful. The pleasure derived from beauty is at the best a dependent uneasy precarious gratification, which holds its existence by the eyes of others, and is liable to excite as many painful as pleasurable sensations in beholders of either sex, sensations which in one shape or another are almost sure to be avenged on the head of their exciter.

However in justice to Dame Nature it must be said that she distributes even her external gifts less partially than the hyperboles of poets and romances, and those tinctured with their spirit, would lead one to imagine. She gives "a matchless eye to Ehione, exquisite hair to Paegnium, to Tarsia a beauteous lip, to Delphia a noble forehead":—it is only the fantastic painter who would crowd all of those beauties together in one face. An ugly young woman and a decidedly beautiful one are equally rare objects:—and in the nature of things it must be so, for "the beautiful strikes us as much as its novelty as the deformed itself":—few only can be *remarkable* either for beauty or its opposite. The diversity of tastes, moreover, prevents the line from being too strongly marked: what has been defined as a "*certain* composition of colour & figure &c" is, as Lord Byron remarks of a *certain* age, one of the most *uncertain* things in the world,—a thing that has indeed "no certain what nor where": and whatever Burke may affirm with regard to fixed principles of taste, whatever rules he may lay down on the subject of beauty,[12] I believe that Nature seldom produces a "set of features or complexion" whose pretensions to elegance & loveliness are viewed in the same light, or nearly the same, by all beholders; for though a clear eye is universally felt to be handsomer than a muddy one, and a smooth cheek than that which is ploughed with wrinkles, yet how far in any particular face, and most faces contain a mixture of beauties and defects, the one may prevail over the other, and what claim the *tout ensemble* may or may not have to be called beautiful,— on this matter I think there will always be some difference of opinion. A swan may to every eye appear handsomer than a goose, but the human face and form afford greater scope for the exercise of fancy and feeling, which will be affected in different persons by different circumstances. Beauty, we are told, cannot be produced by rule; nor can it I think be perceived and admired by rule. The fact is that in every age and country the ideas of mankind have varied on the subject:

> Beauty! thou wild fantastic ape,
> That dost in every country change thy shape!
> Here black, there brown, here tawny, and there white;
> Thou Flatterer! which comply'st with every sight!
> Thou Babel [which confound'st the eye. . . .
> Cowley, "Beauty"]

From whatever cause this may proceed, whether from a greater or lesser degree of sensibility in the beholder or of attention to the object, from habit, association or aught else, it is sufficient for the drift of my argument that the thing is so.

After all, the "best part of beauty is that which a picture cannot express,"[13] or but partially and imperfectly. I speak not of motion, but of countenance as distinguished from feature and complexion. In those faces which at first sight strike the majority of beholders as "rudely stampt" and unhandsome, how frequently on a closer and a longer view does sweetness strength and variety of expression convey to "thinking hearts" a charm far above any of flesh and blood! how does the soul shine through its mask of clay, the coarseness and homeliness of which are unperceived while thus illuminated! I would almost say that though external beauty does not, in my opinion, tend to produce any corresponding internal loveliness, yet the soul which is all symmetry, wherein

---

12. Edmund Burke, *A Philosophical Inquiry into the Origin of Our Ideas of the Sublime and Beautiful.* See in particular the introduction, "On Taste."

13. Bacon, "Of Beauty."

there is "no disproportion," will, in some degree, mould the body to its like-ness. Be this as it may, beauty of expression is far above that of favour, colour, or motion. But we are taught to admire a lovely flower, a glowing landscape,— why then should we be checked from admiring that object wherein, as Whither[14] says, form and colour give most delight, "a worthy woman's face"? —because by fastening our attention too exclusively on what is external we overlook in the woman what we are in no danger of doing with regard to the flower and the landscape—the beauty of the soul.

[1826]

14. George Wither (1588–1667) was a poet best known for his spirited *Juvenilia* (1622).

Nervousness

After some years of suffering from derangement of the nervous system[,] I have satisfied myself that there is no all competent tribunal without ourselves to which we who are weak & miserable, doubly bound to walk circumspectly & continually tempted to stray from the narrow path of prudence & self control, can assuredly appeal on the subject of self management.[1] We must listen with a clear & candid spirit to the opinions of all persons of strong natural sense and receive the fruits of their knowledge & experience; but in the end our own understanding, informed by superior intimacy with our old constitution from childhood and with our present case in all its variations, overruled by a sense of duty, and aided by grace, must determine in the last resort. We may err, for there is no human infallibility: but depend on it in this as on every other point[,] we shall be our own counsellors, if we will but be true to ourselves, & if we have full *information* on the subject in question. Our advisors will differ among themselves; we *must* exert our own judgment to chuse among them; let us also exert it to review their advice. [L]et us give a fair trial to each particular suggestion on matters connected with medical science, but, for the shaping of our general course, for our view of the subject in all its bearings, we must take instructions chiefly from our own *best* selves—which abstract conception I here personify by the name of Good Genius, & into the mouth of this Good Genius I shall put the results of my own long deliberations on the subject of those disorders which affect the mind but do not radically & directly impair the Reason.

Invalid. What can have caused this lamentable failure in my health?

Good Genius. None will deny that the human body, like every other production of nature, is full of mystery: it is mere commonplace to observe that it is a

1. SC wrote this dialogue during the fall of 1834 and sent a shorter version to Emily Trevenen in Jan 1835. Having suffered from "nervous derangement" since early 1832, SC was at the time of composition enjoying a period of relative health that began soon after STC's death in July 1834 and lasted until her major breakdown in Oct 1836. Modeled in part on Landor's *Imaginary Conversations* (1824–29), the dialogue was strongly influenced by Bernard Mandeville's *A Treatise of the Hypochondriack and Hysterick Diseases* (1730) and Marshall Hall's *Commentaries Principally on the diseases of Females* (1830).

subtle intricate labyrinth with a thousand interdependencies which escape our keenest insight. But this like any other acknowledged truth is constantly over-looked in the reasonings of daily talk. Variations in the health take place for which no adequate cause can be assigned, yet lookers-on are sure to find some peg or shelf on which they dispose of the article to their satisfaction. And these like all other misconceptions in theory have some *practical* bad consequences; for from such false or half true premises a false set of references are made & a false code of laws established. Outward causes doubtless often cooperate; but what their share in the result may be it is hard to ascertain, & people will decide on such matters according to their prejudices & prepossessions, often in a very hasty manner. Nervous maladies may arise as spontaneously as consumption, yet they generally seem to have arisen from that which may have only aggra-vated them, & thus from the nature of the complaint which renders the sufferer too much alive to outward impressions, & too full of speculations suspecting them.

Invalid. I do remember how confident I felt at the beginning of my disorder that certain things had caused & would cause certain effects; but further experi-ence has quite unsettled these notions.

Good Genius. Consider what has generally seemed to bear hard upon your health & compare it with what you or others have suggested as the cause of your present bodily depression; but bear in mind that you can only discover what is most *probable* on a subject of this kind.

Invalid. If I could ascertain the cause of my illness[,] I should be better able to regulate myself in the future.

Good Genius. You must recollect however that even if there be an external cause, under different *circes* the same agent may not produce exactly the same effects. Beware too of supposing that the reverse of what may have injured you will be proportionally salutary, nor believe that if your health has decayed from inaction or from bodily or mental fatigue, from want of stimulus or from overt doses of it, that the opposite extreme will be useful. It is excess that has inspired you & you are still less able to bear excess than formerly.

Invalid. I have not strength to make even moderate exertions.

Good Genius. Of course excess & exertion & all such terms are only relative according to the body's capabilities. But keep in mind the principle. Yield to your weakness while it is inferiour, but do not imagine that what is rendered necessary by illness is good for the health in itself: as soon as the need ceases[,] gradually return to a balanced mode of life.

Invalid. I hear on one hand that nervous miseries are caused by indigestion, on the other that the stomach is disturbed in its function by irritation of nerves. The one part of the constitution is never thoroughly well while the other is at fault; there is an action and a reaction going on between them; but which threw the first stone?

Good Genius. It is of the less consequence to settle that point as there is no specific cause for either. Generally speaking[,] whatever is useful to the stomach tends to allay irritability of nerves, & the quieter the nerves are, the better chance there is for the stomach. However, you will find that there are severe stomach complaints without any material ailment of nerves, & some persons have dreadful nervous affections without any settled weakness of digestion, though having the paroxysms of the complaint[,] the stomach is always more or less deranged.

Invalid. Nervous derangement manifests itself by so many different symptoms that the sufferers themselves are puzzled what to make of it, and others, looking at it from different points of view make wrong judgments on the case. Those who perceive only how it affects the mind are apt to forget that it also weakens the body; those who perceive that it is a bodily disease wonder that it should produce any alteration in a well regulated mind.

Good Genius. Mania is also a disease in which the mind is affected through the body; but in the sort of nervousness which we are here discussing[,] Reason, Free Will, & consequently responsibility remain, while what may be called the more sensuous part of the mind, feeling emotion, partakes of the morbid conditions of the body: to consider, to determine, to act are still within our power, but whether we shall be gladsome or gloomy, buoyant with hope or trembling with apprehensiveness, all this depends on the state of the corporeal part.

Invalid. How often we are called upon, when wretchedly disabled, to derive comfort from this source or from that: "to draw honey in a sieve!" It is not material for comfort but the capacity for comfort that is wanting. And how often are we told that cheerfulness & hopefulness are a *duty*.

Good Genius. It is indeed a duty to be as cheerful & hopeful as *we can,* even as it is a duty to be as healthy *as we can,* & our unimpaired Reason may avail not to dispense our distressful sensations by its direct agency, as it might subdue a bit of envy or unjust resentment but to place us under *circes* the most favourable to their being dispersed. What aggravations of our malady may have proceeded from wrong views & ill regulated affections she must cast out. We can less than ever afford to be humoursome.

Invalid. In these cases[,] just as the body is constantly simulating some organic disease[,] so the agitated spirits induce the appearance of certain tempers which arise from diseases of the mind itself & occasion conduct which looks as if it were principled by envy, discontent, cowardice, or the weakest & blindest self love. During the deathly sinkings & persecuting irritations which the malady in its worst stage produces[,] every creature that enjoys a healthy existence seems to make our state more wretched by the contrast of its apparent happiness. Yet this sensation, a common symptom of the complaint, may be felt by one who is not spiritually envious. Far different it is with that truly envious Spirit which, even though possessing happiness from constitution & circumstances, is deprived of enjoyment merely by the sight of fancied good or happiness elsewhere. *This* arises from a vice of the mind which Reason empowered by Grace might correct. I have been in a state of terror for days & nights without any determinate object of terror in my mind: outward objects increased the agitation, & when such presented themselves [they] were often supposed to be the sole cause of it. There is an irascibility that is merely corporeal & does not proceed from want of benevolence: an over anxiety which is not bred of too much care & value for things less needful. That fascination by which the nerves draw the mind of a sufferer ever upon themselves is a different thing from intense selfishness, and those aids to the frail body which are so often placed to the account of self indulgence, are in fact mere accessories to the miserably weak. I have even looked at the gay squares & terraces to which I was conducted for a change of scene, & felt as if *they* made me more miserable by their lightsomeness.

Good Genius. Then nervous & mental affections which originate so differently too often become interfused, acting & reacting upon one another. Unless great vigilance be exerted we are apt to suffer the encroachments of what we may control because much that looks like weakness of will is as involuntary as an ague or a fever. We must look as steadily to see where weakness of body ends & where that of the mind begins as sometimes in a bright clear atmosphere to discern the green sward that bounds the lake from its vivid picture in the smooth sheet of water.

Invalid. Lookers-on fancy that they are without the charmed circle in which they suppose their patient to be confined. Turn a deaf ear they say to those who are under the spell of nervousness—as Ulysses to the Mariners bewitched by a Syren.

Good Genius. The charm consists in this—that the patient's bodily frame is in a new state, a state of which he has not learnt to judge; an infant knows not its strength or its weakness or the capabilities of its body in any respect: in some sort a person whose nervous system is thoroughly deranged is in the same state; he is deceived by his sensations and thinks that they signify & foreshew that which they do not. [B]ut while Reason remains he may still profit by experience —he may learn to measure his powers after a new rate: how far he does this steadily, & sets upon it resolutely[,] must depend on the degree to which he is possessed of discernment & moral energy. For instance, a nervous patient *feels* as if he were too weak to stand on his feet; when induced to make a trial he finds that he can stand, though he cannot stand long, & that sensation will not delude him in the future. After a certain quantity of experience he may reasonably conclude that a certain amount of exertion is more than he can well bear because he finds not merely that it seems as if it would injure at the time but that it really does injure in the end. Sensation therefore is his guide first & last, but he has learnt to interpret his new sensations more fairly than he did in the beginning. But he must never confound a morbid state of sensation with aberration of Reason.[2]

Invalid. They tell me of nervous persons—Hypochondriacs, who are not deluded by the novelty of their sensations merely, but by the workings of their own fancies. One thinks that his head is too big to pass the door. Another believes that his left leg is shrunk though when measured it is proved to be the same size as the right.

> These living teapots stand one arm held out
> One bent; the handle this & that the spout;
> A pipkin there, like Homer's tripod, walks:
> Here sighs a jar, & there a goose pye talks.

Good Genius. Hypochondria of this sort & Mania may be two different species of the same genius—but both are madness if madness be a want of the full use of the reasoning power. However, I can imagine a man to be so overpowered by strong sensations that he may act as if he believed that such things were, while his reason is assuring him that they have no existence. He feels exactly as if he had a glass leg—he cannot bear to treat his leg as if it were not of glass because the imagination of breaking a glass leg lies like a horrid incubus upon his spirits: this may be the intermediate link between madness & morbid sensation. The moment he believes his leg to be really of glass he is mad.

Invalid. The dispute is about words & yet there is a confusion in the minds of many persons on the subject[;] when they are told a man is deluded by sensation they believe he has lost the use of his reason.

Good Genius. The two disorders may often be intermixed—but there is clearly a difference in kind between them & it is the duties of those to whom Reason & consequently conscious responsibility remain that we are now discussing.

Invalid. Well can I remember the horror I have felt as a child from the thought of Ghosts and remembrance of ghostly pictures & stories in the dark. Not that I ever feared that any such frightful objects would actually appear before me, but the copy of them in my mind's eye was more than my nerves

---

2. The importance SC places on Reason in this dialogue anticipates her 250-page essay "Rationalism," which she appended to the 1843 edition of *Aids to Reflection.*

could bear. I believe I was thought superstitious by some who witnessed my fearfulness.[3]

Good Genius. The miserable physical sensations instantly bring thoughts of sorrow and suggest ghostly images of association, as a green leafy tree makes us think of summer.

Invalid. I am perplexed by the conflicting advices which are offered me in regard to medicine, diet, & general management. It is not materials for comfort but the capacity for comfort that is wanting. Motives are suggested[, but] alas what used to be motives are such no longer—healthy sensation alone lends force to the motives of our daily & hourly endeavours & pursuits[,] & till we have lost health of nerves we know not how much we have been acting from the stimulus of animal spirits, inspiring us with hope & joy—how little on reason & religious principle.

Good Genius. Of course. It is not by an insight into our bodily system—by rules drawn from fundamental knowledge of it—that we can be guided: we must proceed experimentally, feeling our way step by step.

Invalid. It is tantalizing to live unrestored in a land of restorations; & you may depend on it, says one of my advisors. Dr. S——— is the man to set you right. I lay on a sofa for 12 months & derived no benefit from the [dawdling?] management of other medical men, but his energetic measures soon brought me round. "O" says another, beware of those goading doctors! I had been ill for some time when a favourable turn in my complaint came on, & I verily believe I should gradually have recovered if I had not fallen into the hands of the dreadful Doctor D——— who forced me to walk when I was fainting with fatigue & thereby plunged me into all my old miseries. Under Dr. Bland's care I got into a comfortable state of health & I am confident that his judicious treatment is just what would suit your constitution. A third is convinced that the complaint has been eradicated by a particular system of diet—a fourth believes that an instantaneous miracle has been wrought in her favour by a quack medicine—a fifth recommends you to try one of the heads of the profession, saying that those who have the widest field of experience and [have been] appealed to in so many desperate cases must have more judgment than others.

Good Genius. The natural powers of the constitution or causes not within man's cognizance come to their aid and the remedy last applied. The medical man who perhaps gives Nature a helping hand when she is beginning in earnest to help herself wins all the credit of the cure: As the fresh water stream meets & mingles with the tide and that seems to be the river which chiefly belongs to the Sea.

3. For a more detailed account of SC's childhood fears, see her autobiography, pp. 265–66.

Invalid. Nervous derangement is seldom cured by medicine[,] and many an ailing medical man may exclaim

> Vei mihi quod nullis nervus est medicibilis herbis
> Nec prosunt domino prae prosunt omnibus artes!
> [Ah, me! that nervousness is not curable by medical herbs
> Nor do those arts profit the Lord or all others before him.]

It is best to try all which appear to have done good in similar cases & which are not likely to be injurious if they fail. As to which is considered generally the fittest for those whose digestion is weakened—we merely adopt the general role to each particular constitution. Otherwise by superstitious strictures we may surrender to many unpleasant & troublesome observances. Invalids have known persons who could not digest mutton—others who were disordered by cheese—others by milk or eggs: but all these are generally digestible. On the other hand, veal is considered uniformly indigestible—yet I have known invalids [who] eat it without feeling the worse.

Good Genius. It is easy to understand how any particular system of prescriptions or prohibitions may gain & maintain credit. Nature is versatile & the nature of man more self-adoptive than that of any other living thing. She accommodates herself to new *circes,* turns all materials to the best advantage, & thus rules of management are determined useful & necessary which are in reality less good or no better than others. While she is striving onward, regardless of our puny endeavours, we[,] like the fly on the Carriage windows[,] fancy that we are effecting the movement. It is absurd however to fancy that diet can be a cure in these cases. The most you can say of it is that it is the [condition?] without which you would not get well. For the details of management we must chiefly rely upon ourselves. Medical advice cannot be the pilot of our voyage—it is only the chart which may aid us in steering ourselves.

Invalid. But how great a reputation some medical men obtain for the treatment of nervous depression & weakness.

Good Genius. The man most likely to give relief in such cases is not so much he who is the most learned & experienced general physician—(such men may perceive that palliation only is in their power & sometimes scarcely that—pay little attention to them—) but he who has studied the particular complaint most carefully, & has the most knowledge of human nature under this particular influence. To infuse confidence, to suggest hopeful considerations, to soothe irritation, to amuse & relieve by temporary shifts & amusive novelties & [appliances?] which can only be suggested by one who has taken pains to know the patient's peculiarities of body & mind—and to do all this with the authority of one who has a name for curing nervousness—all this you will say is the business of a nurse rather than a physician—but I believe it is by such nurse like arts that many a physician has gained immense practice.

But even if all those persons have been cured in the way they suppose[,] it is but a mere chance that your illness will yield to similar treatment.

Invalid. People are apt to forget that it is nervous John or nervous Jane they have to deal with. They seem to be thinking of a certain evil spirit called nervousness, & fancy that when this goblin enters into an unhappy mortal it is to be expelled by the same method, mortified by the same [stripes?], pacified by the same sop, wherever it is to be found.

Good Genius. Diseases are like tulips & auriculas which vary without limit according to unknown differences of soil & situation.

Invalid. Everyone is born a physician—we feel that knowledge & accuracy are necessary before we decide on the class or species of a plant, but we decide upon disorders & assure Miss A. that she is held exactly like Mrs. B. from vague recollections & imaginary resemblance. The stage of growth too is not taken into account—we do not consider whether a malady is or is not ripe for a particular treatment.

Good Genius. The Quackery of applying one specific to all cases which go by the same name is indeed a very general error. Why was Dr. Baillie so great a physician?[4] It is stated in his life that he more than most men had studied & was clear sighted [enough] to apprehend the individual constitution which he had to deal with: looking upon every fresh case in some certain sense a new thing under the sun, yet viewing it under the light of whatever principles there are in medicine as well as of a wide experience of medical facts. Not bearing in mind these distinctions[,] patients attend with undue eagerness to every fresh case they hear of and are the sport of anxious hopes & bitter disappointments, which are succeeded by double despondency; while friends are led to recommend measures and management which may do harm, or at any rate cause further trouble & expense.

———————————

Invalid. With every determination to sacrifice a shorter present to a longer future & to conquer my complaint as far as resolution can do it[,] I often really know not how to act for the best in regard to the degree of exertion which it is proper to make. I am constantly told that habit is everything—but I have not found that perseverance was rewarded by success when I endeavoured to continue the practices of health.

4. Matthew Baillie (1761–1823), author of *The Morbid Anatomy* (1795) and physician to George III, was the first to define what we now call cirrhosis of the liver. His *Collected Works* were published in 1825.

Good Genius. We must do a great deal not with the expectation of being better but in order that we may not be worse. We must take air & exercise for instance long after they have ceased to afford refreshment or that salutary fatigue which promotes sound sleep & every healthy function: they will not avert the impending malady, but they will keep off other evils—muscular inability & the aggravation of illness which inaction & want of fresh air will produce.

Invalid. But must I persevere when my weakness increases the more rapidly the more it is thus resisted? When the very roots of the malady which causes the weakness is increased by it!

> Spesso chi crede il fumo fuggir cade nel fuoco.
> [He who sees little smoke often falls into the fire.]

Good Genius. Habit is good—but don't kill the horse in habitualizing him to live with little food. The lesser necessity must yield to its greater, & a patient may be more irremediably injured by overexertion in one day than by underexertion for years. The bow may be bent to a certain point with impunity or with benefit—one hairsbreadth beyond that point spoils it for ever. Advisors are too apt to forget that the law must be limited by the state of the sufferer—as sufferers are to think the law is to be abrogated when it ought only to be modified. Those who are apart[,] those who have little personal experience[,] are prone to build up theories which are more than half false, because uncorrected by observations of facts, those who are suffering or continually watching a sufferer are so much impressed by the force of the malady that they frequently give into its demands.

Invalid. I hear also that such is the force of habit in the nerves that the oftener they played certain peaks the oftener they are like to play them again: if that be the case how is recovery possible?

Good Genius. Because there are great counteracting causes, unperceived by us, which bring about revolutions for the better as for the worse. But this fact is an argument for soothing the nerves & sacrificing or venturing a great deal in order to stop their paroxysm when they are at their worst. We must meet Nature half way on the first opportunity, not going beyond our strength, nor suffering our powers to rust for want of use.

Invalid. It is said that the poor shall be poorer—& certainly it is so with the poor in health who not only have the malady itself working against them but those privations which the malady induced. During one part of my illness I suffered from a total loss of appetite—with despair I heard that a generous diet was absolutely necessary for me, & saw my friends exerting their calming imaginations to devise concentrated essences of meats, by which the largest possible quantity of nourishment might be conveyed in the narrowest space with least opposition from the shrinking stomach. Then came a craving fit: whatever I took seemed as if it were cast into a yawning gulf and did nothing perceptible toward contracting the gulf, while I felt conscience stricken at every morsel—because how could one with such digestive powers, and without the aids to digestion of air & exercise, profitably or safely dispose of such a load of food?

Good Genius. Nature, as I have already observed, has an adaptive compensatory power. She finds her way out of the Labyrinth which we see but in part. The same bodily state which brings inability brings about that which hinders its effects from being utterly ruinous, & the necessary habits of an Invalid, if adopted by a person in full health, would probably engender disease and misery. One evil neutralizes another as he who is stunned feels the second blow less keenly than that which stunned him. If a man is confined to his bed with a broken leg or lies down—unnecessarily he ruins his health.

Invalid. Ought we then to comply with all the demands of the Appetite?

Good Genius. The demands of the Appetite faithfully indicate the wants of the stomach. The Epicurean is betrayed into surfeit not by his Appetite but by his fanciful palate and [envying?] far more than his share of luxurious enjoyments.

Invalid. This cannot be doubted when the stomach is in a natural state. But surely it is a proverb that one must deny water to the dropsical patient.

Good Genius. As it appears impossible to decide when the appetite is non compos, we must judge as well as we can by trial, but if we have reason on the whole to think that obeying the demands of the body answers better than resisting let us not systematically pursue the latter course from any theory which we may have formed upon the subject.

Invalid. Another case of conscience with me is in regard to the use of stimulants and narcotics, particularly laudanum. Every medical man speaks ill of the drug, prohibits it, & after trying in vain to give me sleep without it, ends with prescribing it himself.

Good Genius. Every other more natural method must be tried fully & fairly before we have recourse to this: we must take air & exercise if possible.

Invalid. I have done so but exertion produces over-fatigue & consequent restlessness: this is not the mere effect of novelty for I have repeated the experiment till it would be folly to repeat it again.

Good Genius. In these cases we must try to make out whether the suffering or the remedy be really the greater evil, being honest with ourselves in this inquiry[;] if we decide in favour of the palliative, it will be our duty to use it as cheerfully & thankfully as we can—not diminishing the relief it affords by dwelling upon the degree of mischief which it may probably be doing to the constitution: that must [be] placed as far out of the mind's reach as possible among the class of inevitable evils. What we do thus cautiously & rationally can never become a bad mental habit, which is the continuance in some undesirable course against the dictates of our better judgment; and it is the liability to become a habit that is the chief evil of laudanum taking, rather than the bodily effects. But we must never suffer it to become a habit—but every time we have recourse to it [we] must ask ourselves if it really be as necessary as it was at first: we must never think of taking it to procure positive comfort, but only to ward off obstinate sleeplessness, and that not so much on account of the immediate suffering as the after injurious effects of irritation and fatigue. "The measure itself is of less consequence than the manner & spirit in which it is pursued." As to the effect on the constitution[,] we must bear in mind how many trying remedies and sense disorders the human frame frequently sustains & yet [is] restored to comfortable health in the end. (Do not take it & keep asking yourself[,] "Can I ever leave it off?" If you have reason to think you shall become a slave to it, give it up whatever it costs you[;] if you have reason to think that you *shall* be able to leave it off hereafter & that it is a useful temporary expedient[,] cease to tease yourself by such questionings.)

Invalid. Many advisors dissuade the nervous from the use of wine and stimulating liquors.

Good Genius. To some constitutions wine may be beneficial[,] and whatever puts the general health into the best condition of course must be favourable to the nerves. It may be wrong to add stimulus in order to meet a weakness which ought to be counteracted by more efficacious & sober means; moderate quantity to which we have been long accustomed generally ceases to affect the nerves sensibly[,] though the withdrawal of it may cause an intolerable sense of faintness.

Invalid. In some cases even the wanted glass of wine causes unwanted irritation when the nerves have become disordered.

Good Genius. Of course, it must then be abandoned. However, during illness we should take stimulants medicinally with a view to the general health & not to the immediate effect. If we have to undergo that which produces very great & unusual exhaustion[,] it may be allowable to fortify ourselves thus—but let us not take a glass of wine the more because we expect an interview with a friend and wish to appear more bright & steady than usual. The nerves will not help themselves if they are thus helped continually. An infant must be carried till it can walk, but if it be borne in arms after it may safely attempt walking[,] its muscles will never gain strength, and if the new supplies of animal vigour are not employed they produce disease instead of health.

Invalid. A notion prevails that nervous incapacity is but imaginary—that by a strong effort of the will it may be dissipated. We are told of the exertions made by persons who seemed in a state of utter prostration when some sudden paramount necessity has arisen[,] and it is alleged that a spirit-stirring event or trance of awful expectation has caused the often moping wretch to spring up into energy & cheerfulness.

Good Genius. Mental stimulus will produce wonderful effects upon the body in cases of functional derangement. A strong excitement has even suspended for a time the pain and powerlessness produced by gout[,] and the story of the addict Linnaeus, who left his bed to which he was confined by this complaint, to examine a young traveller's botanical treasures brought from the Western Hemisphere[,] is well known. But this sort of mental stimulus we cannot procure at will—it is efficacious because it is unforeseen & unprovided by the person on whom it is to act. The force from without—the suddenness—the surprise has wrought the charge, and we cannot surprise ourselves. If I give myself a blow it is not as if another gave it to me.

Invalid. Many persons suppose that a mental medicine is applicable only to the mind. They suppose that patients in such cases are merely put into better humour—better heart and hope. Good sense & energy of mind they think would have enabled them to make the same efforts which the foreign stimulus appears to have done. So they forget that the body is affected through the mind either for good or for bad, although the phrase ["]dying of a broken heart["] is in every body's mouth.

Good Genius. If a man having a wound in some part of his body spoke of it as causing intolerable misery and behaved like a person in severest pain, but upon hearing some piece of good news or striking event, forgets to complain for several hours, & preserves a cheerful countenance, we may fairly infer that the grievance was slighter than he represented it at first—that it might have been borne more patiently. But this is no parallel to the case of the nervous patient who appears lively & at ease after an application of the same kind. In him the bodily affection is actually removed or revived by the mental stimulus—the relaxed nerves are braced up again: while in the wounded man the bodily pain is not assuaged. [T]he wound burns & throbs as before, but his mind being amused he bears it better.

Invalid. Some aver than such Doctrines whether true or no are expedient, as the belief of them in those aroused tends to keep the patient from yielding more than he can possibly avoid to the force of the disorder.

Good Genius. Can any doctrine be salutary in the end that is untrue? If we fancy that by reasoning & perseverance alone we can triumph over that which is a bodily weakness, though affecting the mind & affected by the mind, we mistake the objects which those powers are fitted to deal with as much as if we tried to curb the wind with a bit & bridle or to pierce a shadow with fire and shot; we fail & the failure causes disappointment and irritation: such a notion entertained by others must lead to wrong and harsh judgments expressed or understood, whereby the sufferer's heavy burden is rendered more galling than before, and he is discouraged from those efforts which it is still in his power to make.

Invalid. I can testify by my own experience to this truth. Had I but known as well as I do now what it is possible to achieve & what must be submitted to as inevitable[,] how much regret and bitterness of spirit I should have been spared.

Invalid. On the grounds which you admit[,] however[,] many advocate the use of violent applications and rousing remedies. They would not [hesitate?] to administer an electric shock to the mind and body.

Good Genius. All violence of this kind, [and] I use the words of an intelligent physician, is stabbing in the dark. Many a nervous patient may have been set right by a sudden shock—his whole system revolutionized—but with our present [lights?] surely it is the height of rashness to try such experiments. We hear of the successful cases; those which fail are not spoken of; and I firmly believe that in many suffering has been aggravated & the source of it strengthened by over-strong appliances. The impulse which may by chance force the disordered machine back to its original state will more probably make the dislocation worse if not shatter it to pieces. We fancy that we can see how to direct the force aright, but there lies the fallacy. We cannot see the whole. We cannot see even a part distinctly.

Invalid. It is commonly said that the poor and lowly are free from nervous disorders, leisure & luxury being the promoters of them.

Good Genius. Disorder of nerves may be promoted by almost anything that is injurious to the mind and constitution. Leisure and luxury are not the only circumstances which are unfavourable to perfect sanity & therefore not the only producers of nervousness.

Invalid. It is alleged that refinement of mind, cultivated sensibilities, rich fare, and sedentary habits occasion a more precarious constitution of nerves than falls to the lot of the poor.

Good Genius. The more delicate and exquisite any production becomes the more liable it is to injury, and some habits of the rich are not merely over-refining, but positively conducive to disease. There is truth in the doctrine, but it is stated too broadly. [That] the poor are never nervous is one of those cant sayings which are found highly convenient in helping to prove certain popular theories—they are current coin which pass from hand to hand and which few take the pains to judge for the sake of ascertaining whether they are true money or counters. There is plenty of medical authority for saying that nervous disorders, accompanied with depression, apathy, and a train of miserable mental affections are by no means unknown among the hard-working classes[,] and my experience furnishes me with several lamentable instances.[5] In their case want of rest & comfort were thought to have caused their malady; had they been living at ease & in luxury it would have been said that want of constant employment and the braces of necessity had made them invalids. Both may cause their effects.

Invalid. The poor seldom talk of nerves—they simply say they are ill when they are in a suffering state and deprived of their natural degree of power; when they have learnt from the Doctor that their complaint is beyond the reach of his aid, they trouble themselves little about its nature and definition.

Good Genius. Among those who discourse about the poor & bring forward what they do & suffer[,] how few have more than a superficial acquaintance with their habits and conditions generally.

Invalid. Under the most favourable circumstances[,] derangement of the nervous system must be a heavy trial, but how greatly is it aggravated by our own experience and that of others!

Good Genius. Nervous derangement is in many ways most trying both to those who undergo and them who witness it: those who suffer have to allow for the ignorance in others of what can be recognized by so few outward signs, and those around have great need of charity and candour to put faith in our report, and shew pity for ills with which they cannot sympathize. They who are thus afflicted should feel that since God has chosen to place them in a state so liable to stumbling it is doubly incumbent on them to be vigilant & hold fast by Reason & those faculties that they yet possess fully; while those around should bear in mind that no temptation is so overpowering as that which like nervous

---

5. Anne Parrott, SC's maidservant, was a frequent victim of hysterical fits, and her irregular health was a great source of irritation to the Coleridge family during the 1830s and 1840s.

illness is ever present, arising from the bodily state & not from faculties which are only called into action by particular occasions.

Invalid. Indeed it is not possible that we should be thoroughly understood—except by those who have been fellow sufferers or have watched a fellow sufferer with the anxious eye of affection through all the phases of a similar complaint. Who could conceive thirst that had never been thirsty? Thus instead of soothing [reassurances?] & truly judicious advice from the generally [considerate?,] we receive misapplied maxims and tedious admonitions.

Good Genius. From the dis-courses even of the ignorant or half learned we may gather something that is useful. The commonplace talk made up of what is gleaned from the harvest of popular observation generally contains a portion of truth which is not amiss to be reminded of, and which from having our attention too exclusively occupied with one view of certain topics we might be apt to forget. Let us pick the grain of wheat from the heap that is offered us instead of feeling provoked at the quantity of chaff that it contains.

Invalid. But [consider] the harshness [&] the indelicacy that is often shown toward sufferers—the opportunity which it affords for offensive personality under cover of giving good advice.

Good Genius. Persons alas so rendered irritable and fanciful by nervous weakness are sadly too apt to create or magnify such evilmindedness in others: they themselves do not always distinguish rightly between the suggestions of the disease and those of reason. But even if such unpleasant conduct should be shown[,] let us endeavour to derive good from it.

> If a foe have kenn'd
> A rib of dry rot in thy ship's stout side,
> Think it God's message, & in humble pride,
> With heart of oak replace it;—thine the gains—
> Give him the rotten timber for his pains.
> S.T.C. ["Forbearance"]

Invalid. Once in [a] half angry half merry mood I drew up a paper of Advice to Advisors of the Nervous. I will give you a specimen of it.

Sympathy is like rain on the brown grass. Mingle admonition with sympathy according to the Lucretian prescription—let them feel that they are understood.

To be a fully competent judge of the complaint, as to its trials & requisitions, you should have been within the charmed circle yourself. There is a sort of knowledge which experience only can give—but they who have watched sufferers through all phases of the changeful complaint—one whom they are not predisposed to mistrust [?] must [?] qualified to judge concerning it.

[Do] not wonder at the change in a nervous person & think it inconsistent.

It is the capacity for comfort that is wanting.

Do not joke yourself[,] for like the sun against the fire that will be seen to put out its feeble glimmering of comfort but neither try to then excite your neighbour to joke— & listen with attention in order to excite by vanity or some other stimulus.

Good Genius. In the beginning of a course of illness we cannot manage our minds or bodies so advantageously as we can after we have gained experience: pena ativeduta assai men duole [pain hurts less the second time around]. Could we but foresee all our trials we might present a cuirass of steel instead of an unarmed breast to them—could we but regard a certain quantity of misapprehension as the inevitable accompaniment of such an affliction as ours we should be spared a good deal of needless irritation. We weary ourselves with vain efforts to push off that separate burden which seems as if it did not belong to our proper load—by which means we fling it into a still more uneasy position than before, we fret the poor skin, as well as waste our forces, sending them abroad to combat where a conquest will assuredly cost more than it is worth.

[1834]

On Mr. Wordsworth's Poem Entitled "Lines Left on a Yew-tree Seat"

In the Q[uarterly] Review of Nov[ember] 1834 I read a thought-awakening essay on Mr. W[ordsworth]'s poetical philosophy, or rather on the philosophical nature of his poetry.[1] [I]t struck me that this piece of criticism betokened originating powers as well as deep insights in the author's mind, but that this very originality or decided character of thought has caused him to interpret the language of Mr. W[ordsworth]'s muse in some instances rather according to his own genius than according to that which produced the "Lyrical Ballads," the "White Doe," and the "Excursion." Let me add "Peter Bell"—I will not omit to name that characteristic poem lest it should be suspected that my spirit is reluctant to own fealty there as well as to the kindred creations of the same mind, all of which with "Peter Bell" itself are as alike and as distinctly different, one among another, as it becomes a train of sister poems to be. I felt particularly indisposed to agree with the Reviewer in his ingenious commentary on the Lines left upon a Yew-tree seat. [A] reader who is truly simple, but not silly or frivolous, may sometimes read aright from very simplicity, that is, from resigning himself completely to the will of his author, and not being seduced from submitting to that influence by the suggestions of an autocratic spirit, moulding and colouring the author's materials of thought instead of giving itself to perceive the shapes and hues which he would have them present to the beholder's eye. [A]t any rate freshness of feeling and docility of mind are highly conducive to the power of deeply sympathizing with the sublime yet touching character of Mr. W[wordsworth]'s poetry; to understand every part of it, so as to be able to translate it correctly into prose—as far as that is possible—requires the higher

1. Henry Taylor, "Wordsworth's *Poetical Works,*" *QR* 52 (1834): 317–58. Sir Henry Taylor (1800–86)—dramatist, poet, and well-known man of letters—is chiefly remembered for his 1834 play, *Philip Van Artevelde.* At the time of her essay (Jan 1835), SC was not aware of Taylor's authorship nor was she friendly with him, although the two had met in 1823 when Taylor had visited Southey at Greta Hall. Reintroduced in 1837 by her brother Derwent, SC and Taylor began a friendship which lasted until her death in 1852. Unfortunately, the existing correspondence is slight—only some twenty letters (HRHRC MSS)—but it evidences good will and mutual respect. See above, p. 134 and n.

qualities of intellect, but in Wordsworth as in Shakespeare and every truly great
& popular poet[,] there is something which the understanding alone will not
recognize, and which may be felt by persons of very little power and compass of
thought.[2] I conclude therefore that a reader who has this poetical sense or
susceptibility about him may be delighted with fine and tender harmonies in
Mr. W[ordsworth]'s poetry which will escape the perception of a preoccupied
imagination or a temperament less fitted to receive impressions from the pecu-
liarities of its character, a temperament devoid of poetical sympathies altogether
or one that is filled with poetical sympathies of a somewhat different kind. On
these grounds I can fancy it possible that a person like myself may enter into the
spirit of certain poetical compositions more fully than some who are greatly my
superiors in power of mind: be this as it may[,] for my own gratification[,]
because I love to dwell on Mr. W[ordsworth]'s poetry, holding it up & turning it
round in the light like a wreath of precious stones[,] the colours of which are as
permanent as they are pure & splendid, though it reveals a thousand varying
hues & exquisite veins & markings according to the way in which it is looked at,
I will indulge my humour with discoursing a little upon that same spirit: and as
a young girl busies herself amid her treasure of rich carnations and odorous
jonquils with superfluous & pleasurable industry[,] placing and replacing them
in the flower pot, from the same sort of impulse will I argue with the Reviewer
concerning Mr. W[ordsworth]'s reflections on the Recluse of Esthwaite, taking
up his view of them, as Prince Harry did his Father's crown, putting it on and
pulling it off again, and playfully "trying with it as with an enemy," which had
murderously assaulted some of my long cherished and filially honoured poet-
ical notions.[3]

The interesting poem in question treats of one who owned no common soul,
a man of genius and learning who had gone forth to the world armed against all
enemies but neglect.

> The World, for so it thought,
> Owed him no service. Wherefore he at once
> With indignation turned himself away,
> And with the food of pride sustained his soul
> In solitude.

2. Writing to Mrs. Henry Jones in July 1835, SC noted, "Mr. Wordsworth opens to us a world of
suffering, and no writer of the present day, in my opinion, has dealt more largely or more nobly with
the deepest pathos and the most exquisite sentiment; but for every sorrow he presents an antidote—
he shews us how man may endure as well as what he is doomed to suffer."

3. On 7 Oct 1834, however, SC wrote to her husband, "I do not like some parts of this article in
Blackwood [John Wilson, "Coleridge's *Poetical Works*" 36 (1834): 542–70]. Wordsworth the
master of Coleridge indeed—that is gross flattery of the living Bard."

The poet describes with what a mournful pleasure, when Nature had subdued him to a gentle mood[,] he would think of those "to whom the world, and man itself, appeared a scene of kindred loveliness," and after relating how he lived and died in this melancholy & unfruitful seclusion[, he] philosophizes upon the story in the following lines:

> If Thou be one whose heart the holy forms
> Of young imagination have kept pure,
> Stranger! henceforth be warned; and know that pride,
> Howe'er disguised in its own majesty
> Is littleness; that he who feels contempt
> For any living thing, hath faculties
> Which he has never used; that thought with him
> Is in its infancy. The man whose eye
> Is ever on himself doth look on one,
> The least of Nature's works, one who might move
> The wise man to that scorn which wisdom holds
> Unlawful, ever. O be wiser, Thou!
> Instructed that true knowledge leads to love,
> True dignity abides with him alone
> Who, in the silent hour of inward thought,
> Can still suspect, and still revere himself,
> In lowliness of heart.

This admonition the Reviewer deems only applicable to & only intended for "another philosophic, or rather a pupil apt for becoming such"—by others he conceives that the lesson should be received with some qualification, and he sees a "peculiarity of sentiment" in the doctrine it propounds; whereas my feeling has ever been that the sentiment it avows may be no less generally entertained than those expressed in the words of our Savior—["]Blessed are the meek for they shall inherit the earth, blessed are the pure in heart for they shall see God,["] and ["]Be ye perfect as your Father in Heaven is perfect.["]—nor can I think that the appeal is made to a mind of "rare constitution," but to any mind which is capable of taking an interest in pure & spiritual things—which could be supposed likely to profit by the instructions of a Preacher, a Poet, or a Philosopher.

In addressing one whose heart has been kept pure by the holy forms of young imagination did the poet think only of a man "eminently endowed—one whose gift of imagination has filled his mind with pure & holy forms"? [I]f by these expressions we are to understand an individual possessed of uncommon intellectual qualities I can hardly believe it. Imagination, as we all know, is a part of every human mind, or a state which it is capable of passing into—an imaginative habit must proceed from that which is innate, but depends in some measure on the will of the individual. [P]oetic genius—and a powerful Imagination—are rare gifts, but imaginativeness can hardly be called an uncommon quality, & more or less of Imagination belongs to all. In lines prefixed to the "White Doe" we read that he who sees nothing but what is mournful and perishable in our mortal lot shews himself deficient in the glorious faculty of Imagination which can "colour life's dark cloud with orient rays," can "pluck the amaranthine flower of Faith," & can "bind round the Sufferer's temples wreaths that endure affliction's heaviest shower"[4]—but when Mr. Wordsworth appeals to this truly glorious faculty, what does he [say] more than the Apostle, who in declaiming that to be carnally minded is death, to be spiritually minded life and peace, and that we are saved by Hope [and] looking after things unseen,* appeals to that part of our nature which makes us capable of a Religious Faith? Emily, the heroine of the White Doe, is not a Sappho, but a "blameless Lady"—witness this passage among many others

> If, thou art beautiful, and youth
> And thought endue thee with all truth—
> Be strong;—be worthy of the grace
> Of God, and fill thy destined place:
> A Soul, by force of sorrows high,
> Uplifted to the purest sky
> Of undisturbed humanity!

The relationship between religion & poetry has been pointed out by Mr. Wordsworth in his Supplement to the Preface.[5] One of his later sonnets ends with these lines

---

*"For we walk by faith not by sight" Cor. 2.v.7. "We look not at the things which are seen, but at the things which are not seen" Cor. 2.iv.18.

---

4. From "Weak is the Will of Man," which was prefixed to "The White Doe" in 1815 and 1820.

5. WW writes, "Faith was given to man that his affections, detached from the treasures of time, might be inclined to settle upon those of eternity;—the elevation of his nature, which this habit produces on earth, being to him a presumptive evidence of a future state of existence; and giving him a title to partake of its holiness. The religious man values what he sees chiefly as an 'imperfect shadowing forth' of what he is incapable of seeing. The concerns of religion refer to indefinite objects, and are too weighty for the mind to support them without relieving itself by resting a great part of the burthen upon words and symbols. The commerce between Man and his Maker cannot be carried on but by a process where much is represented in little, and the Infinite Being accommodates himself to a finite capacity. In all this may be perceived the affinity between religion and poetry; between religion—making up the deficiencies of reason by faith; and poetry—passionate for the instruction of reason; between religion—whose element is infinitude, and whose ultimate trust is the supreme of things, submitting herself to circumscription, and reconciled to substitutions; and poetry—ethereal and transcendent, yet incapable to sustain her existence without sensuous incarnation" (*PWW*, p. 808). See also W. *Prose*, 3:62–84.

Then may we ask, though pleased that thought should range
Among the conquests of civility,
Survives imagination—to the change
Superior? Help to virtue does it give?
If not, O Mortals, better cease to live!
        ["The pibroch's note"]

Mr. W[ordsworth] thinks that if progressive improvement in the arts which ministers to luxury tends to sensualize the body of the people and render them less imaginative, in as much as it acts thus, it is impairing that which alone renders the gift of life desirable.

But the poet speaks of *young* Imagination, whose holy forms have power to keep the heart unspotted from the world—and thus in another place he characterizes his Happy Warrior as

The generous Spirit who when brought
Among the tasks of real life, hath wrought
Upon the plan that pleased his childish thought,

herein alluding to that pure and brilliant mirror which he represents the human mind to be when unimpaired in its truth & fidelity by the sullying deadening influences of the world and advancing years. In consonance with the spirit of this thought he tells his sister, in the verses on Tintern Abbey, that neither evil tongues, nor rash judgments, nor the sneers of selfish men, nor greetings where there is no kindness, nor all the dreary intercourse of daily life, will ever prevail to make that imagination grow old which is sustained and fed by the contemplation of Nature, but that even in the latter stages of life a mind so nourished may be the mansion for all lovely forms—while the memory is a dwelling place for all sweet sounds and harmonies.

The high themes with which this truth is connected are "bodied forth" in the Ode on the Intimations of Immortality from Recollections of early Childhood with imaginative splendour befitting the sublime subject; and the inestimable privileges of our early years are there said to be the source of perpetual benedictions in the poet's heart; for it is the purport of that lofty strain to declare that the "motion and the spirit which impels all thinking things, all objects of all thought, and rolls through all things,"[6] is ever working in the mind of men and inspiring those sensations and perceptions, those "obstinate questionings of sense and outward things" which are the tokens of immortality, and that in early childhood these influences of the eternal mind upon the human soul produce

---

6. SC is confused here. These lines are not from the "Intimations Ode" but from "Tintern Abbey."

indistinct glimpses of "worlds not realized" and strive after a state of being inconceivable by our present faculties:

> High instincts before which our mortal nature
> Did tremble like a guilty thing surprised
> ["Immortality Ode"]

These movements of the mind are stronger, these visions more vivid, than when years have brought the inevitable yoke, & custom lies upon us with a weight, heavy as frost and deep almost as life! The text of this poem is taken from a shorter one by the same author:

> The Child is the Father of the Man;
> And I could wish my days to be
> Bound each to each by natural piety.
> ["My Heart leaps up"]

Perhaps we may say that those involuntary motions, those immortal sensations, those "first affections" which seem to be "shadowy recollections" not of a state preexisting in time, but of eternity, from the very passiveness and unconsciousness of the childish mind, exhibit the nature of the soul in the strongest light; in after years such voices within us are not to be distinguished amid those of our conscious being, amid the developed powers of reason & reflection. I pretend now however to interpret this mystic strain, which for most readers can be nothing more than an intimation of certain intimations which a great poet's mind has given him respecting the mysterious nature of his soul; but even those for whom it is not intended, those who have not "been accustomed to watch the flux and reflux of their inmost nature, to venture at times into twilight realms of consciousness, and to feel deep interest in modes of inmost being, to which they know that the attributes of time and space are inapplicable & alien, but which cannot be conveyed save in symbols of time and space";[7] those for whom the ode is not only "high and arduous" but a pure mystery—a series of grand illustrations of a theme which is hidden from their understanding, or like the swelling and peaking of an organ to which a person of deficient musical ear may listen with a sense of grandeur, and the impression that there is a regular harmony in that succession of sounds which it is not in him to unravel—the least poetically or metaphysically disposed reader must acknowledge the vividness of sensations and perceptions when the powers of the mind are new and the greater warmth of the emotions in early youth. [F]or if we do not grow better through reflection as we advance in life, we are pretty sure to grow worse, less

---

7. *BL(CC)*, 2:147. This is the first of many instances in which SC will use unacknowledged quotations from her father. Interestingly, here STC is echoing WW's 1800 Preface—"fluxes and refluxes of the mind" (*W Prose*, 1:126).

innocent, generous, & compassionate. I think it is generally allowed too that youth is an imaginative age; poetical efficiency is a very composite power, and seldom arrives at relative perfection till the whole mind is mature; but it is in our opening years that we are most under the sway of the imagination, and can most afford to be so; & it is interesting to perceive how "lightly tied to earth" are many youthful sufferers—not because they enjoy their temporal condition [less] than older persons, but because the original brightness of their imaginative past is less dimmed by converse with the world, less repressed in its operation by earthly cares & excitements, so that the life to come is more strongly present to their minds & has more hold on their affections.[8] Such being the tone, as it appears to me, of Mr. Wordsworth's sentiments on this subject, I cannot but believe that he addressed his warning and his exhortation, not to some gifted individual who shared his own subtlety of intellect and superior energy of the imaginative power, but to "thinking hearts" in general.

On the maxim [in "The Yew-tree Seat"] that "pride, howe'er disguised in its own majesty, is littleness," the Reviewer observes how "essential it is not only to the philosophic character, but to the moral elevation of any man, that he should regard every atom of pride which he may detect in his nature as something which detracts from dignity, inasmuch as it evinces some want of independence and natural strength." And he is of the opinion that it is "this servility and cowardice of the inmost spirit, together with the artifices or the excesses naturally resorted to in such a state of slavery that Mr. W[ordsworth] detects when he bids us

> 'know that pride,
> Howe'er disguised in its own majesty,
> Is littleness.'"

But it does not strike me that the spirit of the poem is to inculcate a stoical self-sufficiency of soul: in a certain sense, undoubtedly, every well-constituted mind is self-sufficient, insomuch that he who satisfies all that the conscience of a Christian can require may be supposed able to retain his peace of mind even if the whole world should condemn & despise him, and the inconveniences arising from being "unduly dependent on the opinions of others for happiness" are unfelt by him who makes the best of his own nature. Yet it appears to me that pride in this passage is characterized as littleness, not merely or so much

8. SC here slightly revises the opinions expressed by WW at the beginning of his "Essay, Supplementary to the Preface." Whereas WW is not particularly complimentary to the "juvenile Reader . . . in the height of his rapture," and chooses to place more faith in those mature readers who treat poetry "as a study," SC finds a philosophic advantage in youthful "otherworldliness." Her position anticipates a lengthy discussion of the youthful imagination in her review of Tennyson's *Princess*. See pp. 138-40.

because it evinces a "want of that independence and natural strength," which enables the possessor to resist all impressions from without, as because it is the essence of pride to be self-centred—to have no other object but self—and as the poet afterwards nobly announces, "the man whose eye is ever on himself doth look on one the least of Nature's works." A "keen desire of aggrandisement in the eyes of others, a sensitive apprehension of humiliation in their eyes" are doubtless constituents of pride, but what does this excessive anxiety arise from but the exclusive contemplation of self and the "littleness" of soul which is both the condition and the consequence of such a habit, a habit which engenders a feeling of repulsion from our fellow creatures and at the same time slavish dependence on them? For a man is apt to hate those who have power to make him miserable, and this very hatred puts him still more in their power.

Now I think that Mr. Wordsworth condemns the Solitary for having cultivated this self-centredness of spirit—that it was his aim to turn the hearts of men from the worship of that false majesty which pride creates out of selfishness & invests with phantom robes of state.[9] The littleness of such a spirit Mr. W[ordsworth] satirizes in A Poet's Epitaph.

> A Moralist perchance appears;
> Led, Heaven knows how! to this poor sod:
> And he has neither eyes nor ears;
> Himself his world, and his own God;
>
> One to whose smooth-rubbed soul can cling
> Nor form, nor feeling, great nor small;
> A reasoning, self sufficing thing,
> An intellectual All-in-All!

Man, while he dwells only in himself and does not soar upward in love of God and move abroad in love of God's creation, by those good impulses which are the work of grace in the heart, and for which the motives of an enlightened but merely human self-love can never be a substitute; if he does not put on a "better nature than his own," and "raise himself above himself" and out of himself, by growing in all those divine graces which our Savior has declared can alone render us meek partakers of that glory which her merits alone procure; if

---

9. Writing to her husband on 7 Sept 1838, SC remarked of the Wordsworths, "The latter years of that family have not been like the earlier ones which I look back upon, and which are steeped in sunshine. . . . But now there is a settled dulness—no Lyrical Ballads—no Excursion—no White Doe of Rylstone issue from that quarter now. No gladsome Miss Wordsworth and cheerful Miss Hutchinson to say alternately sharp and kind things; no naughty but mirthful Willy at the door— the careless disorder turned to anxious men and women—the bard shorn of his vigour by age, and of his gentleman-like courtesy of manner. For on both points I remember him very different from what he is now."

he thus disobeys the voice of God speaking from within him, well indeed may he be called the "least of Nature's works" and of all created things most miserable because least answering the purposes of his creation. It has long been proved by argument, what indeed the tenour of common discourse shews to be *felt* by most men, though reflected on by comparatively few, that love and charity, like all other special affections, virtuous or otherwise, do not regard self: that the object of every affection, except that of self-love, is something external, though pleasure is inseparable from the attainment of the object for him that seeks it— namely the *subject* of the affection. Those heavenward tendencies which are in the constitution of the soul & form a part of its very idea, and which since the mysterious corruption of the will may be revived by divine influence, those are not one and the same with an enlightened regard to our own well being, and though the Philosopher, after the example of his blessed Instructor & Redeemer, treats through the mediation of that principle in his endeavours to elevate mankind, it is in the hope that he may ultimately bring about a state of feeling in which the consideration of self, *as* self, has no predominance. Thus it may be conceivable that he objects to pride not solely, or chiefly, because it detracts from that ease and comfort, and conscious power and dignity, which results from our feeling independent of others for all those blessings, but looking still further, because, like malice, envy, hatred, anger, revenge, covetedness, and all its kindred evil passions, it is the antagonist of divine love, and represses the germination of those unselfish affections which minister to the perfect happiness of him who has them in his bosom. In one case, as much as in the other, he appeals to the self-love of him whom he seeks to influence, but he appeals to it, according to this hypothesis, on deeper grounds and more pregnant considerations—at least if the distinction which I have attempted to draw be just.

As the Reviewer continues, "the next step takes us into Mr. W[ordsworth]'s peculiar domain." We are told that

> he, who feels contempt
> For any living thing hath faculties
> That he has never used; that thought with him
> Is in its infancy.

"It is here that were we to understand the doctrine as delivered for acceptation by mankind at large we should take some exceptions. The moral government of the world appears to us to require, that in every day intercourse of ordinary man with man, room should be given to the operation of the harsher sentiments of our nature—anger, resentment, contempt. They were planted in us for a purpose, and are not essentially and necessarily wrong in themselves, although they may easily be wrong in their direction." The Reviewer here admits that Mr.

W[ordsworth] is prohibiting contempt & especially that species of it which is produced by the worship of self love; now it appears to me that all passionate contempt of living things may be traced to a selfish source as it might have been in the case of the Solitary. How do we suppose that an angelic nature would be affected toward the most degraded human being? surely not with that sensation which possesses our less holy bosoms when we despise a fellow creature. And if we, even with our finite understanding, made use of all the faculties inherent in the soul, if our thinking part had grown to its full stature, we too should be incapable of this feeling of contempt—still more of a contemptuous frame of mind. [W]e should look on every living thing in a benign spirit, condemning and despising the evil that may be in any individual but having no unkind affection toward the individual himself, being raised far above that temper which makes us view with scorn certain persons on the score of certain qualities belonging to them which in some way or other are causing annoyance to ourselves. It is usual to talk of a cool contempt, and contempt does indeed so far tend to render us cool as it frees us from fear of its object; but contempt for living creatures is always an emotion something different from the mere consciousness that certain things are base and unworthy. Now the only emotion that ought to accompany such a consciousness, according to the law of Christianity, is that of sorrow: every feeling akin to hatred is forbidden by the divine law-giver, be the object what it may.[10] Therefore the poet goes not a hairsbreadth beyond his heavenly guide when he condemns all contempt of persons, even those whose predominating qualities, or whose conduct at any given time, may be truly contemptible. Thus he avers that the man whose eye is ever on himself is the most unworthy of created beings and might prove a wise man to scorn *if* such a passion were not held unlawful by wisdom, and the disposition here condemned is the very source of contempt which is previously reprobated: the man despises others because he looks perpetually on himself, and estimates all men according[ly] as they minister to the gratification of his selfishness. A bigot in religion or politics heartily despises those who differ from him in opinion—a good Christian feels sure that an infidel is greviously in the wrong, but does not despise him. [T]he bigot feels contempt, in reality, not because his opponents have missed the truth but because they will not acknowledge what he wishes to be the truth; the good Christian regards his erring brother with no other *feeling* but that of compassionate sorrow because he has no selfish pride to be offended by the denial of his creed—because he has cultivated the true knowledge that leads to Love.

It may be added that a great part of the mean opinion which we have of individuals arises from the contradiction and partiality of our views—If we

10. Cp. STC on sorrow, *BL(CC)*, 2:235, 244.

could look upon ourselves & others, upon God & the Universe, with eyes that celestial euphony have purged, we should find the relative quantities of and bearings of good & evil, and consequently their value in the balance, to be greatly different from what they appear to our uncleansed vision. It is apparent that the highest intellectual powers will not secure this clear-sightedness, and [the] "hazy mists," which not one ray of Christian light could dissipate, darken many eyes which are embued with the power to see deeper and farther even than those of common mortals. But if men of the most ordinary powers of mind would not but make a full use of all their faculties, constantly improving their moral being "daily self surpassed," instead of living only for those things which must worsen with time, the result would not fail to be blessed and glorious.

On the other hand, a virtuous indignation—a sorrow for sin—a deep conviction that it is devoid of all worth and dignity, whatever aspect it may have to the worldling who beholds it through the mist of prejudice and passion—these sentiments the philosopher must entertain as strongly as any other man; and if the habit of considering things on a great scale, if taking a wide survey of human action, tended to abate our lively sense of particular instances of moral good or evil instead of being a precious gift[,] a philosophic turn of mind would be an infinite disadvantage, as hindering our progress in the knowledge of those things which concern our peace. But such lapses can never take place while our feelings are continually quickened by fresh draughts of that best knowledge to which every other must be subservient. A philosopher, inasmuch as his powers of discernment are superior to those of others[,] will be oftener obliged to perceive and regret the existence of evil; and as far as it is useful to society that the bad conduct of men should be punished, he will feel it his duty to exert himself to that effect, and by outward actions to mark his hatred of inequity, though he feels no hatred against the man who has acted inequitously. He will punish in order to repress crime or misconduct, according to the spirit of British law, not for the sake of avenging himself or others upon the offender—"Vengeance is mine saith the Lord"—not that the supreme Being can be supposed capable of anger, hatred, or revenge, but that according to the working of that universal system of which He is the author[,] retribution must necessarily come upon evil doers; and there is a certain resemblance between such results and those which human anger and revenge are producing upon the earth. Thus you may sentence a culprit to severe punishment without transgressing the precept—"Do unto them as you would they should do unto you." For the man who inflicts pain out of pure benevolence is acting upon the principles on which he desires that every other human being should act, and we all know that the spirit of that injunction is simply that in all our actions we are to be uninfluenced by any preferences of self, but that our consciousness of what is useful and necessary to ourselves is to inform us what is useful and necessary to others.

Doubtless even the unholy passions by God's permission are working to-gether with all other things to bring about his good purposes. Such good may come, yet woe be to them by whom it comes. And is it not a question whether, if any particular individual acted toward his neighbours universally in the same spirit with which a wise and tender parent manages his family, punishing and rebuking out of love and not out of anger and dislike, he might not do more good by his example and influence than he would ever effect by resisting evil at the instigation of his own natural passion. [The Reviewer argues,] "Let the sentiment of justice be paramount and it will lead to such serious consideration of the grounds of our hostile feelings as will in itself and of necessity temper them." But how can he who allows the passion of anger to remain in his heart be sure that it will not get the better of justice: passion would cease to be passion if it rose and fell obedient to the voice of reason, and we shall not long be strictly just if we do not strive to be more than just.[11] [T]here are two powers warring for mastery over us—the flesh and the spirit—in whatever degree we yield to carnal inclinations, a further concession will be demanded.[12] [I]f we follow the spirit, that guide will lead us far beyond mere justice, according to the common acceptation of the word—but if justice be one and the same with the eternal law of righteousness then will justice not only temper our hostile feelings but extinguish them altogether?

It is said [by the Reviewer], "The same sentiments are not to be cultivated by all sorts of minds: the standard of right and wrong is not so ill adapted to human nature as to take no account of its idiosyncrasies, and to make all dispositions equally right or wrong in every frame and fabric of mind in which they are to be found throughout the infinite varieties of moral structures." Certainly the stan-dard of right and wrong is so far adjusted to the varieties of human nature that more or less is required according to what is given, but I cannot believe that a different quality as well as different quantity of virtue is to be expected from different persons. It is quite true that there are "men whose admirable gifts of contemplation, whose clear intellectual insight, whose singular powers of com-municating charitable thoughts would be in part obscured & defeated by the admission of feelings alien to *their* natures," but surely it is not to such men that the warning is exclusively addressed—surely pride is not reprobated only because it is alien to this or that man's temperament, & therefore calculated to

11. Writing to her husband on 7 Sept 1834, SC remarked, "Dequincey's article ["Samuel Taylor Coleridge," *Tait's* 1 (1834): 509–20] makes me despise him for his weakness in betraying his own passion. . . . It is finely written, of course, his intellect is all there though put to base work."

12. Or as STC put it, "The rational instinct, therefore, taken abstractly and unbalanced, did *in itself,* ('ye shall be as gods!' Gen. iii. 5.) and in its consequences, (the lusts of the flesh, the eye, and the understanding as in verse the sixth,) form the original temptation, through which man fell: and in all ages has continued to originate the same" (*SM*, p. 61).

defeat his peculiar mode of doing good, but because it is inimical to the growth of the human soul in divine perfection, because it works contrary to the grace of God. And those men to whose natures harsh sentiments are alien have less need than others to be cautioned against them. It will certainly impede a poet and a philosopher in "the development and operation" of his peculiar gift if he does not cultivate a genial spirit, but his duty as a man of genius is included in his duty as a Christian, and though it may be incumbent on one man, in respect of particular talents which he possesses, to pursue a tranquil vocation, whereas another individual may do better service in contending with the world, yet the various modes of life which are dictated by various tastes and capabilities ought surely to be pursued with exactly the same spiritual principles and aims. Allowing it to be true that some men do most good "by their just antipathies and others by their just sympathies," still the question is not whether we *do* good but whether we *are* good. There can be no merit in doing good by our antipathies unless we cultivate them for this very purpose, and that mind in which the desire to do good is habitual will naturally be more alive to sympathy than to antipathy. He that loves his neighbour as himself will be more shocked at any vice and ungodliness that may truly belong to him than a less benevolent person—but as "love is the very temple of virtue," instead of revelling in sensations of scorn & indignation, & feeling most in his element when he is hurting & humiliating, satirizing and inveighing, and on the contrary as flat and spiritless in the presence of the good & beautiful as the sharp fruits of a temperate clime are apt to become under a too genial sky, he is naturally attracted to all that is just and pure & lovely, as the heliotrope turns to the sun. One individual may be born with more of this kindliness than another, but those who do not seek after it are plainly not pursuing that path which the Gospel assures us is the only one that leads to heaven. We cannot suppose that the principle with some men is to be that they are to do good by not acting on principle but by indulging their passions, that one class of characters are to serve God by the spirit of love and another by the spirit of anger and aversion.[13]

Scorn and resentment may in one sense be "wholesome elements in the great compound of human society"—such as it is now—even as "disease grows [?] unto diseases," they would be altogether superfluous if charity and humility were generally cultivated. [I]n a society where evil was unknown[,] the man of antipathies would have no scope for his peculiar dispositions and powers, and he who indulges such a temper is not educating his spirit for the enjoyment of an existence among good men made perfect.

It is not the vocation of all men to "reason high of Providence, foreknowledge, will, and fate," and few are qualified to "search for final causes and

13. See STC on "animal gratification" and poetry, *BL(CC)*, 2:202–03.

work out abstract results"—yet all of us by revelation are enabled to "look down upon human nature as from an eminence," and the simplest Christian who reads the New Testament with an understanding heart must be fully the master of all the philosophy which [is conducive] to the production of a charitable spirit. It is only individuals of a certain dignified "order of mind" for whom contemplation is the business of life—the immediate means by which they are to benefit the world—but as far as our private welfare is concerned, "meditation is the duty of all and therefore God hath fitted such matter for it which is proportioned to every understanding." For meditation is "an application of spirit to divine things, a searching out of all instruments to a holy life, a devout consideration of them, and a production of those affections which are in a direct order to the love of God and a pious conversation."

It is the belief of many Christians that all men have not within them the power, or that they are not enabled by grace to be good & holy—that they are not elected by God for eternal honour & happiness—and that no man can partake of the feast to whom God has not given the wedding garment: our Saviour says, "No man can come unto me except it were given unto him of my Father." [B]ut even the Calvinists do not imagine that it is only men of peculiar temperament & high intellect who are to be invited to strive after Christian perfection, that the wise and the unwise, according to human estimation, are not alike enjoined to love God with all their hearts.

A system of morals which takes no cognizance of a higher state of being into which humanity is to be developed, in the opinion of a believer in Christianity, can never even collaterally be of any service to religion, can never materially promote the well being of man, because it must necessarily, according to his view of the subject, be founded in error. The inducements it holds out must be either superfluous or nugatory, at the best it can only serve to amuse and justify minds of a peculiar cast,

> And with a pleasing sorcery to charm
> Pain for a while, or anguish, and excite
> Fallacious hope, or arm the obdurate breast
> With stubborn patience, as with triple steel.

The Philosophy of Mr. W[ordsworth]'s poetry is not a plan independent of though reconcilable with Christianity—to me it seems to be Christianity itself, the truths expressed or understood in the Gospel illustrated by the Imagination, the process by which the nature of man is refined and glorified, "brought up into daylight," or made manifest by poetical symbols.

[1835]

[On the British Constitution]

"The British Constitution is *founded* on Public opinion."[1] The institutions and forms of government in which this idea is more or less adequately manifested have been wrought out by public opinion, yet surely the idea itself is not the result & product, but rather the secret guide and groundwork of public opinion, on the point in question, as embodied in definite words & conceptions. But what public opinion was that which moulded our admired policy & fashioned the curious & complicated mechanism of our State machine? Did it reflect the mind & intellects of the majority? or was it not rather the opinions of the best & wisest, to which our *aristocratic* forms of government gave both publicity and prevalence?

Surely we have little reason to say that public opinion taken at *large* is necessarily just & wise by virtue of its being public—necessarily that to which the interests of the nation may be safely entrusted. If we identify it with the opinions of the majority at all times and on all subjects[,] it cannot be identified with the collective wisdom of the age. Like foam on the surface of the ocean, pure if the waters below are pure, vile and brown if they are muddy & turbid, it can but represent the character of that from which it proceeds—the average understanding & morals of the community. How are the masses to be purified and tranquillised—how rendered capable of judging soundly on affairs of state, as far as that is possible to men of humble station? Surely not by the introduction of a vote-by-ballot system, which virtually silences the gifted few and reduces to inaction the highest wisdom of the day? Truth[,] it is said, must ever prevail. But unless utterance is given her—nay more—unless her voice is heard, not drowned by the clamours of the errant, what means has she of

1. This quotation was taken from John James Park's 1832 pamphlet *Dogmas of the Constitution, Four Lectures on the Theory and Practice of the Constitution*. Park (1795–1833), barrister and acclaimed lecturer, was a friend of HNC, who—as a May 1833 letter from SC to Mrs. DC reveals—actually lectured for Park at King's College when the latter was taken ill in the spring of 1833. Park's pamphlet is in part a reaction against STC's 1830 *On the Constitution of the Church and State*. In particular, Park disagreed with STC's declaration that the "Voice of the People . . . is the Voice of God" (*C&S*[*CC*], p. 100). For STC's heated reaction to Park's pamphlet, see *CL* 6:909; and *MN*, pp. 223–28. SC's essay attempts to mediate between Park's position and that of her father. For a helpful summation of STC's argument in *C&S*, see HNC's preface to the 1839 edition. See also Griggs, p. 59.

prevailing? Public opinion is consonant to reason and goodness only inasmuch as it is influenced by the wise and the good. It is often grossly absurd & the public opinion of one year or month is condemned by that of the next.

There is truth in the notion of Miss Martineau, to which by stress of argument she has been driven, that "the majority *will* be in the right."[2] The only rational interpretation of which seems to me to be this, that, *on given points* the majority *ultimately* decide in favour of the truth, because in course of time the opinions of the wisest on those particular subjects are proved by experience & successive accessions of suffrages from competent judges. [T]o be just, they are stamped before the public eye in characters which those who run may read (or as Habakkuk really has it) "he may run who readeth," and on such points public opinion is in fact the adoption of *private* opinion by the public; the judgment approved by the majority is anything rather than that which the majority would have formed by aid of their own amount of sense and talent—for "nel mondo non e se non volgo" [there is nothing but vulgarity in the world]. In *time* the whole lump is leavened with that which emanated from a few—but what practical application should be made of this axiom "the majority will be in the right"? Ought it to be such as would lead us to throw political power without stop or stay directly into their hands, and abide with consequences of their blundering apprenticeship, while on particulars in which the public interests are concerned, in which immediate action is required, they are *learning* to be right? Will it console us under the calamities which their ignorance may inflict that they will know better in the end, and when the commonwealth is in ruins will this after-wisdom restore the shattered fabric or indemnify those who have suffered during its disorganization? This notion of a *ruined commonwealth* appears no visionary bug-bear to those who believe the continuance of a Christian and Catholic government essential to the well-being of the State.[3]

Before we argue about public opinion, before we decide what this great power has already done, or what it ought to do, it would be as well to settle what we mean by the term. The public opinion of *this country,* on *particular points,* in this *age of the world,* is perfectly just and enlightened. On the Newtonian or Copernican systems[,] for instance, public opinion now is identical with that of the philosopher in his closet. But what was public opinion on this same system

---

2. *Society in America* (London, 1837), 3:8. Harriet Martineau (1802–76), the prolific historian and social critic, was a favorite with SC. Although SC frequently disagreed—at times viciously— she read everything Martineau wrote, objecting to her "lack of female modesty" but nevertheless acknowledging her genius. It is Martineau's theories about American democracy, even more than Park's ideas about the constitution, that are being considered in this essay.

3. As STC put it, "I hold it to be the disgrace and calamity of a professed statesman not to know and acknowledge, that a permanent, nationalized, learned order, a national clerisy or church, is an essential element of a rightly constituted nation, without which it wants the best security alike for its permanence and its progression" (*C&S[CC]*, p. 69).

in the age of Kepler and Galileo? (For Newton was anticipated in some measure by those great men). If, however[,] by public opinion be meant the opinions of the multitude taken collectively,—the general body of their opinions concerning all matters of which man can take cognizance,—this can no more be the best possible, than the mass of mankind are as able, moral, & enlightened as a certain number of individuals in every age. But ought not a state to be guided by the best possible opinions? Ought it to be swayed by the uncorrected thoughts of the multitude?

It is not high Tories and Churchmen alone who feel that in America public opinion is a tyrant—because it is a public opinion not sufficiently acted on by the wisest and best individuals. [T]heir voice has utterance and in time is heard, but by the forms of society and of government established there—especially the want of a landed gentry and influential endowed Church—they do not enough prevail over the voices of the crowd, and will of the majority is too much felt for the welfare of the majority themselves. Many Americans are now admitting this and it appears either implicitly or explicitly in the pages of every American traveller. Miss Martineau would have helped us to find it out had we needed her information.[4]

With us government, hitherto, has not been "degraded in its character to that of a machine, the functions of those who are engaged in it being simply this—to ascertain & obey a popular will, like the index of a clock worked by a pendulum." Our laws & institutions have been molded by the suggestions of a wise minority, which the mechanism of our state machinery enabled to come gradually into play—so that the *interests* of the people have been consulted rather than their blind wishes. [T]hus our constitution, considered as an outward thing, has been framed according to an idea of perfection (never in this world to be more than partially realized)—an idea existing equally in the minds of all our countrymen, but more distinctly & effectively developed in those which are aided by an acute & powerful intellect improved to the highest point by education, study, & reflective leisure.[5]

4. De Tocqueville had noted, "In the United States . . . the majority . . . exercise a prodigious actual authority, and a power of opinion which is nearly as great; no obstacle exists which can impede or even regard its progress, so as to make it heed the complaints of those whom it crushes in its path. This state of things is harmful in itself and dangerous for the future" (*Democracy in America*, 2 vols. [1835 & 1840; New York: Alfred A. Knopf, 1945], 1:257). Martineau too had qualified her enthusiasm: "The majority eventually wills the best; but in the presence of imperfection of knowledge, the will is long exhibiting itself; and the ultimate demonstration often crowns a series of mistakes and failures" (*Society in America*, 1:32–33).

5. SC's "idea of perfection" is in keeping with her father's "Idea of a State" as described in *On the Constitution of the Church and State*: "First then, I have given briefly but, I trust, with sufficient clearness the right idea of a STATE, or Body Politic; 'State' being here synonimous with a *constituted* Realm, Kingdom, Commonwealth, or Nation, i.e. where as to constitute, more or less, a moral unit, an organic whole; and as arising out of the Idea of a State I have added the Idea of a Constitution, as the informing principle of its coherence and unity" (*C&S[CC]*, p. 107).

Is it not obvious from Dr. Park's own abstract that our government has never been popular in the sense in which my father denies it to have been such? has it not ever been "a monarchy at once buttressed and limited by the aristocracy"?[6] Was it ever popular as the American government is so? If not, still less has it been popular after such a sort as our modern liberals, our separators of Church & State, will leave no stone unturned to make it. On the other hand, is it not clear as noonday—nay, gloried in by numbers—that notwithstanding the prolonged duration of Parliament—the remnant of Lordly influence in the popular elections & House of Commons—the standing army and national debt—the British State is more democratic in this 19th Century than at any former period?* Ought it to be *still more* democratic, still more the mere representative of the multitude & exponent of their will? Are we likely to fare better under the dominion of the people than this country did in former times when "government had not renounced its right to consult for the benefit of the community, even independently of its inclinations"? On the answer to this question depends the answer to that of Dr. Park—were the acts above named constitutional?

The sage Whig Hallam is of the opinion that the Reform Bill went too far in establishing democratic principles[7]—and as to such politicians as Hume,

---

*We cannot surely imagine that more power & liberty were really enjoyed by the people under the sway of the strong-headed, strong-handed Cromwell, or that their interests were more attended to during the corrupt reign of Charles the 2nd?

A noble national character belongs to the people of England, & grieved indeed should I be to suppose that they wanted "a foundation of moderation and good sense." But how are those good qualities to be most efficiently improved, confirmed, elicited? How does a wise mother act in regard to the children under her care, those children in whom she perceives with delight the germs and first shoots of a thousand amiable affections & excellent dispositions? I need hardly say that she does not trust to them solely, that she remembers of what jarring elements man is a compound, and that she takes care to keep the passions & tempers of her charge in due restraint, in order that their good feelings & seasoning habits may be strengthened and increased? Just so should a paternal government act toward the national family which it has to govern.

Our old borough system involved a certain degree of moral evil, and this in my eyes rendered it objectionable, rather than the predominance which it gave to the aristocracy.

---

6. *C&S(CC)*, p. 95. See also *TT*, 2:52–54; and *MN*, pp. 223–28.

7. Henry Hallam (1777–1859), historian and frequent contributor to the *Ed Rev*, published his *Constitutional History of England* in 1827 and his *Introduction to the Literature of Europe during the Fifteenth, Sixteenth, and Seventeenth Centuries* between 1837 and 1839.

Washington, Roebuck, and their allies, I should imagine they sympathized but little in the anxiety of reasoners like Dr. Park and STC for the balance of powers, and so that they could but succeed in overthrowing the Church & Aristocracy would care much less than a straw for the old & venerable idea of the British Constitution.[8]

These are some of the thoughts which have been suggested to me by the perusal of Dr. Park's instructive abstract. I am aware that they are quite imperfect & inconclusive, but they give a notion of the way in which I have been led to look on the subject of government. I feel very strongly persuaded that an endowed Church, maintaining a body of Catholic doctrine and a State in connection with that Church, are the greatest of public blessings, and it seems to me that the general influence of property and hereditary rank, as well as that which they have hitherto exerted in the national councils has formed a guarantee, to a *certain extent,* for the predominance of talent, intellect, and wisdom—excellence in every department of mind & morals. The wise institutions of the Americans, so far as they *are* wise, are not attributable solely to their popular government. They have had the advantage on many points of our example & experience—they set their chronometer by England, & while the wheels & springs of our ancient timepiece are kept agoing, we cannot know to a certainty how theirs will work, & what degree of accuracy it will preserve, should ours be destroyed.

[1837]

---

8. STC's anxiety was not slight. Speaking of the Emancipation Act, which precipitated his *C&S,* he noted, "The Roman Catholic Emancipation Act—carried on in the violent, and, in fact, unprincipled manner it was—was in effect a Surinam toad;—and the Reform Bill, the Dissenter's admission to the Universities, and the attack on the Church, are so many toadlets, one after another detaching themselves from their parent brute" (*TT,* 2:324 [14 June 1834]).

Reply to Strictures of
Three Gentlemen upon Carlyle

In order to do justice to the views of an author, especially such an author as Carlyle, who less than most men can be understood in fragments, a want of finish in the parts being the characteristic defect of his style, we must take care to place ourselves in his point of view, to possess ourselves of his aim.[1] Now Carlyle's great theme in the work before us is worship—the instinct of "Veneration" in man (but see his limitation of the term, p. 381—or intimation that he has been using it in a limited sense).[2] The religion of nations, as to its superficial and outward part, he considers to be, in great measure, a system of empty forms, dead conventionalisms, and lifeless ceremonies—the worthless remains of a something which once had life. On the other hand, he believes that, in all religions which have ever held sway over masses of men for a considerable time, there has been at bottom a living and life-exciting principle. This principle, which he sets up as the "work of God," against the artefacts of men—vain substitutes for genuine gifts from on high—he maintains to be "Veneration"— the principle or feeling which leads men to bow down before the image of God in the soul of man. Power is an attribute of God—Carlyle maintains that the instinct whereby we are impelled practically to adore and obey mental power, wherever we behold it, is a salutary and high instinct, which instrumentally redeems mankind from the dominion of sense and the despotism of moral evil. (But power in God is joined with benevolence, and so it is in all whom Carlyle sets up as objects of "worship.")

1. This essay was written expressly for Charles John Abraham, with whom SC had argued about Carlyle in October 1843 while on a visit to Eton to see her brother-in-law, Edward Coleridge. In a 25 Oct 1843 letter to her mother, SC refers in passing to a "controversy about Carlyle betwixt the gentlemen and me." Unfortunately, the original MS has not survived, although Edith Coleridge used it for inclusion in her *Memoir and Letters of Sara Coleridge*, where she misdates it. See *ML*(1874), pp. 358–67.

2. The passage to which SC refers discusses Cromwell: "What had this man gained; what had he gained? He had a life of sore strife and toil, to his last day. Fame, ambition, place in History? His dead body was hung in chains; his 'place in History'—place in History forsooth—has been a place of ignominy, accusation, blackness and disgrace" (*On Heroes, Hero-Worship, & The Heroic in History* [London: James Fraser, 1841], p. 381).

In the first passage referred to (*Hero-Worship,* [1841] pp. 22–23),[3] Voltaire is spoken of as a "kind" of hero, a man gifted by God with remarkable "powers" of thought and expression, and who, whatever evil he may have done, exceeding any good that can be ascribed to his authorship, was nevertheless believed by those who "worshiped" him to have devoted his life and abilities to the "unmasking of hypocrisy," and "exposing of error and injustice." Carlyle's proposition seems to me to be simply this: The French nation being such as they were, that is to say, in a comparatively low, dark, unspiritual state, their enthusiasm about Voltaire was a favorable symptom of their mental condition—the spirit evinced therein, a redeeming spirit (in its degree)—their feeling of admiration and veneration for one whom they thought *above* them, in its own nature a noble and blessed feeling. Poor and needy, indeed, must that people be who have no better object of such a feeling than Voltaire. Our author means only to affirm that Frenchmen were better employed in "worshiping" him even for supposititious merits than in groveling along in utter worldliness, pursuing each his own narrow, selfish path, without a thought or a care beyond the gratification of the senses. Here is no intention to set the intellectual above the moral, or to substitute the one for the other, but to insist on the superiority of *natural gifts,* as means of bettering the souls of men, to the vain shows and semblances which commonly pass for religion in the world, according to the author's opinion.

The second passage (pp. 166–67)[4] I remember noting when I first read the work in which it is contained, as announcing a doctrine either wrong in itself or wrongly expressed. But I can not see that it is erroneous by the exaltation of

3. Referred to presumably by Charles Abraham with whom SC was arguing about Carlyle's veneration of the intellect, the passage reads: "Hero-worship endures forever while man endures. Boswell venerates his Johnson, right truly in the eighteenth century. The unbelieving French believe in their Voltaire; and burst-out round him into very curious hero-worship, in that last act of his life when they 'stifle him under roses.' It has always seemed to me extremely curious this of Voltaire. Truly if Christianity be the highest instance of hero-worship, then we may find here in Voltaire one of the lowest! He whose life was that of a kind of Antichrist, does again on this side exhibit a curious contrast. No people ever were so little prone to admire at all as those French of Voltaire. *Persiflage* was the character of their whole mind; adoration had nowhere a place in it. Yet see! the old man of Ferney comes up to Paris; an old tottering, infirm man of eighty-four years. They feel that he too is a kind of hero; that he has spent his life in opposing error and injustice, delivering Calases, unmasking hypocrites in high places;—in short that *he* too, though in a strange way, has fought like a valiant man" (pp. 22–23).

4. The following passage begins a lengthy discussion of Shakespeare's intellectual merits: "Of this Shakespeare of ours, perhaps the opinion one sometimes hears a little idolatrously expressed is, in fact, the right one; I think the best judgment not of this country only, but of Europe at large, is slowly pointing to the conclusion, That Shakespeare is the chief of all Poets hitherto; the greatest intellect who, in our recorded world, has left record of himself in the way of Literature. On the whole, I know not such a power of vision, faculty of thought, if we take all the character of it, in any other man" (pp. 166–67).

intellectual power above goodness, but rather by too bold and broad an affirmation that the former is the measure of the latter. So far I agree with Carlyle, that I believe the highest moral excellence attainable by man is ever attended by a certain largeness of understanding; not that intellectual power is a part of goodness, but that moral goodness can not be evolved, to the greatest extent, without it. Men of high virtue and piety are ever men of insight, the moral and intelligential in their mixed nature reciprocally strengthening and expanding each other. To transfer these remarks to a lower subject, every *great* poet must be possessed not merely of a fine imagination, a lively fancy, or any other particular intellectual faculty, but of a great understanding; he must be one whose mental vision is deeper and more acute than that of other men, who sees into the truth of things, and has a special power of rendering what he sees visible to others. He must be practical, as well as percipient, else he is not a poet, a maker or creator; he must see keenly and (if the expression may be allowed) *feelingly*, else his poetic faculty has no adequate materials to work upon. Shakespeare was inclusively a great philosopher. "Lear," "Hamlet," and "Othello" could never have been produced by one who did not see into the human mind deeply and survey it widely. But to be a Shakespeare, a man must have certain peculiar gifts of intellect added to this great general powerfulness; or, to express myself more distinctly, his mind must be specifically modified, and that from the first—*a priori*. I can not at all agree with Carlyle in thinking that the sole original qualification of every great man of every description is a strong understanding, and that, where there is this common base, circumstances *alone* determine whether the possessor is to be a Caesar or a Shakespeare, a Cowley or a Kant, a Wellington or a Wordsworth. To return to the moral side of the subject, I think that Carlyle expresses himself too broadly when he says that "the degree of vision that dwells in a man is the correct measure of the man," and illustrates his meaning by a reference to Shakespeare.[5] Was Shakespeare as much better than other men as he was deeper and clearer sighted? The truth is that *vision* considered in the concrete, as found in this or that individual, is always specific. The saints and servants of God have a vision of their own—but here let me pause, for I am at the mouth of a labyrinth. Lord Byron, to whom Mr. A[braham] refers, was a very *clever* man; but I think that Carlyle would not allow him any very remarkable "degree of vision;" his "superiority of intellect," *sensu eminente,* he would plainly deny, and, in my opinion, with justice.[6] But

5. "For, in fact, I say the degree of vision that dwells in a man is a correct measure of the man. If called to define Shakespeare's faculty, I should say superiority of Intellect, and think I had included all under that" (p. 171).

6. *Hero-Worship* contains only a passing reference to Byron, but it was one with which SC agreed. Carlyle wrote, "I do not agree with much modern criticism, in greatly preferring the *Inferno* to the two other parts of the divine *Commedia*. Such preference belongs, I imagine, to our general Byronism of taste, and is like to be a transient feeling" (p. 154).

still Byron had a stronger understanding than many a better man, though his fame during life may have been no "correct measure" of his intellectual size (in literary and poetical circles his fame is now fast shrinking into more just proportion therewith). Carlyle's statement is, at best, confused and inadequate, probably because he had not properly thought out the subject when he undertook to speak upon it.

Much waste of words, and of thought too, would be avoided if disputants would always begin with a clear statement of the question, and not proceed to argue till they had agreed upon what it was that they were arguing about. The proposition which I understand Mr. A[braham] to maintain (when he censures Carlyle as a worshiper of intellect, implying that he worships it in a bad sense), and which I venture to deny, is this: That Thomas Carlyle, viewed in his character of author, as appears upon the face of his writings, exalts intellect taken apart from the other powers of the mind—that he sets up mere intellect as the ultimate object of esteem and admiration, and represents a man as truly great and worthy of all honor purely on the score of intellectual gifts, without reference to the use he makes of them. In disproof of this position (or by way of attempting to disprove it), I appeal to the fact that all his heroes, whom he describes as being the deserving objects of what, "not to be too grave about it," he chooses to call "*worship,*" are represented by him as benefactors of the human race, just in proportion as they were *deserving* objects of worship. He describes them as men whose powers have been employed by God's will and their own, for good and noble purposes on a large scale, chiefly for the purpose of leading men, directly or indirectly, from earth to heaven, from the human to the divine. This, indeed, is the keynote of Carlyle's writings—it is the beginning and the end of his whole teaching; it is this which gives a character of elevation to all the productions of his mind, and renders him so widely influential, as, with all his bad taste and frequent crudity and incompleteness of thinking, he certainly is, that in all he puts forth there is an immediate reference to man's higher destiny, under the power of which thought all his other thoughts are moulded and modified. His vocation is that of an *apostle,* in the sense in which the title may truly and reverently be bestowed upon uninspired men. If it be objected to this view of his drift and purpose that Voltaire and Rousseau are mentioned among his heroes, I reply that he has done this, not from blindness to their faults and deficiencies, but from the supposed perception of a certain degree of merit in them not commonly recognized by admirers of goodness. This supposition may be well or ill founded—he may be wrong in supposing those writers to have exerted any beneficial influence; but the character of his aim is to be determined by the supposition and not by the fact. He places them very low in the scale of benefactors, and brings them forward rather as illustrations of his meaning in the lowest instances, than as considering them worthy to be placed by the side of the best and greatest men in the scale of moral greatness. His account of

Cromwell I think very fine as a sketch, and very well framed as an exponent of his doctrine: with regard to its truth in fact, my judgment is suspended. Be that as it may, Carlyle's heroes are all men who have striven for truth and justice, and for the emancipation of their fellow-mortals. He represents them as having been misunderstood by the masses of mankind, in the midst of all their effectivity and *ultimate* influence, simply because the masses of mankind are not themselves sufficiently wise and good and perspicacious to understand and sympathize with those who are so in an eminent degree. There is *some* originality in Carlyle's opinions; but he seems to me to be more original in manner than in matter: the force and feeling with which he brings out his views are more *remarkable* than the views themselves.

Carlyle has somewhere spoken as if he thought that bodily strength gave a just claim to the possession of rule and authority, and this passage has been quoted against him with considerable plausibility. But is it not true that superior strength of body and mind have ever enabled the possessors, sooner or later, to command the herd of their inferiors? This is a fact which Carlyle does not invent, but only reasons upon, and his reasoning is that native strength and other personal endowments, conferred directly by God, without man's inter-vention, convey a better claim to the obedience and service of men, and are a safer ground whereon to erect sovereignty, than arbitrary human distinctions and titles established conventionally, which by a certain theory of theologians are made out to have been instituted by God Himself. The only divine right of kings which he will acknowledge is *native might,* enabling a man to rule well and wisely, as well as strongly. Hereditary sway, pretending to be divine, he looks upon as a mere human contrivance, one that has never adequately answered its purpose, that arose originally from false views and bad feelings, and, as it had in it from the beginning a corrupt root, is ever tending to decay and dissolution. For myself, if it is worth while to say what I think, I can not clearly understand the *divine right* of kings as taught by High Churchmen, but neither do I believe that Carlyle has seen through the whole of this matter, or that there is not much more to be said for conventional sovereignty than appears in his notices of the question. If all men were at all times wise enough to choose the best governors, there need be no such contrivance as hereditary sway—but, till they are, elective sway is no better; and in the mean time, according to Carlyle's own admission, native strength has a sphere of its own, in which it governs with more or less effect, according to its intensity.

Carlyle's *manner* of describing the character of Mirabeau is, perhaps, the most questionable part of his writings; yet even here, I think, his main drift is quite consistent with morality.[7] He is not judging the eminent Frenchman as a

---

7. See Carlyle's "Memoirs of Mirabeau," *West Rev* 26 (1837): 382–439; and his *The French Revolution,* 3 vols. (London: Chapman and Hall, 1842), 2:164–82.

divine, nor examining him as a moralist. His theme is the French Revolution, which he regards as a tremendous crisis, the result of a long series and extensive system of selfishness, cruelties, and injustices, and he views all the persons of his narrative principally in reference to the part they acted, and the effects they wrought, in this great national convulsion. Whatever Mirabeau's private character may have been before God, yet as far as he was a powerful and conspicuous agent in carrying forward the work of the French Revolution, Carlyle was justified, as it seems to me, in setting him forth as an object of interest, and even of admiration, proportioned to the amount and rareness of the gifts which rendered him a potent instrument in the hands of Providence for a particular purpose; and this he might have done without calling evil good, or good evil. But it is abundantly evident that Carlyle did *not* consider Mirabeau's mind and dispositions as *upon the whole* morally bad; he ascribes to him high purposes and public virtues—that is, virtues specially calculated to benefit the public. Whether his account of him be true in fact, or whether it is a fiction, our argument does not require us to consider. The question only is, does Carlyle's language respecting Mirabeau confound the distinction betwixt virtue and vice—does it tend to dim the luster of the first, and to surround the last with a false and falsifying splendor? Now I am inclined to answer this question in the negative, both from consideration of Carlyle's general turn of mind, as displayed in his books, and from a survey of all that he says of Mirabeau, taken in connection with the spirit and principles of the work in which it appears, though I admit that he has not taken sufficient pains to prevent his sentiments from being taken for that which they are not. The writings of Lord Byron are really open, in some measure, to such a charge, because they array in attractive colors imaginary personages to whom no real good or noble qualities are ascribed; they are not reprehensible for that they represent men as worthy to be admired in spite of great vices, but because they tend to produce admiration of the very vices themselves—to detach it from virtue altogether, and place it on inferior objects. Lord Byron's heroes have no higher merits than gallantry and courage; they are invested with a kind of dignity from romantic situation, and the possession of outward elegance, not dignified by their instrumentality in great and important events. Such representations are essentially mean and worthless, but such is not Carlyle's representation in the present instance. He describes Mirabeau, not only as a man of vast energy and amazing political sagacity, but, amid much personal profligacy and unruliness of passion, as being possessed, like his father before him, of a philanthropic spirit, high disinterested aims, and a zeal to serve his country. He affirms, and in this, whatever Macaulay's opinion may be,[8] he is borne out by other authorities, that

8. See "Dumont's *Recollections of Mirabeau*—the French Revolution," *West Rev* 55 (1832): 552–76; repr. *The Works of Lord Macaulay*, 12 vols. (London: Longman & Green, 1898), 8:213–48.

Mirabeau took a right view of the political needs of the French people; that he sought to bring in a limited monarchy on the English model, knowing it to be the only form of public liberty for which the French nation was fit; and that, had God spared his life, and permitted him to go on in the career which he had commenced, he would have been the saviour of his country, so far as this, that, without the horrors of the Revolution, he would have established all that the Revolution ultimately brought abut in so violent and calamitous a manner. Such, according to Carlyle, was Mirabeau's aim; such his insight. That he was in many respects a bad man can not make such an aim not to have been good; the sagacity with which he directed it, and the resoluteness with which he pursued it, not to have been admirable—and to *deny* this character of excellence appears to me to be a confounding of good and evil, not to *affirm* it. Would it not be an approach to the ill practice of lying for God, if we were to refuse all honor to the name of Mirabeau on account of that bad side of his mind and actions, supposing Carlyle's account of him to be correct? Carlyle represents this remarkable man as a voluptuary and a libertine. Libertinism is of the nature of wickedness, but mere libertinism, though it may be accompanied by, and though it tends to produce, hardness of heart, and is a contempt of God's Word and commandments, does not alone constitute the man who is guilty of it "an atrocious villain." It may be villainously pursued, but it is not in itself the same thing as villainy; for a villain, according to the common acceptation of the word, is a man basely malignant as to his general character, incapable of generous thoughts and actions; but libertinism is not absolutely incompatible with generosity and benevolence, however it may *tend* to weaken and fret away all that is better than itself in the mind of the libertine. Again, a *mere* voluptuary is a contemptible being. But Mirabeau, according to Carlyle, was much else besides being a voluptuary. He seems rather to have acted the rake, as a form of activity, than through a slavish subjection to mere sensual appetite; and Carlyle brings forward his exploits in this line, rather to show his multifarious energy—how many different kinds of things he was able to do at once, and with the force of a giant—than with any intention of admitting that he was a selfish sensualist in the main; that this was his distinguishing character. I am afraid his way herein was made all too smooth before him, and that the women sank before his genius with fatal facility. They are too apt to yield their whole heart and mind to men of power and distinction, let their other qualities be what they may, and there was little Christianity in Paris during Mirabeau's career to keep such a disposition in check. However, I am far from defending the *tone* in which Carlyle deals with this part of his subject; there is something of exultation in it highly reprehensible. As a defender of truth, he should not have referred to such things without a mark of reprobation, nor, as a pretender to refinement and elevation of feeling, should he have touched upon them without expressions of disgust and contempt.

On the one other point, however, I do think Carlyle may be defended without sophistry or straining. It was said, as I understood, that whereas this writer treats his own favorites with undue indulgence, he displays a bitter and vehement spirit against their adversaries, and generally all who are not of his school and party. I should say, on the contrary, that Carlyle treats all historical characters that come under his cognizance with leniency; he speaks admiringly and indulgently, for instance, of Marie Antoinette; and I can perceive no *scorn* in his exposure of the weakness and dullness of her husband—which who can deny. In speaking of Laud, he less decries the *man* than the circumstances of which he was the creature.[9] Carlyle, whatever his candor, could not look upon Laud as a large and free-minded man, a martyr in a wholly good cause.

Carlyle is a satirist, but he is not given to satirize individuals, or even parties of men. The object of his satire, as it appears to me, is the weakness and wickedness of *mankind*—systems of opinion, not bodies of believers. He speaks occasionally with contempt, though not always with unqualified contempt (see his last work, *Past and Present* [1843]), of Puseyism, as a resurrection-system of defunct things; but he says nothing of any of the resurrection-men, nor has he ever joined any person or party, that I am aware of, in impeaching the conduct of the Puseyites, considered as a party.[10]

Macaulay's opinion of Mirabeau is cited by Mr. A[braham]. Macaulay may be more correct than Carlyle as to the facts of the case (though I do not see that this has been proved), but I can not think him fit to be trusted with the character of any great man. He is a thorough Utilitarian and anti-Spiritualist, and though he makes judicious remarks upon this person and upon that, yet scarcely sees at all that element of greatness, that spark of the divine in these marked agents of Providence, with Carlyle sees too exclusively. Macaulay finishes fully, but his conceptions are on a confined scale. Carlyle aims at something higher and deeper, his views are more novel and striking, but they are hastily and often inaccurately set forth. Carlyle writes paradoxically about great men. Macaulay, on similar subjects, is liable, in my opinion, to write untruly, from defective perception of a certain side of greatness. I would refer to Carlyle's character of

9. William Laud (1573–1645), chancellor of Oxford and archbishop of Canterbury, was a dominant force in the development of the Anglican church. Writing to JTC on Carlyle's *Cromwell* in September of 1846, SC noted that "it certainly does service to history. . . . The irreverential tone in which Carlyle speaks of 'little Dr. Laud' and the men of 'surplice tendencies' will . . . banish it from the shelves of the 17th Century Anglicans."

10. Edward Bouverie Pusey (1800–82), the English theologian, was a High Churchman and friend of John Keble and J. H. Newman. Seeking to counter religious rationalism, Pusey contributed to the famous *Tracts for the Times* (1833–44). In 1843 he was suspended from his post at Oxford on charges of heresy. He remained a High Anglican and worked with limited success to prevent the succession of many of his followers to Roman Catholicism. Writing to John Taylor Coleridge in August 1843, SC noted that "the *practical* sameness of the teaching of Carlyle with that of Pusey and Newman . . . with Coleridge at the bottom of all, is to me very striking."

Johnson, in his *Essays,* as a most interesting sample of his style and mode of thinking.[11]

In the comparison of Byron and Carlyle, with regard to the moral tendency of their writings, I would add, that if the latter had *invented* the character of Mirabeau, or if the character thus invented was untrue to nature, in representing high and noble qualities in combination with evil ones, so as they never appear in actual life, he might justly be accused of depreciating the former, and varnishing over or softening off the latter. But Carlyle has not been found, I believe, to have misrepresented the life and actions of Mirabeau; nor has it yet been shown that he has misrepresented human nature in his account of them. Neither this nor that, indeed, is the charge against him; but rather that he has described him as a wicked man, and yet has held him up to honor and admiration, on the score of marked talents and striking qualities, apart from virtue. This charge is unsupported, I think, by sufficient evidence; Carlyle has not exalted him as a *man,* still less as a subject of the *Prince of Life,* but as an actor in a great historical drama; nor has he held up his worst actions to positive admiration; he has but given them a place beside his worthier ones, without drawing the line betwixt them with sufficient sharpness. But he was not called upon by the nature of his undertaking to sum up all the points of Mirabeau's character, and decide whether it was good or bad in the eye of God. He had undertaken to describe, and to moralize and philosophize, implicitly rather than expressly, upon the French Revolution; and this I think he does in a deeply religious spirit, ever bearing in mind and bringing before the minds of his readers that there is a God that both ruleth and judgeth the world, and exposing the *moral* bearings of his subject, whether justly or not, yet with a constant regard to the law of conscience and the inward revelations of the Spirit. It was not his province to censure the private vices of Mirabeau (I mean that this was not within the scope of his principal design, though I admit that he ought not to have spoken of them without noting his disapprobation of them more clearly). It was his province to show how the selfishness and godlessness of *numbers,* how spiritual wickedness in high places, gradually reared up a pile of misery and mischief; and how this mass of evil, when at last it exploded with ruinous violence, was at once a remedy from God and a retribution.

[1843]

11. "Boswell's *Life of Johnson,*" *Fraser's Mag* 5 (1832): 379–413. This essay was included in the first (1839) and all subsequent editions of the *Critical and Miscellaneous Essays.*

Reasons for Not Placing "Laodamia" in the First Rank of Wordsworthian Poetry

In what I am about to say I know that I shall be setting myself against general opinion among the readers of Wordsworth. "Laodamia" has perhaps a greater number of admirers than any other of Mr. Wordsworth's poems. I know too how inferiour are my powers to yours in the evolution and defence of critical doctrines and theories, as well as the original devising of them. But Poetry is in part [a] matter of feeling, and I think it is possible that I may have feelings, perceptions not yet awakened in you, that may be material of judgment on this subject which you do not as yet fully possess.[1]

Without further preface I venture to say that in my opinion "Laodamia" is neither as finely conceived as a considerable number of Mr. Wordsworth's poems, nor as happily executed. I venture to say that there is a great want of *feeling,* of *tenderness* and *delicacy,* of *truthfulness* in the representation of Laodamia herself. The speech put into her mouth is as unrefined in tone as it is pompous & inflated in manner. Would any virtuous lady & affectionate wife thus address her husband, on seeing him again after an absence, which has torn her heart with anxiety on his account? Would she accost him so in the style of Sappho to Phaon—or Medea to Jason? Would Homer have put such words into the mouth of Andromache or of Penelope? No—he would have shewn far more dignity & delicacy & tenderness in his conception of the situation & the character. Not only does the Poet make Laodamia speak in this unwifely tone— but he makes a commentary on her feelings, which, if just, would render her utterly unworthy of that deep sympathy & compassion, which yet he claims as her due. He ascribes to her *passions* unworthy of a pure abode—*raptures* such as Erebus disdains. He implies that her feelings belong to mere sense & the lowest part of our nature. There may be women of whom all of this is true—but by

1. This essay was part of several pieces on WW sent from SC to Aubrey de Vere sometime in 1847. De Vere, a poet and man of letters, became a close friend of SC after the death of her husband in 1843, and they maintained a voluminous correspondence right up until SC's death in 1852. Unfortunately, few letters have survived. See de Vere's *Recollections* (New York & London: Edward Arnold, 1897), pp. 195–209; and Griggs, pp. 179–81, 219–22.

what right does the Poet ascribe them to Laodamia—& how can he do so without degrading her far below the purpose of his poem? There is a contradictoriness in this—Laodamia is at once a prey to vulgar passion, and when looked at on the other side, a woman worthy of respect and tenderness—a devoted & deeply loving wife. What wife who *deeply loved* a husband was ever subdued to those inferior feelings? Even when they [become] excited, *affection,* which is so unspeakably deeper & stronger, would absorb and merge them.

Of course, a poor woman is glad to behold the external form of her husband—after absence—"his very step has music in it as he comes up the stair." [R]ight glad she is too to see him with a blooming cheek, proof of his health and welfare—thankful—under circumstances like those of Laodamia, to receive ever so dislocating a squeeze—even to the aching of the bones—a thing to the mere sense unluxurious—nay painful—but comfortable to the heart within, as making assurance doubly sure that she has before her no vision of spectre, like to vanish away—but that *there he is,* the good-man himself, a being confined within the bounds of space, and likely for many a day to be perceptible within that portion of space which is their common home—proof also, or at least a strong sign, that whether or no he be as glad to rejoin her as she to have him back, at all events he is more glad than words express.

Why did Mr. Wordsworth write in this hard, harsh, falsetto style of Laodamia? Was this a sketch taken from *very nature,* as are all his best productions—[or] what I should call such? Was it drawn by the light of the sun in heaven, or by the real moonlight, with all its purity & freshness? No–but by the beams of a purple-tinted lamp in his study—a lamp gaudily coloured but dimmed with particles of smoke & fumes of the candle. Compare with this the feelings embodied in that exquisite little poem, "She was a Phantom of Delight." Can we not see in a moment that Mr. Wordsworth had been gazing intently upon the fine face of Nature herself when he threw forth those verses—that he had been *seeing,* not inventing? Yet is it not far more imaginative than the other? Would any but a great Poet have so seen the face of nature or so portrayed it?

My dear Friend, it is sometimes from a want of fine perceptions that men fail to see what is low & unrefined—but sometimes the coarse escapes their notice from a habit they have of fixing their eyes on ideal purity and elevation, & thus carrying off the image of it & stamping it upon objects to which it does not belong. If I am right in thinking that there is a coarseness in the leading conception of "Laodamia," sure I am that, if you have not perceived this, it is from the latter cause and not from the former. It does appear to me, I own, that there is an essential unspirituality & unrefinement in those theories which attempt to separate off the sensuous from our humanity—to draw so sharp a line between the outward & visible & the inward, in practice. So long as sense *is* thus severed & divorced from our higher being, it *is* a low thing—but may it not be redeemed, & by becoming the mere minister & exponent of what is above itself, become something higher & better than its mere self? I have ever thought those theories "a vaulting ambition which o'er leaps itself & falls on the other side."

Mr. Wordsworth was never *in love,* properly speaking. I have heard him boast of it, in [the] presence of his wife, who smiled angelically, delighted that her husband should be so superior to common men. This superiority, however, entails a certain deficiency. He cannot sympathize with a certain class of feelings in consequence—he cannot realize them. He is always upon stilts when he enters these subjects. He stalks along with a portentous stride & then stamps his great wooden foot down, in the clumsiest manner imaginable. That sonnet among the Duddon ones, about crossing the brook, attempts to describe *loverish* feelings—but even that is forced & sexagenarian—The loves are brought in to clap their wings from a neighboring rock. At what shop did he buy those ready-made Cupids? My Father, on the other hand, though I say it, that shouldn't say it, was *perfect* in this line—faultless as Shakespeare, if not as great as Shakespeare, in his representations of women, & the relation of men to women. Never would he have made a Lady say to her restored Lord—"Come, *blooming* Hero, place thee by my side" &c—making it necessary for Jove to "frown in heaven" & cast upon those ["]*roseate* lips a Stygian hue.["] Indeed my Father never troubled himself about the lips of *men.* They might have been green or orange-coloured for aught he knew or noticed. What came *from them* he was sufficiently observant of; and he admired a brilliant or an elegant looking man—as, for instance, Lord Byron & Mr. H[enry] Taylor—as a *whole,* without entering into particulars.

Now for the *execution* of "Laodamia." It is true that it contains some detached stanzas, or some stanzas which, considered as detached, are very beautiful, but is not a good deal of it, more pompous than truly elevated—slow & dragging rather than majestic? The first two stanzas, the first especially, are abominably still and hard. It is no apology to say they resemble the prologue to the old Greek Tragedy. I don't think any prologue of the kind could have sounded to Grecian ears as those lines do to us—

> With sacrifice before the rising moon
> Performed, my *slaughtered Lord* have I required

Be that as it may, would it be endurable for any poet to write now as Aeschylus did 2000 years ago? Are we in the humour for it? I must repeat in earnest what I once said to you half in jest that your own poetic genius, being cast in an ornate & classic model, prevents you from perceiving the full merit & beauty of Mr. Wordsworth's first style—It eclipses another luminacy by intercepting it, as the moon does when it stands before the sun. Strange indeed it seems to me

that you should see so little in the Brothers—so exquisitely pathetic—so intri-
cated with the beauty of nature, an individualized nature, yet how universal. It
was but lately that I saw such a tribute to that poem—either from John H. Frere
or some man of acknowledged political judgment like him.

[1847][2]

2. Edith Coleridge includes a version of this essay in her *ML*, pp. 273–76. Either she had another draft of the MS now at the HRHRC or she chose to substantially revise the original, deleting the strongest complaints against WW.

[The Autobiography of
Sara Coleridge]

September 8, *1851*.

My dearest Edith,

I have long wished to give you a little sketch of my life. I once intended to have given it with much particularity, but now *time presses:* my horizon has contracted of late. I must content myself with a brief compendium.[1]

I shall divide my history into Childhood Earlier and Later—Youth Earlier and Later—Wedded Life ditto—Widowhood ditto—and I shall endeavour to state the chief Moral or Reflection suggested by each—some maxim which it specially illustrated, or truth which it exemplified, or warning which it suggested.

My Father has entered his marriage with my mother and the births of my three brothers with some particularity in a family Bible, given him, as he also notes, by Joseph Cottle on his marriage; the entry of my birth is in my dear Mother's hand-writing, and this seems like an omen of our life-long separation; for I never lived with him for more than a few weeks at a time. He lived not much more, indeed, with his other children, but most of their infancy passed under his eye. Alas! more than any of them I inherited that uneasy health of his, which kept us apart. But I did not mean to begin with "alas!" so soon, or so early to advert to the great misfortune of both our lives—want of bodily vigour adequate to the ordinary demands of life even under favourable circumstances.

I was born at Greta Hall, near Keswick, December 23rd 1802. My brother Hartley was then six years and three months, born Sep[tember] 19[,] 1796 at Bristol, Derwent, born Sep[tember] 14[,] 1800 at Keswick, four [sic] years and three months old. My Father, married at Bristol Oct[ober] 4[,] 1795, was now 29 years of age, my mother 31[;] their second child Berkeley, born at Nether Stowey May 10th 1798, died while my Father was in Germany, February 10th 1799, in consequence of a cold caught after inoculated small pox, which

---

1. SC's health had been declining steadily, and by September 1851 she thought herself to be in the midst of her "final decline." Although no mention is made of the autobiography in any of SC's other writings and it appears to have been a private gesture from mother to daughter, Edith would eventually publish it in a highly edited form (*Memoir and Letters of Sara Coleridge* [1873]), omitting all passages potentially offensive—even to those long dead.

brought on decline. Mama used to tell me mother's tales, which however were confirmed by my Aunt Lovell, of this infant's noble and lovely style of beauty—his large soft eyes of a London smoke colour, exquisite complexion, regular features, and goodly size. She said that my Father was very proud of him, and one day when he saw a neighbour approaching his little cottage at Stowey, snatched him away from the Nurse half drest, and with a broad smile of pride and delight, presented him to be admired. In her lively way she mimicked the tones of satisfaction with which he uttered, "This is my second son." Yet when the answer was: "Well, this is something like a child," he felt affronted on behalf of his little darling Hartley.

During the November and great part of December previous to my birth, my Father was travelling in Cornwall with Mr. Tom Wedgewood, as I learn by letters from him to my mother.[2] The last of the set is dated December 16, & in it my Father speaks as if he expected to be at Ambleside Thursday evening, Dec[ember] 23rd. He writes with great tenderness to my mother on the prospect of her confinement.[3] I believe he reached home the day after my birth. Several of his letters[,] the last three[,] are from Crescelly, the house of Mr. Allen, father of Lady Mackintosh, and of Mrs. Drew, the mother of Lady Alderson.[4]

Mama used to tell me that as a young infant I was not so fine and flourishing as Berkeley who was of a taller make than any of her other children, or Derwent, though not quite so small as her oldest born. I was somewhat disfigured with redgum. In a few months however I became very presentable, and had my share of *adoration*. "Little Grand Lamas[,]" my Father used to call babes in arms, feeling doubtless all the while what a blessed contrivance of the Supreme Benignity it is, that man in the very weakest stage of his existence, has power in that very weakness. Mere babyhood, even when attended with no special grace, has a certain loveliness of its own, and seems to be surrounded, as by a spell, in its attractions for the female heart, and for all hearts which partake of woman's tenderness, and whose tenderness is drawn out by circumstances in that particular direction.

2. See *CL* 2:879–99.

3. This is true but deceptive. Although the 16 Nov letter is "tender," its context suggests calculation on the part of STC, who was in the midst of a very rocky period of marital relations. To the first letter of the series, Griggs attaches this introduction: "Undoubtedly the missing passages in this letter included an account of the time spent in the company of Sara Hutchinson at Penrith on his way to London. The letters immediately following show that Mrs. Coleridge, cognizant of her husband's intimacy with Sara Hutchinson and thoroughly angered by it, wrote in high dudgeon of this visit. Thus Coleridge was led to berate his wife for her jealousy and to offer analyses of her and of himself; and while he was solicitous about her coming confinement, it is evident that her failure either to look with favour on his affection for Sara Hutchinson and the Wordsworths or 'to give them any Share of your Heart', was an important source of the friction between them" (*CL* 2:879–80).

4. John Barlett Allen was the owner of Crescelly and Wedgwood's father-in-law. See *CL* 2:883.

My Father wrote thus of Hartley and of me in a letter to Mr. Poole of 1803. ["]Hartley is what he always was, a strange, strange boy, 'exquisitely wild,' an utter visionary, like the Moon among thin clouds, he moves in a circle of light of his own making. He alone is a light of his own. Of all human beings I never saw one so utterly naked of self. He has no vanity—no pride—no resentments— and though very passionate I never yet saw him angry with anybody. He is, though seven years old, the merest child, you can conceive—and yet Southey says he keeps him in perpetual wonderment, his thoughts are so truly his own. His dispositions are very sweet—a great lover of truth, and of the finest moral nicety of feelings, and yet always dreaming. He said very prettily, about half a year ago, on my reproving him for some inattention, and asking him if he did not see something: [']My Father,['] quoth he, with flutelike voice—'I see it—I saw it, and tomorrow I shall see it again, when I shut my eyes, and when my eyes are open, and I am looking at other things—but Father, it is a sad pity—but it cannot be helped you know—but I am always being a bad boy when I am thinking of my thoughts.' If God preserve his life for me it will be interesting to know what he will become, for it is not only my opinion, or the opinion of two or of three but all who have been with him talk of him as a Thing that cannot be forgotten."[5]

"My meek little Sara is a remarkably interesting Baby; with the fairest possible skin, and large blue eyes—and she smiles as if she were basking in a sunshine as mild as moonlight, of her own quiet happiness."—In the same letter my Father says: ["]Southey I like more and more. He is a good man, and his industry is stupendous—take him all in all—his regularity and domestic virtues, genius, talent, acquirements and knowledge, and he stands by himself."[6]

Of this first stage of my life of course I have no remembrance, but something happened to me, when I was two years old, which was so striking as to leave an indelible trace on my memory. I fancy I can even now recall, though it *may* be but the echo or reflection of past remembrances, my coming dripping up the Forge Field, after having fallen into the river between the rails of the high wooden bridge that crossed the Greta, which flowed behind the Greta Hall Hill. The maid had my baby cousin Edith, 16 months younger than I, in her arms; I was rushing away from Derwent, who was fond of playing the elder brother, on the strength of his two years' seniority, when he was trying in some way to

---

5. *CL* 2:1014. Misquoted. SC leaves out both the line, "[He is] not generally speaking an affectionate child," and STC's reference to Hartley's "trouble with Worms."

6. Between the two passages quoted above, STC writes, "Mrs. Coleridge enjoys her old state of excellent Health. We go on, as usual—except that tho' I do not love her a bit better, I quarrel with her much less. We cannot be said to live at all as Husband & Wife / but we are peaceable Housemates."

control me, and, in my hurry, slipped from the bridge into the current. Luckily for me young Richardson was still at work in his father's forge. He doffed his coat and rescued me from the water. I had fallen from a considerable height, but the strong current of the Greta received me safely. I remember nothing of this adventure but the walk home through the field. I was put between blankets on my return to the house; but my constitution had received a shock, and I became tender and delicate, having before been a thriving child, & called by my Uncle Southey "fat Sall." As an infant I had been nervous & insomnolent. My mother has often told me how seldom I would sleep in the cradle—how I required to be in her arms before I could settle into sound sleep. This weakness has accompanied me through life.

One other glimpse of early childhood my mind retains. I can just remember sitting by my Aunt Lovell, in her little down stairs wing room, and exclaiming in a piteous tone[,] "I'se miseral!" A poor little delicate low-spirited child I doubtless was with my original nervous tendencies, after that escape from the Greta. "Yes, and you will be miserable," Aunt Lovell compassionately broke out, as mama has told me, "if your mother doesn't put you on a cap." The hint was taken, and I wore a cap till I was 8 years old. I appear in a cap, playing with a doll in a little miniature taken of me at that age by the sister of Sir William Betham, who also made portraits in the same style of my Uncle and Aunt Southey, my mother[,] Aunt Lovell[,] and cousins Edith and Herbert.[7]

I cannot leave this period of my existence without some little [allusion] to my brother's sweet childhood. I often heard from mama what a fine, fair, broad chested little fellow he was at two years old, and how he got the name of Stumpy Canary, when he wore a yellow frock, which made him look like one of those feathery bundles in colour & form. I fancy I see him now, as my mother's description brought him before me, racing from kitchen to parlour & parlour to kitchen, just putting in his head at the door with roguish smile to catch notice, then off again shaking his little sides with laughter. Mr. Lamb and his sister[,] who paid a visit of three weeks to my parents, in the summer of 1802, were charmed with the little fellow, and much struck with the quickness of eye and of memory that he displayed in naming the subjects of prints in books which he was acquainted with.[8] "Pi-pos,—Pot-pos," were his names for the striped and spotted opossum, and these he would utter with a nonchalant air, as much as to say of course I know it all as pat as possible. "David Lesley, Deneral of the Cock

7. Mary Matilda Betham (1776–1852), a poet and portrait miniaturist, corresponded with both STC and SFC. She visited the Lakes several times between 1808 and 1812. In addition to the portraits mentioned by SC, Betham also did one of STC. See *CL* 3:82–83.

8. For a famous description of the visit, see *Lamb Letters* 2:68–71.

Army" was another of his familiars. Mr. Lamb calls him Pi-pos in letters to Greta Hall after his visit to the Lakes.[9]

My parents came to Keswick in 1800. My father writes to my Uncle Southey, urging his joining him in the North, and describing Greta Hall, April 13[,] 1801.[10] My Uncle and Aunt came to G[reta] H[all] at the end of May or beginning of Sep[tember] 1801. My Uncle thought the climate too cold at first & was even disappointed in the country & thought the Lakes diminutive—"All English, perhaps all existing scenery must yield to Cintra—his last summer's residence." In October he went to Ireland to be priv[ate] secretary to Mr. Corry, Chancellor of the Exchequer for Ireland.[11] Margaret was born September 1802. She died at Bristol Aug[ust] 1803. My Uncle & Aunt reached Keswick with Aunt Lovell Sept[ember] 7th 1803, and Greta Hall became their home for the rest of their lives.[12]

Derwent was born at Keswick Sep[tember] 14[,] 1800. I think his parents arrived at G[reta] H[all] in the previous July. He [Coleridge] wrote July 19[,] 1800 from Keswick to D[aniel] Stuart. My mother records thus[:] "My husband came from Germany in the course of that summer 1799. I forget where Southey was then unless he remained at Westbury, where I had visited them after the death of my sweet Berkeley." (In Newfoundland[,] N[orth] Bristol, his father being in Germany[;] Berkeley was born May 10[,] 2½ in [the] morning, 1798[;] died Feb[ruary] 10[,] 1799.)—"After this they came through Stowey with Eliza to go to Minehead, where I visited them, and we all came up to Stowey, and soon S.T.C. quitted me to seek some engagement in London. There he became acquainted with Stuart and the Courier Office, engaged to write the *leading articles,* and having taken lodgings, sent for me and little Hartley, 3 years old. In March, I and the Child left him in London; and proceeded to Rempsford in Gloucestershire, Rectory of Mr. Roskilly; remained there a month. Papa was to have joined us there, but did not, and I and Hartley return[ed] to Bristol[,] I believe[;] I then found you at Mrs. Constance's. Where then were the Southeys?" (My Uncle & Aunt S[outhey] were in Portugal from the end of April 1800—it was May day soon after their arrival[,] the date of my Uncle's first letter to S.T.C.—till June 1801, when they came home & went to Bristol. They

9. See *Lamb Letters* 2:66–68.

10. I here omit SC's marginal note: "See Southey's *Life* Vol. II p. 146."

11. Southey stayed two weeks in Dublin and met Isaac Corry only briefly. See *NL* 1:247, 280.

12. SC's chronology is correct. See either *CL* 2:727–28, 993–1002; or *NL* 1:247, 324, 326. For the grieving Southey, the young SC was a painful reminder of Margaret: "I feel more pain at the sight of little Sara than I apprehended. Coleridge had written much of her fine countenance to me. She is indeed a fine child—but not such as her whom we have lost. Her age, her little voice sting me to recollections that I must blunt and wear out" (324).

went on a *visit* to G[reta] H[all] at the end of Aug[ust] 1801.) "Thence, I went to Stowey to pack up, and sell off the furniture, and prepare for our journey to Keswick. After this, I believe, on getting to Bristol, we took a lodging for a fortnight in Clarence Place, with the two old Misses Estlins, and from thence set off in a post-chaise, with a Mr. Baker to Liverpool, where we paid a very happy visit to the Cromptons—afterward proceeding to Grasmere in a chaise to ourselves in June 1800, where in six or seven weeks my Derwent was born—I mean, when we were settled at G[reta] H[all,] Keswick.—We had stayed at Grasmere a month with the Wordsworths at the small cottage." (They must have entered Keswick in July 1800—there to reside).

"When Derwent was nearly a year old, Southey & Edith came to us at G[reta] H[all,] and he went to Ireland to Mr. Abbot, (no Corry) as Secretary. Edith stayed with me. Then the Southeys went to London—they, Mrs. Southey Sen[ior] & Miss Barker and Aunt Lovell lived at a Silversmiths in the Strand. After Mrs. Southey's death (Jan[uary] 5[,] 1802), the Southeys and Aunt [Lovell] removed to Bristol where Margaret was born. On her death they came to Keswick, there to reside permanently. They arrived Sep[tember] 7, 1803.

My Uncle wrote from Ireland in October[,] joined my Aunt at K[eswick,] and took her to London, either that month or the next. In April 1802 or thereabouts he gave up Corry's place and went to Bristol.

I find in a letter of mama to Aunt Lovell[,] written but not sent, this record of early Greta Hall times:

"Well, after poor Mrs. Southey's death you all removed to Bristol, where the first child, Margaret, was born, and died. Soon after this period, Southey, Edith, and you (Mrs. Lovell) came to Keswick: how well I recollect your chaise driving up the Forge Field. The driver could not find the right road to the House, so he came down Stable Lane, and in at the Forge Gate. My Sara was 7 months old, *very sweet,* and her Uncle called her 'Fat Sal.' I nursed her till their second child, Edith, was born." (about 1—or an hour or two earlier—1804) "She, Sara, was then 16 months old."

"My husband, I think, was then in Malta, where he remained nearly 3 years: there and in Sicily and Rome. When he returned to Keswick[,] sister Edith was confined in the study. This was with Herbert.[13] Soon after this event[,] Coleridge went away with Hartley to the Wordsworths at Coleorton, thence he went to London, and wrote to me to bring the other two children to Bristol, and wait there, in College Street, at Martha's, with Mother, till he should join us to go to Stowey and Ottery together. Accordingly I set off to Penrith, stayed a night at

13. I have followed Edith's lead here and deleted SC's short but very muddled comments on the chronology of STC's trip and Herbert's birth. STC, as SC knew, returned from Malta on 17 August 1806, arrived at Keswick in November, and was at Coleorton with WW by December.

old Miss Monkhouse's, and next day proceeded towards Liverpool, where we were met by Dr. Crompton's carriage, and taken to Eton Hall, 4 miles out of Liverpool, where we stayed a fortnight to the great happiness of Derwent and Sara. Thence we got to Birmingham, stayed a few days with the Misses Lawrence—saw Joseph Lovell & Wife & children, and then proceeded to Bristol, to Martha's, in College St[reet]."[14]

"After some time S.T.C. brought Hartley from London to join us, and we 5 all proceeded to Stowey, to Mr. Poole's most hospitable abode, remaining most pleasantly with him for more than two months, and did not go to Ottery St. Mary at all."[15] (I believe they had illness there.) "We made visits to Ashholt (Mr. Brice's)—to Bridgewater at the Chubb. Then I with my children returned to Bristol, where we stayed a good while hoping to be rejoined by Father. At length he came, but was not for returning with us to Keswick. We set forward with Mr. Dequincey to Liverpool, where we, i.e. myself & children, remained a few days with the Koster family, and were again joined by Mr. De Q[uincey] and reached Grasmere, where we were joyfully received by the Wordsworths at their cottage, and the next day took a chaise to Keswick, on which occasion poor Hartley was so afraid that he should not again be a pet of dear friend Wilsy, that he screamed out of the window of the chaise—'Oh! Wilsy, Wilsy, let me sleep with you.'"

I was in my fifth year during this visit to the South, and my remembrances of it are partial and indistinct—glimpses of memory islanded amid the sea of non remembrance. I recollect more of Derwent than of Hartley & have an image of his stout build and of his resolute managing way as we played together at Bristol. I remember Mrs. Perkins with her gentle Madonna countenance, and walking round the Square with her daughter, who gave me currants when we came round to a certain point. I have faint recollections too of Stowey and of staying at the Kosters at Liverpool. At this time I was fond of reading the original Poems of the Miss Taylors & used to repeat some of them by heart to friends of mama.[16] Aunt Martha I thought a fine lady on our first arrival at College Street. She wore a white veil, so it seems to my remembrance, when I first saw her. I can but just remember Aunt Eliza, then at Mrs. Wa[t]son's, and that there was an old lady, very invalidish at College Street, Mrs. Fricker, my mother's mother. At this time I could not eat meat, except bacon.

14. Joseph Lovell was the brother of Robert Lovell, the coauthor of Southey's first volume of poems (*Poems* [1795]) and the brother-in-law of SFC and Southey's wife, Edith.

15. The Coleridges stayed at Stowey during June and July 1807, where SFC continued her close and lasting friendship with Thomas Poole. See *Minnow*, pp. 6–11.

16. Ann and Jane Taylor published *Original Poems for Infant Minds* (1804) and *Rhymes for the Nursery* (1806). The latter contains "Twinkle, twinkle, little star." The Taylors were obviously an influence in the composition of SC's own book of poems for children, *Pretty Lessons in Verse for Good Children* (1834).

My brothers were allowed to amuse themselves with the noble art of painting, which they practiced in the way of daubing with one or two colours, I think chiefly scarlet, over any bit of a print or engraving in vol[ume] or out of it, that was abandoned to their clutches. It was said of Derwent that upon one of these pictorial occasions, after diligently plying his brush for some time, he exclaimed with a slow solemn half-pitying half-self-complacent air: "Thethe little minute thingth are very difficult!!—but they *mutht* be done!!—*ethpethially* thaitheth." This "*mutht be done*" conveyed an awful impression of resistless necessity!—the mighty force of a principled submission to duty, with a hint of the exhausting struggles and trials of life.

Talking of struggles and trials of life, my mother's two unmarried sisters were maintaining themselves at this time by their own labours. Aunt Martha, the elder, a plain but lively pleasing woman, about 5 foot high or little more, was earning her bread as a dress-maker. She had lived a good deal with a Farmer in the country, Uncle Hendry, who married Edith Fricker, her father's sister; but not liking a female farmer's mode of life, came to Bristol & fitted herself for the business. Uncle Hendry left her a small sum of money—some hundreds—and would have done more doubtless had she remained by him. Burnet offered marriage to my Aunt Martha during the agitation of the Pantisocracy scheme; she refused him scornfully, seeing that he only wanted *a wife in a hurry,* not her individually of all the world.[17]

Aunt Eliza, a year or 20 months younger, about the same height, or but a barleycorn above it, was thought pretty in youth from her innocent blue eyes, ingenuous florid countenance[,] fine light brown hair, and easy light motions. She was not nearly so handsome in face however as my mother & Aunt Lovell, & had not my Aunt Southey's fine figure and quietly commanding air. Her face was too broad (therefore she looked best in a bonnet), her mouth too small, and no feature was really fine. Yet on the whole she was very pleasing, feminine & attractive. Both sisters sang but had never learned music artistically.

Such were my Aunts Martha & Elizabeth Fricker in youth, but they had sterling qualities, which gave their characters a high respectability. Without talent, except of an ordinary kind, without powerful connections, by life long perseverance, fortitude, and determination, prudence & patience & punctuality, they not only maintained themselves, but with a little aid from kind friends, whom their merits won, laid by a comfortable competency for their old age. They asked few favours, accepted few obligations, and were most scrupulous in returning such as they did accept as soon as possible. They united

17. George Burnett (1776?–1811) was a friend of Southey's from Balliol College, Oxford. After the Pantisocracy scheme fell through, he would become convinced that Coleridge and Southey were persecuting him. See *CL* 1:163–73; and *NL* 1:23*n*.

caution and discretion, with perfect honesty & truth, strict frugality and self control, with the disposition to be kind & charitable, and even liberal, as soon as ever it was in their power. Their chief faults were pride & irritability of temper. Upon the whole they were admirable women. I say *were,* but one, Aunt E[lizabeth] F[ricker] still survives on the Isle of Man. Aunt M[artha] died of paralysis at the Isle of Man Sep[tember] 26[,] 1850, at 73. Aunt Eliza is ailing. She must be 73 I believe now—or 72.[18]

Our return to Greta Hall has left an image in my mind and a pleasant one. I can just remember entering the parlour, seeing the urn on the table and teathings laid out, and a little girl very fair with thick yellow hair, and round rosy cheeks seated, I think, on a stool near the fire. That was my cousin Edith, and I thought her quite a beauty. She looked very shy at first, but ere long we were sociably travelling round the room together on one stool, our joint vessel, and our childish noise soon required to be moderated. I was five years old the Christmas after this return, which I believe was latish in Autumn. I remember how Mr. Dequincey jested with me on the journey and declared I was to be his wife, which I partly believed. I thought he behaved faithlessly in not claiming my hand.

I will now describe the home of my youth, dear Greta Hall, where I was born and were I resided till my marriage at 26 years of age in September [1829]. It was built on a hill on the side of the town of Keswick, having a large nursery garden in front. The gate at the end of this garden opened upon the end of the town, consisting of a few poor cottages. A few steps farther was an orchard of not very productive apple trees and plum trees. Below this a wood stretched down to the river side. A rough path ran along at the bottom of the wood and led on the one hand, the Skiddaw side of the vale, to the Cardingmill Field, which the river nearly surrounded. On the other hand the path led below the Forge Field on to the Forge. There was a woody bank between the Forge Field and the path and the river below. Oh that rough path beside the Greta! How much of my childhood, of my girlhood, of my youth, was spent there!

But to return to the house—two houses inter-connected under one roof— the larger part of which my parents and my Uncle and Aunt Southey occupied, while the smaller was the abode of Mr. Jackson, the landlord. The landlord side of the house had 8 rooms, the tenant side 12 rooms, exclusive of back kitchen: the former looked toward Skiddaw. On the ground floor was the kitchen, a cheerful stone flagged apartment looking into the back-place which was skirted by poultry and other out houses, coal house, stick house and so forth, and had trees on the side of the orchard whence it was separated by a gooseberry hedge.

18. As EC notes in *ML*(1873), Eliza Fricker died at Ramsay, on the Isle of Man, in September 1868.

Just in front of the two back rooms, that of our kitchen & the kitchen of Mr. Jackson's abode, was a gravelly bit by which we passed from one house to another. There was a drooping Laburnum tree outside our back kitchen, just in the way as you passed to the Forge Field portion of the kitchen garden. A passage ran from the kitchen to the front door; and to the left of this passage was the parlour which was the dining room & general sitting room. This apartment had a large window looking upon the green which stretched out in front in the form of a long horse shoe, with a flower-bed running round it, and fenced off from the great nursery garden by pales and high shrubs and hedges. There was another smaller window which looked upon another grass plot. The room was comfortably but plainly furnished, and contained many pictures, two oil land-scapes by a friend and several water-colour landscapes. One recess was oc-cupied with a frightful portrait of mama by a young lady.

The passage ran round the kitchen and opened into two small rooms in one wing of the rambling tenement, one which Aunt Lowell sate in by day, another which held the mangle, had cupboards as a pantry but was called the mangling room. Here were kept the lanterns and all the array of clogs & pattens for out of door roamings. The clog shoes were ranged in a row from the biggest to the least & curiously emblemed the various stages of life. The door leading into the backyard had the backkitchen to one side of it. There was another door behind that. The kitchen had a door at each end, one leading to the passage near the back door, the other to the front door passage. As you issued from the front door & down the stone steps you were conducted by a little gravel path to a gate which admitted to you the main walk leading down the hill. There was a little avenue of laurels leading to the Nursery garden gate, the boundary on that side of the G[reta] H[all] premises.

The staircase, to the right of the kitchen, which you ascended from the passage[,] led to a landing place, filled with book cases. A few steps more led to a little bedroom, which mama and I occupied: that dear bedroom, where I lay down in joy or in sorrow nightly for so many years of comparative health & happiness, whence I used to hear the river flowing and sometimes the Forge hammer in the distance, at the end of the field, but seldom other sounds in the night, save of stray animals. A few steps further was another little wing bed-room, then the study, where my Uncle sate all day occupied with literary labours & researches, but which was used as a drawing room for company. Here all the tea-visiting guests were received. The room had three windows—a large one, looking down upon the green with its wide flower border and over to Keswick Lake & Mountains beyond. There were two smaller windows looking toward the lower part of town, seen beyond the nursery garden. The room was lined with books in fine bindings: there were books also in brackets, elegantly lettered vellum covered vol[ume]s lying on their sides in a heap. The walls were hung with pictures, mostly portraits—miniatures of the family and some friends by Miss Betham, of Uncle & Aunt Southey by Downman, now engraved for the Life of Southey, of my cousin Edith and of me by Mr. Nash, and the three children, Bertha, Kate, & Isabel, by the same hand.[19] At the back of the room was a comfortable sofa, and there were sundry tables beside by Uncle's library table: his screen, desk, &c. Altogether, with its internal fittings up, and its noble outlook, and something pleasing in its proportions, this was a charming room. I never have seen its like, I think, though it would look mean enough in my eyes, as a mere room, could I see it now, as to size & furnishings. The curtains were of french grey merino. The furniture covers [were] at one time buff[;] I cannot tell what they were latterly. My Uncle has some fine vol[ume]s of engravings, which were sometimes shewn to visitors—especially, I remember, Duppa's sketches from Raphael & Michael Angelo from the Vatican.

On the same floor with the study & wing bedrooms was a larger bedroom above the kitchen looking onto the backyard. This was my Uncle & Aunt's sleeping apartment. A passage, one side of which was fitted with book shelves, led to the Jackson part of the house, the whole of which, after his decease, and some rooms before, belonged to our party. There was a room, which used to be my Father's study, called the organ room from an old organ which Mr. Jackson had placed there; a bedroom, generally occupied by Aunt Lovell, looking into the backplace—this was a comfortable but gloomyish room. At the end was a wing bedroom. Thence stairs led down to Wilsey's bedroom, Hartley's parlour, Wilsey's kitchen and back kitchen.

In the highest story of the house were six rooms, a nursery, nursery bedroom, landing place, maid's bedroom, another room, occupied by Kate and Isabel at one time, a sort of lumber room, and a dark apple room, which used to be supposed the abode of a boggle. Then there was a way out upon the roof, and a way out upon the leads over one wing of the house, whence we would look far out to the Penrith road, Brow Top, and the Saddleback side of the region.

I must now give one general sketch of the Garden, of which scraps of description have already been attached to that of the house. It was very irregular. In front of the house and the two large windows of the parlour and study was the Green, running out in the form of a long horse shoe with a wide border of flower bed all round and sheltered by a hedge. The kitchen garden was in two parts on either side of this lawn. There was greensward also on the side of the house containing the front door, and there were green palings inclosing this part of the premises. A few steps from the front door of the larger side of G[reta]

19. Edward Nash (1778–1821) entered the Greta Hall circle in 1815. He became a good friend of Southey's and traveled with the poet on his trip to Waterloo in 1815 and on his more extensive European tour of 1817. Nash illustrated Southey's *The Poet's Pilgrimage to Waterloo* (1816) and also completed numerous family portraits.

H[all] was the front door of the landlord's side, and that wing of the building was covered with ivy. The parlour of that part of the house, long called Hartley's parlour, looked out upon a piece of greensward on the other side of our front door. From the backplace a gravel path with laurel bushes on each side led along to the gate of the Nursery garden. To the right was another piece of green with a large copper beech at one end and a sort of shrubbery, below that again a set of beds which were given up to us children as our garden.

That part of the kitchen garden which lay below the hedge that bounded the lawn & flower border was divided into beds for the smaller vegetables—and there was at the lower end, near the palings that separated our domain from Uncle's nursery garden, a little grove of raspberry bushes, white & red—and beyond this, I think, was a plantation of underground artichokes which my Uncle was fond of—and there was a gooseberry hedge, called Hartley's, I think. Why I forget. Peas and beans were in the lower part of the garden abutting on the Forge Field; and that piece of ground was divided by a hedge of beech, privet, evergreen and had an abundance of gooseberry and currant bushes. In the upper compartment of this bower, on the side nearest the house, were the strawberry beds.

My young life is almost a blank in memory from that well remembered evening of my return from our series of Southern visits, till the time of my visit to Allan Bank, when I was six years old. That journey to Grasmere gleams before me as a shadow of a shade. Some goings on of my stay there I remember more clearly. Allan Bank is a large house on a hill overlooking Easedale on one side and Grasmere Lake on the other.[20] Dorothy, Mr. Wordsworth's only daughter, was at this time very picturesque in her appearance with her long thick yellow locks, which were never cut, but curled with papers, a thing which seems much out of keeping with the poetic simplicity of the household. I remember being asked by my Father and Miss Wordsworth, the Poet's sister, if I did not think her very pretty. No, said I, bluntly; for which I [met a] rebuff which made me feel as if I was a culprit.

My Father's wish it was to have me for a month with him at Grasmere, where he was domesticated with the Wordsworths. He insisted on it that I became rosier and hardier during my absence from mama. She did not much like to part with me, and I think my Father's motive at bottom must have been a wish to fasten my affections on him. I slept with him and he would tell me fairy stories, when he came to bed at 12 or one o'clock. I remember his telling me a witch tale too in his study, and my trying to repeat it to the maids afterwards.[21]

20. The following sentence is here scratched out: "We children were very roughly managed, washed in a tub in the stone flagged kitchen, men coming in during the operation."

21. The following sentence is here deleted: "I find among my dear Father's letters to my mother, these reminiscences of my six-year-old self and Allan Bank visit." SC must have seen STC's 9 Sept 1808 letter to SFC. See *CL* 3:120–22.

I have no doubt there was much enjoyment in my young life at that time but some of my recollections are tinged with pain. I think my dear Father was anxious that I should learn to love him and the Wordsworths & their children, and not cling so exclusively to my mother and all around me at home. He was therefore much annoyed when on my mother's coming to Allan Bank I flew to her and wished not to be separated from her any more. I remember his show-ing displeasure with me, and accusing me of want of affection. I could not understand why. The young Wordsworths came in and caressed him. I sate benumbed; for truly nothing does so freeze affection as the breath of Jealousy. The sense that you have done very wrong, or at least given great offence, you know not how or why—that you are dunned for some payment of love and feeling which you know not how to produce or to demonstrate on a sudden—chills the heart & fills it with perplexity and bitterness. My Father reproached me & contrasted my coldness with the childish caresses of the little Words-worths—who felt but lightly, and easily adopted any ways of affection that were required with lively but not deep feeling. I slunk away & hid myself in the wood behind the house, and there my friend John, whom at that time I called my future husband, came to seek me. How much more vividly we remember the painful than the pleasurable. I must have been a cheerful cute thing in the main to judge from these papaish records of my dear Father's own pen.

This was 1808:

[O it was a perfect comedy to see little John on Sara's Entrance—He had screamed with Joy on seeing us come up the Field; but when Sara entered, he ran & crept under the Kitchen-table, then peeped out at her, then all red with Blushes crept back again, laughing half-convulsively yet faintly—at length, he came out, & throwing his pinafore over his face & with both hands upon that, he ran and kissed her thro' and pinafore—. Soon how-ever all was agreed—John has put the Question, & Sara has consented—But (says she) is the Church a far way off?—Nay, replies John—nought but a lile bit—& I'll carry you on my back all the way, & all the way back, after we are married. Sara sleeps with me—She has made the children as happy as happy can be. Every one is delighted with her—indeed, it is absolutely impossible that there can be a sweeter or a sweetlier behaved Child—This is not *my* Speech; but Wordsworth's.—Little John absolutely dotes on her; and she is very fond of him, & very good to all of them. O, she has the sweetest Tongue in the world—she talks by the hour to me in bed—& does not at all disturb me in the night, she lies so very quiet. (*CL* 3:120)]

It was during this stay at Allan Bank that I used to see my Father and Mr. De-quincey pace up and down the room in conversation. I understood not, nor listened to a word they said, but used to note the handkerchief hanging out of the pocket behind, and long to clutch it. Mr. Wordsworth too must have been one of the room-walkers. How gravely & earnestly used STC and WW, & my Uncle Southey also, to discuss the affairs of the nation, as if it all came home to their business & bosoms—as if it were their private concern. Men do not canvass these matters now days, I think, quite in the same tone: domestic concerns absorb their deeper feelings—national ones are treated more as things aloof, the speculative rather than the practical.

My Father used to talk to me with much admiration and affection of Sarah Hutchinson, Mrs. Wordsworth's sister, who resided partly with the Words-worths, partly with her own brothers. At this time she used to act as my Father's amanuensis. She wrote out great parts of The Friend to his dictation. She had fine long light brown hair, I think her only beauty except a fair skin, for her features were plain & contracted[,] her figure dumpy & devoid of grace & dignity. She was a plump woman of little more than five foot. I remember my Father talking to me admiringly of her long light locks, and saying how mildly she bore it when the baby pulled them hard in play.

Miss Wordsworth, Mr. W[ordsworth]'s beloved sister, of more poetical eye and temper, took a great part with the children. She told us once a pretty story of a primrose, I think, which she spied by the wayside when she sent to see me soon after my birth, though that was at Christmas, and how this same primrose was still blooming when she went back to Grasmere.

Our dear friends, the Wordsworths, were rather rough & rustic in their management of children; there was a greater care and refinement in these matters at my own home, though nothing like the delicacy and softness of the present day. I remember how we children sometimes left our beds at 4 o'clock & roamed about the kitchen barefoot before there was any one to dress us. But this may have been only once. I have a dim vision too of being washed in a tub in the kitchen, in an exposed sort of way, and of some men or man coming in & out during the operation.

The Wordsworths and my Father boasted that I was rosier after a month's stay at Grasmere than I had been at Keswick. But I have not a comfortable remembrance [of] nursery arrangements and accommodations. Nursery indeed if I recollect rightly, there was none of any regular description. I remember telling my cousin Edith, with childlike ingratitude, or rather incapability of seeing & feeling, that there was aught to be grateful for, that I had suffered a [great] deal of "*miserality*" at Grasmere. Long afterwards I heard from Miss Crump at Allan Bank a scornful account of the untidy tenancy of the W[ords-worth]s—horrid smoke, which indeed I remember, the dirt, the irregular Scotchy ways, the mischief inflicted on the walls by the children, who were chid & cuffed freely enough, yet far from kept in good order. The extreme order, cleanliness[,] and neatness of Rydal Mount presented a strange contrast to former W[ordsworth] residences to those who remembered them in the Grasmere hut, in this for them too large & roomy mansion, and again in the shabby once Vicarage house near the Church. At Alfoxden, there were but two—the Poet and his Sister, no wife[,] children or sister-in-law, and a single but united pair *can* live rustically & simply without such disorder and uncleanliness as are sure to appear, where there is a numerous family, and no well considered arrangements and provisions made for their comfort. A single lady keeps herself neat without servant's aid, if she be well trained & handy; so does a man. But children are sure to be dirty untidy & riotous unless time and trouble of grown persons are bestowed in keeping them clean & neat & quiet and cheerful contended.

My Father had particular feelings and fancies about dress, as had my Uncle Southey & Mr. Wordsworth also. He would not abide the scarlet socks which Edith and I wore at one time. I remember going to him when mama had just drest me in a new stuff frock. He took me up and set me down again without a caress. I though he disliked the dress—perhaps he was in an uneasy mood. He much liked everything feminine and domestic, pretty and becoming, but *not* fine ladyish. My Uncle Southey was all for gay bright cheerful colours & even declared he had a taste for the *grand,* in half jest. Mr. Wordsworth loved all that was rich and picturesque, light & free in clothing. A deep Prussian blue or purple was one of his favourite colours for a silk dress. He wished that white dresses were banished, & that our peasantry wore blue and scarlet and other warm colours instead of sombre, dingy black, which converts a crowd that might be ornamental in the landscape, into a swarm of magnified ants. I remember his saying how much better young girls looked of an evening in bare arms even if the arms themselves were not very lovely—it gave such a lightness to their general air. I think he was looking at Dora when he said this. White dresses he thought cold—a blot and disharmony in any picture in door or out door. My Father admired white clothing, because he looked at [it] in reference to woman as expressive of her delicacy & purity, not merely as a component part of a general picture.

My Father liked my wearing a cap. He thought it looked girlish & domestic. Dora and I must have been a curious contrast—she with her wild eyes, impetuous movements, and fine long floating yellow hair & I with my timid large blue eyes[,] slender form & little fair delicate face muffled up in lace border & muslin. But I thought little of looks then: only I fancied Edith S[outhey] on first seeing her most beautiful.

I attained my sixth year on the Christmas after this my first Grasmere visit. It must have been the next summer that I made my first appearance at the dancing school, of which more hereafter. All I can remember of this first entrance into public is that our good humoured able but rustical dancing master, Mr. Yewdale, tried to make me dance a minuet with Charlie Denton, the youngest of our worthy Pastor's home flock—(he had ten children, 7 boys & 3 girls)—a very pretty rosy-cheeked large black eyed compact little laddikan. But I was not *quite* up to the business. I think my beau was a year older. At all events it was I who broke down, & Mr. Y[ewdale,] after a little impatience, gave the matter up. All teaching is wearisome, but to teach dancing [is] of all teaching the wearisomest.

The last event of my earlier childhood which abides with me is a visit to Allonby, when I was 9 years old, with Mrs. Calvert—I think this was Mr. Calvert's doing.[22] I remember the ugliness & meanness of Allonby, the town, a cluster of red-looking houses, as far as I recollect, and being laughed at at home for describing it as a "pretty place," which I did conventionally, according to the usual practice, as I conceived, of elegant letter-writers. The sands are really fine in their way, so unbroken & extensive, capital for galloping over on poney-back; I recollect the pleasures of these sands, and of the seaside animation and vegetation, the little close white Scotch roses, the shells, the crabs of every size, from Liliputian to Brobdingnagian, crawling in the pools, the sea anemones with their flower-like appendages which we kept in jugs of salt water, delighted to see them draw in their petals or expand them by a sudden blossoming, the sea weed with its ugly berries, of which we made hideous necklaces. All these things I recollect but not what I should most regard now, the fine forms of the Scotch hills on the opposite coast, sublime in the distance, and the splendid sunsets which give to this sort of outline a gorgeous furnishing.

Of the party, beside John & Raisley Calvert, and Mary their sister, who was two years younger than I[,] were Tom & William Maude, two sons of Mrs. Calvert's handsome portly eldest sister, Mrs. Maude. We used to gallop up & down the wide sands on two little ponies, a dark one called Sancho, and a light one called Airey behind the boys. Mary and I sometimes quarreled with the boys and of course, in a trial of strength, got the worst of it. I remember Raisley & the rest bursting angrily into our bedroom & flingling a pebble at Mary, enraged at our having dared to put crumbs into their porridge & not content with which inroad & onslaught they put mustard into ours next morning, the sun gone down upon their boyish wrath without quenching it. One of them said[,] "It was all that little vixen, Sara Coleridge; Mary was quiet enough by herself."

I remember we made acquaintance with Harriet Graham, a sprightly handsome Miss, of a year older than I, a younger daughter of some family of Grahams

22. Mary Calvert, later Mrs. Joshua Stranger, was SC's closest friend outside of the Greta Hall/Allan Bank circle. The Calverts lived in Keswick, and their large family provided SC with needed social diversions.

residing at Carlisle; and there were some dull Miss Clifts, too, of whom we saw something, and Anne & Helen Faucitt, daughters of a Cockermouth clergyman.

I had a leaven of malice I suppose in me, for I remember being on hostile terms with some little old woman, who lived by herself in a hut, and took offence at something I did, as it struck me, unnecessarily. She repaired to Mrs. Calvert to complain; the kend & kind of her accusation was, "That' un" (meaning me) "ran up & down the mound before [my] door." Mrs. C[alvert] thought this no heinous offence, but it was done by me, no doubt, with an air of derision. The crone was one of those morose ugly withered, ill-conditioned ignorant creatures, who, in earlier times, were persecuted as witches, and tried to be such. Still I ought to have been gently corrected for my behavior, and told the duty of bearing with the ill temper of the poor & ignorant and afflicted.

At this time, on coming to Allonby, I was rather delicate. I remember that Mrs. Calvert gave me a glass of port wine daily, which she did not give to the other children.

Oh me! How rough those young Calverts & Maudes were; and yet they had a certain respect for me mingled with a contrary feeling, or at least with great rudeness. I was honoured among them for my extreme agility—my power of running & leaping. They called me "Cheshire Cat" because I grinned. "Almost as pretty as Miss Cheshire," said T[om] Maude to me one day of some admired girl.

Such are the chief *historical* events of my little life, up to nine years of age. But can I in any degree retrace what being I was then—what relation my then being held to my maturer self? Can I draw any useful reflection from my childish experience, or found any useful maxim upon it?

What was I? In person very slender and delicate, not habitually colourless, but often enough pallid and feeble looking. Strangers used to exclaim about my eyes, & I remember remarks made upon their large size both by my Uncle S[outhey] and Mr. W[ordsworth]. I suppose the thinness of my face, & the smallness of the other features, with the muffling close cap increased the apparent size of the eye, for only artists, since I have grown up, speak of my eyes as large & full. They were bluer too in my early years than now.

I had great muscular activity, which I cultivated into agility: great were my feats in the way of jumping, climbing and race-running.

My health alternated as it has done all my life, till the last ten or twelve years when it has been unchangeably depressed, between delicacy and a very easy comfortable condition. I remember well that nervous sensitiveness and morbid imaginativeness had set in with me very early. During my Grasmere visit I used to feel frightened at night, on account of the darkness. I then was a stranger to the whole host of night-agitators—ghosts, goblins, demons, devils, boggles, burglarists, elves and witches. Horrid ghastly tales & ballads, of which crowds afterwards came in my way, had not yet cast their shadows over my mind. And yet I was terrified in the dark, and used to think of lions[,] the only form of terror which my dark-engendered agitation would take. My next bugbear was the Ghost in Hamlet. Then the picture of Death at Hellgate in an old edition of Par[adise] Lost, the delight of my girlhood—last & worst came my Uncle Southey's ballad horrors, above all the Old Woman of Berkeley. Oh the agonies I have endured between nine & twelve at night, before mama joined me in bed[,] in presence of that hideous assemblage of images:—the horse with eyes of flame! Oh! I dare not, even now, rehearse these particulars for fear of calling up some of the old feeling, which indeed I have never in my life been quite free from. What made the matter worse was, that like all other nervous sufferings, it could not be understood by the inexperienced and consequently subjected the sufferer to ridicule and censure. My Uncle S[outhey] laughed heartily at my agonies. I mean at the cause—he did not enter into the agonies. Even mama scolded me for creeping out of bed after an hour's torture and stealing down to her in the Parlour, saying I could bear the loneliness and the night fears no longer. But my Father understood the case better. He insisted that a lighted candle should be left in my room, in the interval between my retiring to bed & mama's joining me. From that time forth my sufferings ceased. I believe they would have destroyed my health had they continued. I preferred sleeping with Miss Hutchinson at Allan Bank to sharing my Father's bed because he was late in joining me.

Yet I was a most fearless child by daylight—ever ready to take the difficult mountain path and outgo my companions' daring in tree-climbing. In those early days we used to spend much of our summer time in trees, greatly to the horror of Mrs. Rickman and some of our London visitors.[23]

On reviewing my earlier childhood I find the predominant reflection . . .

23. John Rickman (1771–1840), the good friend of Lamb and Southey's, served as clerk assistant at the House of Commons. He favored the practical world of politics over the imaginative world of literature but was no less welcome at Greta Hall because of it.

N O T E S

CHAPTER 1. INTRODUCTION

1 "Sara Coleridge," in *Death of the Moth and Other Essays* (New York: Harcourt Brace Jovanovich. 1970), pp. 111–18. The essay originally appeared in *The New Statesman and Nation* (26 Oct 1940).

2 In 1822, at the age of nineteen, Sara published *An Account of the Abipones,* a three-volume translation of a work in Latin by Martin Dobrizhoffer. Three years later, she published *The Right Joyous and Pleasant History of the Facts, Tests, and Prowesses of the Chevalier Bayard,* a two-volume translation from medieval French. Originally intended to assist her brother Derwent with college expenses, neither translation was to be anything more than an amusement for Sara, chores to keep her busy during her long and often strained engagement to her first cousin, Henry Nelson Coleridge. Like Mary Kingsley, the marginalized "heroine" of Woolf's 1938 polemic *Three Guineas* (New York: Harcourt Brace Jovanovich, 1966), Sara contributed much to "Arthur's Education Fund" (3).

3 *Pretty Lessons in Verse for Good Children* (1834), a collection of poems originally written for daughter Edith and son Herbert, was quite successful and went through five editions. In 1837, Sara published another children's book, *Phantasmion,* a long and rambling prose fairy tale.

   After Coleridge's death in 1834, Sara and her husband began what proved to be a protracted defense of the poet's reputation. Making use of the most effective strategy possible, they brought out STC's unpublished material and republished that which was out of print, maintaining high editorial standards and frequently including noteworthy critical essays as either introductions or appendixes. Between 1834 and 1843, they were responsible for publishing two volumes of *Table Talk,* four volumes of *Literary Remains,* the third edition of *The Friend,* the fourth and fifth editions of *Aids to Reflection,* a single volume including both the *Constitution of Church and State* and the two *Lay Sermons,* and last, the *Confessions of an Inquiring Spirit.* After Henry's death in 1843, Sara continued their project by publishing the *Biographia Literaria* in 1847, *Notes and Lectures upon Shakespeare* in 1849, *Essays on His Own Times* in 1850, and *The Poems of Samuel Taylor Coleridge* in 1852.

   In addition to her editorial work, Sara published two reviews for the *Quarterly Review,* one of Tennyson's *The Princess* in March 1848 and another on Dyce's edition of Beaumont and Fletcher in September 1848.

4 According to Noel Annan, Leslie Stephen thought STC "the seminal mind of the century" (314) and insisted that his daughter read STC, as well as Carlyle, in great quantity (*Leslie Stephen: The Godless Victorian* [New York: Random House. 1984], pp. 313–15). Like Matthew Arnold before him, Stephen had some trouble in coming to grips with STC's personal weaknesses and so found it difficult to balance the poet's private faults against his public virtues. Unlike Arnold, however, Stephen chose to applaud the virtues in print rather than denigrate the vices.

5 The quotation marks signify an informed wariness about the ideological baggage that has accompanied and continues to accompany discussions of female illness. The term is meant not in the inherited and uncritical sense of Woolf's biographer, Quentin Bell, for whom it seems to represent the logical culmination of a whole series of "natural" female traits—emotionalism, irrationality, disorganization, etc.—but rather in the sense of its ties to nineteenth-century hysteria and of its decidedly ambivalent stance in relation to the "cult of female invalidism" which fostered it. As Barbara Ehrenreich and Deirdre English have argued in their *Complaints*

and Disorders: The Sexual Politics of Sickness, hysteria involved both the acceptance of society's definition of woman as inherently "sick" and a powerful protest against "an intolerable social role" (42–43). For enlightening discussions of Woolf's "madness," see Susan M. Kenny, "Two Endings: Virginia Woolf's Suicide and *Between the Acts,*" *University of Toronto Quarterly* 44 (Summer 1975): 265–89; and Jane Marcus, "Virginia Woolf and her Violin: Mothering, Madness, and Music," in *Mothering the Mind: Twelve Studies of Writers and Their Silent Partners* (New York: Holmes & Meier, 1984), pp. 181–201. See also *Suffer and Be Still: Women in the Victorian Age,* ed. Martha Vicinus (Bloomington: Indiana University Press, 1973).

6   From "S. T. Coleridge," *Reflector* 1 (1888): 300-09; reprinted in *Hours in a Library* (London: Smith, Elder, 1892). 3:339–68.

7   This passage and all other passages designated either "Letter" or "Diary" are, unless otherwise noted, taken from the MSS housed at the Harry Ransom Humanities Research Center, the University of Texas at Austin, where they form part of the extensive Coleridge family papers.

Similar passages recur throughout SC's late diaries. In Sept 1848 she had written, "I am at this time employed on that most tedious work—mastering the adoptions of the Lit Remains from Schelling & Schlegel—a sentence from this page, a sentence or two from that, here a free translation, there an expansion, or interpolated paraphrase. These editorial labours are in one sense well worth while: it is setting a matter in order—giving a correct statement—to last as long as my father's works are read—in another point of view it is a most ungrateful labour—unseen—unnoticed—very time-consuming—and neither profit nor credit rewards it in any least adequate degree" (Diary [28 Sept 1848]).

8   *A Room of One's Own* (New York: Harcourt Brace Jovanovich, 1957) contains Woolf's most celebrated discussion of "minor" women writers. There she argues that "masterpieces are not solitary births" (68) but are dependent upon and indebted to a whole tradition of lesser known predecessors (61-81). Nevertheless, as I shall argue, the standards by which works are judged to be either "major" or "minor" are left unquestioned; the cultured reader, Woolf implies, is automatically capable of recognizing "a work of genius" (53). Similarly, in another early piece, "The Lives of the Obscure" (*Dial* [May 1925], pp. 381–90), Woolf defends and applauds the "invincible mediocrity" (381) of second-string autobiographers as essential to the appreciation of "good books." To understand a literary period, she argues, one must be intimately familiar with its "gradations of merit." But *how* those gradations come into being and by what process they order the literary universe remains a nonproblem.

9   *The Death of the Moth and Other Essays,* pp. 187–97. The essay appeared originally in the *Atlantic Monthly* (April 1939), pp. 506–10.

10 Although my criticism here immediately recalls similar censures by Queenie Leavis, E. M. Forster, and Quentin Bell, my position could not be more different. I have no intention of denying Woolf's political vision, the political content of her novels, or her dependence on the world of "sober fact." On the contrary, I insist on all three: Woolf's "highbrow" responsibility for and dependence upon "lowbrow . . . vitality" has been copiously and convincingly documented—first in "Lives of the Obscure" and *A Room of One's Own,* and later in *Three Guineas,* "Sara Coleridge," and "Middlebrow." See also Jane Marcus, "No more horses: Virginia Woolf on Art and Propaganda," *Women's Studies* 4 (1977): 265–90. There, Marcus refutes the criticisms of Leavis, Forster, and Bell, but fails, I think, to recognize how Woolf's rage against "middlebrows" is in danger of turning an otherwise useful polemic into a prejudicial and exclusionary critical practice.

11 *The Diary of Virginia Woolf,* ed. Anne Oliver Bell (New York: Harcourt Brace Jovanovich, 1974–84), 1:211.

12 This is not to suggest that the author of *Three Guineas* desired either a police state or a literary canon exclusively "highbrow." It is to suggest, however, that Woolf's need to rethink patriarchal institutions encountered understandable difficulties when it came to the institution of art. By "institution" I mean—following Peter Bürger—the structure of assumptions and beliefs which mediates both the production and reception of art in society. According to Bürger (*The Theory of the Avant-Garde* [Minneapolis: University of Minnesota Press, 1984]), it was only

during the first decades of the twentieth century that this mediation was exposed and questioned. The challenge came, significantly, not from critics but from avant-garde artists who were displeased with the commodification of art in bourgeois society. By attempting to destroy the cherished notions of artistic autonomy so much a part of late-nineteenth-century aestheticism, they had hoped to reintegrate art into social praxis. With its alternating chapters of fact and fiction, Woolf's experimental novel *The Pargiters* could also be seen as evidencing such a hope.

13　*Virginia Woolf: A Feminist Slant,* ed. Jane Marcus (Lincoln: University of Nebraska Press, 1983), p. 2. See also Marcus's "A Niece of a Nun: Virginia Woolf, Caroline Stephen, and the Cloistered Imagination," ibid., pp. 7–36.

14　My position has important ties to various recent works by Raymond Williams, Terry Eagleton, Fredric Jameson, and Edward Said—not to mention Jerome McGann. All depend in one way or another upon an understanding of literary culture argued originally by Williams. Anticipated in his classic *Culture and Society* (1959) and elaborated in both *Keywords: A Vocabulary of Culture and Society* (1976) and *Marxism and Literature* (1977), this history traces the word *literature* from the fifteenth century to the present in order to illuminate a process of increasing separation from social praxis. During the fourteenth and fifteenth centuries, the word referred to a level of experience, a state of being widely read in all kinds of writings: one "had literature" in the general sense of having a broad education. By the late Renaissance, it had come to mean specifically the objects of that education, all types of books. Later still, during the eighteenth and nineteenth centuries, the term took its present meaning—the objects exclusively of imaginative production. This same process Peter Bürger (*Theory of the Avant-Garde*) discusses as the formation of "autonomous art," the gradual "detachment of art from [its] practical contexts" (46). He identifies three phases—Sacral Art, Courtly Art, and Bourgeois Art—and examines the changing modes of production and reception in terms of intended social function (35–54). Eagleton gives a related account in his *Literary Theory: An Introduction* (Minneapolis: University of Minnesota Press, 1983), pp. 1–53.

15　Sara Coleridge's autobiography appears in *ML* (1874), pp. 33–49. For an unexpurgated version, see the appendix, pp. 249-66.

16　The Wordsworth household(s) provides an obvious example of women playing an integral but unacknowledged role in the production of romantic literary texts. Dorothy's journal, for instance, records the daily activities of a domestic economy whose primary aim was to ensure that William maintained his poetic productivity: not only did Dorothy Wordsworth, Mary Wordsworth, Sara Hutchinson, and later Dora Wordsworth make it possible for William to work unencumbered by routine chores, they also labored directly on behalf of his texts—copying and recopying his poems, listening to his recitations, and discussing his latest efforts. For an insightful reading of the Wordsworths' domestic economies, see Kurt Heinzelman's essay "The Cult of Domesticity: Dorothy and William Wordsworth at Grasmere," in *Romanticism and Feminism,* ed. Anne Mellor (Bloomington: Indiana University Press, 1988).

17　Mary Poovey, *The Proper Lady and the Woman Writer: Ideology as Style in the Works of Mary Wollstonecraft, Mary Shelley, and Jane Austen* (Chicago: University of Chicago Press, 1985).

18　Poovey's analysis of the contradictions of bourgeois womanhood during the beginning of the nineteenth century is further substantiated—both theoretically and historically—by two extremely helpful essays in Annette Kuhn and AnnMarie Wolpe, *Feminism and Materialism: Woman and Modes of Production* (London: Routledge and Kegan Paul, 1978). The first, "Patriarchy and Relations of Production" by Roisin McDonough and Rachel Harrison, outlines crucial distinctions between patriarchy and capitalism, employing early-nineteenth-century Britain as an example of a period during which the two forces were in contention. The second essay, "Structures of Patriarchy and Capital in the Family" by Annette Kuhn, concentrates specifically on the family as the locus of that conflict between economic and patriarchal ideologies. See pp. 11–41, 42–67.

19　Janeway's ambitious study, *The Powers of the Weak* (1980), explores the hidden relationships between the empowered and the powerless, assuming from the outset that "what women know, learned and relearned in our long sojourn in the country of the weak, is the geography of an uncharted territory of human existence" (5). Once this territory is charted, Janeway argues, women will be encouraged to pursue their political potential and "reinvent" their future without the oppressive constraints of patriarchy (pp. 1–21, 304–21).

20 In addition to Margaret Homans, *Women Writers and Poetic Identity* (Princeton: Princeton University Press, 1980), two notable exceptions come to mind: Mary Kelley, *Private Woman, Public Stage: Literary Domesticity in Nineteenth-Century America* (Oxford: Oxford University Press, 1984): and Julia Swindells, *Victorian Writing and Working Women: The Other Side of Silence* (Minneapolis: University of Minnesota Press, 1985).

21 Arno J. Mayer, *The Persistence of the Old Regime: Europe to the Great War* (New York: Pantheon Books, 1981).

CHAPTER 2. "CASTLES IN THE AIR"

1 In nineteenth-century Britain, as recent feminist scholarship has amply demonstrated, superior intelligence by no means guaranteed the exceptional woman even partial economic autonomy. She could not, of course, attend a university or vote in governmental elections. But neither could she—once married—sign a contract, own the money she earned, or hold the titles to property originally hers. Even her children belonged legally to her husband. Female selflessness, then, was not simply a cultural myth but a legal mandate. For two excellent examples of revisionist biography, both of which shed light on SC's situation, see Celia Morris Eckhardt, *Fanny Wright: Rebel in America* (Cambridge: Harvard University Press, 1984): and Jean Strouse, *Alice James: A Biography* (New York: Bantam, 1982).

2 In April 1816, for instance, SFC reported to Thomas Poole that she had not heard from STC in "almost three years" (*Minnow* 44).

3 Dorothy Wordsworth's censures of SFC ("Her radical fault is want of sensibility . . . what can such a woman be to Coleridge?") are often cited—unfairly I think—as proof of her irremediable shortcomings. See *D. Wordsworth,* pp. 124–31, 207–27. Molly Lefebure's recent biography of SFC, *Bondage of Love: A Life of Mrs. Samuel Taylor Coleridge* (New York: W. W. Norton, 1987), provides the much-needed corrective to this unusually harsh view. See in particular pp. 15–18.

4 "[S]hould it be *necessary,*" Wordsworth wrote, "she [Sara] will be well fitted to become a Governess in a nobleman's or gentleman's family" (*W Letters* 3:209).

5 Henry Crabb Robinson agreed at least in part. Visiting Greta Hall in Sept 1816, he found Hartley "a boy pedant" with a "starch and affected manner" (*Diary* 1:340).

6 This subordination found its rationale in the doctrines of "Female Influence" popularized by the French writer Louis Aime-Marin (*De l'éducation des mères de famille* [1834]). Sarah Ellis, a disciple of Aime-Marin, wrote a typical answer to the hotly debated "female question" of the mid-nineteenth century: "Women, in their position in life, must be content to be inferior to men; but as their inferiority consists chiefly in their want of power, this deficiency is abundantly made up to them by their capability of exercising influence" (*The Daughters of England* [London, 1845], p. 47). For STC's very similar position, see *CL* 5:152–58.

7 SC's sole excursion out of the Lake district occurred in Dec 1819 when her mother took her to Liverpool to be fitted with a back brace. As Dorothy Wordsworth reported, "We expect Mrs. Coleridge and Sara next week on their way from Liverpool. Mrs. C took Sara thither to get her fitted with steel stays or supporters for her Back. She has long had a weakness there; and the spine has been almost imperceptibly forming a slight curve in one part. The stays have been made under the direction of a Surgeon eminent for skill in such cases, and he entertains no doubt of a perfect cure provided her health is good. To attain this she ought to be allured from standing as much as possible and *must* lie on her back for at least two hours in the day" (*W Letters* 3:571). The "eminent" surgeon must have known his business, for there is no record of Sara having further trouble with her back.

8 Neither Dora nor Edith had studious inclinations, and a frequent theme in the letters of both Dorothy Wordsworth and Mrs. Coleridge considers how well off the three girls would be for a more equitable distribution of talents. Dorothy writes, "Often do we wish that Dorothy [Dora] was like her [Sara] in this respect—*half* like her would do very well, for with all Dorothy's idleness there are many parts of her character which are much more interesting than corresponding ones in Sara, therefore, as good and evil are always mixed together, we should be very contented with a moderate share of industry, her talents being quite enough" (*W Letters* 3:320).

9 See *HC Letters,* pp. 8–11; *Minnow,* pp. 51, 84; and *CL* 5:37n.

10 As I shall explain, Southey withdrew his encouragement for SC's projects once she became engaged. "[S]uch employment," he wrote to John Rickman, "disqualif[ies] her for those duties which she shall have to perform whenever she changes from the single to the married state" (*NL* 2:280).

11 For a complete account of the Oriel affair, see *CL* 5:57–132; and *HC Letters,* pp. 30–56.

12 As many of SFC's letters attest, SC was anxious to meet with her father. In April 1819, for example, SFC wrote to Poole, "Sara is still very uneasy about not seeing her father. I hope I shall be able to take her to Town next year, when she may be gratified with a reintroduction to him" (*Minnow* 75).

13 Upon his death in 1827, Sir George would leave £100 to Mrs. Coleridge as well as to Wordsworth and Southey. Coleridge, much to his disappointment and anger, was not provided for.

14 STC was enamored of the painting and called it "the most beautiful Fancy-figure, I ever saw." It hung over his desk until his death in 1834. See *CL* 4:878, 891; and Griggs, pp. 32, 38.

15 See Auerbach's *Woman and the Demon* (Cambridge: Harvard University Press, 1982), pp. 1–62; and Ehrenreich and English's *Complaints and Disorders,* pp. 15–44. For the latter, disease, beauty, and the "essence of Womanhood" have to be seen as intimately related. For example, "The association of TB with innate feminine weakness [during the middle decades of the nineteenth century] was strengthened by the fact that TB is accompanied by an erratic emotional pattern. . . . The behavior characteristic for the disease fit expectations about woman's personality, and the look of the disease suited—and perhaps helped to create—the prevailing standards of female beauty. A romantic myth rose up around the figure of the female consumptive and was reflected in portraiture and literature" (21).

16 HNC was not, however, the first man to have had matrimonial designs upon SC. The summer before traveling to London she had been courted by John May, Jr., who appealed unsuccessfully to his father for permission to wed SC. Because of opposition from various corners, including the Southeys, SC put an end to the affair. But much to her displeasure, May proved persistent, and SC finally had to appeal to JTC in April 1823 for help in putting an end to May's attentions. It was not until the spring of 1824, however, that the situation was resolved. See *Minnow,* p. 110.

17 SC did in fact become a "Quarterly Reviewer," but she did not accept Southey's conservatism as gospel any more than she would accept her father's doctrines without first altering them to suit her own purposes. Speaking of Wordsworth and Southey, she told Henry Reed, "I never adopted the opinions of either *en masse,* and since I have come to years of secondary and more mature reflection, I have been unable to retain many which I received from them" (Reed, 64).

18 Lamb's awareness of Coleridge's estrangement from his family is also evident from an earlier remark recorded by Henry Crabb Robinson on Jan 8, perhaps just after Lamb saw the Coleridges together at Moreton House: "He [STC] ought not to have had a wife or children; he should have a sort of diocesan care of the world,—no parish duty" (*Diary* 1:481).

19 As I discuss at length in chapters 4 and 5, STC also conceived of his illness as something peculiarly intellectual. Two days after SC's birth, for example, he wrote Southey, "God have mercy on us!—We are all sick, all mad, all slaves!—It is a theory of mine that Virtue & Genius are Diseases of the Hypochondriacal & Scofulous Genus—& exist in a peculiar state of Nerves, & Diseased Digestion" (*CL* 2:478). SC's editorial labors will thus become an attempt to "cure" both her own "Disease," her marginalized female intellect, and her father's, his fragmentary and miscellaneous texts.

20 In his biography of SC, *Coleridge Fille,* Griggs includes a description of an evening Lamb spent at Highgate during which this tension made itself felt: "The evening passed pleasantly enough, though there was one source of irritation. Coleridge, it seems, launched forth in a long theological monologue, but as he touched on various controversial questions, Sara interrupted with, 'Uncle Southey doesn't think so'. Lamb, sensing Coleridge's irritation but ever ready to see the humorous side of things, was greatly amused, and as he rode homeward in a gig later was heard to chuckle to himself, 'Uncle S-Southey d-doesn't think s-so' " (40). Griggs treats the incident lightly, eager to portray father and daughter in an uncomplicated relationship of mutual adoration. Unfortunately, he fails to document the anecdote.

21 A list of the contributors to SC's three surviving commonplace books read like a Who's Who of the Romantic period. In addition to all of the various Coleridges, Southeys, and Wordsworths, the list includes Joanna Baillie, Caroline Bowles, Barron Field, C. J. Fox, Elizabeth Fry, J. H. Fryer, Mary Jane Jewsbury, Charles Lamb, Basil Montagu, Thomas Poole, W. M. Praed, Edward Quillinan, Henry Crabb Robinson, Henry Taylor, C. H. Townsend, Emily Trevenen, and Aubrey de Vere, among others.

22 STC admitted as much in a letter to John Anster, where after lamenting at length the "idleness" and "vanity" of Derwent, he suddenly contrasted the accomplishments of his daughter: "On the other hand my Daughter, who with her Mother spent some weeks at our House on their journey to my Brothers, is a good & lovely Girl & every thing (save that her Health is delicate) that the fondest & most ambitious Parent could pray for. The young men, & some of their elders, talk in raptures of her Beauty. She is exceedingly industrious" (*CL* 5:335–36).

23 Quoted in Lord Coleridge's *The Story of a Devonshire House* (London: T. Fisher Urwin, 1905), p. 282. The colonel's letter, dated March 22, also reveals that on the basis of Sara's "charms" he decided to increase his sister-in-law's annual stipend by £20.

24 Although no letters from HNC to SC written before 1827 have survived, there are numerous indications that they corresponded regularly.

25 *Amadis de Gaul,* the Spanish romance, was translated by Southey and published in 1803.

26 As I suggested earlier, the strategies of compensation employed by SC find their theoretical substantiation in Elizabeth Janeway's *Powers of the Weak.* Janeway argues that much feminist scholarship remains locked within the very power structures (i.e., patriarchal) that it wishes to revise and that by focusing only on those women who radically challenged the status quo, feminists have tended to ignore the strategies by which the majority of nineteenth-century women deflected and appropriated male power for their own purposes. The quotation from Victor Turner and Edith Turner's *Image and Pilgrimage in Christian Culture* (1978) that gives Janeway her title is particularly relevant to SC's religious stance: "INFERIORITY: A value-bearing category that refers to the powers of the weak, countervailing against structural power, fostering continuity, positing the model of an undifferentiated whole whose units are whole human beings. The powers of the weak are often assigned in hierarchic and stratified societies to females, the poor, autochthons, and outcasts."

27 For interesting and informative accounts of opium use in the nineteenth century, see A. Calkins, *Opium and the Opium Habit* (London: Lippincott, 1871) and Althea Hayter, *Opium and the Romantic Imagination* (New York: Faber, 1968).

28 SC's manuscript was completed but never published; it is now part of the Coleridge collection at HRHRC.

29 Letter of March 1837. Quoted in Winifred Gerin, *Charlotte Brontë: The Evolution of Genius* (Oxford: Oxford University Press, 1967), p. 110.

30 Writing to her cousin, John Taylor Coleridge, she commented, "I sometimes cannot help lamenting . . . that [STC] does not write more popularly, but I repress the thought as unworthy of his daughter" (Letter [24–25 June 1825?]).

31 See *Minnow,* pp. 92–93. The letter, incorrectly dated 1822, was actually written during the early spring of 1826.

32 Southey's love for his books has been well documented, and at his death his library contained some fourteen thousand volumes. Even with Edith Southey's help, Sara's chore lasted approx-

imately four months. See *Minnow*, p. 95; SFC's letter was written during the spring of 1826, not 1822 as Stephen Potter, the editor, suggests.

33 DC's letter has not survived. His words are quoted in SC's response to her brother dated 2 Feb 1826.

34 See also *CL* 4:404–09, where STC lists a provocative series of guidelines for an unidentified young man considering marriage. He ends his advice by asking his correspondent to ponder carefully the following questions: "Are we suited to each other? Does she *seriously* adopt my opinions on all important subjects? Has she at least that known docility of nature which, uniting with true wifely love, will dispose her so to do?"

35 See also *Marginalia* 2:92–93.

36 Specifically, SC's essay is a reaction against a "sprightly morceau" by Caroline Bowles, the poet and later the second wife of Robert Southey. Bowles's essay appeared originally in *Blackwood's Edinburgh Magazine* before being republished as chapter three of *Chapters on Churchyards* (1829). As early as Feb 1821 SC has written to Elizabeth Crumpe, "I perfectly agree with you in your strictures on *external loveliness*. You will think me trite perhaps if I say that beauty unaccompanied by mental endowments is a mere toy 'that wears but till the gilding frets away,' as your favorite poet has it" (Letter DCL [19 Feb 1821]).

37 Mary Wollstonecraft, *Vindication of the Rights of Woman* (New York: Penguin Books, 1972), p. 319.

38 See Francis Bacon, "Of Beauty" in *Essays and New Atlantis* (New York: Walter J. Black, 1942), pp. 180–81. Interestingly, SC uses Bacon, Bowles, Cowper, and Quarles as cited references but only alludes to Coleridge and Wordsworth.

39 *The Familiar Letters of Sir Walter Scott* (Edinburgh: David Douglas, 1894) 2:342. Scott and Lockhart visited Greta Hall together in Aug 1825. SC remarked that "Lockhart is handsome but looks satirical" (Letter DCL: SC to E. Crumpe [19 Oct 1825]).

40 For varying accounts of SC's aborted effort, see Griggs, pp. 60–61; and *CL* 6:558n.

41 The occasion of SC's letter was her gift to HNC of a copy of Wordsworth's poem "The White Doe of Rylstone." She explained, "This poem has solaced me during the dreary years of my absence from you—It has, I think, done me more real good than all the vain consolations . . . of those around me—a thousand times more than new scenes, gay faces, or aught that is recommended for the heartache by careless advisors. . . . You are right, I doubt not, in saying that I overrate this poem—my own peculiar feelings may give it for me a merit it cannot possess for the world in general. . . . To me, however, it is still a most exquisite production."

42 While in London SC tutored JTC's son John Duke Coleridge, and on her journey home she wrote him a letter: "You must persuade your papa to bring you some day or other to the Lakes; it is a fine land for little boys and girls. All the gaieties and festivities that go on there, they can enter into and enjoy as much as grown people. We have not hot crowded parties, where the company sit up late and where there is nothing to amuse little lads and lassies, but we go on the lake in a nice large boat, take out dinner and tea-apparatus, land on an island or one of the bays or promontories, on the shores of the lake, pick up sticks to light a fire, and then sit upon stones or rocks and regale ourselves" (*Life and Correspondence of John Duke Lord Coleridge* [London, 1904], pp. 21–22).

43 "I must be patient," Sara wrote Elizabeth Crumpe in April 1829, "& hope for the best, & we have both had so many disappointments that we ought to have acquired the virtue of fortitude. I must try to employ the long period which must elapse ere our union can be accomplished in acquiring all those dispositions & faculties which may fit me to render my beloved happy & comfortable, & may enable me to discharge my duties as a wife in a more effectual manner than I might have done ere I had been disciplined by sorrow & reflection" (Letter DCL [13 Apr 1829]). Henry, however, was less willing to be patient: "His extreme eagerness for wedded bliss," SC noted with some amusement, "rather I fear unsettled his mind. . . . Never did my poor man more hanker for a wife to *make him easy*" (Letter DCL: SC to E. Crumpe [5 July 1828]).

CHAPTER 3. "THE HOUSE OF BONDAGE"

1 In addition to Ehrenreich and English, *Complaints and Disorders,* and Vicinus, *Suffer and Be Still,* see Ilza Veith, *Hysteria: The History of a Disease* (Chicago: University of Chicago Press, 1965).

2 Ironically, two months earlier Henry had written his father that "The Reform Bill & the Whigs are as good as gone to the Devil. The Times itself abuses both, & said yesterday that the country would not have been in such a condition, if the Duke of W[ellington] were in power" (Letter: HNC to James Coleridge [25 Aug 1831]). According to SC, HNC's pamphlet, "Notes on the Reform Bill" (1831), was "much admired by the Anti-reformers & talked about by both parties. 3300 copies have been sold" (Letter DCL: SC to E. Wardell [4 July 1831]).

3 The intermittent use of opium was in SC's day as socially acceptable as the taking of aspirin today; and like aspirin, opium was used to treat a wide variety of commonplace disorders. Carrying none of today's social stigmas, heavy dependence on the drug indicated only the moral weakness of its user, for the physiological nature of addiction was simply not understood. Similarly, the symptoms of withdrawal were not identified as drug-related but as the natural illnesses of the addict; so once the pains began, opium was invariably administered for relief, perpetuating a vicious cycle.

4 See, for example, Alexander Hamilton, *A Treatise on the Management of Female Complaints* (Edinburgh, 1792).

5 For a good example of the theory of the hysteric as spoiled child, see Robert B. Carter, *Pathology and Treatment of Hysteria* (London, 1854). For a helpful overview of hysteria in the nineteenth century, see "The Hysterical Woman: Sex Roles and Role Conflict in Nineteenth-Century America," in Carroll Smith-Rosenberg, *Disorderly Conduct: Visions of Gender in Victorian America* (New York: Alfred A. Knopf, 1985), pp. 197–216.

6 Almost twenty years after SC's death, John Stuart Mill would write, "All women are brought up from the very earliest years in the belief that their ideal of character is the very opposite to that of men; not self-will, and government by self-control, but submission, and yielding to the control of others. All the moralities tell them that it is the duty of women, and all the current sentimentalities that it is their nature, to live for others; to make complete abnegation of themselves, and to have no life but in their affections" (*The Subjection of Women* [London, 1869], p. 27).

7 Elizabeth Poole Sandford, the popular author of conduct books for women, was the niece of STC's old friend Thomas Poole.

8 Hannah More, *Strictures on the Modern System of Female Education,* 2d ed., 2 vols. (London: Cadell & Davies, 1799), 2:13.

9 More's *Strictures on the Modern System of Female Education* (1799) was followed by Sandford's *English Female Worthies* and *Woman in Her Social and Domestic Character* and by Ellis's *The Daughters of England* (1845).

10 "I think with the *Spectator,*" Sara wrote in August 1834, "that Mrs. More's very great notoriety was more the work of circumstances, and the popular turn of her mind, than owing to a strong original genius. . . . Mrs. More's steady devotion to the cause of piety and good morals added the stamp of respectability to her works. . . . though such a passport can not enable any production to keep its hold on the general mind if it is not characterized by power as well as good intention." See *ML*(1873), pp. 77–79.

11 Martineau visited STC at Highgate in July 1833. Although SC would no doubt have heard of the visit, her letters indicate she had already become familiar with Martineau's work. For the only surviving firsthand account of the meeting, see *Harriet Martineau's Autobiography* (London: Verso Press, 1983) 1:396–98. See also Vera Wheatly, *The Life and Work of Harriet Martineau* (New Jersey: Essential Books, 1957); Robert Webb, *Harriet Martineau: A Victorian Radical* (New York: Columbia University Press, 1960); and Valerie Pichanick, *Harriet Martineau: The Woman and Her Work, 1802–76* (Ann Arbor: University of Michigan Press, 1980).

The latter is a particularly perceptive account of Martineau's intellectual life, an account that nicely illumines SC's struggles by emphasizing the numerous obstacles facing nineteenth-century women writers.

12 The *Monthly Repository* 18 (1823): 80.

13 Martineau later claimed that her economic want as a young woman ultimately became her greatest blessing, for it forced her to live by her pen. See Wheatley, *Life and Work,* pp. 55–72.

14 HNC also grieved: his commemorative lines, "On Berkeley and Florence Coleridge," were included in STC's *PW*(1834) 2:149; they were reprinted in Griggs, *Coleridge Fille,* p. 76.

15 Letter: SC to HNC (2 April 1834).

16 See Griggs, pp. 121–22; and *HC Letters,* p. 268.

17 The essay is undated, but it is mentioned to ET in a letter postmarked 5 July 1834, two months before the publication of *Pretty Lessons.* Evidently, SC never sent the complete MS, but she did send, in Jan 1835, a much-condensed version, which she referred to as her "nonsensical notes upon nervousness."

18 See also Griggs, pp. 98–100.

19 For a contemporary evaluation of SC's "solution," see David Erdman. *EOT(CC)* 1:lx–lxvii.

20 Henry Taylor, "Wordsworth's *Poetical Works,*" *Quarterly Review* 52 (1834): 317–58. Taylor, the dramatist and the man of letters, would later become good friends with SC. At the time of her essay, however, she had not seen Taylor for many years and was not aware of his authorship.

C H A P T E R   4.   "T H E   G R E A T   A R T"

1 The Wordsworths were similarly upset. Sara Hutchinson wrote Edward Quillinan, "If you have seen the English Papers you will know that poor C. Lamb is dead—He died of Erysipelas—& was only ill 3 or 4 days—This was a great shock to us" (*SH Letters,* 437–38).

2 See D. Wordsworth, pp. 388–400; and Cuthbert Southey, *The Life and Correspondence of the Late Robert Southey,* 6:239–85. The most recent and most detailed account of DW's illness is to be found in Robert Gittings and Jo Manton, *Dorothy Wordsworth* (Oxford: Clarendon Press, 1985), pp. 250–83.

3 The York Retreat was the first mental institution in Great Britain to insist upon humane care of its inmates. See Samuel Tuke, *A Description of the Retreat* (London, 1813); and Elaine Showalter's history of women and mental illness, *The Female Malady,* pp. 8, 30, 35, 52–53.

4 See Showalter, *Female Malady,* pp. 23–98; and Michael Donnelly, *Managing the Mind: A Study of Medical Psychology in Early Nineteenth-Century Britain* (New York: Tavistock, 1983), pp. 3–29, 68–105, 137–40.

5 Official report from the Retreat quoted by Southey in a letter of November 1834 to John May (Ramos, 269).

6 See D Wordsworth, pp. 393–400. De Selincourt's last chapter is somewhat misleadingly entitled "Posthumous Life." As his account of Dorothy's reaction to her brother's death makes clear, her mind had not "died" completely, if at all.

7 Quoted in Showalter, *Female Malady,* p. 29; and Donnelly, *Managing the Mind,* pp. 137–38.

8 Shoshana Felman, "Woman and Madness: The Critical Phallacy," *Diacritics* 5 (1975): 2–10.

9 See also *HC Letters,* pp. 203–04.

10 Although evidence of opium usage during this period is slight, SC did maintain a regular dependence on the drug, and her addiction must be seen as an ongoing factor in the patterns of her illness.

11 SC's criticism of Martineau was perhaps especially harsh when written to HNC, who was unable to abide liberalism in even its tamest forms.

12 Molly Lefebure, *Samuel Taylor Coleridge: A Bondage of Opium* (New York: Stein and Day, 1975), pp. 334–35, 480–91.

13 Although the movement officially began in July of 1833 with a sermon by John Keble on apostolic succession, it did not attract the public's attention until E. B. Pusey joined the party in

early 1835. See R. W. Church, *The Oxford Movement* (rept. Chicago: University of Chicago Press, 1970), pp. 23–29, 94–98.

14 An important exception was F. D. Maurice, whose response to Newman, *Subscription No Bondage,* SC liked immensely. See Charles Sanders, *Coleridge and the Broad Church Movement* (Durham: Duke University Press, 1942), pp. 210–42.

15 The term *wondertale* is Vladimir Propp's. See his *Theory and History of Folklore,* trans. Adriadna Martin and Richard Martin (Minneapolis: University of Minnesota Press, 1984), pp. 102–23.

16 See Newman's "Literature" in *The Idea of a University* (London, 1852).

17 SC and HNC had moved from Hampstead to Regent's Park, London, in June 1837. The new residence was more convenient for HNC, whose law offices were located at Lincoln's Inn, and more spacious for SC, whose children desperately needed a larger house.

18 Park's 1832 pamphlet, *Dogmas of the Constitution, Four Lectures on the Theory and Practice of the Constitution,* took issue with STC's declaration that the "Voice of the People . . . is the Voice of God" (*C&S*[*CC*], p. 100). For STC on the "clerisy," see *C&S*[*CC*], pp. 42–60.

19 Harriet Martineau, *Society in America,* 3 vols. (London, 1837), 3:297–301.

20 De Tocqueville concurred: "In the United States . . . the majority . . . exercise a prodigious actual authority, and a power of opinion which is nearly as great; no obstacle exists which can impede or even retard its progress, so as to make it heed the complaints of those whom it crushes in its path. This state of things is harmful in itself and dangerous for the future" (*Democracy in America,* 2 vols. [1835 & 1840; New York: Alfred A. Knopf, 1945], 1:257). Even Martineau qualified her enthusiasm: "The majority eventually wills the best; but in the presence of imperfection of knowledge, the will is long exhibiting itself; and the ultimate demonstration often crowns a series of mistakes and failures" (*Society in America,* 1:32–33).

21 SC's letter evidently precipitated a reply from Reverend Plummer, for she responded to his objections several weeks later by writing a short essay, "Dogmatism Defended—by a Protestant—against Popery, Dissent, & Extremes in every direction." It remains unclear whether or not the essay was actually sent.

22 This is precisely the argument that SC makes in her introduction to the 1847 *Biographia Literaria.* See *BL*(1847), 1:v–clxxxiii.

23 HNC's preface to the fifth edition of *Aids to Reflection* (1843) is dated October 1842, although SC was the one who finally saw the book through the press during the spring of 1843. HNC also worked on a new edition of the *Biographia Literaria,* an edition that would eventually become the well-known 1847 *Biographia.* As is clear from the notes in that edition, HNC had barely begun the task before having to relinquish it to SC.

24 HNC was not, however, too sick to attempt severing all connections with STC's old publisher William Pickering and making a new agreement with Edward Moxon. At SC's insistence, and with John Taylor Coleridge and Joseph Henry Green in full accord, HNC wrote to Pickering because the publisher had long been careless about financial matters—especially about making the proper payments. Concerned for the welfare of his family, HNC hoped Moxon would prove more lucrative. Much to HNC's disappointment, however, Pickering was unwilling to change his terms. See Griggs, pp. 137–38.

25 That SC was aware of the importance of those boundaries is evident in this revealing passage from a letter of SC's to Dora Wordsworth written some eight months after HNC's death: "I should not like to see her [Dorothy W] now though beautiful & impressive as the ruin of her noble mind and intellect may be. I wish to preserve my remembrance of her, as she was in her best days, uncrossed by the image of her present state. There is nothing that I so dread for dearest friends,—that visits me so in my most terrible dreams,—as *any form* of derangement" (Letter DCL [13 Sept 1843]).

CHAPTER 5. "THE BUSINESS OF LIFE"

1 J. F. Ferrier, The Plagiarisms of S. T. Coleridge," *Blackwood's Edinburgh Magazine* 47 (Mar 1840): 287–99. For De Quincey's charges, see *Tait's Edinburgh Magazine* 1 (Sept 1834): 509–20.

2 At STC's death Green was named the official literary executor and was assigned STC's "opus maximum" to prepare for publication. It quickly became apparent, however, that he could not control the literary estate without assistance from the Coleridge family. Almost immediately, SC and HNC assumed de facto control, and after HNC's death the governing responsibilities naturally fell to SC.

3 Hartley did, however, recognize the unpopularity of SC's position: "She must be aware, that it will not please all—too high-church for liberal-latitudinarian or evangelical; while to a large portion both of the high and low church the very word Reason is so terribly odious, that I verily suspect they think it was invented by Tom Paine" (*HC Letters* 268).

4 B. M. G. Reardon, *Religious Thought in the Nineteenth Century* (Cambridge: Cambridge University Press, 1966), p. 254. See also Sanders, *Coleridge and the Broad Church Movement,* pp. 179–262.

5 SC's friendship with Maurice, however, was not without its tensions. To her sister-in-law she wrote, "[He is] always instructive—but he won't let one enjoy one's own opinions *much*—he either snatches them out of one's hands or tosses them over the hedge on to a dung-hill, or crumples them and takes the shine out of them so that one's ashamed to ask for them back" (Letter: SC to Mrs. DC [1846?]).

6 For an in-depth discussion of Carlyle on Coleridge, see Sanders. *Coleridge and the Broad Church Movement,* pp. 146–76. See also his *Carlyle's Friendships* (Durham: Duke University Press, 1977), pp. 36–60.

7 Unfortunately, nothing more is known about Abraham. He met SC at Eton and argued with her there about Carlyle. SC thought enough of him to address her essay "Reply to the Strictures of Three Gentlemen upon Carlyle" to him specifically. Evidently that was the end of their correspondence.

8 The MS has not survived, but EC published it in her *Memoir and Letters of Sara Coleridge* where she misdates it. See *ML*(1874), pp. 358–67.

9 For a useful discussion of the importance of hero-worship to the mid-Victorian sensibility, see Walter Houghton, *The Victorian Frame of Mind 1830–1870* (New Haven: Yale University Press, 1957), pp. 305–40.

10 See above, pp. 77-81.

11 See above, pp. 99-101.

12 Norman Fruman, "Aids to Reflection on the New *Biographia,*" *SiR* 24 (1985): 141–42.

13 Aubrey de Vere (1814–1902), the Irish poet and man of letters, became a close friend of SC after the death of her husband, and they maintained a voluminous correspondence until a year or so before SC's death in 1852. Other than the letters published in EC's *ML,* however, nothing of their correspondence has survived. Because the friendship had romantic possibilities (never realized), SC most likely asked that the letters be destroyed. See de Vere's *Recollections* (New York & London: Edward Arnold, 1897), pp. 195–209; and Griggs, pp. 179–81, 291–22.

14 SC's intellectual broadmindedness was characteristic of her widowhood. To Mary Stanger, she wrote, "We can not have clear, definite views, or know well what our professed tenets really are, or why we ought to hold them, unless we reflect upon them, and compare them with the opposite ones which we reject. Persons who never do this . . . are apt, I think, to become narrow, superstitious, and bigoted, to think their own belief the only one that any wise and good person can hold" (*ML*[1874] 221).

15 J. C. Hare, "Samuel Taylor Coleridge and the English Opium-Eater," *British Magazine* 7 (Jan 1835): 15–27; McFarland, *Coleridge and the Pantheist Tradition* (Oxford: Oxford University Press, 1969), pp. 1–52.

16 This is precisely the position taken by two recent studies of the *Biographia:* see Kathleen Wheeler, *Sources, Processes and Methods in Coleridge's 'Biographia Literaria'* (Cambridge: Cambridge University Press, 1980); and Catherine Wallace, *The Design of the 'Biographia Literaria'* (London: George Allen & Unwin, 1983).

17 This essay, attributed to Samuel Wilberforce, is an attempt to make STC into a High Church theologian by quoting him out of context. See *Chr M* 2 (1842): 109–36.

18 Her argument maintains that Newsman's *Lectures on Justification* (1838) inadvertently establishes the very position it attacks—namely Luther's. See *BL*(1847), 1:xcii–cxxvi.

19 Henry Taylor (1800–86), the dramatist, poet, and man of letters, is chiefly remembered for his 1834 play *Philip Van Artevelde*. A friend of Robert Southey, Taylor met SC first at Keswick but did not become a close acquaintance until after HNC's death. See Griggs, pp. 180–81.

20 Primarily because of the three positive reviews that greeted the first of Tennyson's publications—W. J. Fox in the *Westminster Review* (Jan 1831), A. H. Hallam in the *Englishman's Magazine* (May 1831), and John Wilson in *Blackwood's Edinburgh Magazine* (May 1832)—the poet was hailed as a promising young genius, but at the same time, paradoxically, his poetry generated much derision. The savage sarcasm of J. W. Croker's 1833 review of Tennyson's second volume became the well-known cause of the poet's famous "ten-year silence" and the morbid sensitivity both to publication and criticism that continued throughout his life. By 1842 Great Britain had largely accepted Tennyson as the next great British poet, but disagreement continued as to the path his genius should follow. The four major reviews of the 1842 *Poems* offered various recommendations but were unable to hide an uneasiness about Tennyson's ability to live up to his already acknowledged talent. Thus, *The Princess* was intended by the author to be that poem which would finally settle his account with the critics.

21 For a detailed account of *The Princess* and the "woman question," see John Killham, *Tennyson and 'The Princess': Reflections of an Age* (London: Athlone, 1958), pp. 1–141.

22 SC's review appeared in the *Quarterly Review* early in 1848, although not as she originally intended. Lockhart deleted all references to Keats and altered several passages to make SC's criticism of Tennyson more strident. The text reproduced here is the printed version but with the deleted passages restored in angle brackets. The original MS is now part of the Coleridge Collection at the University of Texas at Austin.

23 SC's reference to "sphere of action" indicates a familiarity with French theories of "Female Influence," an idea popularized by Louis Aime-Marin in his 1834 *De l'éducation des mères de familles*. According to Aime-Marin, women are highly moral creatures who could—without having to participate in the marketplace—exert their influence on the rest of the world by way of love and piety. Sara's remarks here and elsewhere closely resemble the general outlines of Aime-Marin's doctrines, indicating that although she assumed an apolitical attitude toward women's rights, she believed that her spirituality had political ramifications.

24 Christopher Ricks, *Tennyson* (New York: Macmillan, 1972), p. 190.

25 John Jump, *Tennyson: The Critical Heritage* (New York: Barnes & Noble, 1967), p. 7. Tennyson's sensitivity to reviewers was notorious even in his own day. Robert Browning wrote in Feb 1845, "Tennyson reads the 'Quarterly' and does as they bid him, with the most solemn face in the world—out goes this, in goes that, all is changed and ranged . . . Oh me!" (*The Letters of Robert Browning and Elizabeth Barrett,* ed. E. Kinter, [1969], 1:19).

26 "That review," SC informed her sister-in-law, "is not *altogether* as I wrote it. . . . Almost one third was cut out. What I grieved to part with—(the only passage I cared much about) was a critique upon Keats, doing him, as I thought, due honour. Mr. L. cut that out because the former critic (who cut up Endymion) would not 'swallow laudations of Keats.' He—Croker no doubt—was very wroth about Sterling's article" (Letter: SC to Mrs. DC [Sept 1848]).

27 "Review of Alexander Dyce's *The Works of Beaumont and Fletcher* . . . and George Darley's *The Works of Beaumont and Fletcher,*" *Quarterly Review* (Sept 1848).

CHAPTER 6. "PUTTING IN ORDER A LITERARY HOUSE"

1 The collection of poetry, *Poems of Hartley Coleridge,* did not appear until 1851, when it was issued with another edition, *Essays and Marginalia of Hartley Coleridge*. Both were two-volume sets, edited by Derwent Coleridge and published by Edward Moxon.

2 To her sister-in-law, SC expressed the same opinion: "I fancy I perceive that Miss Trevenen has the same feeling—that H's life is disgraceful and to be thrown into the shade if possible. I do

not think it altogether such, and am possessed with a very strong sense that the main truth— Fact considered as characteristic—ought not to be suppressed" (Letter: SC to Mrs. DC [May? 1849]).

3 The "representation" of Stuart's to which SC refers was "Anecdotes of the Poet Coleridge," *Gentlemen's Magazine* 10 (1838).

4 "Dear Miss F——, the trouble I have taken with this book is ridiculous to think of—it is a filial phenomenon; no one will thank me for it, and no one will know or see a twentieth part of it" (*ML*[1874] 300).

5 See also *EOT(CC)* 1:lxxxiv–xc.

6 When they had first met in 1837, SC had not been particularly impressed: "A clever, agreeable man," she noted, "though rather fond of shewing off in conversation." She was similarly offended by the "audacious utilitarianism of his remarks on Bacon's philosophy," which she had read in the *Edinburgh Review* that July. See Griggs, pp. 177–78.

7 See James Morris, *Heaven's Command: An Imperial Progress* (New York: Harvest, 1973), pp. 152–74.

8 SC debated with great vigor de Vere's opinions of Keats, Shelley, and Tennyson as he had articulated them in the *Edinburgh Review* (90 [Oct 1849]: 388–438). See *ML*(1874), pp. 407–11.

9 See also, SC to Isabella Fenwick (14 Aug 1850); and *ML*(1874), p. 454.

10 See above, p. 146 and *n*.

11 See William Hazlitt, *Political Essays* (London, 1819), pp. 190–241.

12 For Erdman's confirmation of SC's claim, see *EOT(CC)*, 1:lxiv–lxv.

13 Anne Marsh (1791–1874)—author of *The Admiral's Daughter, Emilia Wyndam, Norman's Bridge,* and others—and Anna Jameson 1794–1860)—author of *Legends of the Saints and Martyrs* and *Sacred and Legendary Art*—had both become acquainted with SC during the 1840s, as had the actress Fanny Kemble (1809–93), whom SC thought too "cold and high" for any kind of steady acquaintance.

14 Catherine Gore (1799–1861), the prolific novelist parodied by Thackeray in *Lords and Liveries,* was once a favorite with SC; she admired in particular *Mothers and Daughters* (1831) and *The Banker's Wife* (1843).

15 Reed, professor of English at the University of Pennsylvania and devotee of Coleridge and Wordsworth, had written SC in 1849 for permission to publish an American edition of STC's poetry. A correspondence ensued with books and articles regularly exchanged. Yarnall, a friend of Reed's from Philadelphia, was introduced to SC in 1850. He proved a lively correspondent, reporting in detail his frequent trips around the States.

16 Brodie (1783–1862) had seen both STC and HNC, the former only once, the latter several times. HNC died in January 1843 of a degenerative nerve disease, and Brodie had treated him by letting blood and blistering his back. For references to STC and Brodie, see *CL*. 6:851, 909.

17 Edith Coleridge included a version of the autobiography in *ML*(1874), but because that version is heavily edited, this passage and all following passages are quoted directly from the MS at HRHRC.

18 Berkeley did not survive infancy. He died on February 11, 1899, while STC was in Germany with the Wordworths.

19 As SC might have realized, her father's famous poem to Sara Hutchinson, "Ode to Dejection," was composed within weeks of SC's conception, making for yet another irony in their father–daughter relationship.

20 Writing on a spare page in the same notebook in which she wrote her autobiography, for example, SC listed some forty prospective essays she hoped to write, on topics ranging from Wordsworth to Kant to demonic possession.

21 "[Young Sara] is to come in the spring," Dorothy wrote to Catherine Clarkson, "and Mrs. C is desirous to put off the evil day, for she dreads the contamination which her lady-like manners must receive from our rustic brood, worse than she would dread illness, I may almost say *death.* As to poor little Sara, she had behaved sweetly ever since her Mother left her, but there is

nothing about her of the natural wildness of a child. She looks ill and has a bad appetite" (*W Letters* 2:373).

22 Southey's ballad was particularly disturbing to the young SC perhaps because it focuses on an evil mother who, with help from the devil, terrorizes small children. Unlike *Hamlet* or *Paradise Lost,* "The Old Woman of Berkeley" ends with the forces of evil victorious. The poem concludes:

> The Devil he flung her on the horse,
>   And he leapt up before,
> And away like the lightening's speed they went,
>   And she was seen no more.
>
> They saw her no more, but her cries
>   For miles round they could hear,
> And the children at rest at their mother's breast
>   Started, and scream'd with fear.

INDEX

Except for main entries, the abbreviations listed by the author are used in the index.